Democracy, Civic Culture and Small Business in Russia's Regions

This book adopts a novel analytical approach to understanding how Russia's stalled democratization is related to the incomplete liberalization of the economy. Based on extensive original comparative study of Russia's regions, the book explores the precise channels of interaction that create the mutuality of property rights, entrepreneurship, rule of law, norms of citizenship and liberal democracy. It demonstrates that the extent of democratization varies across regions, and that this variation is connected to the extent of liberalization of the economy. Moreover, it argues that the key factor in producing this linkage is the relative prominence of small business owners and their supporters in articulating their interests vis-à-vis regional and local administrations, especially through the institutionalization of networks and business associations. The book develops its key theses by means of detailed analysis of the experiences of four case study regions. Overall, the book provides a major contribution to understanding the path of democratization in Russia.

Molly O'Neal is a Visiting Research Scholar at Johns Hopkins University's School of Advanced International Studies in Washington, DC.

Routledge Contemporary Russia and Eastern Europe Series

While Russia's political system has become steadily less democratic in recent years, Molly O'Neal's impressive *Democracy, Civic Culture and Small Business in Russia's Regions* shows that small business associations have been a key factor working against this trend. Well grounded in hard statistical analysis, the heart of the book is its vivid case studies of four different regions that grow out of the author's research on location. Each case study features personal profiles of small business association leaders and fascinating accounts of their efforts to influence policymaking, efforts O'Neal shows also tend to promote political pluralism. The regional accounts also call attention to exceptions, providing a rich sense of the often-overlooked geographic variety that Russian politics features and that this book shows are rooted firmly in history. This study will be of interest to anyone who cares about Russia, democracy, and connections between politics and economics.

Henry Hale
Elliott School of International Affairs,
George Washington University

Impressive . . . excellent . . . original . . . addresses large and profound issues, in a sophisticated way . . . could well have an appeal beyond the Russian studies audience.

Philip Hanson
Chatham House and University of Birmingham

This fascinating study, of Putnam-esque ambition, brings a fresh perspective to the forces shaping Russia's trajectory over the past generation. Focusing on the nascent small business community in four different regions, O'Neal's richly textured analysis highlights post-communism's complex interplay of politics, economics and history.

William Pyle
Frederick C. Dirks Professor of
International Economics
Middlebury College

This substantial work investigates the sources and limits of democratization in Russia during the past two decades. Most previous studies of this subject have concentrated on country-wide Russian political trends; by contrast, this one compares sub-national Russian regions whose levels of democratization vary substantially from one another. The book combines quantitative analysis of a large data set covering all of Russia's federal regions with four case studies that examine processes of democratization (and non-democratization) in depth. The result is a well-crafted appraisal of the role of small businesses in regional political development since the breakup of the USSR.

Bruce Parrott
Johns Hopkins University

Democracy, Civic Culture and Small Business in Russia's Regions

Social processes in comparative historical perspective

Molly O'Neal

Routledge
Taylor & Francis Group

LONDON AND NEW YORK

First published 2016
by Routledge

2 Park Square, Milton Park, Abingdon, Oxfordshire OX14 4RN
711 Third Avenue, New York, NY 10017

*Routledge is an imprint of the Taylor & Francis Group,
an informa business*

First issued in paperback 2017

British Library Cataloguing in Publication Data
A catalogue record for this book is available from the British Library

Library of Congress Cataloging-in-Publication Data
O'Neal, Molly.
   Democracy, civic culture and small business in Russia's regions : social
processes in comparative historical perspective / Molly O'Neal.
      pages cm. — (Routledge contemporary Russia and Eastern Europe
series ; 65)
   1. Small business—Russia (Federation)   2. Entrepreneurship—
Russia (Federation)   3. Democracy—Russia (Federation)   4. Russia
(Federation)—Economic conditions.   5. Russia (Federation)—Social
conditions.   I. Title.
   HD2346.R8O54 2016
   322'.30947—dc23
   2015008602

ISBN: 978-1-138-90269-5 (hbk)
ISBN: 978-0-8153-6464-1 (pbk)

Typeset in Times New Roman
by Apex CoVantage, LLC

For Russia's small business owners:
heroes of resilience, bearers of hope.

Contents

Preface

The central concerns of this project arose from my professional involvement in American and multilateral foreign economic policy related to the post-communist transformation in Europe beginning in 1989. Perhaps the single most important source of institutional support for the project is the Center for International Private Enterprise (CIPE). I would like to thank John Sullivan, Andrew Wilson and Mark Schleifer in the Washington headquarters of CIPE and Alexander Raevsky and Tatiana Titova of CIPE's Moscow office. In 2002–2009, under a project funded by USAID, CIPE worked in Russia with regional Chambers, OPORA affiliates and other local business associations to identify and articulate interests common to all small business owners. The first eight regions in the project were Irkutsk, Khabarovsk, Krasnodar, Perm, Primorsk, Samara, Saratov and Volgograd, joined later by the Altai, Astrakhan, Kamchatka, Kirov, Nizhniy Novgorod, North Ossetia-Alania, Rostov, Sakha-Yakutia and Smolensk regions. The second phase of the project also shifted the emphasis specifically to anti-corruption efforts. I am grateful to Dina Krylova, former OPORA vice president, and Georgiy Satarov of INDEM for sharing their insights and experience of the CIPE project's work with business associations on anti-corruption advocacy. The network of Russian entrepreneurs having taken part in the programs of the Center for Citizen Initiatives led by Sharon Tennison was also a vital source of advice and support for this project, especially in Rostov.

I also received expert advice and insights from Victor Sedov, Sharon Tennison, Ambassador James Collins, Timothy Tarrant, Igor Mikhalkin, Mikhail Mamuta, Victor Ermakov, Gail Buyske, Vladimir Medoev and Igor Danchenko. Olga Plotnikova and Andrei Shubin of OPORA and Alexander Rybakov of the Russian Chamber were also generous with time and advice. I am above all grateful to those interviewed for this study in Samara, Togliatti, Rostov, Taganrog, Smolensk, Perm and Kungur.

Russian scholars whose insights were important to this project were Andrey Yakovlev, Viktoria Golikova, Alexey Titkov, Alexey Zudin, Irina Semenenko, Aleksandr Chepurenko, Nikolai Petrov, Alla Chirikova, Oleg Podvintsev, Petr Panov and Natalya Zubarevich.

Bruce Parrott, Mitchell Orenstein, Frank Fukuyama and Andrew Kuchins provided critical advice that shaped this project throughout. Henry Hale of George

Washington University deserves special thanks for his sustained interest and advice. I would also like to thank Will Pyle, Robert Orttung, Alex Sokolovski, Anders Aslund, Thane Gustafson, Jonathan Harris and Harley Balzer for advice, criticism and guidance on the project. The Institute of Qualitative and Multi-Method Research (IQMR) held in Syracuse, New York, in 2009 provided very important insights at a formative stage of the research design.

For very important support and guidance in the quantitative aspects of the project, I would like to acknowledge the invaluable advice and insights of Professor Leo Feler of Johns Hopkins University's School of Advanced International Studies (SAIS), as well as SAIS colleagues Pete Peterson, Alex Etra, Tariq Khan and Saurabh Shome, and Assen Assenov and Ivanova Reyes at American University.

The fieldwork in Russia for this book was supported by a grant from the International Research and Exchanges Board. I also thank the International Relations department at the Moscow State Institute for International Relations (MGIMO) for serving as a base for my research in Moscow and for scholarly and practical advice.

Molly O'Neal
Washington, DC

Abbreviations and terms

CCI	Center for Citizen Initiatives
CIPE	Center for International Private Enterprise
Cooperatives	*de facto* private companies organized under 1988 Soviet law
CPRF	Communist Party of the Russian Federation
CPSU	Communist Party of the Soviet Union
Delovaya Rossiya	business association for medium-sized and newer firms
DemRossiya	Democratic Russia (movement and proto-party)
DVR	Democratic Choice of Russia
EBRD	European Bank for Reconstruction and Development
FAS	Federal Anti-Monopoly Service
FSB	Federal Security Service
GRP	gross regional product
IISP	Independent Institute for Social Policy
INDEM	independent research institute "Information for Democracy"
Kadet	Constitutional Democratic Party
Komsomol	youth affiliate of CPSU
Komuch	Committee of Members of the Constitutional Assembly
Kray	territory treated as subject of Russian Federation
LDPR	Liberal Democratic Party of Russia
MED	Ministry of Economic Development
MVD	Ministry of Internal Affairs
NDR	Our Home Is Russia (party)
NP	Non-commercial partnership
Oblast'	region treated as subject of the Russian Federation
OOO	limited liability company
OAO	open stock company
OPORA	Union of Entrepreneurs' Organizations of Russia (Ob'edinenie Predprinimatel'skich Organizatsii Rossii)
PGU	Perm State University
Pravoe Delo	Right Cause (party)
RRAPP	Rostov Regional Agency for Entrepreneurship Support
RSPP	Russian Union of Entrepreneurs and Industrialists

SME	Small and Medium Enterprise
SPS	Union of Right Forces (party)
SR	Just Russia (party)
TPPRF	Chamber of Commerce and Industry of the Russian Federation
Zemstvo	Local government councils established in 1864

1 Small business owners and regional democracy

"In our view, post-communist studies should spend more time in the realm of verification and less time in the realm of discovery."

Frederic Fleron and Erik Hoffman (1993:13)

"What then are the most promising avenues for future research? The first focuses
on the shaping of the socioeconomic order and the impact that this may have on
political development. Much work has been done on the development of a Russian
middle class, but it has tended to focus on consumption patterns and orientations to
issues of self-development, while the fundamental question about the implications
of the emergence of new sources of class power has been neglected. . ."

Richard Sakwa (2008:494)

"It will be apparent that the abundance of hypotheses about the determinants of the
performance of democracies is not matched by an abundance of information about
Russia pertinent to them."

Harry Eckstein (1998:349)

"Modernization, whatever else it may be, means social change."

Dankwart Rustow (1968:47)

The empirical puzzle

The empirical puzzle at the heart of this book is a theoretically compelling empirical *regularity* – the positive association of small business 'prevalence' (small
company numbers relative to the workforce) and the extent of democratization in
the federal subjects of Russia from 1992 to 2008. Three major threads of political theory could potentially account for the association of small firm prevalence
with democratization. The first, modernization theory, would suggest that differences in the prevalence of small firms are merely a proxy for differential levels of
the 'real' socioeconomic causal variables: economic development, urbanization
and education. By contrast, comparative historical analysis would emphasize the
association of small firm prevalence with the attitudes and expectations of an
emerging middle class, of which entrepreneurs would be one constituent group.
Finally, the 'civic culture' tradition would suggest that small firm prevalence is

associated with democratization through the *sociocultural* implications of entrepreneurs acting as a defined social or civic group.

The contrasting experience of Russia's regions provides an intriguing challenge
to these three theoretical traditions in that here, as in all the post-communist democratizations beginning in the late 1980s, the emergence of private enterprise was sudden and novel, contemporaneous with democratization, not therefore conceivably
part of the 'social requisite' or structural conditions often underlying democratic
breakthroughs.[1] The fact that private entrepreneurs, as social and economic agents,
arose in the case of Russia and, for that matter in all the cases of post-communist
Europe, only in the aftermath of, and in response to, deliberate and 'exogenous' policy change rather than from incremental, spontaneous social development allows us
an analytically promising way of delimiting temporally the role that private enterprise owners may have played relative to the process of democratization.

This book seeks to answer these questions: "Does variation in the prevalence of
small firms explain some of the variation in democracy at a regional level in Russia?
Can we specify the means through which the emergence of private entrepreneurs may
have contributed to sustaining or reinforcing democratization at a regional level?"

The cited passages at the head of this chapter illuminate various aspects of the
research design: its emphasis on theory testing or verification, its focus on an
aspect of macro-social change, and its emphasis on collecting and reporting, as
Eckstein recommended, information about Russia pertinent to "hypotheses about
the determinants of the performance of democracies."[2]

Table 1.1 shows the pattern of correlation between a measure of small business prevalence by region and an index of democracy by region for the periods
1991–2001, 2000–2004 and 2005–2009. The variable that we will call *small firm*

Table 1.1 Correlation: Small Business Prevalence and the Regional Democracy Index

Small Firm Prevalence in Year	Democracy Index 1991–2001	Democracy Index 2000–2004	Democracy Index 2005–2009
1995	0.1757	0.1560	0.1173
	(0.1238)	(0.1727)	(0.3064)
2000	**0.4051***	**0.3733***	**0.3198***
	(0.0002)	(0.0007)	(0.0041)
2002	**0.3883***	**0.3681***	**0.3164***
	(0.0004)	(0.0008)	(0.0045)
2004	**0.3915***	**0.3663***	**0.3201***
	(0.0004)	(0.0009)	(0.0040)
2006	**0.4347***	**0.3968***	**0.3237***
	(0.0001)	(0.0003)	(0.0036)
2008	**0.4396***	**0.3703***	**0.3644***
	(0.0001)	(0.0008)	(0.0009)

P values shown in parentheses. Asterisk denotes significance at 0.01 level.

Source: Rosstat data on small firms and regional labor force by year, Regional democracy index.

$N = 79$

prevalence is defined as the number of incorporated small firms (those with up to 100 employees) relative to 1,000 people in labor force of a given region. (Goskomstat 2001; Rosstat 2002, 2008, 2010) The degree of regional democracy is an index of periodical expert evaluations of each of Russia's 83 regions in the time periods 1991–2001 (baseline), 2000–2004 and 2005–2009. (IISP 2006; Petrov and Titkov 2013)

The data in Table 1.1 show that the two variables are positively correlated, but this correlation appears only after the year 2000, or nearly ten years after the democratic breakthrough of 1991. This suggests that, even if both democratization and entrepreneurship at a regional level are in part the consequence of antecedent levels of socioeconomic modernization (urbanization, education levels) or sociocultural factors such as pre-revolutionary civic traditions, the democratic breakthrough nevertheless 'enabled' in a direct sense the emergence of small firms.

The more elusive question we will seek to explore, however, is whether the correlation between levels of democratization and small firm prevalence by region in subsequent years is in part the effect of different levels of small business prevalence on the persistence or consolidation of regional democratization over time. The book uses both a 'variables' approach and a 'case' approach in analyzing this question. Adopting the cross-sectional regression analysis from a comprehensive regional dataset allows us to test whether variations in small firm prevalence have independent explanatory power over the outcome 'democracy.' We do this by constructing a model controlling for differentials in economic growth or development, average levels of education and urbanization. The analysis traces the interaction of these two variables using their temporal sequence to draw inferences about causation.

Although small firm prevalence and democratization are correlated positively, any expectation that they are inextricably linked is not supported by considerable number of cases (regions) in our sample. The 79 regions in our sample are distributed as shown in Table 1.2, using the democracy index of 2000–2004 and 'small firm prevalence' in 2004:

Table 1.2 Cross-Tabulation of Small Firm Prevalence, Regional Democracy Index

	Small Firm Prevalence 2004 Above Average	*Small Firm Prevalence 2004 Below Average*	*Total*
Dem 2000–2004 score above average	24 regions	13 regions	37 regions
Dem 2000–2004 score below average	15 regions	27 regions	42 regions
Total	39 regions	40 regions	79
Pearson chi² = 6.6873		**Pr = 0.010**	

Source: Rosstat *Regiony Rossii,* Regional Democracy Index

Table 1.2 shows that from 2000 to 2004, 61 regions conformed to theoretical expectations by having 'matched' outcomes on the two variables and 28 regions had 'deviant' outcomes. This evidence suggests that the relations between the two variables of interest are conditioned and altered by other variables and potentially also by temporal sequences and lags.

A qualitative model of the interactions among the variables guides the design of the case studies of four regions. This model is proposed on the basis of the findings of the regression analysis presented in Chapter 2. The model is depicted in Figure 1.1:

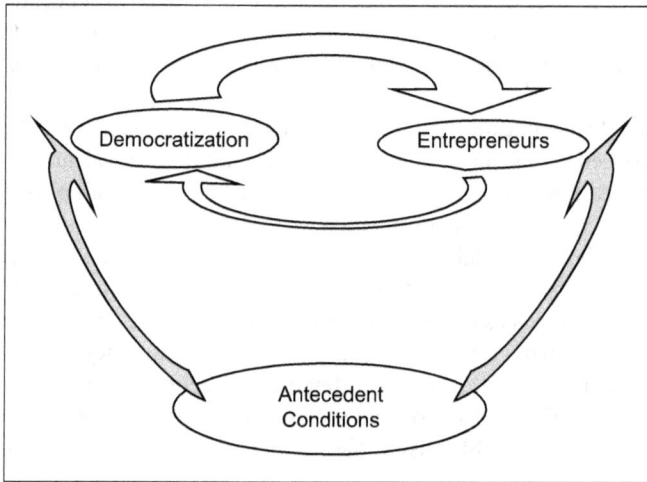

Figure 1.1 Schematic Model of Interactions Among Variables

Robert Putnam's influential study *Making Democracy Work* adopts as a point of departure an interactive model somewhat analogous to the one depicted here, where social demands through political interactions shape government's policy choices and implementation, giving rise to more societal demands. (Putnam 1993) The processes in our model, by contrast, are initiated by an exogenous 'shock' at the level of state policy, that is by the democratic breakthrough of the early 1990s. The effect of this democratic breakthrough is represented by the large arrow at the top of the diagram. The 'feedback' arrow running back to democratization from entrepreneurs is analogous to the 'societal demands' in Putnam's model. The interaction between the exogenous shock of democratization and the emergence of entrepreneurs is to be understood as taking place in a contemporary setting, beginning in 1991. The role of historically antecedent conditions, unique to each region of Russia, is hypothesized to influence both democratization and entrepreneurial development. These antecedent conditions are understood as both structural and ideational.

The effects of antecedent structural conditions – urbanization, education levels, average incomes and poverty rates – will figure in the regression analysis. The effects of ideational antecedent conditions – reflected in the explicit application of historical precedents to today's civic life and to the interaction of the business community with regional political authorities – will be a focus of the qualitative case studies. The accessibility and relevance of the 'usable past' may be important to varying regional outcomes on democratization and on the extent to which small business – and business more broadly – adopts a 'civic' identity. These ideational currents relate critically to the contemporary awareness among business and governing elites of regions' participation in Russia's economic modernization and industrialization from around 1870 up to 1917 and of the part played by regions in democratic political developments from the revolution of 1905 through the end of the Civil War.

Unlike Putnam's model, the model proposed above does *not* map all the processes in a given polity: our model focuses instead on the role of only one set of social actors – small entrepreneurs. The broader evolution of democratization obviously does not depend exclusively on these actors. Narrowing the analysis in this way nevertheless helps to clarify what contribution such actors have made to democratization and by what means. As in partial equilibrium analyses, the *ceteris paribus* assumption has to be borne in mind.

The four case study regions are selected so that two – Samara and Smolensk– have levels of small business development 'matched' with their levels of democratization, and two others – Rostov and Perm– show one of the variables markedly weak relative to the other. The four contrasting case studies delve into why and how this association comes to be in the cases where it seems to hold, and what might explain divergent cases. The case studies will seek to reveal what processes and combinations of actors, styles and structures of interaction and characteristics of organizations tend to produce or not produce the theoretically predicted result. The case studies draw on interviews with entrepreneurs, regional and municipal officials and legislators, business association leaders, and regional academic experts, extensive documentary sources from business associations relative to their goals and accomplishments and regional and municipal small business promotion programs.

The conception of democracy and democratization adopted in this study closely parallels that of Lipset (1959:73): "Democracy is not a quality of a social system which either does or does not exist, but is rather a complex of characteristics which may be ranked in many different ways." Lipset's formulation emphasizes two characteristics that are central to the approach of this study. First, we take democracy to be a continuous variable. Second, democracy is taken to characterize the *social system,* rather than solely the functioning of political or governmental institutions.

Diamond (1992) uses the ungainly but useful word "democraticness" in reviewing the cross-sectional statistical analyses testing Lipset's claim that economic development is requisite to democracy.[3] Diamond adopts as the dependent variable the Freedom House scheme of 'shades' of democracy to categorize existing political regimes. The 'degrees' of democracy are shown in Table 1.3:

Table 1.3 'Shades' of Democracy – Freedom House Categories

State hegemonic, partly open
Non-competitive, partially pluralist
Semi-competitive, partially pluralist
Competitive, partially illiberal
Competitive, pluralist, partially institutionalized
Liberal democracy

Source: Diamond 1992:457

The degrees on this scale characterize both the political regime *and* characteristics of the social system and assume, problematically perhaps, that the two are always in a fixed correspondence. Democracy, in this conception, is both a quality of political regime and a description of social reality. For purposes of this study, then, the variable 'democracy' is continuous in a cross-sectional sense – a matter of measurable degree allowing comparison of many cases at any point in time. Differences of degree can matter analytically even if *none* of the cases studied approaches the fully democratic end of the scale of measurement.

We also take democracy to be, following the argument of Charles Tilly, separable analytically into multiple contemporaneous *processes* of democratization and de-democratization within a given polity. (Tilly 2004) In Tilly's formulation, an analytic refinement of that of Barrington Moore, the term 'democracy' covers a dynamic and unceasing process of becoming and unbecoming. For Moore, democracy is

> a long and certainly incomplete struggle to do three closely related things: 1) to check arbitrary rulers, 2) to replace arbitrary rules with just and rational ones, and 3) to obtain a share for the underlying population in the making of rules.
>
> (Moore 1966:414)

The present study analyzes the interactions of a single category of social actors across divergent regional experiences within Russia beginning in the early 1990s. No attempt is made to map all processes in play in the Russian polity, nor is there any intention to minimize the significance of powerful processes of de-democratization contemporaneous to those processes studied here.

Macro-social processes present unique challenges to the study of comparative politics, because they are, as Paul Pierson (2003) wrote, "invisible and slow." From the vantage point of the future, historians often find that crucial political outcomes were the result of gradual and almost imperceptible macro-historical changes. The dispersion of ownership rights and the gradual institutionalization of their secure recognition is a resonant macro-historical process, especially in the Russian context. The combination of a 'variables' and a case study approach across Russia's regions adopted in this study is an attempt to make perceptible one dimension of an unfolding 'invisible and slow' macro-social process.

The Russian regions together experienced a sudden 'shock' of institutional change in late 1991, analogous to, if immeasurably sharper than, the abrupt regional devolution in Italy, which framed Putnam's 1993 study. For a period lasting through Yeltsin's presidency the *de facto* and *de jure* devolution of power to regions and republics promoted a divergence of outcomes. (Ross 2002; Stepan 2000; Treisman 1999) The regions of Russia differ by per capita income and other social indicators considerably more widely than do the regions of Italy. At exactly the same time in every region of Russia, private firms and entrepreneurs were allowed to establish themselves formally. This, as we have previously argued, provides an opportunity to isolate and study the impact of this social category in a tightly circumscribed time period in many different settings. Finally, there is, as in Putnam's cases, a divergence of historical experience and underlying civic culture among the Russian regions.

The Putin federal reforms beginning in 2002 recentralized power and aimed to homogenize regional outcomes. However, the first decade of Russia's independence produced persistent variations in the two principal variables in this study: democratization and the extent of small firm development within the business community. Remington (2009:3) argues, "A substantial body of literature testifies that Russia's regions feature widely different types of regime." Remington notes that case studies of Russian regions by political scientists have been fairly common, but large-N comparative studies of Russian regions by political scientists have been few.[4]

Remington (2010) and Marsh (2004) are similar in methodology to this book in that both attempt to explain variations in regional democratization. Remington uses the Petrov democracy index as the dependent variable in his study, and Marsh devises his own index based on a study of the extent of electoral competition only. Remington finds that structural factors such as per capita income and urbanization explain a great deal of the regional variation in democratization, but emphasizes that the considerable variation left unexplained by these structural factors suggests the decisive role played by historically contingent and non-material factors such as political leadership and receptiveness to democratic norms. Marsh's index of regional democracy is based exclusively on the extent of competition in and fair conduct of regional elections from 1999–2002. He finds that variations in civil society development and economic liberalization explain much of the variation in regional democracy as he defines it. Sharafutdinova (2010) uses regression across the cases of Russia's regions to query the relationship between public perceptions of corruption and the extent of electoral competition by region.

This study differs from the approaches adopted by Remington, Sharafutdinova and Marsh while having much in common with them. By contrast to each of them, this study posits the 'agency' of a specific set of social actors – small business owners – applying both a 'variables' and a case study approach to the study of this group's influence upon the process of democratization.

In keeping with Tilly's approach to analytically separable processes of democratization and de-democratization, this study sets itself the goal of closely analyzing one aspect of ongoing process and change at a societal level. It seeks to understand what conditions, actors and institutions have tended to produce the generally strong association of regional 'democratic-ness' with intensity of small business activity, and why in other cases this association seems not to hold.

The four regional case studies in this book trace the role of organizations representing small business vis-à-vis regional and municipal governments, the entry of entrepreneurs into political or administrative office, the 'weight' of small business relative to incumbent (Soviet-era) or 'oligarch' owned big companies and how the business community in a given region has influenced the development of regional media and broader civic life.

A nexus of conceptual ladders

The conceptual nexus that justifies the focus in this study on the role of private entrepreneurs can be illustrated by use of three conceptual ladders (adopted from the framework of Giovanni Sartori) from general to associated specific sub-concepts. (Collier and Gerring 2009) Doing this exposes the interesting overlapping 'supporting' role that entrepreneurs, firms and organized business interests play in three theories about the social underpinnings of democracy. The three ladders are shown in Table 1.4:

Table 1.4 'Social' Explanations of Democratization: Conceptual Ladders

	Modernization Theory	*Civic Culture*	*Comparative Social History*
Explanation	Socioeconomic development	Social capital	Social structural change
Central concept	Modernity	Civic associations	Middle class
Sub-concept	Industrialization	Business associations	Entrepreneurs

These approaches range from structural to historically contingent explanations, but are not mutually incompatible. An exemplary synthetic approach is Huntington's *The Third Wave,* which explains 29 cases of democratization from 1974 to 1990 by reference to socioeconomic modernization as well as sociocultural or ideational change. (Huntington 1991) Putnam (1993) emphasizes sociocultural explanations for democracy, but adds to these explanations the role of historical path dependence in producing divergent levels of institutional performance in his Italian regional cases. Both scholars check the insights of one theoretical framework against others to produce a richer understanding of the outcome they seek to explain.

These three approaches define methodological choices, ranging from the application of probabilistic logic to a large number of similar cases, through interpretation based on a stylized paradigm of class conflict and accommodation, to the tracing of open-ended and contingent interplay among self-organized groups and between such groups and agents of state authority. The sub-concepts highlighted in all three instances are, of course, only one of several constituent sub-concepts that underlie the encompassing concepts of modernity, the middle class and civil society. But in each 'ladder,' a key sub-concept is related either to markets, business or entrepreneurship.

Modernization theory

One of the strongest empirical regularities in social science is the correspondence of higher levels of economic development and liberal democracy. Theoretical explanations for this association reach back to Aristotle, who argued that democracy could be sustained only where basic wants of citizens were satisfied. Otherwise, he reasoned, there would be unconstrained distributional conflict.

According to the classic formulation by Lipset (1959), socioeconomic modernization is a composite of four closely related factors: per capita income or wealth, industrialization, urbanization and high general level of popular education. Lipset's central claim has been tested in empirical studies using different country groups, different time periods and different measures of both the dependent variable (political regime) and independent variable (socioeconomic modernization). Diamond (1992) shows that the work of three decades of empirical testing of Lipset's hypothesis tends broadly to support it.

But modernization theory seems to explain outcomes or results rather than cast any real light on path or process. This is a serious weakness, because, as Rustow reminds us, modernization *is* change.[5] Even if, as Diamond shows, the core hypothesis of modernization theory tends to be supported by empirical evidence, we remain unsatisfied because, as Diamond writes, most of the studies "tell us little about why development tends to generate democracy, how it does so, and under what circumstances it fails to do so, or does the reverse." (Diamond, 1992:472)

Timothy Frye (2003) and Steven Fish (2005) are two examples of attempts to draw inferences about the role of business owners to democratization in contemporary Russia. Frye's survey evidence shows that entrepreneurs in Russia tend on average to be more supportive of liberal democracy than other groups.[6] Fish (2005) presents cross-national comparative evidence for his claim that that one of the principal reasons that democratization stalled in Russia was the incomplete liberalization of the economy.[7] This book may be seen partly as a test of Fish's finding using sub-national comparative data, adopting Frye's intuition, supported by his survey evidence, that entrepreneurs as a group may supply some of the 'agency' missing from structural, cross-sectional analyses.

The modernization thesis meets a stubborn challenge in the post-communist democratizations beginning in the late 1990s. Most narrative accounts of the

democratic breakthrough in the Soviet Union and Russia emphasize the historically contingent rather than the structural, and in particular the leadership of Gorbachev. (Brown 1996, McFaul 2001) It is worth noting, however, that Gorbachev
himself both contemporaneously and in his subsequent writings claimed that
'society' demanded reforms and he understood himself to be acting on its behalf.

One line of argument asserting the conclusive power over events of societal
modernization in the late Soviet period emphasizes the role of 'decay' or the
waning of ideological norms and an awakening of new expectations and values.
Hosking (1990), Lewin (1990), Lapidus (1989), Zaslavsky (1995) Ruble (1987,
1990), Starr (1988), Dallin (1992) and Rigby (1992) are examples of a society-
based revisionist outlook in Soviet studies that sought explanations for attempts to
reform the Soviet political regime in state-society relations, including by reference
to social differentiation, changing attitudes, values and expectations. T. H. Rigby
remarked that there was, beginning in the Brezhnev years "a profuse flowering of
what I have called the covert 'market in ideas,' a blossoming vastly greater than
what was apparent publicly." (Rigby 1992:18)

If, in reality, social conditions were at the source of the decisive shift in Soviet
policy in the mid-1980s, this change was 'invisible and slow' because much of it
took place outside the public sphere in networks of like-minded educated circles
and in informal and illegal economic activity. Neither of these easily could be analyzed in the 'variables' framework most conducive to the modernization strand of
comparative political science, nor were narrative or etiological sources of understanding easily accessible.

Civil society, interest groups and the civic outcome

Scholarship in this tradition emphasizes the role of self-organized social groups
sharing values or interests in explaining democratic outcomes. The norms and
habits of citizenship and civic engagement are in this view the sociocultural
underpinnings of democracy. The pioneering text in this tradition, Almond and
Verba (1963) emphasizes values and attitudes that generate different levels of
social optimism and engagement including in self-organized groups across different polities. The survey research of Richard Rose (2000), Rose, Mishler and
Munro (2006) applies an approach similar to that of Almond and Verba to post-
communist Russia, in that it explains political outcomes by reference to normative
and attitudinal change at the mass level.

In Tocqueville's 'strong' formulation of this tradition, what is crucial is that
groups in society self-organize, even for goals and interests that are outside the
political sphere:

> An association, be it political, industrial, commercial, or even literary or sci-
> entific, is an educated and powerful body of citizens which cannot be twisted
> to any man's will or quietly trodden down, and by defending its private inter-
> ests against the encroachments of power, it saves the common liberties.
>
> (Tocqueville 1840/1969:697)

Associations embody values and norms and, at the same time, project and articulate interests vis-à-vis the state. Robert Putnam argues that "Civil associations contribute to the effectiveness and stability of democratic government, it is argued, both because of their 'internal' effects on individual members and because of their 'external' effects on the wider polity." (Putnam 1993:89) The interests associations pursue derive from the adoption by group members of certain distinctive norms and values. "What interest groups and social movements share is a set of norms, beliefs or values that keep the 'interests' intact. These shared orientations are the glue binding together the group constituency, leading it to act as a coherent entity." (Bashevkin 1996:135)

Putnam (1993) seeks to prove the decisive role of civil society in the performance of democratic institutions. Like Tocqueville, he emphasizes civic norms and values that ensure that the interests civic groups pursue are 'enlightened' and supportive of, rather than 'myopic,' and thence inimical to, the public good. He explores the possibility that performance of institutions is "shaped by the social context within which they operate." (Putnam 1993:8) Putnam's fundamental question is "Is there any connection between the civic-ness of a community and the quality of its governance?" (Putnam 1993:91) His hypothesized independent variable is the variation in degree of 'civic-ness' among Italian regions, a composite measure at the regional level of the vibrancy of associational life, the breadth of newspaper readership, voter turnout on policy referenda and the frequency of party list (programmatic) versus 'preference' (clientelistic) voting.

Having produced evidence for the importance of 'civic-ness' as an independent variable, Putnam then turns to consideration of 'civic-ness' as a dependent variable or outcome. The roots of divergent degrees of 'civic-ness' are, he concludes, in distinctive historical trajectories of regions. He identifies as one factor in producing a civic tradition the role of banking and commerce in the economic progress of the more civic regions, built, as Putnam argues, on the 'social capital' of interpersonal trust and vibrant associational life. (Putnam 1993)

The present study adopts the advice of the cautions made explicit in Tarrow (1996), a critique of Putnam's use of comparative history in social science explanation. The imputed contributions of antecedent conditions to the outcomes of interest (democratization and entrepreneurialism) are grounded where possible in structural data (such as the character of natural resource endowments and economic geography). The impact of ideational antecedent conditions is adduced from evidence of contemporary elite awareness of and explicit reference to the 'usable' precedent of the late Tsarist period of economic and social modernization under market conditions.

In research applying the 'puzzle' explored by Putnam (1993) to the study of post-communist Russia, Marc Howard (2002, 2003) explains the pervasive weakness of voluntary associations by appealing to the persistence of informal 'friendship networks' based on the habits and norms of the Soviet era. These, he argues, serve to overcome the limitations in interpersonal trust that hamper the development of formally constituted associations.

Instead of emphasizing the role of formal and institutionalized civic associations, Tilly (2004) posits the importance to democratization of 'trust networks' among citizens and agents of state authority. One of the principal processes of democratization is, in this theory, the extension of trust networks across the boundary between state and society. Democratization, Tilly writes, "consists of a set of changes in citizen-agent relations: broadening them, equalizing them, protecting them, and subjecting them to binding consultation." (Tilly 2004:15) Three dimensions of change in 'citizen-agent' relations are crucial to democratization: segregating 'categorical' inequality from public politics, integrating trust networks into public politics, and increasing breadth, equality, enforcement, and security of mutual obligations between citizens and government agents. (Tilly 2004)

Diamond defines civil society as "the realm of organized social life that is voluntary, self-generating, (largely) self-supporting, autonomous from the state, and bound by a legal order or a set of shared rules." (Diamond 1994:5) He cites and endorses the contention of Lipset and Huntington that the democratic function of civil society is to provide the basis for the limitation of state power. Among the wide array of groups that form civil society, according to Diamond, are interest-based groups such as business associations, while private firms themselves and the interactions of the market belong instead to 'economic society.' Business associations, labor unions and consumer associations are civil society groups having close relations with but lying outside of economic society in Diamond's conception.

Among the questions probed by Steven Fish (1995) in his study of pro-democracy civil society groups and political movements in four Russian regions was the link between economic liberalization and civil society development. He found that the continued role of the state as employer frustrated the development of civil society's autonomy and, in one of his four case regions, emerging private business was a significant source of financial and other backing for democratic groups. In anticipation of further changes, Fish writes,

> If privatization does engender some basis for popular capitalism in Russia, it may foster political parties, trade unions, and interest associations based on class, profession and sector. If, however, it concentrates the lion's share of wealth in a thin stratum of state officials and enterprise directors, it may beget patterns of interest representation based on communal, patron-client, familial, and personalist relations. The changes in social structure that privatization will induce will not determine fully the character of intermediary institutions, but they will powerfully reshape the interest basis of politics.

> (Fish 1995:223)

Tocqueville's argument for the decisive role of self-organized civil society is the ultimate source of the 'pluralist' model of interest articulation. (Dahl 1970; Keane 1998; Truman 1951) This tradition emphasizes the potentially contentious encounter of groups in the public sphere and in particular their role in making demands on the state. Truman's formative work in the pluralist tradition defines interest groups this way:

> As used here, 'interest group' refers to any group that, on the basis of one or more shared attitudes, makes certain claims upon other groups in society for the establishment, maintenance, or enhancement of forms of behavior that are implied by the shared attitudes . . . These afford the participants frames of reference for interpreting and evaluating events and behavior.
>
> (Truman 1951:33)

Because interest groups' *raison d'etre* is to affect governmental policy, they can be categorized by the character of their relations to political authority along a continuum from pluralist to corporatist. The character of coordination between the state and interest groups representing business gives rise to various 'types of capitalism' related to the underlying pluralist to corporatist character of interest articulation. (Hall and Soskice 2001; Streeck and Yamamura 2001)

The definitions of pluralism and of corporatism by Schmitter (1974) help to guide the analysis of business associations in the case studies of this book and to support inferences about the contribution of small and new firms to the character of business-state coordination in the four case study regions. Pluralist forms of business-state coordination may be seen as compatible with 'enlightened' or civic interest articulation. In authoritarian corporatism, by contrast, the state dominates business, replacing reciprocal relations with clientelism and patronage:

> Pluralism can be defined as a system of interest representation in which the constituent units are organized into an unspecified number of multiple, voluntary, competitive, non-hierarchically ordered and self-determined (as to type or scope of interest) categories which are not specifically licensed, recognized, subsidized, created or otherwise controlled in leadership selection or interest articulation by the state and which do not exercise a monopoly of representational activity within their respective categories.
>
> (Schmitter 1974:96)

> Corporatism can be defined as a system of interest representation in which the constituent units are organized into a limited number of singular, compulsory, noncompetitive, hierarchically ordered and functionally differentiated categories, recognized and licensed (if not created) by the state and granted a deliberate representational monopoly within their respective categories in exchange for observing certain controls on their selection of leaders and articulation of demands and supports.
>
> (Schmitter 1974:93)[8]

In general, a normative controversy surrounds the study of groups in politics: Does group activity enhance or undermine equality or participation in democracies? The controversy reaches back to Rousseau's dread of 'faction' and contrasts with the opposite claim advanced by Tocqueville. As Putnam says,

> Citizens in the civic community are not required to be altruists. In the civic community, however, citizens pursue what Tocqueville termed "self-interest properly understood," that is, self-interest defined in the context of broader public needs, self-interest that is "enlightened" rather than "myopic."
>
> (Putnam 1993:88)

Putnam's crucial variable, "civic-ness," is founded on social equality and an ethos of participation, cooperation and collaboration. Putnam contrasts the "horizontal" relations of reciprocity and cooperation with "vertical relations of authority and dependency" which are inimical to "civic-ness." (Putnam 1993:88) Without the social equality that underpins the cooperative and reciprocal social relations of the civic community, the activity of groups can be uncivic, where power and information are unequally distributed and groups pursue interests narrowly defined and contrary to the interests of other groups and society at large. Ledeneva (1998, 2006) argues that a culture of favors and clientelism dominates Russian business-state relations. Unlike Howard, she does not posit the existence of informal, collaborative 'social capital,' but clientelistic networks based on social inequality and domination. Putnam argues that the prevalence of such networks reliably predicts the poor performance of democratic institutions.

Mancur Olson insisted upon the distorting and socially sub-optimal outcomes for general welfare when groups are able to bend state policy to their narrow interest. Olson was particularly concerned, as was Adam Smith, by the problem of 'combinations' of economic interests acting to preserve monopolistic market access through the exercise of political influence. (Olson 1982) Interest groups in Olson's formulation would not, as in the corporatist case, be dependent upon or subservient to the state and therefore not independent, but would be so powerful as to be able to effect 'state capture.'

From this literature it is possible to devise a typology of business – state coordination associated with different forms of interest articulation, as shown in Table 1.5.[9]

Table 1.5 Modes of State-Business Coordination and Associated Forms of Interest Articulation

Basis of Coordination	Interest Articulation
Rule-bound exchange	Pluralist
Patrimonial exchange	Moderate corporatist
Business captured by state	Authoritarian corporatist
State captured by business	Olson's dystopia – weak state

The building of capitalism in the Russian context 'from scratch' has spawned a political economy literature emphasizing the emergence of the phenomenon of state capture by emergent industrialists' interests and the corrosive effects of industrial lobbying in either obstructing further reform (Hellman 1998, 2000), distorting electoral outcomes, and inhibiting the development of independent media and political parties. (Goldman 2003; Reddaway and Glinski 2001; Rutland 2001) Throughout the 1990s, state capture was the widely accepted characterization of business-state coordination in Russia. (Barnes 2003, 2006; Orttung 2004; Rutland 2001, 2006; Volkov 2002) During Putin's presidency, according to many scholars, the state capture of the 1990s was replaced by 'business capture' consistent with authoritarian forms of corporatism. (Aslund 2007; Hanson and Teague 2005)

Several studies based on surveys of company owners across the spectrum of firm size and sector address the question of business-state coordination. (Frye 2002; Golikova 2007; Pyle 2006a, 2006b) Frye (2002) pointed to the emergence of an emerging 'elite exchange' framework for business lobbying. The median size of the 500 firms in Frye's sample was 150 employees. Sixty-five percent of the firms surveyed were privatized, 20% were *de novo,* and 15% were state owned. Thirty percent were members of business associations. Frye's main conclusion was that 'state capture' was not an accurate characterization of business-state coordination in Russia, when a representative sample of Russian companies (as opposed to the highly visible 'oligarch' companies) was considered.

Among firms reporting success in lobbying in Frye's survey, half reported lobbying through business associations, but all also reported lobbying through personal contacts with municipal agencies (52%), regional agencies (38%), mayors (33%), regional legislatures (27%), city legislatures (27%) and governors (20%). A third reported using the press and media in lobbying. Frye, Yakovlev and Yasin (2009) present evidence that the business community as a whole (as distinct from the very large oligarch or state-owned firms) is generally in a form of 'exchange' with the state, rather than either dominating or being dominated.

Yakovlev (2006b), Frye (2002), Pyle (2006a), Golikova (2007, 2009), Semenenko (2001), Duvanova (2007) and Markov (2007) study the role and functions of business associations in Russia since the 1998 financial crisis. These scholars understand business associations, much in the mode of economic historian Douglass North, as adaptive institutional innovations lowering information and transactions costs, rather than as instruments for state capture or rent seeking.

Surveys by the World Bank in 1992–1994 (Recantini and Ryterman 2001) found that firms joined associations to try to reduce transaction costs in dealing with unknown other firms. Raiser, Rousso and Steves (2003) found business associations were in effect trust networks among firms. Duvanova (2007) sought to explain what conditions drove the emergence of business associations in four countries. Using World Bank-EBRD firm survey data from Russia, Croatia and Kazakhstan, Duvanova found that an initial level of intensity of bribe-extraction by officials, along with excessive administrative requirements, stimulated the creation and development of business associations. She concluded that formation of business associations was a rational defensive strategy of firms to bureaucratic predation.

Golikova (2009) finds evidence that business association membership is increasingly serving as an instrument of for advocacy of a more favorable legal environment for business. Around 20% of Golikova's survey respondents found business associations useful in 'preparing legislation.' This was up from about 10% in a comparable 2002 survey. Golikova infers that association membership is a hedge against risk of unfavorable change in business conditions because of state action. Supporting Frye's 'elite exchange' paradigm, Golikova finds that association members are more likely to benefit from various policies to promote business development (e.g. preferential credit programs) by municipal authorities and are in turn more often than non-members to report that they have actively supported local governments' social initiatives.

This literature draws upon the insights of institutional economics in understanding the emergence of business associations as market-supporting institutions. This scholarship, of which the progenitors are Olson and North, shares with the civic culture perspective of Putnam an emphasis on enlarging and reinforcing interpersonal trust.

Comparative historical analysis

Dankwart Rustow derided modernization theorists' 'tally ho' method of probabilistic reasoning, because, he contended, such an approach could not explain whether democracy causes economic development or vice versa, or if both are caused by an unknown anterior cause. Rustow therefore called for comparative historical analysis aimed at producing theoretical insights applicable to comparable countries (although not necessarily those in a single region). (Rustow 1968) As Lipset himself acknowledged,

> The data . . . support strongly the conclusion that a more systematic and up-to-date version of Aristotle's hypothesis concerning the relationship of political forms to social structure is valid. Unfortunately . . . this conclusion does not justify the optimistic liberal's hope that an increase in wealth, in the size of the middle class, in education, and other related factors will necessarily mean the spread of democracy or the stabilizing of democracy.
>
> (Lipset 1959:73)

Diamond concludes that, "A careful reading of Lipset's thesis reveals that economic development promotes democracy only by effecting changes in political culture and social structure." (Diamond 1992:488) According to Huntington (1991:65), "Economic development appears to have promoted changes in social structure and values that, in turn, encouraged democratization."

Whereas modernization theory built probabilistic generalizations on composite descriptive data on large number of countries in a particular historical moment, comparative macro-analytical social history traces comparable processes in a few cases over time. Causation is imputed by application the logic of 'etiology' or narrative, by what influential actors and events were present or absent in contrasting cases. (Moore 1966; Skocpol 1979)

For Barrington Moore, anything true in all places and all times was "either trivial or false."[10] Nevertheless, his classic study of paths to the modern world led him to a sweeping and memorable generalization: "No bourgeoisie, no democracy." (Moore 1966) In a fundamental sense, the approach of Moore shares with that of modernization theorists an underlying set of assumptions about the roles of social classes – landowners, industrial workers, townspeople, peasantry – that arises from classical political economy. Social class is an outgrowth of economic relations and, therefore, is related to distributional tensions, potential conflict and accommodation.

Moore's approach is to see democracy or autocracy as the result of certain patterns of contention and accommodation among social classes over a long historical period. From this perspective, socioeconomic modernization is at most a kind of backdrop or background condition for the emergence of the broad categories of social actors whose interactions cause democratization or, in some cases, the emergence of alternative political regimes.

Some scholars adopting the methods of comparative macro-historical analysis argue that the conclusive role in democratic outcomes belongs to the working class, rather than the bourgeoisie. (Luebbert 1991; Rueschemeyer, Stephens and Stephens 1992) They argue that full political participation within a universal suffrage regime of the working class would, without a stable constitutional order governing property rights, result in disruptive and potentially violent distributional conflict. In effect, they recast Moore's famous dictum to say, in effect, "No working class reconciled to pursuit of its interests within the liberal democratic framework, no democracy." Considerably less pithy or memorable than Moore's formulation, this claim nonetheless makes the important point that democracy as an outcome is best explained not by the activity of a single social group, but by the character of interaction or contention among groups.

A number of social historians turned, especially since 1985, to a re-examination of the role played by capitalists (merchants and industrialists) in the parliamentary politics of late Tsarism and in social and civic life. (Roosa 1997; Shanin 1985; West 1991) The work of these social historians is implicitly comparative in two senses. First, it emphasizes the distinctiveness of Russia relative to the industrial and social modernization experienced in 18th-century England and elsewhere in Western Europe in the 19th century. Second, either explicitly or implicitly, this work draws parallels and contrasts between the late imperial period and more contemporary late Soviet and Russian experience.

Gill (2008) is explicitly comparative in the tradition of Moore, in that it studies the emergence of the contemporary Russian commercial bourgeoisie in the framework of the historical rise of the bourgeoisie in Britain, France, Germany and the United States. Mau and Starodubrovskaya (2002) claim that Russia's experience should be studied in the comparative framework of great social revolutions, as, using different analytical approaches, do McFaul (2001), Hough (1997), Fish (1995) and Weigle (2000).

Pipes (1999) ascribes to weakly established property rights in Tsarist Russia much responsibility for the failure of constitutional liberalism to gain a stable footing. Russia's peculiar vulnerability to revolutionary paroxysm as opposed to evolutionary change is, in Pipes's argument, in considerable measure because of the weakness of such commercial and business elites that did emerge in the late Tsarist period and the reliance of many of them on favor from state policy.

Fischer (1958) and Carr (1989) agree that a fundamental weakness of early 20th-century Russian liberalism was the absence of any substantial base outside the intelligentsia and in particular the absence of any firm support among commercial and industrial elites. Carr argues that liberalism's success in Britain, parts of Western Europe, and in the English-speaking world came because it could in the 18th and much of the 19th century still claim to be the leading and most dynamic proponent of social reform, sponsored by a rising entrepreneurial class.

Not only was the Russian commercial bourgeoisie small in numbers at the turn of the 20th century but also Russian business was criticized for

> the clear supremacy of traders over industrialists within it, 'provincial' narrow-mindedness, 'backward' business practices and extreme despotism towards the employees and members of their own families, the political indifference of the majority coupled with monarchist, xenophobic and anti-liberal political tendencies of most of those who were ready to commit themselves.
>
> (Shanin 1985:119)[11]

In a social history of Moscow's merchant-industrialists from 1855 to 1905, Owen (1981) finds much the same traditionalism, parochialism and political inertness cited by Shanin. However, Owen traces a clear evolution of the younger 'sons' of leading merchant-industrialists toward a more modern, progressive outlook up to and especially after 1905. Nevertheless, returning to the same questions, Owen (1991) stresses the impediments – state tutelage, foreign ownership and the ethnic heterogeneity of the business elite – that kept Russian commercial and industrial interests from forming a cohesive and politically significant class self-awareness.

Hosking (1973) documents how leading business figures such as the Riabushinsky brothers (bankers) and Moscow textiles manufacturer Alexander Konovalov attempted to expand the role of the business elite beyond the Progressist party where it had been centered in the Third Duma and through the newspaper *Utro Rossii,* financed by the same circle of industrialists. This expanded Progressist Party expressed almost complete agreement with program of the Kadets, but argued that the intelligentsia needed support from business interests, whose opinions the government would be more likely to heed. A statement of the Progressist policy agenda in *Utro Rossii* moreover declares that "the Russian merchantry has always been inspired by and has always shown liberal political tendencies. . . ."[12] Emphasizing the emergence of business lobbying rather than direct participation by business elites in duma politics, Roosa (1997) studies the formation the Association of Industry and Trade in 1906, its leading figures, public declarations and interaction with the state until it was dissolved in 1917. The contemporary Russian Chamber of Commerce and Industry claims direct descent from this Association.

The case study regions in this project consider the role in contemporary elite self-awareness played by precedents set by regional merchant-industrialists of the late Tsarist period in civic, political, associational and philanthropic life. The activities of the regional chapters of the Chambers of Commerce and Industry are a focus of the case studies. These regional Chambers make frequent reference to the 'ancestry' of the contemporary Chamber in the late Tsarist period in shaping the ethos of members and the *raison d'être* of the Chamber's positions on economic policies.

Conclusions and plan of the book

The late USSR was an ostensibly 'modern' country without a commercial and industrial bourgeoisie. In post-communist societies such as Russia, entrepreneurs are a social novelty, making it easier to gain analytical purchase on their specific influence on democratization than in other settings. Structural comparative analysis is the theoretically informed analysis of empirical puzzles. (Kohli 2002) Our puzzle – the positive association of small business development and regional democracy – is one that can be considered in the light of modernization theory, historical comparative analysis and theory related to the formation, identity and purposes of interest groups and their relations to broader civil society.

Diamond argues that democracy consists of three dimensions: competition, participation and liberty. (Diamond 1992:455) This study focuses on participation by a single category of citizens. Private entrepreneurs are, this study argues, one of the main sources of social innovation in Russia. They are the social category that least resembles any antecedent group in Soviet society.

A key hypothesis is that small firm prevalence is related to the quality and diversity of the associational environment for business, which varies across Russia's regions. Business associations, in turn, may tend to support democratization through their role within broader associational milieu, through the articulation of interests in the public sphere including in the media, through the development of an identified set of attitudes and aspirations for entrepreneurs in general, through philanthropic activities and through serving as a staging point for aspirants to regional and municipal legislative and executive office.

Chapter 2 summarizes the development of small business in Russia and uses regression techniques to explore the relationship between small firm prevalence and regional democracy. Chapter 3 elaborates the qualitative model introduced at the beginning of this introductory chapter and, drawing on the regression findings, explains the rationale for case selection and the organization of the four case studies. Chapter 4 takes up the case of the Samara region, Chapter 5 the Smolensk region, Chapter 6 the Rostov region, and Chapter 7 the Perm region. The final chapter is a structured comparison of the cases that draws conclusions from both the quantitative and qualitative analysis.

Notes

1 The term 'region' is used here and throughout the book to denote a province or 'subject' of the Russian federation. The Russian term '*oblast*' (or '*kray*' in the case of the Perm region) is used with equivalent meaning to 'region' where otherwise there could be any ambiguity.
2 Surveying Soviet studies in the aftermath of the collapse of the USSR, Fleron and Hoffmann conclude that, "Our focus on elites and bureaucracies has ill-prepared us for comprehending powerful social forces and popular movements, and our perspective 'from the top' rather than 'from the bottom' has been of little help in explaining, let alone predicting the demise of the Soviet political system." (Fleron and Hoffman 1993:11) One might say that mainstream Soviet studies only tardily and incompletely 'brought society back in.'
3 Diamond, 1992, pp. 470 tabulates the basic findings of cross-sectional tests of the Lipset hypothesis by various scholars from 1963 to 1991.
4 Regional case studies and comparisons include Gel'man, Ryzhenkov and Brie 2003; Melvin 1998; Ruble, Koehn and Popson 2001; Mitchneck 2007; Stoner-Weiss 2006; Stavrakis, deBardeleben and Black 1997; Matsuzato 2001; and Hughes 1997. Ahrend (2002) exemplifies the economics literature adopting large-N regression analysis to Russia's regions.
5 Przeworski and Limongi (1993) show that economic growth, as opposed to a given level of economic development, bears a complex or equivocal relationship to democratization.
6 The much larger survey evidence of Maleva et al. (2004) places entrepreneurs in the inner core of the emergent middle class characterized by aspirational values.
7 Fish and Choudry (2007) makes the case from cross-national data that economic liberalization has a positive long-term effect on democratization.
8 Schmitter distinguishes between the democratic of neo-corporatism of Western European social democracies and authoritarian corporatism. His argument is essentially a matter of historical sequence, in that neo-corporatism emerges only within a polity where pluralist interest articulation has previously been dominant. Schmitter and Guillermo O'Donnell posited that different forms of interest articulation, especially rigid forms of corporatism, might explain cases such as Argentina and other Latin American dictatorships, where trends of socioeconomic modernization (industrialization, urbanization, generalized education) did not bring democratization. (O'Donnell 1973)
9 This scheme is partly derived from Yakovlev 2006a.
10 Moore quoted by Rustow (1968).
11 This assessment by Shanin synthesizes the view of several key Russian sources of the period.
12 *Utro Rossii*, 4 April 1912 (cited by Hosking 1973:191).

References

Ahrend, Rudiger. (2002) Speed of Reform, Initial Conditions, Political Orientation, or What? Explaining Russian Regions' Economic Performance. *DELTS Working Papers*: Ecole Normale Superieure.

Almond, Gabriel A. and Sidney Verba. (1963) *The Civic Culture: Political Attitudes and Democracy in Five Nations*. Thousand Oaks, CA: Sage Publications.

Aslund, Anders. (2007) *Russia's Capitalist Revolution: Why Reform Succeeded and Democracy Failed*. Washington, DC: Peterson Institute for International Economics.

Barnes, Andrew. (2003) Russia's New Business Groups and State Power. *Post-Soviet Affairs* 19 (2):154–186.

Barnes, Andrew. (2006) *Owning Russia: The Struggle Over Factories, Farms, and Power*. Ithaca, NY: Cornell University Press.

Bashevkin, Sylvia. (1996) Interest Groups and Social Movements. In LeDuc, L., Niemi, R. G and Norris, P. (eds.) *Comparing Democracies: Elections and Voting in Global Perspective*. Thousand Oaks, CA: Sage Publications.

Brown, Archie. (1996) *The Gorbachev Factor*. Oxford: Oxford University Press.

Carr, E. H. (1989) "Liberalism in Alien Soil" In *From Napoleon to Stalin and Other Essays* (pp. 60–67). New York: St. Martin's Press.

Collier, David and John Gerring (eds.) (2009) *Concepts and Method in Social Science: The Tradition of Giovanni Sartori*. London: Routledge.

Dahl, Robert. (1970) *Polyarchy*. New Haven, CT: Yale University Press.

Dallin, Alexander. (1992) Causes of the Collapse of the USSR. *Post-Soviet Affairs* 8 (4):279–302.

Diamond, Larry. (1992) Economic Development and Democracy Reconsidered. *American Behavioral Scientist* 15:450–499.

Diamond, Larry. (1994) Rethinking Civil Society. *Journal of Democracy* 5:5–17.

Duvanova, Dinissa S. (2007) *Interest Groups in Post-Communist Countries: A Comparative Analysis of Business and Employer Associations*. Doctoral Dissertation. Political Science, Ohio State University, Columbus, OH.

Eckstein, Harry. (1998) Russia and the Conditions of Democracy. In Eckstein, H., Hoffmann, E. and Reisinger, W. (eds.) *Can Democracy Take Root in Russia? Explorations in State-Society Relations*. New York: Rowman & Littlefield Publishers.

Fischer, George. (1958) *Russian Liberalism: From Gentry to Intelligentsia*. Cambridge, MA: Harvard University Press.

Fish, M. Steven. (1995) *Democracy from Scratch: Opposition and Regime in the New Russian Revolution*. Princeton, NJ: Princeton University Press.

Fish, M. Steven (2005) *Democracy Derailed in Russia: The Failure of Open Politics*. New York: Cambridge University Press.

Fish, M. Steven and Omar Choudry. (2007) Democratization and Economic Liberalization in the Postcommunist World. *Comparative Political Studies* 40 (3):254–282.

Fleron, Frederic J. and Erik P. Hoffman. (1993) Communist Studies and Political Science: Cold War and Peaceful Coexistence. In Fleron, F. and Hoffmann, E. (eds.) *Post-Communist Studies and Political Science: Methodology and Empirical Theory in Sovietology*. Boulder, CO: Westview Press.

Frye, Timothy. (2002) Capture or Exchange? Business Lobbying in Russia. *Europe-Asia Studies* 54 (7):1017–1036.

Frye, Timothy. (2003) Markets, Democracy, and New Private Business in Russia. *Post-Soviet Affairs* 19 (1):24–45.

Frye, Timothy, Andrei Yakovlev, and Yevgeny Yasin. (2009) The "Other" Russian Economy: How Everyday Firms View the Rules of the Game in Russia. *Social Research: An International Quarterly* 76 (1):29–54.

Gel'man, Vladimir, Sergei Ryzhenkov, and Michael Brie. (eds.) (2003) *Making and Breaking Democratic Transitions*. Lanham, MD: Rowman & Littlefield.

Gill, Graeme. (2008) *Bourgeoisie, State and Democracy: Russia, Britain, France, Germany and the USA*. Oxford, New York: Oxford University Press.

Goldman, Marshall I. (2003) *The Privatization of Russia: Russian Reform Goes Awry*. New York: Routledge

Golikova, Victoria. (2007) Uchastie Rossiyskikh Kompaniy v Biznes Assotsiatsakh. In Yakovlev, A. (ed.) *Rossiyskaya Korporatsiya*. Moscow: State University Higher School of Economics.

Golikova, Victoria. (2009) Business Associations: Incentives and Benefits from the Standpoint of Corporate Governance. In Dolgopyatova, T., Iwasaki, I., and Yakovlev, A. (eds.)

Organization and Development of Russian Business: A Firm-Level Analysis, London: Palgrave/Macmillan.

Goskomstat Rossii. (2001) *Regiony Rossii*. Moscow: State Committee of the Russian Federation for Statistics.

Hall, Peter and David Soskice (eds.) (2001) *Varieties of Capitalism: The Institutional Foundations of Comparative Advantage*. Oxford: Oxford University Press.

Hanson, Philip and Elizabeth Teague. (2005) Big Business and the State in Russia. *Europe-Asia Studies* 57 (5):657–680.

Hellman, Joel. (1998) Winners Take All: The Pitfalls of Partial Reform. *World Politics* 50 (2):203–234.

Hellman, Joel. (2000) Measuring Governance, Corruption and State Capture. How Firms and Bureaucrats Shape the Business Environment in Transition Economies. *World Bank Policy Research Paper*. Washington, DC: World Bank.

Hosking, Geoffrey. (1973) *The Russian Constitutional Experiment*. Cambridge, UK: Cambridge University Press.

Hosking, Geoffrey. (1990) *The Awakening of the Soviet Union*. Cambridge, MA: Harvard University Press.

Hough, Jerry F. (1997) *Democratization and Revolution in the USSR 1985–1991*. Washington, DC: Brookings Institution.

Howard, Marc M. (2002) Postcommunist Civil Society in Comparative Perspective. *Demokratizatsiya: The Journal of Post-Soviet Democratization* 10 (3):285–305.

Howard, Marc M. (2003) *The Weakness of Civil Society in Post-Communist Europe*. New York: Cambridge University Press.

Hughes, James. (1997) Sub-National Elites and Post-Communist Transformation in Russia: A Reply to Kryshtanovskaya and White. *Europe-Asia Studies* 49 (6):1017–1037.

Huntington, Samuel P. (1991) *The Third Wave: Democratization in the Late Twentieth Century*. Oklahoma City: University of Oklahoma Press.

Independent Institute for Social Policy (IISP) Moscow. (2006) *Demokratichnost' Rossiskikh Regionov*. Petrov, Nikolai and Titkov, Alexei. http://atlas.socpol.ru/indexes/index_democr.shtml. Accessed November 10, 2010.

Keane, John. (1998) *Civil Society: Old Images, New Visions*. Cambridge, MA: Polity Press.

Kohli, Atul. (2002) State, Society and Development. In Katznelson, I. and Milner, H. (eds.) *Political Science: State of the Discipline*. New York: W. W. Norton & Company and American Political Science Association.

Lapidus, Gail W. (1989) State and Society: Toward the Emergence of Civil Society in the Soviet Union. In Bialer, S. (ed.) *Politics, Society and Nationality: Inside Gorbachev's Russia*. Boulder, CO: Westview Press.

Ledeneva, Alena V. (1998) *Russia's Economy of Favours: Blat, Networking, and Informal Exchange*. Cambridge, UK: Cambridge University Press.

Ledeneva, Alena V. (2006) *How Russia Really Works: The Informal Practices That Shaped Post-Soviet Politics and Business*. Ithaca, NY: Cornell University Press.

Lewin, Moshe. (1990) *The Gorbachev Phenomenon*. Berkeley: University of California Press.

Lipset, Seymour Martin. (1959) Some Social Requisites of Democracy: Economic Development and Political Legitimacy. *American Political Science Review* 53:69–105.

Luebbert, Gregory M. (1991) *Liberalism, Fascism, or Social Democracy: Social Classes and the Political Origins of Regimes in Interwar Europe*. New York: Oxford University Press.

Maleva, Tatiana, E. Avraamova, M. Mikhailiuk, L. Nivorozhkina, A. Ovsiannikov, L. Ovcharova, . . . N. Firsova. (2004) *Srednie Klassy v Rossii: Ekonomicheskie i Sotsial'nie Strategii*. Moscow: Moscow Carnegie Center.

Markov, Stanislav. (2007) *Capitalists of All Russia, Unite! Business Mobilization Under Debilitated Dirigisme*. Conference Paper. American Political Science Association.

Marsh, Christopher. (2004) Measuring and Explaining Variations in Russian Regional Democratization In Ross, C. (ed.) *Russian Politics Under Putin*. Manchester: Manchester University Press.

Matsuzato, Kimitaka (2001). From Ethno-Bonopartism to Centralized Caciquismo: Characteristics and Origins of the Tatarstan Political Regime, 1990–2000. *Journal of Communist Studies and Transition Politics* 17 (4):43–77.

Mau, Vladimir and Irina Starodubrovskaya. (2002) *The Challenge of Revolution: Contemporary Russia in Historical Perspective*. New York: Oxford University Press.

McFaul, Michael. (2001) *Russia's Unfinished Revolution: Political Change from Gorbachev to Putin*. Ithaca, NY: Cornell University Press.

Melvin, Neil J. (1998) The Consolidation of a New Regional Elite: The Case of Omsk 1987–1995. *Europe-Asia Studies* 50 (4):619–641.

Mitchneck, Beth. (2007) Governance and Land Use: Decision-Making in Russian Cities and Regions. *Europe-Asia Studies* 59 (5):735–760.

Moore, Barrington. (1966) *The Social Origins of Dictatorship and Democracy: Lord and Peasant in the Making of the Modern World*. Boston: Beacon.

O'Donnell, Guillermo. (1973) *Modernization and Bureaucratic Authoritarianism*. Berkeley: Institute of International Studies, University of California.

Olson, Mancur. (1982) *The Rise and Decline of Nations: Economic Growth, Stagflation and Social Rigidities*. New Haven, CT: Yale University Press.

Orttung, Robert. W. (2004) Business and Politics in the Russian Regions. *Problems of Post-Communism* 51 (2):48–60.

Owen, Thomas C. (1981) *Capitalism and Politics in Russia: A Social History of the Moscow Merchants 1855–1905*. Cambridge, UK: Cambridge University Press.

Owen, Thomas C. (1991) Impediments to Bourgeois Consciousness in Russia, 1880–1905: The Estate Structure, Ethnic Diversity and Regionalism. In Clowes, E., Kassow, S. and West, J. (eds.) *Between Tsar and People: Educated Society and the Quest for Public Identity in Late Imperial Russia*. Princeton, NJ: Princeton University Press.

Petrov, Nikolai and Alexei Titkov. (2006) *Demokratichnost' Rossiskikh Regionov*. http://atlas.socpol.ru/indexes/index_democr.shtml. Accessed November 10, 2010.

Petrov, Nikolai and Alexei Titkov. (2013) *Reyting Demokratichnosti Regionov Moskovskogo Tsenta Karnegi: 10 Let v Stroyu*. Moscow: Carnegie Moscow Center. http://carnegie.ru/publications/?fa=55853. Accessed December 1, 2014.

Pierson, Paul. (2003) Big, Slow, and. . . . Invisible: Macro-Social Processes in the Study of Comparative Politics. In Mahoney, J. and Rueschemeyer. D. (eds.) *Comparative-Historical Analysis in the Social Sciences*. New York: Cambridge University Press.

Pipes, Richard. (1999) *Property and Freedom*. New York: Alfred A. Knopf.

Przeworski, Adam and Fernando Limongi. (1993) Political Regimes and Economic Growth. *Journal of Economic Perspectives* 7 (3):51–69.

Putnam, Robert. (1993) *Making Democracy Work: Civic Traditions in Modern Italy*. Princeton, NJ: Princeton University Press.

Pyle, William. (2006a) Collective action and post-communist enterprise: The economic logic of Russia's business associations. *Europe-Asia Studies* 58 (4):491–521.

Pyle, William. (2006b) Russia's Business Associations: Who Joins and Why? *CIPE Economic Reform Feature Service*. Washington, DC: Center for International Private Enterprise.

Raiser, Martin, Alan Rousso, and Franklin Steves. (2003) Trust in Transition. *Working Papers*. London: European Bank for Reconstruction and Development.

Recantini, Francesca and Randi Ryterman. (2001) *Disorganization or Self-Organization: The Emergence of Business Associations in a Transition Economy.* World Bank Policy Research Working Paper Series, No. 2539.

Reddaway, Peter and Dmitry Glinski. (2001) *The Tragedy of Russia's Reforms: Market Bolshevism Against Democracy.* Washington, DC: United States Institute of Peace Press.

Remington, Thomas F. (2010) *Accounting for Regime Differences in the Russian Regions: Historical and Structural Influences.* Emory University School of Law. Public Law & Legal Theory Research Paper Series No. 10–119, Law & Economics Research Paper Series No. 10–78. Social Science Research Network Electronic Paper Collection. http:// ssrn.com/abstract=1648230. Accessed February 12, 2011.

Remington, Thomas F. (2009) *Helping Hands or Grabbing Hands? The Business Environment in Russia's Regions. Democracy and Inequality in the Postcommunist Transition.* Presented at Midwestern Political Science Association Conference, Chicago, IL.

Rigby, T. H. (1992) The USSR: End of a Long, Dark Night? In Miller, R. (ed.) *The Development of Civil Society in Communist Systems.* Sydney, Australia: Allen & Unwin.

Roosa, Ruth AmEnde. (1997) *Russian Industrialists in an Era of Revolution: The Association of Industry and Trade, 1906–1917.* Edited by T. C. Owen. Armonk, NY and London: M. E. Sharpe.

Rose, Richard. (2000) Uses of Social Capital in Russia: Modern, Pre-modern, and Anti-modern. *Post-Soviet Affairs* 16 (1):33–56.

Rose, Richard, William Mishler, and Neil Munro. (2006) *Russia Transformed: Developing Popular Support for a New Regime.* Cambridge, UK and New York: Cambridge University Press.

Ross, Cameron. (2002) *Federalism and Democratisation in Russia.* Manchester: Manchester University Press.

Rosstat (Federal'naya Sluzhba Gosudarstvennoy Statistiki). (2002, 2008, 2010) *Regiony Rossii: Sotsial'no-Ekonomicheskie Pokazateli.*

Ruble, Blair A. (1987) The Social Dimensions of Perestroika. *Soviet Economy* 3 (2): 171–183.

Ruble, Blair A. (1990) The Soviet Union's Quiet Revolution. In Breslauer, G. (ed.) *Can Gorbachev's Reforms Succeed?* Berkeley: University of California, Center for Slavic and East European Studies.

Ruble, Blair A., Judi Koehn, and Nancy E. Popson (eds.) (2001) *Fragmented Space: The Russian Federation.* Washington, DC: Woodrow Wilson Center Press.

Rueschemeyer, Dietrich, Evelyne H. Stephens and John D. Stephens. (1992) *Capitalist Development and Democracy.* Chicago: University of Chicago Press.

Rustow, Dankwart A. (1968) Modernization and Comparative Politics. *Comparative Politics* 1 (1): 35–51.

Rutland, Peter. (ed) (2001) *Business and the State in Contemporary Russia.* Boulder, CO: Westview Press.

Rutland, Peter. (2006) Business and Civil Society in Russia. In Evans, A, Henry, L. and Sundstrom, L. (eds) *Russian Civil Society: A Critical Assessment.* Armonk, NY and London: M. E. Sharpe.

Sakwa, Richard. (2008) Two Camps? The Struggle to Understand Contemporary Russia. *Comparative Politics* 40 (4):481–500.

Schmitter, Philippe C. (1974) Still the Century of Corporatism? *Review of Politics* 36: 85–131.

Semenenko, Irina S. (2001) *Gruppy Interesov na Zapade i v Rossii: Konseptsii i Praktiki.* Moscow: IMEMO.

Sharafutdinova, Gulnara (2010) What Explains Corruption Perceptions? The Dark Side of Political Competition in Russia's Regions. *Comparative Politics* 42 (2):147–170.

Shanin, Teodor. (1985) *The Roots of Otherness: Russia's Turn of Century.* 3 vols. Vol. 1, *Russia As a 'Developing Society'.* New Haven, CT and London: Yale University Press.

Skocpol, Theda. (1979) *States and Social Revolutions: A Comparative Analysis of France, Russia and China.* Cambridge, UK: Cambridge University Press.

Starr, S. Frederick. (1988) Soviet Union: A Civil Society. *Foreign Policy* (70):26–41.

Stavrakis, Peter J., Joan deBardeleben, and Larry Black. (eds.) (1997) *Beyond the Monolith: The Emergence of Regionalism in Post-Soviet Russia.* Washington, DC and Baltimore, MD: Woodrow Wilson Center Press and Johns Hopkins University Press.

Stepan, Alfred. (2000) Russian Federalism in Comparative Perspective. *Post-Soviet Affairs* 16 (2):133–176.

Stoner-Weiss, Kathryn. (2006) *Resisting the State: Reform and Retrenchment in Post-Soviet Russia.* Cambridge, UK: Cambridge University Press.

Streeck, Wolfgang and Kozo Yamamura. (eds.) (2001) *The Origins of Nonliberal Capitalism: Germany and Japan in Comparison.* Ithaca, NY: Cornell University Press.

Tarrow, Sidney. (1996) Making Social Science Work Across Space and Time. *American Political Science Review* 90 (2):389–397.

Tilly, Charles. (2004) *Contention and Democracy in Europe, 1650–2000.* New York: Cambridge University Press.

Tocqueville, Alexis de. (1969). *Democracy in America.* London: Fontana Press. (Original work published 1840)

Treisman, Daniel. (1999) *After the Deluge.* Ann Arbor: University of Michigan Press.

Truman, David B. (1951) *The Governmental Process: Political Interests and Public Opinion.* New York: Alfred A. Knopf.

Volkov, Vadim. (2002) *Violent Entrepreneurs: The Use of Force in the Making of Russian Capitalism.* Ithaca, NY: Cornell University Press.

Weigle, Marcia A. (2000) *Russia's Liberal Project: State-Society Relations in the Transition from Communism.* University Park: Pennsylvania State University Press.

West, James L. (1991) The Riabushinsky Circle: Burzhuaziia and Obshchestvennost' in Late Imperial Russia. In Clowes, E. W., Kassow, S. D. and West, J. L. (eds.) *Between Tsar and People: Educated Society and the Quest for Public Identity in Late Imperial Russia,* edited Princeton, NJ: Princeton University Press.

Yakovlev, Andrei. (2006a) The Evolution of Business – State Interaction in Russia: From State Capture to Business Capture? *Europe-Asia Studies* 58 (7):1033–1056.

Yakovlev, Andrei A. (2006b) *Agenty Modernizatsii.* Moscow: State University Higher School of Economics.

Zaslavsky, Victor. (1995) From Redistribution to Marketization: Social and Attitudinal Change in Post-Soviet Russia. In Lapidus, G. (ed.) *The New Russia: Troubled Transformation,* Boulder, CO: Westview Press.

2 Small business owners and regional democracy

Quantitative analysis

This chapter begins with a survey of the extent of small business development in Russia, briefly tracing its emergence within the context of the broader Russian business community beginning in the late 1980s. The second part of the chapter probes the relationship over the period since 1991 between the prevalence of small firms by region and an index of regional democratization. The term 'region' is used here to denote a 'subject' of the Russian Federation, of which there are 83. Russian state statistical service (Rosstat) publications give complete time series from 1992 to 2008 for all the variables used in the analysis in this chapter for no fewer than 76 of the regions.[1] The chapter ends with an interpretation of the regression results and the framing of four regional case studies.

Small business in Russia: scope, trends, context

The Russian business community can be seen as embracing three large 'generational' categories: 'incumbent' business, 'oligarch' business and 'new' business. Gazprom and state-owned or state-dominated strategic conglomerates of the Putin era are incumbent businesses, as are many regionally significant industrial concerns, heirs of Soviet-era enterprises, whose leadership typically descends in a more or less direct lineage from the Soviet period. The flamboyant 'oligarch' businesses born in the Yeltsin era arose from the 1990s privatizations especially in the extractive sector, and many of their owners trace their roots in business to the cooperatives movement beginning in 1988. Cooperatives feature in the business biographies of 21 of the top 50 in the 2010 *Forbes* ranking of Russian billionaires. (*Forbes* Russian Edition, May 2010)

The third category, 'new' business, includes the small and medium-sized companies that are the focus of this study, but encompasses some larger companies as well. They are also referred to as *de novo* companies, in that they have no relationship to privatization or any Soviet antecedent enterprise. These companies are concentrated in the service sector of the economy, including telecommunications, IT, retail, finance, construction and transport. Frye, Yakovlev and Yasin (2008) and Yakovlev (2006b) argue that the role of *de novo* companies in shaping the institutions of business-state coordination has been underestimated.

A representative sample of 606 Russian companies from six industrial sectors surveyed in 2004 illustrates that small companies are much more likely to have

Table 2.1 Enterprise Size by Year of Creation

Date of Creation	Small Enterprise		Large Enterprise		Total	
	Number	*Percent*	*Number*	*Percent*	*Number*	*Percent*
1988 to 2004	169	68.70	116	32.22	285	47.03
1918 to 1987	73	29.67	215	59.72	288	47.52
Before 1918	4	1.63	29	8.06	33	5.45
Total	246	*100*	360	*100*	606	*100*

$CHI^2 = 80.2021$; Pr = 0.000

Gamma = -0.5842; ASE = 0.055

Source: Pyle (2004)

been founded since 1988 than large companies. (Pyle 2004; see Table 2.1) This unsurprising finding nevertheless supports the claim that although not all new firms are small, small firms are almost always new. The fact that small firms are typically new is important to understanding why they would be a source of innovation or change in pre-existing patterns of interaction with state structures.

The variable at the center of our analysis – small firm prevalence – is the number of incorporated small companies with up to 100 employees in a given region relative to the economically active population (labor force) of that region. These data are collected and reported annually by the state statistical service (Rosstat) and are supported by two studies by the independent Russian SME Resource Center (2004, 2006) on behalf of USAID. Incorporated small firms are registered under Russian company law as limited liability companies, most frequently as "obshchestvo s ogranichnnoy otvetstvennostiyu (OOO)."[2] Microenterprises – those with up to 15 employees – are considered a sub-category of small firms. Figure 2.1 shows the numbers of incorporated small companies (including microenterprises) by year:

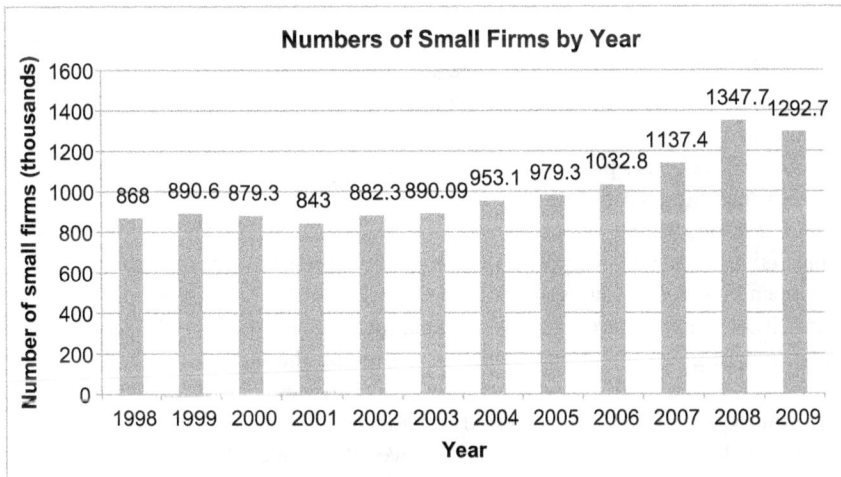

Figure 2.1 Number of Small Firms by Year 1998–2009

Source: Rosstat

Numbers of incorporated small firms have been collected and published by region since 1992, allowing analysis of their cross-sectional and temporal variation. Small firms produce 13–17% of GDP and account for about 20% of employment. (OECD 2009)

The other legal form of small business in Russia is the individual entrepreneur, known also by the term "*predprinimatel' bez obrazovanii yuridichestkogo litsa*" (entrepreneur without formation of a juridical person). Ahrend and Tompson (2005:39) and Buyske (2007:96) note that Russian official statistics on the scope of small business typically do not encompass these individual entrepreneurs, resulting in underestimation of the extent of small business development in Russia. Official statistical publications began to report the numbers of individual entrepreneurs by region only from the mid-2000s. (Rosstat 2009; Russian SME Resource Center 2004, 2006) Individual entrepreneurs substantially outnumber incorporated small companies in Russia, and they also employ others, exactly as incorporated microenterprises do.

The continued preference shown by entrepreneurs for the category of unincorporated self-employment is taken by most business people interviewed for this study as symptomatic of the continuing inadequacies of the regulatory and legal environment for doing business. Crossing the threshold to incorporation offers opportunities for growth and expansion but also exposes entrepreneurs to new risks and vulnerabilities. Ahrend and Tompson (2005) estimated that small and micro firms and individual entrepreneurs taken together grew in numbers by 15–20% annually in the first half of the 2000s.

The 2007 federal law "On the Development of Small and Medium Entrepreneurship" established for the first time the formal definition of SMEs. (Russian Federation 2007) Consistent with practice in the European Union, the law defines an SME as a business entity meeting the following criteria: state and foreign ownership together not to exceed 25%; ownership by non-SME entities together not more than 25%; number employed not to exceed 250 employees for medium, 100 for small and 15 for micro-enterprises. Annual turnover maximum thresholds (to be adjusted every five years) were set in 2008 at 60 million rubles for micro-enterprises, 400 million rubles for small firms, and 1 billion rubles for medium-sized firms.

The 2007 law also provides for a number of measures to advance SME development including simplified accounting and taxation, preferential access to government procurement contracts, protection against excessive inspections and financial and advisory support. These features in the law were the result of public and open engagement between the Russian Chamber of Commerce and Industry and OPORA, as the two principal associations representing small business, and the principal government interlocutor in designing the legislation, Deputy Prime Minister Igor Shuvalov, as well as with key Duma members. *Kommersant* (2007) and other press sources of the period confirm that the Ministry of Economy, supported by business lobbying, prevailed over the objections of the Ministry of Finance with respect to tax relief measures to be applied to small firms and independent entrepreneurs.

Several legislative accomplishments for small business were clustered in the period 2000–2003 that saw the adoption of the laws on inspections in 2001, on licensing in 2002, on company registration in 2002, on standardization and certification in 2003 and the law establishing the Simplified Tax System for small firms in 2003. Passage of the 2007 Small Business Development law was followed by adoption of a law on disposition of real property held by municipalities and the law further circumscribing the scope and frequency of inspections, both in 2008. (Buyske 2007; CEFIR 2006; Russian Federation 2007, 2008a, 2008b) Buyske (2007) traces the development of public assertion of the interests of small business and their input to economic policy to the first All Russia Conference of Small Business in 1996. These conferences continued to attract participation from entrepreneurs and policymakers under sponsorship of the Russian Chamber of Commerce and Industry and OPORA.[3]

The Russian Chamber of Commerce and Industry (2009b) reports 5,192,363 SMEs in Russia, broken down into categories established by the 2007 SME development law:

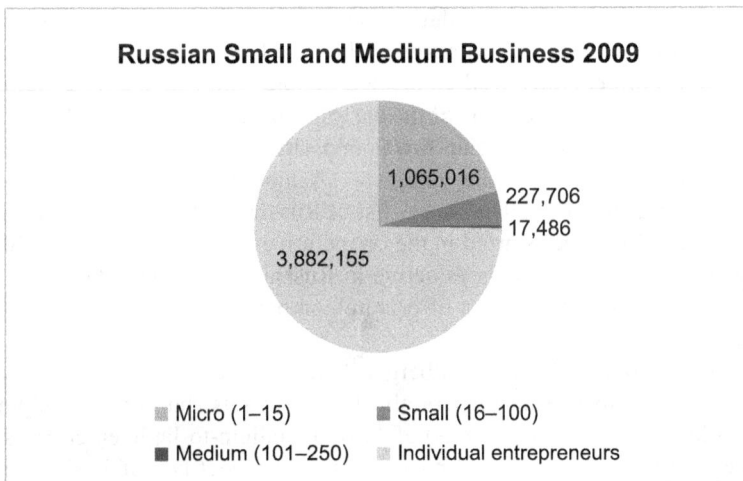

Figure 2.2 Russian Small and Medium Business 2009

Source: Russian Chamber of Commerce (2009)

Figure 2.2 clearly illustrates the dominant role within small business played by individual entrepreneurs, the large role played by microenterprise among small companies, and the fairly small number of firms in Russia that meet the legal definition of medium-sized enterprises. While the total scope of small business viewed comprehensively is larger than is widely appreciated, the composition by size of SMEs suggests that impediments and disincentives persist in inhibiting the expansion of incorporated small and medium-sized firms.

The emergence of private business is often associated with social and political outcomes through its tendency to make economic power more diffuse and less concentrated. (Fish 2005, Fish and Choudry 2007) The OECD (2009) reports that almost 60% of the Russian labor force is employed in the private sector. The World Bank (2005) found that the predominance of Financial Industrial Groups (FIGs; oligarch-owned private business) is not as great when viewed from the standpoint of employment as it is when considered from the perspective of sales or production. Private companies not belonging to FIGs accounted for more than 70% of employment in the principal industrial subsectors, 77% in transport and communications and more than 90% of employment in construction and trade. It is precisely in their role of creating employment independent of the state that the social and potential political importance of private business lies, and this role is underestimated when companies are considered only in terms of their contribution to GDP.[4]

Gill (2008) sees the origins of Russian capitalism in three initial sources: the "cooperatives" of late perestroika, spontaneous privatization and informal market trading and the mass privatizations of 1992–1994. Russian small business initially arose from three main sources: cooperatives (where entrepreneurs were young and typically well-educated and well-connected members of Komsomol, on the lower, ambitious rungs of the elite ladder), shuttle traders (often women and not generally well-connected people who adapted as a matter of survival to the harsh conditions of the early 1990s and supplied the kiosk markets that came to typify Russian towns and cities) and privatization of small enterprises through the voucher program. (Aslund 2007; Gill 2008; Schleifer and Treisman 2000) The 2010 Forbes list of Russia's richest shows a considerable number of fortunes started in the cooperatives movement. (*Forbes* 2010)[5] However, most small companies active in Russia by the mid-2000s were created after 1998, when numbers of private companies in general began to rise steeply.[6]

According to Desai and Goldberg (2008:99), the landmark mass privatizations passed to private owners all physical assets (buildings, equipment, inventories, transport and utilities) of 17,000 medium-to-large enterprises and hundreds of thousands of small businesses. The Soviet law of 1988 allowing the founding of cooperatives opened the door to legal private entrepreneurship in Russia.

Since 2008, the 20th anniversary of passage of the (Soviet) Law on Cooperatives, May 26, 1988, the date of the law's passage has been observed as a holiday honoring entrepreneurs. Jones and Moskoff (1991) document the largely negative public image of the cooperatives and their close identification with the young and politically connected Komsomol. Cooperatives were superseded by the collapse of the Soviet Union and by passage in 1992 of the Russian Law on private enterprise. Many small firm owners built their businesses from the early-to-mid 1990s from informal market trading, where the vast majority of individual entrepreneurs remain engaged. (CIPE 1992)

The 1998 crisis appears in retrospect as a watershed both in the emergence of a more 'normal' business environment in Russia and in establishing the rudiments of more arms-length business-government coordination mechanisms. (Frye 2002; Frye and Yakovlev 2007; Frye et al. 2008; Yakovlev 2006a, 2006b) After 2000, the role of business associations became more prominent as a means of moving from improvised to more structured and 'categorical' approaches to interest articulation by business. According to Yakovlev (2006b), this change was driven by the devaluation's improved profit potential for new investments and increased production, a settlement offer from tax authorities regarding companies' arrears, the end of large privatizations and, perhaps most crucially, the perceived risk that communist and other left-wing forces within the government headed by Prime Minister Yevgeny Primakov might rescind the property rights of oligarchs who flouted tax and other laws.

From this point onward, Yakovlev argues, large firms were numerous enough to make it attractive to deal with the state on a collective footing. A look at the 'demography' of companies in Russia over time reinforces Yakovlev's point by showing the vigorous expansion in numbers of private companies (see Table 2.2). It is also an indicator of the institutionalization of legal norms, in that these data are based on legal company registrations.

By inference, the large ramp-up in newly registered firms must be mainly due to the founding of *de novo* companies, because the privatization process was largely complete after 1996. The increase in numbers from 1996 to 2001 reflects both the economic recovery and the improved business conditions after the 1998 devaluation that stimulated the emergence of companies serving the domestic market. (RLMS 2006)It is important to recognize, however, that many new companies are founded as subsidiaries of established firms. In addition, some legally registered companies are likely to be 'shells' created to take advantage of legal tax benefits. Finally, some entrepreneurs set up new small companies to pursue new activities rather than expanding their existing companies, in part to benefit from the simplified tax regime available to small companies. The numbers of new company

Table 2.2 Russian Enterprises and Organizations by Ownership Category (Thousands)

	1996	2001	2003	2004	2005	2006	2007	2008
State	322	151	157	161	159	160	149	142
Municipal	198	217	239	246	248	252	264	263
Private	1426	2510	2957	3238	3499	3838	3639	3855
Foreign & joint venture	181	209	234	247	245	265	215	203
Private Non-profit	95	223	244	252	253	253	239	212
Total	2222	3310	3831	4144	4404	4768	4506	4675

Source: Rosstat 2008 Statistical Yearbook

registrations in Russia relative to the existing 'population' is large as these World Bank data in Figure 2.3 show:

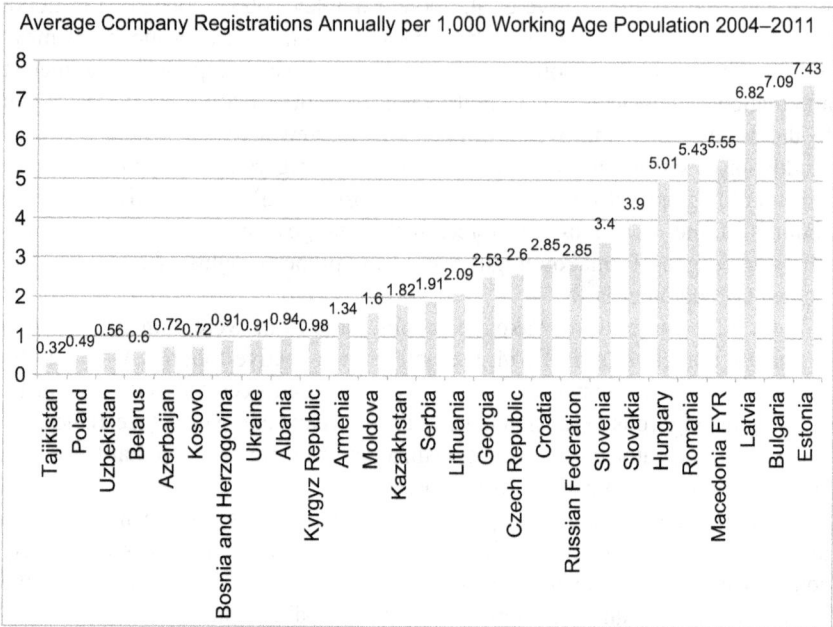

Figure 2.3 New Firm Registrations in Post-Communist Europe and Eurasia

Source: World Bank IFC Entrepreneurship Database http://www.doingbusiness.org/data/exploretopics/entrepreneurship accessed June 10, 2013.

Note: Not all cases report data for all years in the period 2004-2011. The average shown is of the available years in this period for each reporting country.

Despite the vigorous growth in numbers of private companies in Russia, international comparative indices generally rate the investment climate of Russia worse than in other leading emerging economies such as India, China and Brazil, and much worse than in OECD countries. The World Bank's *Doing Business* database measures the impact of ten aspects of business regulation in terms of time, complexity and expense: starting a business, dealing with construction permits, employing workers, registering property, getting credit, protecting investors, paying taxes, trading across borders, enforcing contracts and closing a business. These measures are assessed in the main business city of a given country. Russia's overall ranking in 2010 was 120th among the 183 countries in the study: worse than China, but ahead of Brazil and India. (World Bank and International Finance Corporation 2009, 2010)

The periodic monitoring of business owners in the Business Environment and Enterprise Performance Survey (BEEPS) conducted by the European Bank for Reconstruction and Development (EBRD) and the World Bank reports entrepreneurs' assessments of the business climate in post-communist transition countries of Europe and Eurasia. (EBRD and World Bank 2008) In much the same vein, the Moscow-based Centre for Economic and Financial Research (CEFIR) conducted six rounds of surveys of small firm owners from 2001 to 2006. (CEFIR 2001–2006)

The BEEPS and CEFIR surveys suggest that business owners perceived some improvements in business conditions as a result of the round of federal legislation in the first half of the 2000s. Nevertheless, problems in the regulatory and legal environment, and especially corruption, remained significant, according to respondents in these surveys. (CIPE 2003a, 2003b) In general, the formal changes to legislation, while welcomed by entrepreneurs, encountered entrenched bureaucratic resistance and habits on the part of officials and many businesspeople. Optimistic developments such as the greater recourse of entrepreneurs to the *arbitrazh* (commercial) courts to resolve disputes sat alongside a widely held perception that the problem of corruption, including in egregious and potentially violent forms such as *reyderstvo* (raiding), became worse from the mid-2000s onward.

Business associations in Russia have focused much of their interest articulation and policy advocacy on the legal and regulatory sphere affecting the conduct of business. The associations have acknowledged the central grievance of many small business owners is corruption and addressed this by the adoption of a set of proposed remedies that involve allowing legal experts from business associations to review and suggest re-drafting of proposed legislation as it affects the business climate and also seeking avenues for public consultation on the conduct of police, tax enforcement and related official functions. (CIPE 2003–2009, 2006, 2008, 2010; INDEM and CIPE 2009; Satarov, Parkhomenko, Krylova and Rostovikova 2007) The manifest growth from the early 2000s onward in the caseload of arbitrazh courts, where disputes among private actors and between companies and tax and other officials are adjudicated, can be interpreted as a degree of institutionalization of predictable rules of the game for business. (Hendley 1998, 1999, 2003; Hendley, Ickes, Murrell and Ryterman 1997; Hendley, Murrell and Ryterman 2000)

Regression analysis

As discussed in Chapter 1, the prevalence of small firms within the business community may help to explain different outcomes as to regional democracy through small firms' contribution to economic development and growth, through entrepreneurs' influence on changing social attitudes and norms, or through their role in the public articulation of their interests within a civic framework.

The measure of regional democratization used in the analysis is an index designed by Nikolai Petrov and Alexei Titkov of periodic structured evaluations of each region's performance by a group of prominent Russian scholars of regional politics. The composite democracy index is available for three periods: 1991–2001 (the so-called baseline assessment), 2000–2004 and 2005–2009. (Petrov and Titkov 2006, 2013)

The composite index is the sum of ten sub-indicators, each measured on a scale of 1–5. This means that a perfectly democratic region would have a score of 50, and the lowest possible composite score would be 10. The ten sub-indicators are as follows:

1 regional political system (balance among executive, legislative and judicial branches; limitations on, or protection of, citizens' rights);
2 openness (transparency of regional policy process, availability of public information);
3 conduct of elections (national, regional and local, role of 'administrative resources');
4 political pluralism (parties within regional parliaments);
5 media independence;
6 prevalence and extent of corruption;
7 economic liberalization (including the scope and conduct of privatizations under regional jurisdiction);
8 civil society (visibility and activities of NGOs and civic activism);
9 character of elites (extent of replacement, turnover as well as levels of professionalism); and
10 local governments (competitive elections to municipal posts, influence and autonomy of municipalities relative to the regional authorities).[7]

The index is a continuous measure of '*democratichnost*' ('democraticness'). The conceptualization of democracy as continuous is shared by Lipset: "Democracy is not a quality of a social system which either does or does not exist, but is rather a complex of characteristics which may be ranked in many different ways." (Lipset 1959:73) This formulation emphasizes two characteristics that are central to the approach of this study. First, we take democracy to be a continuous variable. Second, democracy is taken to characterize the social system, rather than solely the functioning of political or governmental institutions. The Petrov index adopts precisely such an analytical approach.

Table 2.3 summarizes the data on this variable.

The regional measure of small firm prevalence used in this analysis is the number of incorporated small companies for each 1,000 people in the economically active population (labor force). The analysis uses this variable for the years 1995, 2000, 2002, 2004, 2006 and 2008. (Goskomstat 2001; Rosstat 2002, 2004, 2008, 2010)

It is important to note that this measure of small business development does not directly measure the *economic* impact of such companies. It says nothing directly about their efficiency, competitiveness or profitability. Scaling the number of small companies to the workforce is rather, we will argue, an indicator of

Table 2.3 Descriptive Summary of Regional Democracy Index

Democracy Index Period	Observations	Mean	Std. Dev.	Min	Max
1991–2001	79	27.9	6.22	14	45
2000–2004	79	29.0	6.28	17	45
2005–2009	80	30.1	6.05	18.5	43

the *social* salience of such firms. The more prevalent they are, the more likely in general they will be to have a shared identity and defined interests in the civic sphere. The summary picture of small business intensity across Russia's regions by this measure is summarized in Table 2.4:

Table 2.4 Descriptive Summary of Variable 'Small Firm Prevalence' by Region

Small Firm Prevalence	Observation	Mean	Std. Dev.	Min	Max
1995	78	11.6	4.71	5.24	33.76
2000	79	9.48	6.09	2.08	44.54
2002	79	9.32	5.52	1.30	35.23
2004	79	11.05	5.88	5.08	43.78
2006	79	10.76	5.74	3.50	41.70
2008	80	14.91	8.85	3.10	58.80

As was shown in Chapter 1, small business prevalence in the years 2000, 2004, 2006 and 2008 is correlated positively with the regional democratization index scores for all three periods. (see Table 1.1). We also found that regions rated more democratic than average tended to be those with greater prevalence of small firms and, conversely, those less democratic than average tended to have fewer than average small firms relative to the workforce. (see Table 1.2). The chi-squared measure supported the intuition of close association between these variables. At the same time, the relatively large number of cases that are deviant on this simple approach to analysis of the relationship between these two variables suggests the role of other factors, some of which can be incorporated into a multi-variate regression analysis.

As previously discussed, incorporated small companies are outnumbered by as much as 3 to 1 by unincorporated entrepreneurs. We have data on the numbers by region of independent entrepreneurs scaled relative to each 1,000 of the economically active population for 2004 and 2008. Table 2.5 shows the correlations between the prevalence of independent entrepreneurs by region and the regional democracy index in its three periods. It will be seen that, unlike the prevalence of incorporated small firms with democratization, the correlations here are not significant:

Table 2.5 Pairwise Correlation of Democracy and Intensity of Individual Entrepreneurs

	Dem Index 1991–2001	Dem Index 2000–2004	Dem Index 2005–2009
Individual entrepreneurs 2004	0.0095 (0.9337)	0.0405 (0.7231)	0.0189 (0.8690)
Individual entrepreneurs 2008	−0.0462 (0.6857)	−0.0793 (0.4870)	0.0037 (0.9739)

P values shown in parentheses. Asterisk denotes significance at 0.01 level.

The contrast between the prevalence of small firms and the analogous measure applied to individual entrepreneurs with respect to their association with the democracy index suggests that the relationship between democracy and small firm prevalence is not exclusively related to their contribution in the economic sphere. As has been previously noted, individual entrepreneurs are functionally, but not formally, the same as microenterprises. One might therefore expect the prevalence of individual entrepreneurs to manifest a similar association with the regional democracy index.

Using the time path from 1991 to 2008 in the two principal variables and in relevant control variables, we are able to explore two questions: whether variation in regional democratization explains the scope of small firm development, and whether, conversely, the scope of small firm development reinforces regional democratization. Then, by disaggregating the democracy index into its sub-indicators, we can inquire as to which dimensions of democratization may have been influenced positively by the scope of regional small firm development. Finally, by employing the two stage least squares technique with an instrumental variable applied to the small firm prevalence, we attempt to address and diminish the impact of endogeneity between small firm prevalence and democratization.

For reference, the variables used in the regressions throughout this chapter are defined in Table 2.6 along with the years or periods for each.

Regression 1: explaining regional variation in small firm prevalence

Democratization in Russia was at the outset intimately associated with pro-market economic reforms, including the legalization of private enterprise and the legal

Table 2.6 Summary Description of Variables

Variable Label	Description	Years
DEM	Regional democracy composite index (three periods)	1991–2001, 2000–2004, 2005–2009
SMALLFIRM	Number of incorporated firms up to 100 employees relative to 1,000 of the economically active population	1995, 2000, 2002, 2004, 2006, 2008
STUDT	Number of post-secondary students per 1,000 population by academic year	1995–1996, 2001–2002, 2005–2006
NEWS	Newspapers printed per 1,000 population	2000, 2004, 2008
INCMONTH	Average per capita monthly income in rubles (current)	2000, 2004, 2008
PCTPOV	Share of population with income below poverty line	2000, 2004, 2008
URBAN	Share of population living in cities	2000, 2004, 2008
INDENTREP	Number of unincorporated (independent) entrepreneurs per 1,000 of the economically active population	2004, 2008
PCS	Number of personal computers per 100 households	2000, 2004, 2008
MOSCOW	Dummy variable =1 for Moscow, 0 for all others	

and institutional changes that allowed companies to come into being. The enact-ment of legal changes allowing companies to be formed does not by itself ensure the creation of new firms by private actors at any given or fixed level of intensity, however. By modeling this relationship, we can discover the effects on small firm prevalence of the scope and duration of democratization by region as well as the effects of other variables on the scope of small firm development. This question is formulated in a set of regressions depicted as Model 1.

Using the variables as previously defined, the general form of Model 1 is as follows:

$$\text{SMALLFIRM} = \beta_0 + \beta_1(\text{DEM}) + \beta_2(\text{STUDT}) + \beta_3(\text{NEWS})$$
$$+ \beta_4(\text{INCMONTH}) + \beta_5(\text{PCTPOV}) + \beta_6(\text{URBAN}) + \beta_7(\text{PCS})$$
$$+ \beta_8(\text{INDENTREP}) + \beta_9(\text{MOSCOW})$$

This general form is estimated in six different variations, which are shown in Table 2.7. The specifications allow us to trace the effects of democratization on small firm development through the period 1991–2008. Table 2.8 shows the effect of the democratic opening on small firm prevalence.

The key finding from the estimation of this set of regressions is that the democracy index score of regions is statistically significant in explaining regions' outcome on small firm prevalence with a lag of at least two years from the close of the period for which democratization is measured. It is particularly noteworthy

Table 2.7 Specifications of Model 1

$\text{SMALLFIRM\_02} = \beta_0 + \beta_1(\text{DEM91\_01}) + \beta_2(\text{STUDT\_0001}) + \beta_3(\text{NEWS\_00})$
$\quad + \beta_4(\text{INCMONTH\_00}) + \beta_5(\text{PCTPOV00}) + \beta_6(\text{URBAN00}) + \beta_7(\text{PCS\_00}) + \beta_8(\text{MOSCOW})$

$\text{SMALLFIRM\_04} = \beta_0 + \beta_1(\text{DEM91\_01}) + \beta_2(\text{STUDT\_0001}) + \beta_3(\text{NEWS\_04})$
$\quad + \beta_4(\text{INCMONTH\_04}) + \beta_5(\text{PCTPOV04}) + \beta_6(\text{URBAN04}) + \beta_7(\text{PCS\_04})$
$\quad + \beta_8(\text{INDENTREP\_04}) + \beta_9(\text{MOSCOW})$

$\text{SMALLFIRM\_06} = \beta_0 + \beta_1(\text{DEM91\_01}) + \beta_2(\text{STUDT\_0506}) + \beta_3(\text{NEWS\_04})$
$\quad + \beta_4(\text{INCMONTH\_04}) + \beta_5(\text{PCTPOV04}) + \beta_6(\text{URBAN04}) + \beta_7(\text{PCS\_04})$
$\quad + \beta_8(\text{INDENTRP\_04}) + \beta_9(\text{MOSCOW})$

$\text{SMALLFIRM\_08} = \beta_0 + \beta_1(\text{DEM91\_01}) + \beta_2(\text{STUDT\_0506}) + \beta_3(\text{NEWS\_08})$
$\quad + \beta_4(\text{INCMONTH\_08}) + \beta_5(\text{PCTPOV08}) + \beta_6(\text{URBAN08}) + \beta_7(\text{PCS\_08})$
$\quad + \beta_8(\text{INDENTREP\_04}) + \beta_8(\text{MOSCOW})$

$\text{SMALLFIRM\_06} = \beta_0 + \beta_1(\text{DEM00\_04}) + \beta_2(\text{STUDT\_0506}) + \beta_3(\text{NEWS\_04})$
$\quad + \beta_4(\text{INCMONTH\_04}) + \beta_5(\text{PCTPOV04}) + \beta_6(\text{URBAN04}) + \beta_7(\text{PCS\_04})$
$\quad + \beta_8(\text{INDENTREP\_04}) + \beta_9(\text{MOSCOW})$

$\text{SMALLFIRM\_08} = \beta_0 + \beta_1(\text{DEM00\_04}) + \beta_2(\text{STUDT\_0506}) + \beta_3(\text{NEWS\_08})$
$\quad + \beta_4(\text{INCMONTH\_08}) + \beta_5(\text{PCTPOV08}) + \beta_6(\text{URBAN08}) + \beta_7(\text{PCS\_08})$
$\quad + \beta_8(\text{INDENTREP\_08}) + \beta_9(\text{MOSCOW})$

Note: The regression results tables throughout the chapter report results using robust standard errors where the standard error of the coefficient estimate for the principal independent variable of interest (*SMALLFIRM* or *DEM*) is larger than the estimate obtained from the standard OLS regression.

Table 2.8 OLS Regression: Dependent Variable: Small Firm per 1,000 Persons in Workforce

VARIABLE			COEFFICIENTS			
	1a	1b	1c	1d	1e	1f
dem	0.0855	**0.224****	**0.262****	**0.500*****	**0.205****	**0.402****
	(0.11)	(0.110)	(0.112)	(0.188)	(0.0957)	(0.189)
studt	**0.0154****	**0.0223****	**0.0166****	**0.0200****	**0.0174*****	**0.0201****
	(0.006)	(0.0096)	(0.0082)	(0.00844)	(0.00442)	(0.00862)
news	0.005	**0.00140***	**0.00144****	0.00102	**0.00139***	0.00137
	(0.002)	(0.000800)	(0.0007)	(0.00132)	(0.000782)	(0.00133)
incmonth	−0.0001	0.00042	−3.94e-06	−0.00048	−0.000140	**−0.000584***
	(0.002)	(0.00048)	(0.000395)	(0.000332)	(0.000404)	(0.000337)
pctpov	0.070	−0.0317	−0.0255	−0.057	−0.0368	−0.111
	(0.053)	(0.0769)	(0.0597)	(0.2168)	(0.0785)	(0.218)
urban	**0.169****	0.0294	0.0324	0.0598	0.0647	0.0866
	(0.063)	(0.0683)	(0.0561)	(0.106)	(0.0627)	(0.107)
pcs	0.14	−0.114	−0.00525	0.0114	−0.00738	0.0186
	(0.326)	(0.103)	(0.087)	(0.0976)	(0.0836)	(0.100)
indentrep		−0.0289	0.00699	0.0253	0.0171	0.0314
		(0.316)	(0.0258)	(0.096)	(0.0257)	(0.0980)
moscow	−17.26	−5.308	2.598	6.614	3.540	4.727
	(16.52)	(10.79)	(9.594)	(12.98)	(7.788)	(13.20)
constant	−13.54	−2.804	−6.593	−7.078	−7.117	−5.222
	(7.473)	(7.543)	(7.398)	(10.48)	(5.538)	(10.63)
Observations	77	76	76	78	76	78
R-squared	0.5862	0.551	0.583	0.364	0.567	0.342

Standard errors in parentheses   ***** $p < 0.01$, ** $p < 0.05$, * $p < 0.1$**

Robust standard errors are reported for equations 1a, 1b, 1c, and standard OLS regression results for equations 1d, 1e and 1f.

that the democratic index for the period 1991–2001 explains *more* of the variation in small firm prevalence as the time lag lengthens, with the coefficient rising to 0.5 when the baseline democracy rating (1991–2001) is used to explain variation in small firm prevalence in 2008. The same rising pattern seems to hold for the power of the democratization index in 2000–2004 in explaining small firm prevalence in 2006 and 2008 (specifications 1e and 1f). The R-squared measure of overall 'fit' suggests that this model in all its variations does a good job of explaining the variation in small firm prevalence.

The number of students in higher education relative to the population also is a significant determinant of the variation in small firm prevalence throughout all the years considered, and the number of newspapers printed relative to the population was a significant determinant in three time periods. Different degrees of urbanization seem only to have been significant in the earliest of the time frames considered (specification 1a). Urbanization, a variable that changes only very incrementally from year to year, is the best approximation we have in this cross-sectional analysis of the durable antecedent structural factors that may have influenced the path of both of our principal variables of interest: democracy and small firm prevalence.

Regression 2: explaining regional variation in democratization

This section turns to the question of what structural factors may contribute to explaining the variation in the extent of regional democratization. Regression 2 tests the hypothesis that variations in small firm prevalence are part of the explanation, taking into account the effects of control variables.

The general form of Regression 2 is as follows:

$$\text{DEM} = \beta_0 + \beta_1(\text{SMALLFIRM}) + \beta_2(\text{INCMONTH}) + \beta_3(\text{PCTPOV})$$
$$+ \beta_4(\text{URBAN}) + \beta_5(\text{STUDT}) + \beta_6(\text{NEWS}) + \beta_7(\text{PCS})$$
$$+ \beta_8(\text{INDENTREP}) + \beta_9(\text{MOSCOW})$$

The five variations estimated are presented in Table 2.9:

Table 2.9 Five Specifications of Model 2

$\text{DEM00\_04} = \beta_0 + \beta_1(\text{SMALLFIRM\_95}) + \beta_2(\text{INCMONTH\_04})$ (2a)
  $+ \beta_3(\text{PCTPOV\_04}) + \beta_4(\text{URBAN04}) + \beta_5(\text{STUDT\_0001}) + \beta_6(\text{NEWS\_04})$
  $+ \beta_7(\text{PCS\_04}) + \beta_8(\text{INDENTREP\_04}) + \beta_9(\text{MOSCOW})$

$\text{DEM05\_09} = \beta_0 + \beta_1(\text{SMALLFIRM\_95}) + \beta_2(\text{INCMONTH\_08})$ (2b)
  $+ \beta_3(\text{PCTPOV\_08}) + \beta_4(\text{URBAN08}) + \beta_5(\text{STUDT\_0506}) + \beta_6(\text{NEWS\_08})$
  $+ \beta_7(\text{PCS\_08}) + \beta_8(\text{INDENTREP\_04}) + \beta_9(\text{MOSCOW})$

$\text{DEM05\_09} = \beta_0 + \beta_1(\text{SMALLFIRM\_00}) + \beta_2(\text{INCMONTH\_08})$ (2c)
  $+ \beta_3(\text{PCTPOV\_08}) + \beta_4(\text{URBAN08}) + \beta_5(\text{STUDT\_0506}) + \beta_6(\text{NEWS\_08})$
  $+ \beta_7(\text{PCS\_08}) + \beta_8(\text{INDENTREP\_08}) + \beta_9(\text{MOSCOW})$

$\text{DEM05\_09} = \beta_0 + \beta_1(\text{SMALLFIRM\_02}) + \beta_2(\text{INCMONTH\_08})$ (2d)
  $+ \beta_3(\text{PCTPOV\_08}) + \beta_4(\text{URBAN08}) + \beta_5(\text{STUDT\_0506}) + \beta_6(\text{NEWS\_08})$
  $+ \beta_7(\text{PCS\_08}) + \beta_8(\text{INDENTREP\_08}) + \beta_9(\text{MOSCOW})$

$\text{DEM05\_09} = \beta_0 + \beta_1(\text{SMALLFIRM\_04}) + \beta_2(\text{INCMONTH\_08})$ (2e)
  $+ \beta_3(\text{PCTPOV\_08}) + \beta_4(\text{URBAN08}) + \beta_5(\text{STUDT\_0506}) + \beta_6(\text{NEWS\_08})$
  $+ \beta_7(\text{PCS\_08}) + \beta_8(\text{INDENTREP\_08}) + \beta_9(\text{MOSCOW})$

The results of OLS regression of the five formulations of Regression 2 are presented in Table 2.10.

Small firm prevalence is significant in explaining variations in regional democratization only in the final formulation, where this variable as measured in 2004 explains a considerable part of the variation in the democracy index in 2005–2009. In addition, when equation 2d is estimated with non-robust standard errors, the coefficient on the variable for small firm prevalence (measured in 2002) is significant at the 90% confidence level. From the standpoint of traditional structural explanations of democratization, it is interesting that neither average money

Table 2.10 OLS Regression: Dependent Variable: Regional Democracy Index

	COEFFICIENTS				
MODEL	2a	2b	2c	2d	2e
smallfirm	0.127	0.202	0.163	0.227	**0.250****
	(0.172)	(0.149)	(0.122)	(0.138)	(0.115)
incmonth	−0.00008	−0.000164	0.0000887	−0.000067	−0.0000733
	(0.00055)	(0.000219)	(0.000206)	(0.000144)	(0.000200)
pctpov	−0.111	−0.170	−0.152	−0.134	−0.139
	(0.101)	(0.134)	(0.131)	(0.124)	(0.128)
urban	**0.226*****	**0.137****	**0.112***	0.0907	**0.107***
	(0.075)	(0.0640)	(0.0637)	(0.0573)	(0.0622)
studt	−0.0002	−0.00575	−0.00658	−0.00644	−0.00776
	(0.006)	(0.00535)	(0.00545)	(0.00545)	(0.00531)
news	0.00074	**0.00141***	0.00115	0.00124	0.00103
	(0.0098)	(0.000786)	(0.000794)	(0.000787)	(0.000777)
pcs	0.099	**0.0213*****	**0.199*****	**0.211*****	**0.206*****
	(0.108)	(0.0606)	(0.0575)	(0.045)	(0.0563)
indentrep	0.045	0.0218	0.012	0.00708	0.0234
	(0.032)	(0.067)	(0.059)	(0.05239)	(0.0584)
moscow	−14.93	**−21.55*****	**−19.15****	**−21.47*****	**−18.92****
	(9.933)	(7.889)	(7.700)	(5.5434)	(7.543)
constant	11.71	14.92**	17.72***	17.60***	16.27***
	(6.822)	(6.535)	(6.215)	(6.496)	(6.016)
Observations	76	77	78	78	78
R-squared	0.359	0.410	0.441	0.451	0.464
Standard errors in parentheses				*** $p < 0.01$, ** $p < 0.05$, * $p < 0.1$	

OLS with robust standard errors results reported for equation 2d only, and standard OLS results for equations 2a, 2b, 2c and 2e.

incomes nor the share of the population in poverty is significant in explaining variations in democracy.

The degree of urbanization by region is a good predictor of democracy in 4 of the 5 specifications, consistent with a central claim of modernization theory. As suggested in the discussion of the first set of regressions, regional variations in urbanization may reflect historical tendencies that predate the collapse (or even the birth) of the USSR.

While urbanization changes little over the time period of this analysis, the number of personal computers per 100 households rose sharply over the period since 1990. In 4 of 5 specifications of the model, this variable is highly significant in explaining the outcome on the democracy index. The pervasiveness of personal computers is indirectly a measure of average incomes and is related to income differentials among regions. But, at the same time, this variable seems to measure a qualitative aspect of human development. The speed and pervasiveness of adoption of personal computers is likely a manifestation of some kind of 'social capital,' assuming that personal computers are generally a medium of connectedness through the internet. Like the number of students relative to the population, this variable is related to human capital resources, but perhaps also gets at an aspect of voluntary engagement and information sharing among all age groups. Interestingly enough, the number of students relative to the population is a strong predictor of small firm prevalence in all specifications, whereas the personal computers variable is not. On the other hand, the number of personal computers per 100 households explains variations in democracy but not of small firm prevalence.

Comparing the results of regressions 1 and 2

Tables 2.11 and 2.12 highlight the key findings from Regressions 1 and 2, allowing them to be interpreted together.

Table 2.11 Model 1: Dependent Variable: Small Firms per 1,000 People in Workforce

Dependent variable	SmallFirm02 (1a)	SmallFirm04 (1b)	SmallFirm06 (1c)	SmallFirm08 (1d)	SmallFirm06 (1e)	SmallFirm08 (1f)
Independent variable	Dem91–01	Dem91–01	Dem91–01	Dem91–01	Dem00–04	Dem00–04
Coefficient	0.127	**0.224****	**0.262****	**0.500*****	**0.205****	**0.402****
Stat sign. variables	studt+ urban+	studt+	studt+ news+	studt+ news+	studt+	studt+ incmonth–
R-squared	0.5862	0.551	0.583	0.364	0.567	0.342
						$p < 0.01, p < 0.05, p < 0.1$

Table 2.12 Model 2: Dependent Variable: Regional Democracy Index Scores

Dependent variable	Dem00–04 (2a)	Dem05–09 (2b)	Dem05–09 (2c)	Dem05–09 (2d)	Dem05–09 (2e)
Independent variable	SmallFirm95	SmallFirm95	SmallFirm00	SmallFirm02	SmallFirm04
Coefficient	0.127	0.202	0.163	0.227	**0.250****
Stat. sign. variables	urban+	urban+ news+ pcs+ moscow–	urban+ pcs+ moscow–	pcs+ moscow–	urban+ pcs+ moscow–
R-squared	0.359	0.410	0.441	0.451	0.464
					$p < 0.01, p < 0.05, p < 0.1$

Note for Table 2.11: *** $p < 0.01$, ** $p < 0.05$, * $p < 0.1$

Note for Table 2.12: *** $p < 0.01$, ** $p < 0.05$, * $p < 0.1$

Regressions 1 and 2, each of them in the several specifications shown above, attempted to trace the interaction of democracy and small firm prevalence over the period 1991–2008. This is a way of grappling analytically with the problem of endogeneity between small firm prevalence and democracy. It also takes into account the close association of both these variables with variations among regions in urbanization, availability of public information and the share of the population in higher education at a given period. It is noteworthy that the purely economic variables (per capita income or poverty rates) are not generally significant in explaining variation in either democracy or small firm prevalence.

The contrast between the R-squared measures of Models 1 and 2 shows that the chosen approach explains small business prevalence better than the same set of variables explains different outcomes with respect to democracy. Human agency by political leaders is likely a large part of the unexplained variation in regional democratization. The two aforementioned summary tables allow us to see that democratization influences the prevalence of small firms quite significantly. The coefficient on the variable small firm prevalence *(smallfirms)* in the OLS estimations of Model 1 shows statistical significance beginning with the small firm prevalence in 2004 and intensifying after that. Indeed the model suggests that the achievement of a greater degree of democratization in the 1990s explains variations in small firm prevalence *more* decisively in each of the years ending with 2008.

Centrally important to the analysis of this chapter is the question posed in Model 2: whether variations in small firm prevalence explain any of the variations in regional democratization. We find evidence for this in the final specification (2e), summarized in the Table 2.12. The coefficient estimate for small firm prevalence *(smallfirm)* in equation 2e is 0.25. This means that for every additional small company per 1,000 of the workforce the predicted democracy score for a region in 2005–2009 rises by 0.25.

Regression 3: two stage least squares (2SLS) and instrumental variable

Using 2SLS and an instrumental variable for the prevalence by region of small firms in 2004 presents a more rigorous test of the finding that small firm prevalence in 2004 explains some of the variation in the democracy index by region in 2005–2009. The instrumental variable must be highly correlated with small firm prevalence in 2004, but not with the democracy index score in 2005–2009. Estimating Model 2 in versions 2b and 2c (see Table 2.10) showed that small firm prevalence in 1995 (2b) and 2000 (2c) were not significant in predicting the democracy index score in 2005–2009. However, each of these variables is strongly correlated with small firm prevalence in 2004, 2006 and 2008.

The basic OLS model we begin with is as follows:

$$\text{DEM05\_09} = \beta_0 + \beta_1(\text{SMALLFIRM\_04}) + \beta_2(\text{PCS\_08})$$
$$+ \beta_3(\text{PCTPOV\_08}) + \beta_4(\text{STUDT\_0506}) + \beta_5(\text{NEWS\_08})$$

The results of this regression are shown in Table 2.13. The coefficient estimate on the variable measuring small firm prevalence in 2004 is 0.29 and is significant at the 90% confidence level.

As was seen in Table 1.1 relating democracy to small firm prevalence, the variable small firm prevalence in 1995 is not correlated with democracy index scores in any of the three periods. It is, however, highly correlated with small firm prevalence in subsequent years. The measure of small firm prevalence in 2000 is weakly correlated with the democracy index in 2005–2009, but is strongly and positively correlated with small firm prevalence in subsequent years. Using *both* of these variables together as an instrument to stand in place of the measure of small firm prevalence in 2004 (SMALLFIRMS_04) satisfies the first crucial test of validity when used in the first stage equation that follows:

$$\text{SMALLFIRM\_04} = \beta_0 + \beta_1(\text{SMALLFIRM\_95}) + \beta_2(\text{SMALLFIRM\_00})$$
$$+ \beta_3(\text{PCS\_08}) + \beta_4(\text{PCTPOV\_08}) + \beta_5(\text{STUDT\_0506}) + \beta_6 (\text{NEWS\_08})$$

The results of running this first stage regression gives us a predicted value of the variable SMALLFIRMS_04 based exclusively upon the explanatory power of the first stage equation. The results are shown in Table 2.13:

Table 2.13 OLS First Stage Regression: Dependent Variable Small Firm Prevalence 2004

VARIABLES	SMALLFIRM_04
SMALLFIRM_95	−0.0800
	(0.0775)
SMALLFIRM_00	0.920***
	(0.0698)
PCS_08	−0.0267
	(0.0233)
PCTPOV_08	−0.0699
	(0.0516)
STUDT_0506	0.00210
	(0.00258)
NEWS_08	5.32e-05
	(0.000312)
Constant	4.517***
	(1.533)
Observations	77
R-squared	0.867

*** $p < 0.01$, ** $p < 0.05$, * $p < 0.1$

The first stage estimation shows that SMALLFIRM_00 strongly predicts small firm prevalence in 2004. Although small firm prevalence in 1995 does not enter significantly in this first stage, it is nonetheless necessary to include both instruments to satisfy all the statistical tests of validity in the regression using the

Instrumental Variable (IV). The version of Regression 3 using the instruments is shown as follows, along with the results of estimating the model using unadjusted and robust standard errors:

$$\text{DEM05\_09} = \beta_0 + \beta_1(\text{SMALLFIRM\_04=SMALLFIRM\_95}$$
$$\text{SMALLFIRM\_95}) + \beta_2(\text{PCS\_08}) + \beta_3(\text{PCTPOV\_08})$$
$$+ \beta_4(\text{STUDT\_0506}) + \beta_5(\text{NEWS\_08})$$

Table 2.14 OLS and IV Estimation: Dependent Variable - Democracy Index Score 2005–2009

	(1)	(2)	(3)
VARIABLES	OLS	IV	IV-robust
SMALLFIRM_04	0.29*	0.24	0.24*
	(0.119)	(0.136)	(0.120)
PCS_08	0.22***	0.21***	0.21***
	(0.046)	(0.047)	(0.044)
PCTPOV_08	−0.24*	−0.23*	−0.23*
	(0.108)	(0.108)	(0.094)
STUDT_0506	−0.01	−0.01	−0.01
	(0.006)	(0.005)	(0.005)
NEWS_08	−0.00	0.00	0.00
	(0.001)	(0.001)	(0.001)
Constant	25.92***	26.36***	26.36***
	(3.211)	(3.124)	(3.064)
Observations	78	77	77
R-squared	0.360	0.325	0.325
F-stat		117.32	119.56
Sargan/Hansen J stat		0.949	1.172

Standard errors in parentheses
*** $p < 0.001$, ** $p < 0.01$, * $p < 0.05$

The variable SMALLFIRM_04 that enters this equation is the one that emerges from the estimation in the first stage shown in Table 2.14. This is the value that is predicted by the two instruments and the control variables in Model 3. Based on the estimation of the various specifications of Regression 2, we know that neither SMALLFIRMS_95 nor SMALLFIRMS_00 is significant in explaining variation in the democracy outcome in 2005–2009. The first stage estimate of SMALLFIRMS_04 cannot be endogenous to DEM05_09, because DEM05_09 cannot logically be the cause of small firm prevalence in 1995 or 2000. The coefficient on the variable SMALLFIRM_04 in the robust errors version of the model is significant at the 95% confidence level, and the analogous coefficient with unadjusted standard errors is significant at the 90% confidence level. The F-stat and Sargan/Hansen J-stat values also support the validity and strength of the instruments used.

Regression 4: explaining variations in the democracy index sub-indicators

In Equation 2e in Table 2.10 we found that the prevalence of small firms in 2004 is statistically significant in explaining variations in the democracy index score in 2005–2009. This finding withstood in addition the 2SLS and IV refinement of the forgoing section (Regression 3).

In order to refine the interpretation of this result, we estimate in this section the same set of independent variables as in Equation 2e but replace the dependent variable, the democracy index score in 2005–09 with the scores for each region on the 10 sub-indicators of which the 2005–2009 index is the sum.

It will be recalled that the Democracy index in 2005–2009 is a composite of the scores on the following sub-indices rated from 1 to 5:

1   regional political system (division of power, independence of courts and law enforcement bodies, extent of respect for citizens' rights);
2   openness (transparency, responsiveness to public);
3   fairness in the conduct of elections;
4   political pluralism, in particular the role of political parties;
5   the extent of independence of the media;
6   corruption (in particular the interplay of business and political elites);
7   economic liberalization;
8   civil society development (including NGO range and activity levels, referenda, demonstrations);
9   elites (how fixed or changeable through time, how diverse); and
10   local governments (quality and influence of elected municipal governments, relative to the governor and regional administration).

(The abbreviations *POL, OPEN, ELEC, PLUR, MEDIA, CORR, ECON, CIV, ELIT, LOC* denote in order the sub-indicators 1–10 previously defined.)

Regression 4 follows the form of Regression 2, with each sub-indicator score in the Democracy index of 2005–2009 replacing the composite index as the dependent variable. The 10 variations of Regression 4 are shown in Table 2.15. The estimation of these equations is tabulated in Table 2.16.

These regressions show that the coefficient on the variable small firm prevalence in 2004 is significant and positive when the dependent variable is dispersion of political authority *(POL)*, openness in the conduct of government *(OPEN)*, media independence *(MEDIA)* or civil society development *(CIV)*. The coefficient on the small firm prevalence variable is significant at the 99% confidence level for explaining variation in the openness, media, and civil society sub-indicators and at the 90% level for explaining variations in the dispersion of political authority. The magnitude of the effect of variations in small firm prevalence is also substantial in these four specifications, when it is recalled that each sub-indicator varies only over the range of 1 to 5.

It is perhaps surprising that small firm prevalence is not significant in explaining the variation on either of the principal *economic* variables in the democracy

Table 2.15 Model 3: Dependent Variable: Dem05_09 Sub-Indicators Individually

$POL05\_09 = \beta_0 + \beta_1(SMALLFIRM\_04) + \beta_2(INCMONTH\_08) + \beta_3(PCTPOV\_08) + \beta_4(URBAN\_08) + \beta_5(STUDT\_0506) + \beta_6(NEWS\_08) + \beta_7(INDENTREP\_08) + \beta_8(PCS\_08) + \beta_9(MOSCOW)$

$OPEN05\_09 = \beta_0 + \beta_1(SMALLFIRM\_04) + \beta_2(INCMONTH\_08) + \beta_3(PCTPOV\_08) + \beta_4(URBAN\_08) + \beta_5(STUDT\_0506) + \beta_6(NEWS\_08) + \beta_7(INDENTREP\_08) + \beta_8(PCS\_08) + \beta_9(MOSCOW)$

$ELEC05\_09 = \beta_0 + \beta_1(SMALLFIRM\_04) + \beta_2(INCMONTH\_08) + \beta_3(PCTPOV\_08) + \beta_4(URBAN\_08) + \beta_5(STUDT\_0506) + \beta_6(NEWS\_08) + \beta_7(INDENTREP\_08) + \beta_8(PCS\_08) + \beta_9(MOSCOW)$

$PLUR05\_09 = \beta_0 + \beta_1(SMALLFIRM\_04) + \beta_2(INCMONTH\_08) + \beta_3(PCTPOV\_08) + \beta_4(URBAN\_08) + \beta_5(STUDT\_0506) + \beta_6(NEWS\_08) + \beta_7(INDENTREP\_08) + \beta_8(PCS\_08) + \beta_9(MOSCOW)$

$MEDIA05\_09 = \beta_0 + \beta_1(SMALLFIRM\_04) + \beta_2(INCMONTH\_08) + \beta_3(PCTPOV\_08) + \beta_4(URBAN\_08) + \beta_5(STUDT\_0506) + \beta_6(NEWS\_08) + \beta_7(INDENTREP\_08) + \beta_8(PCS\_08) + \beta_9(MOSCOW)$

$CORR05\_09 = \beta_0 + \beta_1(SMALLFIRM\_04) + \beta_2(INCMONTH\_08) + \beta_3(PCTPOV\_08) + \beta_4(URBAN\_08) + \beta_5(STUDT\_0506) + \beta_6(NEWS\_08) + \beta_7(INDENTREP\_08) + \beta_8(PCS\_08) + \beta_9(MOSCOW)$

$ECON05\_09 = \beta_0 + \beta_1(SMALLFIRM\_04) + \beta_2(INCMONTH\_08) + \beta_3(PCTPOV\_08) + \beta_4(URBAN\_08) + \beta_5(STUDT\_0506) + \beta_6(NEWS\_08) + \beta_7(INDENTREP\_08) + \beta_8(PCS\_08) + \beta_9(MOSCOW)$

$CIV05\_09 = \beta_0 + \beta_1(SMALLFIRM\_04) + \beta_2(INCMONTH\_08) + \beta_3(PCTPOV\_08) + \beta_4(URBAN\_08) + \beta_5(STUDT\_0506) + \beta_6(NEWS\_08) + \beta_7(INDENTREP\_08) + \beta_8(PCS\_08) + \beta_9(MOSCOW)$

$ELIT05\_09 = \beta_0 + \beta_1(SMALLFIRM\_04) + \beta_2(INCMONTH\_08) + \beta_3(PCTPOV\_08) + \beta_4(URBAN\_08) + \beta_5(STUDT\_0506) + \beta_6(NEWS\_08) + \beta_7(INDENTREP\_08) + \beta_8(PCS\_08) + \beta_9(MOSCOW)$

$LOC05\_09 = \beta_0 + \beta_1(SMALLFIRM\_04) + \beta_2(INCMONTH\_08) + \beta_3(PCTPOV\_08) + \beta_4(URBAN\_08) + \beta_5(STUDT\_0506) + \beta_6(NEWS\_08) + \beta_7(INDENTREP\_08) + \beta_8(PCS\_08) + \beta_9(MOSCOW)$

composite: corruption or economic liberalization. This finding tends to support the intuition that the relationship of small firm prevalence with democracy does not work through or by means of changes in economic outcomes as such. With one exception, measures of average welfare – monthly per capita income or poverty rates – also do not explain the variation of the democracy sub-indicators. The one interesting exception to this is that higher poverty rates tend to diminish regions' scores on economic liberalization. This makes intuitive sense, because those regions where poverty is most pervasive might be the ones where considerations of social dislocation and unemployment might have most heavily weighed against reforms such as enterprise restructuring, withdrawal of subsidies and privatization.

Urbanization, which we have posited may be a proxy for antecedent structural determinants of both small firm prevalence and democracy, contributes

Table 2.16 OLS Regression: Dependent Variable: Regional Democracy Index Sub-indicators

VARIABLES	COEFFICIENTS									
	pol	open	elect	plural	media	corr	econ	civ	elit	loc
SmallFirms04	0.0261*	0.056***	0.0180	0.0102	0.0452***	0.000885	0.0187	0.0657***	0.0167	-0.00770
	(0.0155)	(0.018)	(0.0214)	(0.0182)	(0.0170)	(0.0151)	(0.0150)	(0.0183)	(0.0152)	(0.0168)
incmonth08	1.01e-05	-6.08e-06	-8.64e-06	-1.38e-05	-1.73e-05	-2.47e-05	-3.95e-05	2.66e-05	2.74e-05	-2.76e-05
	(1.93e-05)	(0.00003)	(0.000026)	(3.17e-05)	(2.96e-05)	(2.62e-05)	(1.82e-05)	(3.25e-05)	(2.43e-05)	(2.92e-05)
pctpov08	-0.0212	-0.0216	-0.0123	0.0135	-0.0128	-0.00852	-0.0359**	0.00212	-0.0138	-0.0288
	(0.0142)	(0.0203)	(0.02133)	(0.0202)	(0.0189)	(0.0167)	(0.0164)	(0.0195)	(0.0138)	(0.0186)
urban08	0.00289	0.00053	0.0130	0.0179*	0.0136	0.0176**	0.0159**	-0.00531	0.0124*	0.0187**
	(0.005927)	(0.0099)	(0.01104)	(0.00986)	(0.00921)	(0.00815)	(0.00697)	(0.00896)	(0.00637)	(0.00908)
studt0506	-0.000664	-0.00126	-0.00130	-0.00102	-0.000627	-0.000499	-0.00111	-0.000356	-0.000650	-0.000269
	(0.000609)	(0.0085)	(0.00109)	(0.000842)	(0.000786)	(0.000696)	(0.000742)	(0.0007621)	(0.000712)	(0.000776)
news08	0.000161**	0.0001489	0.0000283	0.000167	0.000232**	-5.10e-05	0.000208**	9.01e-05	9.83e-05	-5.21e-05
	(8.03e-05)	(0.000124)	(0.000149)	(0.000123)	(0.000115)	(0.000102)	(9.02e-05)	(0.000125)	(0.000127)	(0.000113)
indentrep08	-0.00114	0.00382	0.00481	0.00417	0.00166	-0.00258	0.00738	0.000902	0.00209	0.00230
	(0.00587)	(0.0093)	(0.00874)	(0.00926)	(0.00865)	(0.00766)	(0.00647)	(0.00798)	(0.00638)	(0.00853)
pcs08	0.0176***	0.0206**	0.0314***	0.0161*	0.0231***	0.0138*	0.0306***	0.0243***	0.0146**	0.0143*
	(0.00531)	(0.009)	(0.00984)	(0.00891)	(0.00832)	(0.00737)	(0.00683)	(0.00779)	(0.00655)	(0.00821)
moscow	-3.324***	-1.44	-1.840*	-2.470**	-1.828	-0.496	-1.809**	-2.095**	-1.855***	-1.841*
	(0.696)	(1.132)	(1.02)	(1.195)	(1.117)	(0.989)	(0.725)	(0.936)	(0.799)	(1.102)
constant	2.297***	2.63	1.279	1.211	0.864	1.681**	1.602**	1.449	1.145	2.137**
	(0.660)	(4.6)	(0.9997)	(0.953)	(0.891)	(0.789)	(0.771)	(0.992)	(0.754)	(0.879)
Observations	78	78	78	78	78	78	78	78	78	78
R-squared	0.410	0.296	0.297	0.232	0.442	0.208	0.487	0.390	0.409	0.298

Standard errors in parentheses

*** $p < 0.01$, ** $p < 0.05$, * $p < 0.1$

OLS with robust standard error result shown for equations 3a, 3b, 3g, 3h, 3j

to explaining the outcomes on the sub-indicators for extent of corruption, economic liberalization, turnover of elites and autonomy of local (municipal) administrations. Variation in the print-run of all publications scaled to the population explains some of the variation in 3 of the sub-indicators. The Moscow dummy variable is significant and negative on 7 of the 10 sub-indicators.

Finally, the number of personal computers per 100 households is significant and of substantial magnitude on all of the sub-indicators. Surprisingly, the coefficient on this variable is positive and significant when the dependent variable is the corruption sub-indicator. This suggests that the level of information about corruption and public awareness of it may be reflected in the corruption sub-indicator, instead of, or in addition to, the underlying comparative prevalence of corruption.

Conclusions

This analysis supports the hypothesis that variations in small firm prevalence are in considerable part explained by variations in the extent and scope of the democratic breakthrough in the formative years 1991–2001. The analysis also suggests that, beginning in 2004, regional variations in small firm prevalence contributed to explaining variations in regional democracy outcomes. The disaggregation of the democracy index into its constituent sub-indicators suggests, moreover, that the contribution of small firm prevalence to regional democracy is related to four sub-indicators: the dispersion of political authority among executive, legislative and judicial institutions; media independence; civil society activism and development; and the openness of political decision-making, including both transparency and the existence of institutions of public participation. The approach taken in the four regional case studies is to inquire into the processes that involve entrepreneurs in the outcomes on these constituent factors in the democracy index.

Notes

1 Over the period of this study, the number of regions has declined as several formerly fully autonomous subregions were absorbed into the larger territories within which they were located. The Federal Statistics Service (Rosstat) annual publication *Regiony Rossii* does not publish full data series for Chechnya. The autonomous okrugs within Arkhangelskaya, Tyumenskaya oblasts and Krasnoyarskiy kray are reported as part of the larger territories, bringing the number of regions for which most series are complete to 79.
2 Incorporated small firms can also take the form of OAO (Otkrytoe Aktsionernoe Obshchestvo) or ZAO. (Zakrytoe Aktsionernoe Obshchestvo)
3 The author attended the 10th entrepreneurs' conference in 2010, devoted to the design of policy 'infrastructure' to support small business development.
4 Household income and expenditure surveys conducted under the Russia Longitudinal Monitoring Survey (RLMS) conducted by the University of North Carolina, Chapel Hill on behalf of USAID in the years 1992 to 2006 are consistent with the Rosstat data with respect to the rapidly growing importance of private enterprise employment as a source of income for the population. (RLMS summary report 2005)
5 Gill (2008) and Fish and Choudry (2007) show that a substantial part of the Russian elite has a commercial origin, contrasting with the findings of Kryshtanovskaya and White

(2003, 2005) who argue that the elite is dominated by figures of silovik (intelligence or military) origins.

6 Business surveys typically find *de novo* companies – companies not based on privatization – are the majority among smaller companies and are substantial and growing share of all company size categories.

7 For convenience, the index will be referred to as the Petrov index.

References

Ahrend, Rudiger and William Tompson. (2005) Fifteen Years of Economic Reform in Russia: What Has Been Achieved? What Remains to Be Done? In *Economics Department Working Paper*. Paris: Organisation for Economic Co-operation and Development.

Aslund, Anders. (2007) *Russia's Capitalist Revolution: Why Reform Succeeded and Democracy Failed*. Washington, DC: Peterson Institute for International Economics.

Buyske, Gail. (2007) *Banking on Small Business: Microfinance in Contemporary Russia*. Ithaca, NY: Cornell University Press.

Centre for Economic and Financial Research (CEFIR). (2001, 2002, 2003, 2004, 2005, 2006) Monitoring the Administrative Barriers to Small Business Development, Rounds 1–6. *CEFIR surveys*, www.cefir.ru. Accessed July 2010.

Center for International Private Enterprise (CIPE). (1992) *Who Are Russia's Entrepreneurs?* CIPE Washington Conference background.

Center for International Private Enterprise (CIPE). (2003–2009) *Semi-Annual Reports on Russian SME Advocacy Program*, USAID Moscow.

Center for International Private Enterprise (CIPE). (2006) Strengthening Local Democracy in Russia: The Case for Business Associations. *Economic Reform Case Study*. Washington, DC: Center for International Private Enterprise.

Center for International Private Enterprise (CIPE). (2008) *CIPE's USAID-Funded "SME Policy Advocacy" Project: Facts and Figures at a Glance*. Washington, DC.

Center for International Private Enterprise (CIPE). (2010) *Twenty-Five Year Impact Evaluation*. Washington, DC.

Center for International Private Enterprise (CIPE) and Russian Chamber of Commerce and Industry. (2003a) *Assessment of Needs of the Business Community, Representing Small Business in Russia*. (Report Produced for USAID in Project Design Phase for SME Advocacy Project) USAID Moscow.

Center for International Private Enterprise (CIPE) and Russian Chamber of Commerce and Industry. (2003b) *Business Association Diagnostic Review*. Moscow: U.S. Agency for International Development.

Desai, Raj M. and Itzhak Goldberg (eds.) (2008) *Can Russia Compete?* Washington, DC: World Bank and Brookings Institution.

European Bank for Reconstruction and Development and World Bank. (2008) *EBRD-World Bank Business Environment and Enterprise Performance (BEEPS): Summary Presentation BEEPS at a Glance*.

Fish, M. Steven. (2005) *Democracy Derailed in Russia: The Failure of Open Politics*. New York: Cambridge University Press.

Fish, M. Steven and Omar Choudry. (2007) Democratization and Economic Liberalization in the Postcommunist World. *Comparative Political Studies* 40 (3):254–282.

Forbes Russian edition. (2010) The 100 Richest Businessmen, May, 2010.

Frye, Timothy. (2002) Capture or Exchange? Business Lobbying in Russia. *Europe-Asia Studies* 54 (7):1017–1036.

Frye, Timothy and Andrei Yakovlev. (2007) *Reforms in Russia Through the Eyes of Business: What Has Changed in Seven Years*. Moscow: Higher School of Economics.

Frye, Timothy, Andrei Yakovlev and Yevgeny Yasin. (2008) The "Other" Russian Economy: How Everyday Firms View the Rules of the Game in Russia. *Social Research: An International Quarterly* 76 (1):29–54.

Gill, Graeme. (2008) *Bourgeoisie, State and Democracy: Russia, Britain, France, Germany and the USA*. Oxford, New York: Oxford University Press.

Goskomstat, Rossii. (2001) *Regiony Rossii*. Moscow: State Committee of the Russian Federation for Statistics.

Hendley, Kathryn. (1998) Remaking an Institution: The Transition in Russia From State 'Arbitrazh' to 'Arbitrazh' Courts. *American Journal of Comparative Law* 46 (1):93–127.

Hendley, Kathryn. (1999) Rewriting the Rules of the Game in Russia: Neglected Issue of the Demand for Law. *East European Constitutional Review* 8 (4):89–96.

Hendley, Kathryn. (2003) Reforming the Rules for Business Litigation in Russia: To What End? *Demokratizatsiya: The Journal of Post-Soviet Democratization* 11 (3):363–380.

Hendley, Kathryn, Barry W. Ickes, Peter Murrell and Randi Ryterman. (1997) Observations on the Use of Law by Russian Enterprises. *Post-Soviet Affairs* 13 (1):19–41.

Hendley, Kathryn, Peter Murrell and Randi Ryterman. (2000) Law, Relationships and Private Enforcement: Transactional Strategies of Russian Enterprises. *Europe-Asia Studies* 52 (4):627–656.

INDEM and CIPE. (2009) *Sudebnaya Vlast' i Predprinimateli: Resultaty Sotsiologicheskogo Analiza*. Moscow.

Jones, Anthony and William Moskoff. (1991) *Ko-ops: The Rebirth of Entrepreneurship in the Soviet Union*. Bloomington: Indiana University Press.

Kommersant. (2007, April 4) *Malomu biznesu okazali predpochtenie*. http://www.kommersant. ru/doc/760237. Accessed December 15, 2012.

Kryshtanovskaya, Olga and Stephen White. (2003) Putin's Militocracy. *Post-Soviet Affairs* 19 (4):289–306.

Kryshtanovskaya, Olga and Stephen White. (2005) The Rise of the Russian Business Elite. *Communist and Post-Communist Studies* 38 (3):293–307.

Lipset, Seymour Martin. (1959) Some Social Requisites of Democracy: Economic Development and Political Legitimacy. *American Political Science Review* 53:69–105.

OECD. (2009) *OECD Economic Surveys: Russian Federation*. Paris: Organisation for Economic Co-operation and Development.

Petrov, Nikolay and Alexei Titkov. (2006) *Demokratichnost' Rossiskikh Regionov*. http:// atlas.socpol.ru/indexes/index_democr.shtml. Accessed Novermber 10, 2010.

Petrov, Nikolay and Alexei Titkov (2013) *Reyting Demokratichnosti Regionov Moskovskogo Tsenta Karnegi: 10 Let v Stroyu*. Moscow: Carnegie Moscow Center. http://carnegie. ru/publications/?fa=55853. Accessed December 1, 2014.

Pyle, William. (2004) [Dataset of survey results: Entrepreneurs and business association leaders]. Unpublished raw data.

Rosstat (Federal'naya Sluzhba Gosudarstvennoy Statistiki). (2002, 2004, 2008, 2010) *Regiony Rossii: Sotsial'no-Ekonomicheskie Pokazateli*.

Rosstat (Federal'naya Sluzhba Gosudarstvennoy Statistiki). (2009) *Maloe i Srednee Predprimatel'stvo v Rossii*.

Russia Longitudinal Monitoring Survey (RLMS). (2005) *Monitoring Economic Conditions in the Russian Federation 1992–2004*. Chapel Hill: University of North Carolina.

Russia Longitudinal Monitoring Survey (RLMS). (2006) *Monitoring Conditions in the Russian Federation, 1992–2005*. Chapel Hill: University of North Carolina.

Russian Chamber of Commerce and Industry. (2009a) *Monitoring Sostoyaniya Malogo i Srednego Predprinimatel'stva v Subyektakh Rossiyskoy Federatatsii*. Moscow.

Russian Chamber of Commerce and Industry. (2009b) *Dannye o Kolichestve Deystvyyush-chikh Subyektov Malogo i Srednogo Predprinimatel'stva*. Moscow.

Russian Federation. (2007) Federal Law 209-ф3 of 24 July 2007 *"O Razvitii Malogo i Sredenogo Predprinimatel'stva v Rossiiskoy Federatsii*. Moscow Federal Assembly of the Russian Federation. http://www.gov.ru/main/page4.html. Accessed May 10, 2010.

Russian Federation. (2008a) Federal Law 159-ф3 *(Ob Osobennostakh Otchuzhdeniya Ned-vizhmogo Imushchestva, Nakhodyagosya v Gosudarstvennoy Sobstvennosti Sub'ektov Rossiiskoy Federatsii ili v munitsipal'noy sobstvennosti i arenduemogo sub'ektami mal-ogo i srednogo predprinimatel'stva*. Moscow: Federal Assembly of the Russian Federation. http://www.gov.ru/main/page4.html. Accessed May 15, 2010.

Russian Federation. (2008b) Federal Law 294-ф3 *"O zashite prav yuridichestkikh lits i individualnykh predprinimatel'ey pri osushchestvlenii gosudarstvennogo kontrola (nad-zora) i munitsipal'nogo kontrola*. Moscow: Federal Assembly of the Russian Federation. http://g2b.perm.ru/section/show/6443#352. Accessed June 2, 2010.

Russian SME Resource Center and United States Agency for International Develop-ment. (2004) *Analysis of the Role and Place of Small and Medium-Sized Enterprises in Russia*. Moscow: Russian SME Resource Center and U.S. Agency for International Development.

Russian SME Resource Center and United States Agency for International Development. (2006) *Analysis of the Role and Place of Small and Medium-Sized Enterprises in Russia: Statistical Reference*. Moscow: U.S. Agency for International Development.

Satarov, Georgiy; Sergey Parkhomenko, Dina Krylova and Yuliya Rostovikova. (2007) *Business Without Corruption: An Action Guide*. Moscow: USAID, CIPE, INDEM, and OPORA Rossii.

Schleifer, Andrey and Daniel Treisman. (2000) *Without a Map: Political Tactics and Eco-nomic Reforms in Russia*. Cambridge, MA: MIT Press.

World Bank. (2005) From Transition to Development. *Country Economic Memorandum*. Washington, DC.

World Bank and International Finance Corporation. (2009) *Doing Business in Russia 2009*. Washington, DC.

World Bank and International Finance Corporation. (2010) *Doing Business 2010: Compar-ing Regulation in 183 Economies: Russian Federation*. Washington, DC.

Yakovlev, Andrei. (2006a) The Evolution of Business – State Interaction in Russia: From State Capture to Business Capture? *Europe-Asia Studies* 58 (7):1033–1056.

Yakovlev, Andrei. (2006b) *Agenty Modernizatsii*. Moscow, Russia: State University Higher School of Economics.

3 Elaborated process mapping and case selection

The regression findings from the preceding chapter allow us to elaborate upon the qualitative model introduced in schematic form in Chapter 1 and to outline a temporal and conceptual structure for the regional case studies in Chapters 4–7. The elaboration of the model is presented in the first part of this chapter. A key element of the elaboration of the model will be to introduce the role of business associations intermediating between the two key variables under study: small firm prevalence and regional democratization.

The second part of the chapter examines the distribution of Russia's regions relative to their performance on the two key variables – small firm prevalence and democracy index scores – and explains the selection of the four case study regions: Samara, Smolensk, Rostov, Perm. The third and final section compares the four case study regions with respect to several key social, political and economic variables and introduces the case studies.

Factor analysis, antecedent conditions, business associations as civic actors

The qualitative model shown in schematic form in Chapter 1 (Figure 1.1) is a conceptual interpretation of the interplay of democratization and small firm prevalence supported in broad terms by the regression findings. Those findings suggested that the strength and decisiveness of the democratic breakthrough in any given region in 1991–2001 heavily influenced the numbers of small firms relative to the working population, controlling for per capita income and all the other variables in the regression model. The qualitative model shown in Figure 3.1 introduces several refinements based upon the regression evidence as well as hypothesizing a key role for business associations representing the small business constituency. It is important to note that the model as depicted here represents the case where both democratization and numbers of small firms relative to the workforce are substantial. Among the case studies in this project, this 'ideal' case applies most closely to the Samara region.

The explanatory power of the extent of democratization in the period 1991–2001 on the outcome small firm prevalence was, as we saw in Chapter 2, very substantial and robust. This result is depicted in the model as the thick arrow

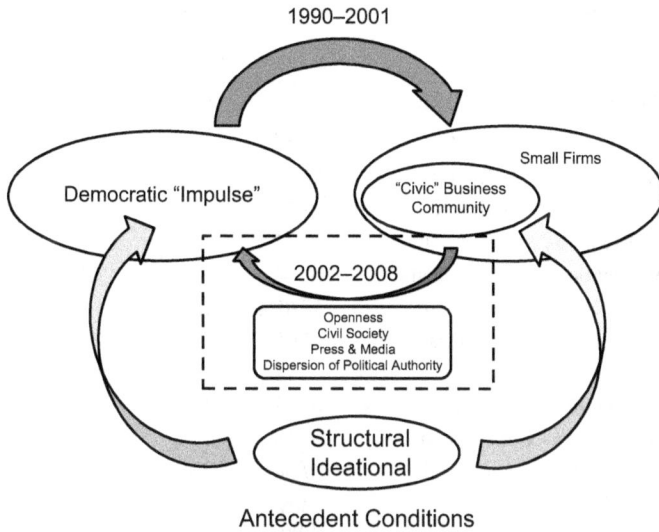

Figure 3.1 Elaborated Qualitative Model

running from *Democratic "Impulse"* to *Small Firms*. The size of each of these 'balloons' is intended to reflect, in this ideal case, the substantial exogenous impulse from the democratic breakthrough to the concentration of small firms. The regression evidence strongly supported the intuitively reasonable idea that the numbers of small firms relative to the working population is in substantial measure a consequence of the extent of the democratic opening of the 1990s. Furthermore, if the regression evidence is to be believed, small firm concentrations from 2000 onward were still strongly and positively related to the extent of the first decade's democratic opening.

Table 3.1 compares the four case study regions in this study in terms of the results on federal and gubernatorial elections in 1991–2002. The presentation adopts from Sakwa (2008) a scheme categorizing Russian political parties of the period into four large 'camps': reformers, centrists, national-patriots and communists. (Sakwa 2008:139)

The late *perestroika* political elite encompassed three major groups: hardline traditionalists, centrist reformers devoted to Union-wide reforms, and liberal reformers assigning a greater priority to democratization and market reforms than to preservation of the Union. The relative strengths of these three categories of elites across the four regions are manifest in the 1991 presidential election in the Russian Soviet Federal Socialist Republic (RSFSR). The 'impulse' that affected the strength of small business development seems to depend on three things: relative reformist stance of the post-1991 governor, strength and length of tenure of reformers in legislatures and mayoral office, and abiding influence and electoral strength of the traditional anti-reform elements of the Communist Party of the Soviet Union (CPSU), reorganized as the Communist Party of the Russian

Table 3.1 Key Election Results: Case Study Regions (Percentage of Support)

	Samara	Perm	Rostov	Smolensk
1991 Presidential Election - Yeltsin Vote	63.98	71.13	53.48	37.57
1993 Constitutional Referendum - "Yes"	55.40	77.70	50.30	42.10
1993 Duma Elections - Reformers	25.04	35.36	19.74	16.08
1993 Duma Elections - Centrists	6.74	5.00	6.24	5.74
1993 Duma Elections - National-Patriots	19.67	14.81	22.28	32.63
1993 Duma Elections - Communists	16.44	6.91	17.31	16.15
(Share of vote parties meeting 5%)	*67.89*	*62.08*	55.57	70.6
1995 Duma Election - Reformers	5.05	11.37	14.11	7.58
1995 Duma Election - Centrists	22.78	26.56	12.91	7.91
1995 Duma Election - National-Patriots	16.63	14.75	19.68	22.74
1995 Duma Election - Communists	26.18	11.08	26.99	40.06
(Share of vote parties meeting 5%)	*70.64*	*63.76*	*73.69*	*78.29*
First Elected Governor	Titov 1996	Igumnov 1996	Chub 1996	Glushenkov 1993
Governor Election - 1st Round Percentage Winner	63.39	42.38	62.15	39.3
Yeltsin Appointee?	yes	no*	yes	no
1996 Presidential Election - 1st Round Percentage Yeltsin	28.38	55.27	29.08	21.98
1996 Presidential Election - 1st Round Percentage Zyuganov	41.59	16.12	34.99	44.57
1999 Duma Election - Reformers	25.7	22.21	13.13	10.45
1999 Duma Election - Centrists	24.84	29.85	38.17	33.26
1999 Duma Election – National-Patriots	5.42	7.51	4.98	6.94
1999 Duma Election - Communists	26.13	14.15	28.48	31.48
(Share of vote parties meeting 5%)	*82.09*	*73.72*	*84.76*	*82.13*
2000 Presidential Election 1st Round Percentage Putin	40.86	60.79	53.33	52.48
2000 Presidential Election 1st Round Percentage Zyuganov	29.85	19.97	32.54	34.78
2000 Presidential Election 1st Round Percentage Yavlinsky	2.79	7.3	5.18	3.27
2000 Presidential Election 1st Round Percentage Zhirinovsky	1.75	3.47	2.42	3.04
2000 Presidential Election 1st Round Percentage Titov	20.24			
2000 Governor Elections	Titov 53%	Trutnev 52%	Chub 78%	Maslov** 41%

Source: Orttung (2000) and Central Electoral Commission, www.cifrf.ru

*Igumnov was the deputy of Yeltsin appointee Kuznetsov who resigned to take up his Duma seat in 1993.

**Maslov elected in 2002.

Federation (CPRF). Of the four cases, the reformist counter-elite in Smolensk was the weakest.

The reformers' electoral success in the 1993 Duma elections in Samara and especially in Perm had been heralded by these two regions' powerful support for Yeltsin in the 1991 presidential election. The single digit outcome in 1993 for the CPRF in Perm is symptomatic of the enthusiasm for renewal in that region. The democratic 'impulse' of the very early 1990s was unusually strong in these two regions. This is evident as well from the comparatively weak comeback by the CPRF in the 1995 elections, compared with their performance in the other two regions. The Perm region's peculiarity is again borne out by Yeltsin's decisive win in the first round of the 1996 presidential elections. The majorities in the Rostov region for Yeltsin in 1991 and for the constitutional referendum he favored in 1993 were not reflected in a strong performance by reformers in the 1993 Duma elections. Rostov and especially Smolensk were regions of relative success for the national-patriot Liberal Democratic Party of Russia (LDPR), which made its surprising breakthrough in 1993. The CPRF's recovery in the 1995 elections was considerable across Russia and in all four case study regions, but in Smolensk was particularly sweeping. CPRF candidate Zyuganov decisively defeated Yeltsin in the first round presidential elections of 1996 in the Smolensk oblast. In the 1999 Duma elections, reformers recovered somewhat, most notably in Perm and Samara regions.

The gubernatorial elections in these four regions show the elections were most closely contested in Perm and Smolensk regions. In both these regions, incumbent governors lost elections, once in Perm, and three times in Smolensk, in the period from 1991 to 2002. Samara's Konstantin Titov and Rostov's Vladimir Chub were both Yeltsin appointees in 1991, and both were among the most 'durable' of Russia's regional leaders. Titov, however, faced much more genuine electoral competition than did Chub after his first election in 1996. Titov's margin of victory in 2000 was much smaller than Chub's.

The gubernatorial election results in general bear out the idea that regional politics were more open and contested in the Perm and Samara regions than in the Rostov region. In both Samara and Perm, the protagonists of competitive regional politics emerged from the democratic ferment of the late 1980s and early 1990s, and their tenure in office produced a degree of institutionalization of elite competition in which liberal and reformist views continued to be significant. In Smolensk, gubernatorial elections were frequent, and incumbents defeated, but, after 1992 or so, the fledging 'democratic' camp had dissolved, leaving no obvious trace on the region's politics.

This electoral evidence and the democracy index scores for the four regions support the claim that the democratic 'impulse' was strongest and most durable in the Perm and Samara regions, weaker and more equivocal in the Rostov region, and weaker still in the Smolensk region. An obvious source of variation in the model shown in Figure 3.1 is this difference in the initial democratic 'impulse' among our four case study regions.

Returning to our discussion of the schematic model, therefore, our particular focus will be on the hypothesized 'feedback' arrow, depicting the reinforcement of democratization exerted by the concentrations of small firms relative to the work-force, and relative to the business community as a whole, in any given region. The 'feedback' arrow is placed within a box for emphasis. This arrow's thickness depicts its intensity, which depends to a large extent on the engendering of small firms depicted by the thick arrow of the democratic 'impulse' in the initial time period 1991–2001.

Factor analysis of the democracy index sub-indicators

The regressions in Model 4 (Chapter 2, pp. 45 ff.) found that 'small firm prevalence' in 2004 explained some of the variation in four sub-measures of the democracy index in 2005–2009: those measuring civil society development, the independence and diversity of press and media, the openness of (transparency and scope for public participation in) the conduct of regional and municipal governments and the dispersion of political authority (among governors, mayors, legislatures). (Petrov 2004, 2005, 2006; Petrov and Titkov 2006, 2013)

Applying factor analysis to all ten sub-indicators in the index (using the period 2005–2009) shows that two underlying factors explain 71% of the variation among the sub-indicators. This result is shown in Table 3.2. Only two factors have eigenvalues above 1, which means that the democracy index is, in effect, a measure of two principal underlying factors.

Table 3.2 Factor Analysis Table Sub-Indicators Democracy Index 2005–2009

Factor	Eigenvalue	Difference	Proportion	Cumulative
Factor 1	5.99	4.84	0.60	0.60
Factor 2	1.15	0.37	0.12	0.71

Table 3.3 shows the factor loadings of these two principal factors for each of the 10 sub-indicators in the index:

Table 3.3 Factor Loadings by Sub-Indicator of the Democracy Index 2005–2009

Variable	Factor 1	Factor 2	Uniqueness
Openness	0.80	−0.32	0.25
Elections	0.80	0.077	0.36
Pluralism	0.82	−0.18	0.29
Media	0.86	−0.17	0.23
Economic Reform	0.84	0.25	0.23
Civil Society	0.74	−0.43	0.27
Political Dispersion	0.85	−0.01	0.28
Elite Turnover	0.80	0.19	0.32
Corruption	0.40	0.81	0.18
Local Government	0.71	0.18	0.46

The factor loadings reveal that the civil society, media diversity and independence, openness in the conduct of government, political power dispersion, and pluralism indicators are strongly associated with the principal underlying factor in the democracy index. *The first four of these five sub-indicators are those where the regression analysis showed a significant positive effect from small business prevalence.* The sub-indicators most associated (in relative terms) with the second factor are elections, economic reform, elite turnover, corruption, and the powers and effectiveness of local governments.

The first principal factor is obviously much more influential than the second one in the index. The cluster of sub-indicators where it is strongest suggests that Factor 1 relates to public participation and engagement at a societal level. For simplicity, we will call this underlying factor '*civic-ness.*' The sub-indicators loaded relatively more heavily on the second factor, by contrast, are related to the *quality* of governance and to state autonomy: impartiality, administrative coherence and the insulation of policymaking from popular pressures or excessive dependence on interest lobbying. This second factor can be called '*governance.*'

The important finding from this analysis is that *small firm prevalence affects democratization principally as a manifestation of social or civic participation.* This is despite the fact that small firm lobbying and advocacy through business associations is, as we have seen, directed explicitly at outcomes covered by the 'governance' factor of the democracy index: curbing corruption and improving bureaucratic and regulatory quality.

Based on this analysis, the elaborated model schematized at the beginning of this chapter suggests that the variable 'small firm prevalence' has its effect on democratization through the contribution such firms make to the '*civic-ness*' of the business community as a whole. The model depicts the 'civic business community' as lying within the broader population of small firms.

Accordingly, the case studies of four regions will trace the effects of small firm owners on civic life through their involvement in business associations, the relationship of small firms to the regional press and the role that entrepreneurs have played in regional and municipal political office as well as within regional ministries. These processes exemplify the influence of small firm prevalence on the outcomes of openness, media diversity and independence, civil society activism and political power dispersion. These four sub-indicators are shown on the elaborated version of the model as processes within the 'feedback' arrow.

The size of the 'civic business community' relative to the broader business community is the qualitative variable that underlies the effect that small firm prevalence has on democratization in the regression findings of Regression 2 in Chapter 2 (see pp. 39 ff.). For this to be true, we need not establish that the civic business community in a given region is dominant, relative to the business community as a whole. We need only show that small firm prevalence generally reliably predicts of the *relative* 'civic-ness' of the regional business community.

The relative 'civic-ness' of the business community should be considered within a context where significant countercurrents of both big and small company interactions with government are non-transparent, informal, improvised and anti-competitive. (Ledeneva 1998, 2006) The explanatory power of the model does not depend in principle on there being *any* region in Russia where local monopolies and clientelism are not predominant. What matters is the extent of the civic business community within the business community as a whole. If, for example the ratio of firms exposed to competitive conditions (which tend to be smaller and/or *de novo*) to incumbent and oligarch firms were 1/8 compared with 1/20, this would affect the 'feedback' arrow in our model.

The role of antecedent conditions

The model also postulates an important role for structural and ideational antecedent conditions affecting both the extent of democratization and the emergence of small firms. The regions of European Russia typically trace an unbroken ancestry from Tsarist *gubernii* (provinces) and have distinctive economic and human geographies. These distinctive characteristics support substantial political and administrative divergences and, to varying degrees, distinctive social, economic and cultural identities.

The model hypothesizes that, although democratic governance and private entrepreneurship have been mutually reinforcing in the nearly two decades that are the focus of our study, both are to some degree affected by antecedent conditions. The regression model attempted to capture some of the antecedent structural conditions by including the variable 'urbanization' which has considerable historical persistence.

The ideational part of the antecedent conditions will be one focus of the qualitative case studies. As will be seen, regional and municipal administrations, business associations and other civic groups have participated in a revival of interest in the pre-revolutionary past and to a re-evaluation in particular of the role played by private merchant-industrialists in Russia beginning in the second half of the 19th century. The unearthing of this experience is part of the self-awareness of many regional entrepreneurs and serves as an identity shaping 'usable' past.

Business associations as civic actors

The obvious and most visible means through which small business owners are engaged in civic life in the regions is through business associations. The work of associations therefore will receive considerable attention in the regional case studies. Putnam (1993) observes that civic associations have 'internal' effects on their members and 'external' effects on the wider polity. Using Putnam's terminology, one could say that business associations are both 'bonding' and 'bridging' social capital. They bind members with shared identity and interests, and they bridge members' concerns in relations with regional and municipal administrations and with other social groups. The public statements and published materials of business associations such as the Russian Chamber or OPORA explicitly link the promotion of the interests of small businesses to the broader social ends of employment creation, income growth, innovation and economic diversification.

A survey by William Pyle of 606 Russian firms across six industrial subsectors in 2004 found that business association membership and firm size are highly correlated. Just under a third of the 246 surveyed companies with up to a hundred employees reported belonging to at least one association, while more than half of the 360 large companies in the sample belonged to at least one association. (Pyle 2004)[1] Pyle's survey data are useful for probing the possibility that motivations for joining business associations and the usefulness of associations to members are a function of firm size. It is important to realize, however, that Pyle's firm survey covers industrial companies only, rather than a representative sample of all firms. With this caveat in mind, comparing the views of large and small company respondents with respect to the effectiveness of business associations gives an interesting result summarized in Figure 3.2 and Table 3.4.

The three functions where the small firms in Pyle's sample considered associations to be more effective than large firms, and where this difference is statistically significant, are all in the area of trust building and enforcement: dispute resolution, ethical standards and the provision of information, marketing and legal expertise. These results also suggest that large companies' role in associations has a distinctly corporatist nuance: both through structuring labor relations and providing input to industrial policy. *For small companies, the importance of business associations can be construed as in promoting the 'bonding' social capital of intra-group trust.*

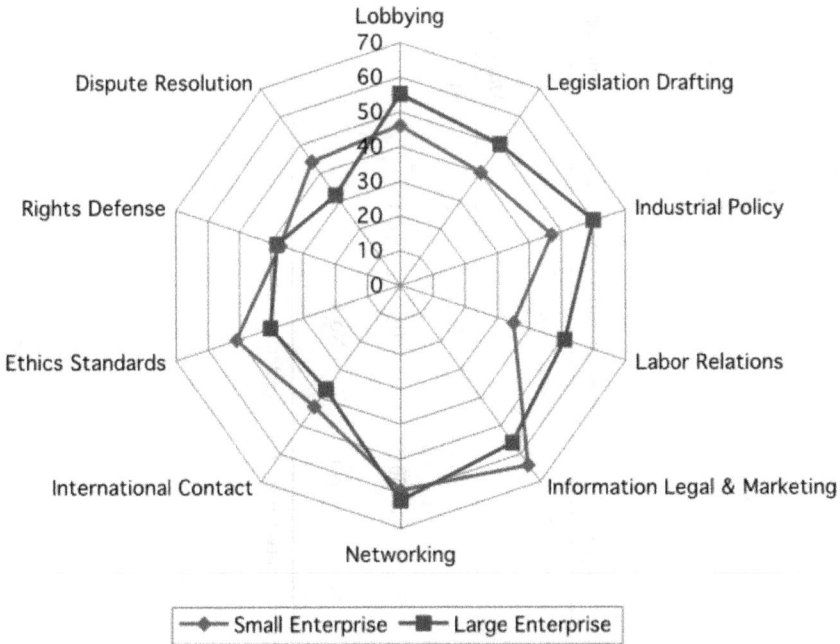

Figure 3.2 Contrasting Small and Large Firms' Assessments of Business Associations' Effectiveness

Source: Pyle Survey data, author's calculations

Table 3.4 Percentages of Business Association Members Rating Association Activities 'Moderately' to 'Strongly' Effective

	Lobbying	Legislation Drafting	Industrial Policy	Labor Relations	Information Legal & Marketing	Networking	International Contact	Ethics Standards	Rights Defense	Dispute Resolution
Small Enterprise	46	40	47	35	64	59	43	51	37	44
Large Enterprise	55	50	60	51	56	62	37	40	38	32
CHI2 Significant	No	No	No	Yes	Yes	No	No	Yes	No	Yes

Source: Pyle (2004) survey data, author's calculations

Interviews in the case study regions for this project support the inference that business association membership for small companies can best be understood in a social capital and trust-building perspective. Because of their contribution to employment and tax revenue, the largest regional companies (either 'incumbent' or 'oligarch' businesses) have easy and direct access to regional governors and a direct 'partnership' (whether they seek it or not) on matters such as education, skills training, housing, healthcare and other social priorities. (Chirikova 2007; Peregudov 2009)

Russia's most prominent exponent of institutional economics, Alexander Auzan, observed that business associations began to grow and develop seriously in Russia when many entrepreneurs came to believe that they would still be in business in five years' time. (Golikova 2007) Auzan's insight neatly captures the idea that informal networks built on favor from persons in elected or bureaucratic office are not adaptable over longer periods.

As the Soviet Union ebbed away, transactions based on market prices expanded on the margins of the formal economy. This unofficial business was of necessity done '*po poniatiam*' – by (informal) understanding. (Howard 2002, 2003; Ledeneva 1998, 2006; Petrova and Tarrow 2007; Zaslavsky 1995) Contemporary business associations are overlaid upon and, to some degree, may be the visible expressions of previously existing informal networks.[2] The crucial difference, however, between informal networks and business associations is the latter's social visibility and accessibility to new entrants on transparent terms.

In the framework of Douglass North (1990), business associations can be understood as the product of decisions by a limited number of state and private actors to institutionalize (depersonalize and formalize) business-state coordination, placing these relations within a framework of rules understandable by and transparent to both sides of the interaction and available to all firms categorically. They reflect an attempt to have institutions perceptible, accessible and applicable to the whole category of entrepreneurs, actual and potential. Olson (1982) holds that the more encompassing a business association, the more closely its objectives will be compatible with economic efficiency and a competitive environment for business. As Pyle and Solanko (2010) argue, encompassing business associations may be expected to advocate a 'pro-market' (as opposed to a pro-business) set of policy aims, seeking advantageous but universally applicable business conditions, for example simplified administrative rules and an effective legal framework.

Four business associations in Russia can be considered 'encompassing' using the terminology of Olson, because they represent the businesses across a wide range of sectors. Three of Russia's encompassing associations would also meet the customary definition of 'peak' organization, because their membership includes sector-based associations in addition to firms or individuals. The three peak organizations are the Chamber of Commerce and Industry of the Russian Federation (known by its Russian initials TPPRF), the Russian Union of Industrialists and Entrepreneurs (RSPP) and OPORA, the union of entrepreneurial organizations of Russia (*Ob'edinenie Predprinimatel'skikh Organizatsii Rossii*).

RSPP was founded in 1990 as an organization of directors of state-owned industrial concerns. (Gill 2008; Hanson and Teague 2005). RSPP's immediate antecedent was the all-Union Scientific-Industrial Union *(Nauchno-Promyshlen-nyi Soyuz)*. (Zudin 1997) Hanson and Teague (2005) see the elevation by Putin of the RSPP after 2000 as the embrace of a state corporatist model of business-state coordination. Although membership in the RSPP is not mandatory (a characteristic of corporatism in the fullest sense), its member companies claim to represent about 60% of GDP.

Membership in the Russian Chamber (TPPRF) is open to the whole spectrum of businesses from large to small, including unincorporated individual entrepreneurs. OPORA is an umbrella organization (legally constituted as a 'non-commercial partnership') for 129 sectoral and multi-sectoral associations of small and medium sized companies and entrepreneurs, and an affiliated but separate civic association of small and medium entrepreneurs. Delovaya Rossiya is a national association of medium to large companies in the 'new' economy: airlines, telecommunications, information technology, retail and consumer goods manufacturing. Delovaya Rossiya has about 2,000 members across most of Russia's regions. Although both the Chamber and RSPP were founded in the first half of the 1990s, they have developed most vigorously since 1998. (Golikova 2009; Pyle 2006a, 2006b)

As president of the TPPRF for more than a decade beginning in 2001, former foreign and prime minister Yevgeny Primakov fostered the revival and expansion of the Russian Chamber. An unlikely agent of social transformation, the neo-traditional Russian Chamber nevertheless contributed significantly to advancing the interests of new and small companies. The Chamber is the most fully established business association across Russia's regions and even in many municipalities, attracting to its ranks many smaller companies. The small firm membership in regional and municipal Chamber affiliates has contributed to the institutional evolution of the Chamber as a whole.

The Chamber traces its origins to the Moscow stock market committee *(birzhevoi komitet)* formed by entrepreneurs in 1869, which was the basis for the founding of the first national Chamber of Commerce, drawing together regional business organizations, under the Provisional Government in 1917. Its founder was Alexander Konovalov, a Duma deputy and leading business figure of the age. (Owen 1981; Pastukhov et al. 2007, Roosa 1997) The pre-revolutionary Chamber was transformed into the Soviet Chamber of Commerce, a quasi-official agency involved exclusively in the sponsorship of Soviet international trade.

The contemporary Chamber's emphasis on its history in Russia's nascent capitalism of the 19th and early 20th centuries includes an explicit borrowing of civic, philanthropic and patriotic themes from that period. Its handsomely restored offices in the mid-19th century Moscow stock exchange building are a tangible reference to this past era. The Russian Chamber was reconstituted through the passage of a founding law in 1993. (Russian Federation 1993) In its renewed institutional shape, the Chamber borrowed from the continental European model of Chambers of Commerce its role as provider of fee-based business services.

From British and American models, the Russian Chamber adopted the principle of voluntary membership and services made available to non-members on reasonable terms. (Rybakov and Fedotov 2009)[3] Although the Soviet antecedent institution had virtually no presence in the provinces, the Chamber has an expanding network of regional affiliates. The 1993 law provides that an affiliate Chamber may be set up with at least 15 initiating members.

Chambers are given the legal right to give independent legal expertise on draft legislation related to the economy and to foreign economic relations and other questions affecting the interests of entrepreneurs. They are also expected to "represent and defend the legal interests of their members." (Russian Federation 1993:Article III)

The law also sets out the services that Chambers of Commerce can provide to support business activity. They include the registering of patents and trademarks, provision of certificates of origin, and appraisals of value in addition to certifying quality, quantity and content, maintaining and allowing access to a register of companies' financial standing and reliability, organizing and sponsoring trade shows and missions, publishing bulletins and journals with business information and providing arbitration services to resolve disputes among companies. The law further provides that Chambers' legal documentation related to these services will be recognized throughout Russia. Some Chambers also provide fee-based training.

The TPPRF committee for development of small and medium business has been among its most prominent and active.[4] The committee's leadership includes leading figures on SME promotion policy in Russia. Among these figures are committee chairman Viktor Ermakov, director of the Russian Agency for Support of Small Business, Alexander Ioffe, the former director of the city of Moscow's small business development programs, Mikhail Mamuta, director of the Russian Microfinance Center, Yevgeny Borisov, head of the SME development programs of the Samara regional administration, Dina Krylova, a former OPORA vice president and anti-corruption activist, and Russian SME Center director Igor Mikhalkin.

OPORA was created in 2001 as an early 'project' of the presidential administration under Putin. (Rutland 2006) OPORA was founded not as an association, but as an umbrella for the many already existing business associations representing small business. OPORA was constituted under Russian law as a non-commercial partnership (NP) of business associations. OPORA claims 100 organizations in the membership.[5] OPORA's leadership claims to represent more than 300,000 people, taking account of all those employed by companies belonging to associations under the OPORA umbrella.

OPORA's other affiliated structure is a nationally registered civic organization *(Obshcherossiiskaia Obshchestvennaia Organizatsia Malego i Srednogo Predprimatel'stva)*. OPORA is present in Russia's regions *only* in this form, and only at the initiative by a local entrepreneur or group of entrepreneurs to establish a regional association. The number of members of OPORA as a civic association is not made public and is likely not to exceed 5,000 people.[6]

The immediate forerunner of OPORA was the Confederation of Russian Entrepreneurs, headed by Vladimir Shumeiko, a strong advocate of Yeltsin's early economic reforms, who later became deputy prime minister and federation council speaker. The period 1990–1992 saw the rise of many proto-parties and associations in Russia, generated unambiguously 'from below' typically with a recognized and charismatic leader, and the Confederation was one such association. (Zudin 1997) According to Victor Sedov, who served as executive director of the Confederation, the organization languished after Shumeiko left and had dwindled away by the late 1990s.[7]

The Charter of OPORA's civic association was adopted at a founding congress in September 2002. The charter sets out the governing structure headed by an elected president at the national level. There are to be regional and municipal associations with their own elected leadership. (OPORA 2006) The goals of the organization set out in the charter can be summarized as follows:

- To engage entrepreneurs in seeking favorable political, economic, legal conditions for business
- To offer expert input from society in the decisions of state bodies relating to small and medium business
- To participate in developing means to reduce the economic foundations of corruption
- To form public awareness about civil society as the aggregation of interests of the population and to build up a middle class on the best traditions of entrepreneurship and Russian business culture
- To form public awareness of the positive role of entrepreneurs
- To participate in developing programs of support for entrepreneurship
- To give policymakers objective information about issues affecting SMEs
- To participate in development of mechanisms to aid in implementation of laws related to SMEs
- To support activism by businesspeople and the high social and moral standing of business
- To cooperate in the development of market structures and mechanisms, relations to property and freedom of entrepreneurship
- To cooperate in the development of social and legal guarantees for entrepreneurs
- To create institutions of mutual support and financing among entrepreneurs
- To create a single open information space of the community of entrepreneurs

The charter language reveals that OPORA's purpose is not only to represent the small business that now exists, but also to shape and encourage a small business community that is reputable, civically engaged and diversified across new sectors. This marks OPORA as a promotional organization as much as a purely representative one. (Semenenko 2001)

In addition to regional Chamber and OPORA affiliates, regions typically are home to local entrepreneurs' associations with a small business vocation. TPPRF's national policy is to interact with and support these local entrepreneurs' associations in the regions, as well as to cooperate closely with OPORA. There is little evidence of rivalry or dissension at the regional level between OPORA, regional Chambers, or Delovaya Rossiya. Personalities involved may occasionally not be compatible, but the organizations seem generally to be convinced that their influence is magnified by working together. This may be partly the consequence of the formation of coalitions fostered by cooperation of many of the associations with CIPE programs.

A survey of small business people in 35 Russian regions carried out by OPORA in 2007–2008 gives a sense of how varied are the concerns of small business people across Russia's regions. (OPORA 2008) The survey questioned entrepreneurs in 35 regions, including the Perm, Rostov and Samara regions. Survey respondents were asked to identify those obstacles affecting their business from a list, with no rank order among the obstacles and no limit on the number a given respondent could cite as affecting him or her. Their responses suggest interesting contrasts among these three regions, shown in Table 3.5. The percentage of respondents in a given region identifying a given constraint or obstacle is shown. (Our fourth case study region, Smolensk, was not among those surveyed.)

The categorization of the issues into the broad categories of 'economic' and 'political' is an interpretation given the survey results by the author of the present study. The characterization of some of the problems respondents cited as 'economic' implies that they are principally constraints emerging from relationships among market participants and do not depend mainly on policy decisions by the governing authorities. By contrast, those problems labeled 'political' are those where the framework of laws and policies is the direct source of the constraint. For example the economic problem *par excellence* is finding qualified personnel, a manifestation of tightening labor markets and the intensity of competition for talented and well-trained staff. (Underlying this, however, might be inadequacies in advanced business and management curricula in regional universities, a policy variable.) 'Political' impediments are those that directly relate to problems in governance, official abuse of power, failure to enforce laws impartially or conflicts of interest. Unfair competition can be understood to imply rigged competition from market participants enjoying special official sponsorship. The purchase or lease of land and buildings by small firms is generally under the jurisdiction of municipal authorities. Corruption and regulations are both obviously a matter of the quality of the legal framework relating to businesses.

Table 3.6 creates a cumulative weight for political and economic obstacles to small business owners as the sum of the percentages of respondents citing obstacles in each of these two large categories in the OPORA survey. This provides a revealing illustration of the relative impact of political versus economic constraints on small business development as seen from the standpoint of the surveyed entrepreneurs in three of our case study regions. St. Petersburg is also included in this table for comparison in that it has the largest small firm prevalence of any region in Russia throughout the period under study.

Table 3.5 Obstacles to Business Success Identified by Small Business Owners by Region

Problems	Economic Issues				Political Issues				Other
	Finding Staff	Credit Access	Weak Demand	Equipment Costs/ Availability	Unfair Competition	Property Lease/Buy	Corruption	Regulations	
Perm Region	34%	27%	23%	not cited	22%	6%	not cited	39%	12%
Samara Region	67%	not cited	33%	17%	33%	25%	not cited	8%	not cited
Rostov Region	26%	14%	19%	19%	45%	not cited	18%	21%	not cited

Source: OPORA regional index 2007–2008

Note: 'Not cited' means no respondent named the given issue as a major obstacle.

Table 3.6 Relative Weight of Political and Economic Obstacles by Region

Cumulative Scores	Economic	Political	Total	Ratio Political/Economic
Perm	84	67	163*	0.8
Samara	152	32	184	0.2
Rostov	78	84	162	1.1
St. Petersburg	95	61	156	0.6

*The sum includes the 12% in Perm who cited unspecified 'other' obstacles affecting their businesses.

Source: OPORA survey data

The fact that economic constraints far outweighed political ones in the Samara region is indicative of the greater levels of market competition among companies in that region. The ratio of political to economic constraints is greatest in the Rostov region, and intermediate in Perm. Perm respondents' assessment of the climate for small business is relatively benign when it comes to political impediments. They saw 'unfair' competition, which means the sponsorship of certain market players by politicians or officials, as less serious than in Rostov or Samara.

An insight that comes from these survey results is that relatively low political impediments to business do not by themselves translate into greater prevalence of small businesses or their share in output or employment. Economic constraints are at least as influential on that outcome. In the Rostov region, entrepreneurs rate the 'political' impediments as very serious, but the economic constraints are less binding than in Perm or Samara. It is worth noting that Rostov respondents rated the availability of finance better than others and also did not see insufficient market demand as limiting their expansion. Conversely, where political impediments are generally low as in Perm, this has not translated into larger numbers of small firms, or to a bigger share for small firms in employment or output. On the basis of the survey's findings, the OPORA study ranked the 35 regions as to where corruption (in the judgment of the surveyed entrepreneurs) posed the greatest obstacle to small business. In a rank ordering from the least to the most affected by corruption, the Perm region was in 9th place, Samara in 10th and Rostov in 30th place. (St. Petersburg was in 11th place on this ranking.) (OPORA 2008)

The forgoing discussion of the problems faced by small business owners may give an idea of the interests and demands of the constituency that business associations claim to represent. The interviews with business association leaders and members, as well as with regional and municipal officials who serve as their interlocutors, in the regional case studies probe the external and internal (or bridging and bonding) functions of the associations. In the internal dimension, the principal issues are the extent of the association's autonomy from state authority, its inclusiveness or representativeness, the scope of its own initiative, leadership and 'expert-ness.' On the external dimension, important issues are the association's *effectiveness* or tangible achievements, its '*public-ness*' in pursuit of its goals and the intensity, substance and frequency of interactions with regional and municipal authorities. According to Diamond (1994) the organizations of civil society need not be adversarial to the governing authority, but must have enough independent standing to be credible.

Table 3.7 summarizes the principal analytical questions guiding the case study inquiries into the work of business associations in the regions:

Table 3.7 Framework for Evaluating Business Associations

Internal

Does the association have legitimacy among business community? To what extent does it serve members' goals and those of the broader business community?

What is its reputation with and distance from the regional or municipal administration?

How open and transparent is its internal governance? Who sets its agenda and priorities? How inclusive is it? How is it disposed to small business?

What is the professional background of associations' leadership? (e.g. business, politics or administration) What is the process of selection of leadership?

How 'expert' or professional is the association's staff?

How oriented is it to a well-defined agenda of achievable goals built on consultations within membership?

How engaged and involved are members, for example on sectoral or thematic committees?

External

How open is it in terms of information made publicly available?

How public is it in terms of its profile in media and public events? How effective is its public articulation of interests?

How active, substantive and diverse are the channels of interest articulation vis-à-vis regional administrations, municipalities and legislatures? How critical is the view of business associations to the formulation and implementation of small business promotion programs?

How prominent are educational or philanthropic initiatives of the associations and what are their links to other civil society associations?

Context

Do institutions other than associations perform some of the same functions of training, information sharing, group identity formation and trust building?

How open and diverse is the association landscape? How do small local associations relate to larger ones?

The rationale for case selection

Figure 3.3 plots the relationship between small firm prevalence in 2004 (shown on the horizontal axis) and the democracy index score for each region in 2005–2009 (see equation 2e, Table 2.10). The four regions selected as case studies – Samara, Smolensk, Rostov and Perm – are shown with larger dots, as are the two cities that are themselves federation subjects – Moscow and St. Petersburg.

The graph illustrates how exceptional Moscow and St. Petersburg are in terms of the numbers of incorporated small firms relative to the workforce. The dashed line

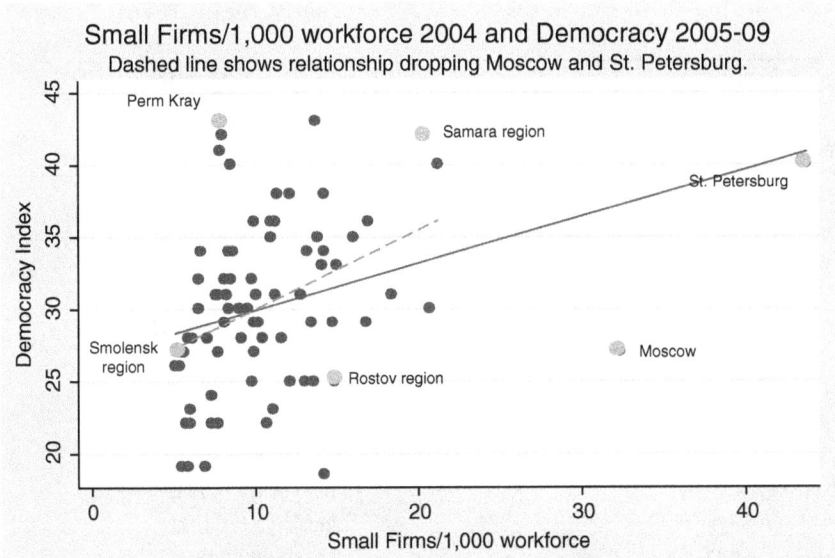

Figure 3.3 Regression Line Showing Case Study Regions

in the figure plots the regression line between the two variables when St. Peters-burg and Moscow are left out of the calculation. The positive slope of the dashed line shows that the relationship between the two principal variables, accounting of course for all the control variables in the model, is *even more robust* if Russia's two principal cities are not included in the analysis. The Smolensk region lies directly on the regression line when Moscow and St. Petersburg are dropped. Rostov, like Moscow, is an outlier in the sense that small firms are more prevalent than would be predicted by the regions' performance on the democracy index. The Samara region is an 'overachiever' on both variables, and the Perm region *(kray)* 'over-achieves' on the democracy index relative to its numbers of small firms.

Table 3.8 arranges the 79 regions of Russia that are the focus of our analyses into four broad categories, based on their democracy index scores for 2005–2009 and the numbers of small firms relative to the labor force in 2004. The mean of the democracy index in 2005–2009 is 30.14, and the mean number of small firms relative to the workforce in 2004 is 11.05. The four groups of regions in Table 3.8 are defined by how each region falls relative to the mean on these two variables. The 'consistent' cases include those regions (numbering 19) that score above the mean on both variables, and those (numbering 29) that fall below the mean on both variables. The 'deviant' cases are those where the democracy index score is above average but small firm prevalence is below average, or, conversely, where small firms are comparatively common, but the democracy index score is below average.

The rationale for the selection of the four regional cases is based on their being representative of the cases in one of the four quadrants of Table 3.8. The Samara region is an obvious strong performer on both measures, whereas the Perm and Rostov regions are challenging 'deviant' cases.

Table 3.8 Cross-Tabulation of Russia's Regions: Small Firm Prevalence 2004 and Democracy Index 2005–2009

'Consistent' Cases I'	**'Consistent' Cases II**
Dem 2005–2009 > Mean *Small Firms 2004 > Mean*	*Dem 2005–2009 < Mean* *Small Firms 2004 < Mean*
Sverdlovskaya (UFD)	Altai Republic (SibFD)
Samarskaya (PFD)	Astrakhanskaya (SFD)
St. Petersburg	Tulskaya (CFD)
Novosibirskaya (SibFD)	Amurskaya (FEFD)
Yaroslavskaya (CFD)	Vologodskaya (NWFD)
Kareliya Republic (NWFD)	Ulyanovskaya (PFD)
Nizhegorodskaya (PFD)	Penzenskaya (PFD)
Leningradskaya (NWFD)	Kostromskaya (CFD)
Pskovskaya (NWFD)	Ivanovskaya (CFD)
Tomskaya (SibFD)	Tambovskaya (CFD)
Sakhalinskaya (FEFD)	Chitinskaya (SibFD)
Altaisky Kray(SibFD)	Tatarstan Republic (PFD)
Kaluzhskaya (CFD)	Orlovskaya (CFD)
Kalingradskaya (NWFD)	Smolenskaya (CFD)
Voronezhskaya (CFD)	Sakha Republic (FEFD)
Primorskiy Kray (FEFD)	Bryanskaya (CFD)
Ryazanskaya (CFD)	Khakasiya Republic (SibFD)
Udmurtskaya Republic (PFD)	Dagestan Republic (SFD)
Stavropolskiy Kray (SFD)	Karachaevo-Cherkesskaya Rep (SFD)
	Kurganskaya (UFD)
	Kalmykia Republic (SFD)
	Baskortostan Republic (PFD)
	North Ossetia-Alaniya Republic (SFD)
	Kurskaya (CFD)
	Evreyskaya AO (FEFD)
	Tyva Republic (SibFD)
	Kabardino-Balkariya Republic (SFD)
	Mordovia Republic (PFD)
	Chukhotskiy AO (FEFD)

(*Continued*)

Table 3.8 (Continued)

'Deviant' Cases I Democracy Over-perform	'Deviant' Cases II Small Firm Prevalence Over-perform
Dem 2005–2009 > Mean *Small Firms 2004 < Mean*	*Dem 2005–2009 < Mean* *Small Firms 2004 > Mean*
Permskaya (PFD)	Magadanskaya (FEFD)
Krasnoyarskiy Kray (SibFD)	Lipetskaya (CFD)
Irkutskaya (SibFD)	Krasnodarskiy Kray (SFD)
Arkhangelskaya (NWFD)	Moskovskaya (CFD)
Volgogradskaya (SFD)	Omskaya (SibFD)
Chelyabinskaya (UFD)	Saratovskaya (PFD)
Vladimirskaya (CFD)	Moscow
Tverskaya (CFD)	Adygeya Republic (SFD)
Komi Republic (NWFD)	Rostovskaya (SFD)
Murmanskaya (NWFD)	Mary El Republic (PFD)
Kamchatskaya (FEFD)	Belgorodskaya (CFD)
Novgorodskaya (NWFD)	Kemerovskaya (SibFD)
Chuvashskaya Republic (PFD)	Ingushetiya Republic (SFD)
Tyumenskaya (UFD)	
Khabarovskiy Kray (FEFD)	
Buratiya Republic (SibFD)	
Orenburgskaya (PFD)	
Kirovskaya (PFD)	

Notes:

1. Regions in each category are listed in descending order by their democracy index score for 2005–2009

2. Unless otherwise noted, the regions are formally 'oblasts'

3. CFD denotes the Central Federal District

   SFD denotes the Southern Federal District

   UFD denotes the Urals Federal District

   NWFD denotes the Northwestern Federal District

   PFD denotes the Privolzhe (Volga) Federal District

   SibFD denotes the Siberian Federal District

   FEFD denotes the Far Eastern Federal District

The lower left quadrant, where both democracy and small firm prevalence are below the mean, is both crowded and eclectic, making the choice of a representative case from this category difficult. The Smolensk region was chosen from this group because it has seen fairly vigorous development of small firms since 2005, even if it underperformed on this measure significantly in 2004. Moreover, although measured as a laggard on the democracy index, the Smolensk region has nevertheless experienced several gubernatorial elections from 1993 to 2002 with outcomes undetermined before the fact. In a sense, then, the Smolensk region presents another puzzle or challenge for the analysis.

The case study regions in broad comparison

Figure 3.4 shows the pattern of change of per capita monthly income in constant rubles from 2000–2008, relative to the national average over the period.

This chart reveals the strong growth performance of the Rostov region from 2004 and a tendency for a narrowing of differences among the four regions by 2008 relative to the immediately preceding years. Both of these points are emphasized in the World Bank's comparative regional study. (World Bank 2009)

Figure 3.5 allows a comparison of the four regions by the share of the population in the principal city and in cities with a population greater than 50,000. The regional capital Rostov represents only roughly a quarter of the oblast's population, whereas in the other three cases, this share is at least one third. The share of regions' population in cities with more than 50,000 is greatest in the Samara

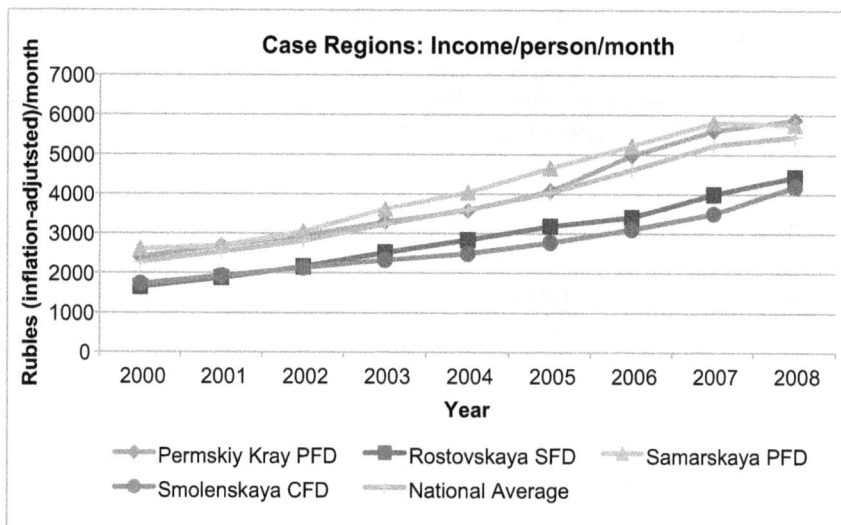

Figure 3.4 Case Study Regions Per Capita Monthly Income Compared

Source: Rosstat

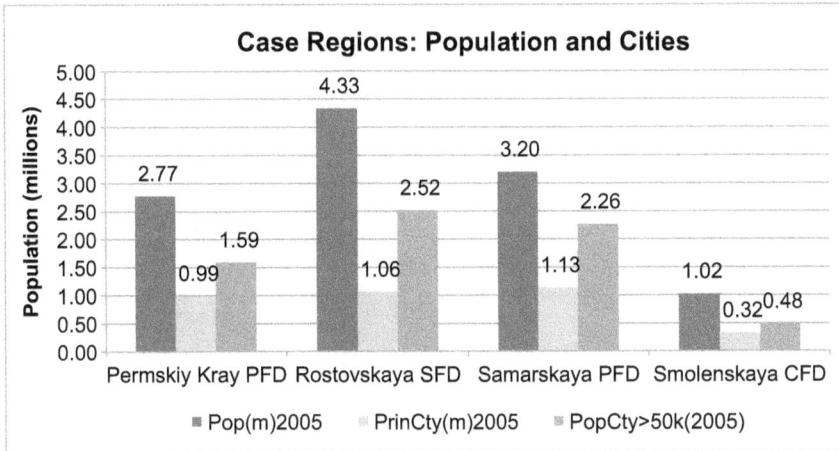

Figure 3.5 Urbanization by Case Study Region
Source: Rosstat *Goroda Rossii* 2010

region, followed closely by the Perm region. This figure gives insight into differences in the structural variable 'urbanization', which the regression evidence in Chapter 2 suggested are part of the explanation for differences in small firm prevalence and in democratization across regions.

Figure 3.6 shows how the four regions have performed relative to each other on the measure of small firm prevalence, central to the analysis in this study.

Using the year 2008, Table 3.9 gives the numbers of micro-, small- and medium-sized companies in the four case study regions. Micro-enterprises are legally incorporated firms with 10 or fewer employees; small companies are here defined as those with 11–100 employees.[8] Medium-sized enterprises are those with up to 250 employees and meeting turnover and ownership rules defined in the 2007 federal law on Small Business.

Figure 3.7 shows how the four regions compare on the democracy composite index by period, relative to the national average. The democracy index for Moscow is also shown for comparison.

Conclusions and case study structure

This chapter has presented a model synthesizing conceptually the interactions and processes explored in the regressions of Chapter 2. This model will structure the case studies. The factor analysis of the regional democracy sub-indicators allowed us to see more clearly how those aspects of democratization shaped by small firm prevalence are related. The role of business associations in the formation of the civic business community has been postulated, and an approach to comparative analysis of the role of business associations has been defined. We have seen how differences among the four case study regions justified their selection.

Small Firms per 1000 Labor Force (Year)

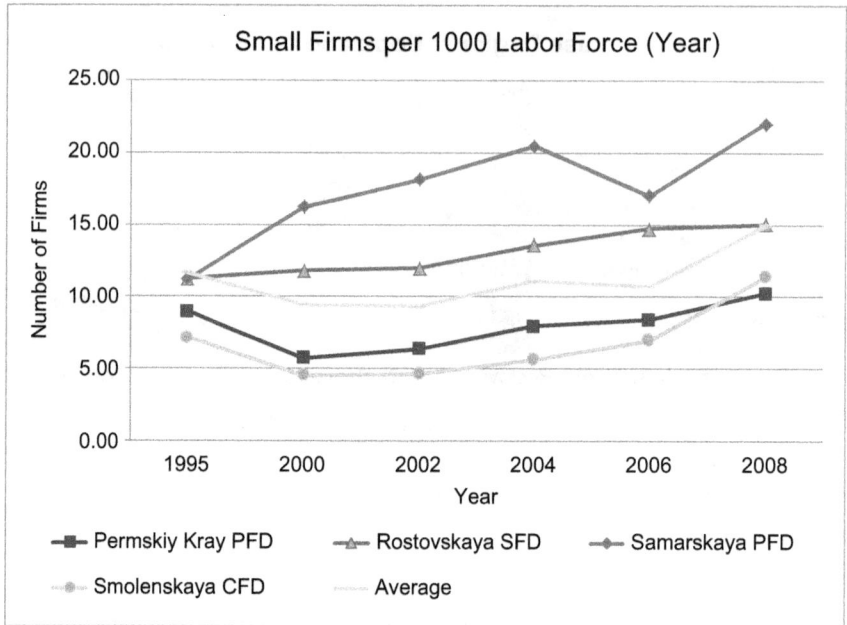

Figure 3.6 Trends in Small Firm Prevalence by Case Study Region

Source: Rosstat *Regiony Rossii*, various years

Table 3.9 Micro, Small and Medium Enterprises in Case Study Regions, 2008

Micro, Small and Medium Enterprises in Case Study Regions, 2008

REGION	Medium Enterprise	Small Enterprise	of which, micro-enterprises
Perm	251	14783	10431
Rostov	450	33490	26296
Samara	311	39331	28943
Smolensk	128	5934	4259
RUSSIA	14170	1347667	1065016

Source: Rosstat 2009

Each of the four regional case studies in Chapters 4–7 trace the interactions depicted in the elaborated model diagram. Each case study begins with a discussion of the region's economic geography and business history to establish the role of *antecedent structural conditions* affecting small firm development. Next, each case study assesses the extent of the *democratic 'impulse'* and its institutionalization in 1991–2001. From there, each case study presents a comparative overview of small business development in each region, which is to a considerable degree a consequence of the democratic breakthrough of period 1991–2001.

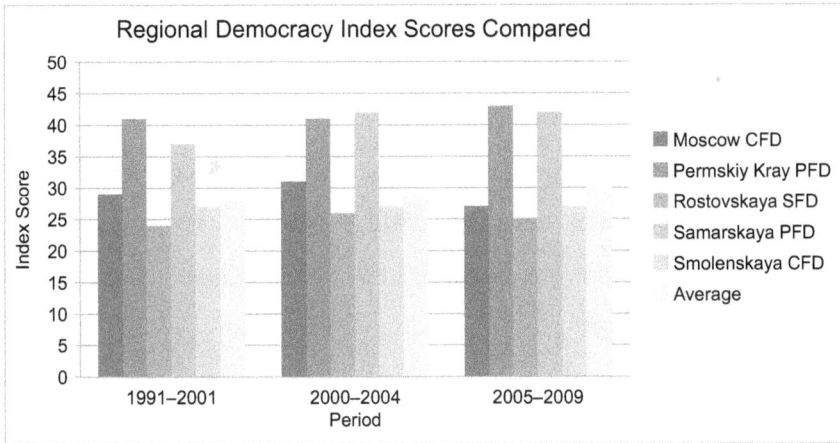

Figure 3.7 Regional Democracy Index Scores Compared

The ensuing sections of each case study chapter zero in on the civic business community, manifest in the work of business associations, relative to four aspects of democratization: civil society development, openness on the part of regional and municipal administrations and the scope of public participation, media independence and diversity, and the dispersion of political authority. Each case study analyzes the role and effectiveness of business associations in that region and character of interactions of business associations with regional and, where appropriate, with municipal administrations. The role of small firms and the business community relative to the regional press and the extent of civic or philanthropic activities by business are reviewed. In view of the hypothesized role that small firm prevalence plays in the dispersion of political authority, the extent of elite 'crossovers' from small business to legislative office is analyzed in each region. A final section considers how distinctive ideational antecedent conditions seem to have affected both democratization and the extent of entrepreneurship in each region.

Notes

1 Surveys suggest that only about 20–30% of companies are members of business associations. Among large companies, membership in one or more business associations reaches 55–60%. (Frye 2002, Frye and Yakovlev 2007, Golikova 2007, 2009, Pyle 2006b) Because small companies in Russia are overwhelmingly in trade and services, the small companies in Pyle's 2004 survey are not representative of all Russian small companies. However, the only way in which they differ from the other companies in the sample is size, so that it may be reasonable to impute any differences in the small company respondents' outlook, especially as it relates to the role and functions of business associations, to company size.

2 Several surveys of entrepreneurs show that calling acquaintances in regional administrations persists as a problem-solving preference relative to more formal means of solving business problems. (CEFIR 2002, 2006; OPORA 2008)

3 Personal interview, Alexander Rybakov, Director, Department for Regional Chamber Development, TPPRF Moscow, October 7, 2009.
4 The web address in Russian is http://www.tpprf.ru/ru/interaction/committee/komrazv/ members/ Accessed November 12, 2014. Mamuta, Ermakov, Mikhalkin, Krylova, Borisov and Ioffe were all interviewed for this study
5 The OPORA website shows list at www.opora.ru/np.
6 This is the author's inference based on the numbers of members in various regional chapters.
7 Personal interview, Victor Sedov, director, U.S. Russia Center for Entrepreneurship, Moscow, September 28, 2009.
8 Our central variable, small firm prevalence is based on the numbers of firms having up to 100 employees.

References

Centre for Economic and Financial Research (CEFIR). (2002, 2003, 2004, 2005, 2006) Monitoring the Administrative Barriers to Small Business Development, Rounds 1–6. *CEFIR surveys*, www.cefir.ru. Accessed July 2010.

Chirikova, Alla E. (2007) *Vzaimodeystvie Vlasti i Biznesa v Realizatsii Sotsialnoy Politki: Regional'naya Proektsia*. Moscow: Independent Institute of Social Policy.

Diamond, Larry. (1994) Rethinking Civil Society. *Journal of Democracy* 5:5–17.

Frye, Timothy. (2002) Capture or Exchange? Business Lobbying in Russia. *Europe-Asia Studies* 54 (7):1017–1036.

Frye, Timothy and Andrei Yakovlev. (2007) *Reforms in Russia Through the Eyes of Business: What Has Changed in Seven Years*. Moscow: Higher School of Economics.

Gill, Graeme. (2008) *Bourgeoisie, State and Democracy: Russia, Britain, France, Germany and the USA*. Oxford, New York: Oxford University Press.

Golikova, Victoria. (2007) Uchastie Rossiyskikh Kompaniy v Biznes Assotsiatsakh. In Yakovlev, A (ed.) *Rossiyskaya Korporatsiya*. Moscow: State University Higher School of Economics.

Golikova, Victoria. (2009) Business Associations: Incentives and Benefits from the Standpoint of Corporate Governance. In Dolgopyatova, T., Iwasaki, I. and Yakovlev, A. (eds.) *Organization and Development of Russian Business: A Firm-Level Analysis*, London: Palgrave/McMillan.

Hanson, Philip and Elizabeth Teague. (2005) Big Business and the State in Russia. *Europe-Asia Studies* 57 (5):657–680.

Howard, Marc M. (2002) Postcommunist Civil Society in Comparative Perspective. *Demokratizatsiya: The Journal of Post-Soviet Democratization* 10 (3):285–305.

Howard, Marc M. (2003) *The Weakness of Civil Society in Post-Communist Europe*. New York: Cambridge University Press.

Ledeneva, Alena V. (1998) *Russia's Economy of Favours: Blat, Networking, and Informal Exchange*. Cambridge, UK: Cambridge University Press.

Ledeneva, Alena V. (2006) *How Russia Really Works: The Informal Practices That Shaped Post-Soviet Politics and Business*. Ithaca, NY: Cornell University Press.

North, Douglass. (1990) *Institutions, Institutional Change and Economic Performance*. New York: Cambridge University Press.

Olson, Mancur, (1982) *The Rise and Decline of Nations: Economic Growth, Stagflation and Social Rigidities*. New Haven, CT: Yale University Press.

OPORA Rossii. (2006) *Ustav Obshcherossiyskoy Obshchestvennoy Organizatsii Malogo i Srednogo Predprinimatel'stva "OPORA Rossii"*. Moscow.

OPORA Rossii. (2008) *Razvitie Malogo i Srednogo Predprinimatel'stva v Regionakh Rossii "Index OPORY"*. Moscow.

Orttung, Robert W. (ed.) (2000) *The Republics and Regions of the Russian Federation: A Guide to Politics, Policies and Leaders*. Edited by E. W. Institute. Armonk, NY and London, UK: M. E. Sharpe.

Owen, Thomas C. (1981) *Capitalism and Politics in Russia: A Social History of the Moscow Merchants 1855–1905*. Cambridge, UK: Cambridge University Press.

Pastukhov, B. N., G. A. Bordyugov, S. N. Katyrin, A. G. Poznyak, A. M. Rybakov, and V. I. Fedotov. (2007) *Sluzhenie Rossii: Torgovo-Promyslennaya Palata Rossiyskoy Federatsii (1917–2007)*. Moscow: Russian Chamber of Commerce and Industry.

Peregudov, Sergey P. (2009) Business and State Bureaucracy in Russia: Dynamics of Interaction. *Russian Politics and Law* 47 (4):43–57.

Petrov, Nikolai. (2004) Regional Models of Democratic Development. In McFaul, M., Petrov, N. and Ryabov, A. (eds) *Between Dictatorship and Democracy*. Washington, DC: Carnegie Endowment for International Peace.

Petrov, Nikolai. (2005) Democratichnost' Regionov Rossii. *Carnegie Moscow Center Briefing* 7 (9).

Petrov, Nikolai (2006) Naznacheniya Gubernatorov: Itogi Pervogo Goda. *Carnegie Moscow Center Briefing* 8 (3).

Petrov, Nikolai and Alexei Titkov. (2006) *Demokratichnost' Rossiskikh Regionov*. http://atlas.socpol.ru/indexes/index_democr.shtml. Accessed Novermber 10, 2010.

Petrov, Nikolai and Alexei Titkov (2013) *Reyting Demokratichnosti Regionov Moskovskogo Tsenta Karnegi: 10 Let v Stroyu*. Moscow: Carnegie Moscow Center. http://carnegie.ru/publications/?fa=55853. Accessed December 1, 2014.

Petrova, Tsveta and Sidney Tarrow. (2007) Transactional and Participatory Activism in the Emerging European Polity: The Puzzle of East-Central Europe. *Comparative Political Studies* 40 (1):74–94.

Putnam, Robert. (1993) *Making Democracy Work: Civic Traditions in Modern Italy*. Princeton, NJ: Princeton University Press.

Pyle, William. (2004) [Dataset of survey results: Entrepreneurs and business association leaders]. Unpublished raw data.

Pyle, William. (2006a) Collective Action and Post-Communist Enterprise: The Economic Logic of Russia's Business Associations. *Europe-Asia Studies* 58 (4):491–521.

Pyle, William. (2006b) Russia's Business Associations: Who Joins and Why? *CIPE Economic Reform Feature Service*. Washington, DC: Center for International Private Enterprise.

Pyle, William and Laura Solanko. (2010) *The Composition and Interests of Business Lobbies: Testing Olson's Hypothesis of the 'Encompassing Organization'*. Unpublished manuscript.

Roosa, Ruth AmEnde. (1997) *Russian Industrialists in an Era of Revolution: The Association of Industry and Trade, 1906–1917*. Armonk, NY and London: M. E. Sharpe.

Rosstat. (2009) *Maloe i Srednee Predprimatel'stvo v Rossii*. Moscow: State Statistics Service.

Russian Federation. (1993) Federal Law of 7 July 7, 1993 N.5340-I *"O Torgovo-Promyshlennykh Palatakh v Rossiiskoy Federatsii"*. Moscow: Federal Assembly of the Russian Federation, http://www.gov.ru/main/page4.html. Accessed January, 10, 2011.

Rutland, Peter. (2006) Business and Civil Society in Russia. In Evans, A. B., Henry, L. and Sundstrom, L. (eds) *Russian Civil Society: A Critical Assessment*, Armonk, NY and London, UK: M. E. Sharpe.

Rybakov, A. M. and V. I. Fedotov. (2009) *Vovlechenie v Chlenstvo*. Moscow: National Endowment for Democracy and CIPE.

Sakwa, Richard. (2008) *Russian Politics and Society*. Fourth ed. London and New York: Routledge.

Semenenko, Irina S. (2001) *Gruppy Interesov na Zapade i v Rossii: Konseptsii i Praktiki*. Moscow: IMEMO.

World Bank. (2009) Russian Federation Regional Development and Growth Agglomerations: The Longer Term Challenges of Economic Transition in the Russian Federation. *Country Economic Memorandum*. Washington, DC: World Bank.

Zaslavsky, Victor. (1995) From Redistribution to Marketization: Social and Attitudinal Change in Post-Soviet Russia. In Lapidus, G. W. (ed.) *The New Russia: Troubled Transformation*. Boulder, CO: Westview Press.

Zudin, Alexey. (1997) *Sistema Predstavitel'stva Rossiyskogo Biznesa: Formy Kollektivnogo Deystviia*. Moscow: Tsentr Politicheskikh Tekhnologiy.

4 The Samara region

A tale of two cities

The Samara oblast has been one of Russia's more economically dynamic, with greater than average political competition and social activism. The regional democracy indicators put the Samara region in the top five outcomes in the three time periods: 1991–2001, 2000–2004 and 2005–2009. (Petrov and Titkov 2006, 2013) The Independent Institute for Social Policy (IISP) notes that Samara region's advantages include "high human capital, high levels of education and mobility and adaptiveness of the population to the market economy as well as developed market supporting institutions and good quality of regional management." (IISP 2008) Among the four case study regions in this study, Samara closely edges out Perm over the period 1991–2008 in per capita money incomes, with both regions showing growth rates closely tracking the national averages. The Samara region is more urbanized than Russia as a whole at just above 80% as compared with around 73% for the entire country. (Rosstat 2010b)[1] Together, the two principal cities of the Samara region – Samara and Togliatti – form an urban agglomeration of almost 2 million people, the country's third largest. Roughly two thirds of the oblast's population lives in either Samara or Togliatti.

Economic geography and business history – antecedent structural conditions

Settlement of the Samara region by ethnic Russians began with the founding of a fort *(krepost)* on the site of the city of Samara in 1586, where the river traces a huge loop around the forested Zhiguli Hills. Samara's pleasant, long river embankment attracts strollers, bathers and boaters. (The city's historically resonant original name, restored in 1991, replaced its clumsy Soviet moniker Kuibyshev.) The deep and wide river surrounded by fertile grain-producing land produced the conditions for substantial settlement by Russians beginning in the 15th century. (Figes 1989) Ethnic Russians account for a stable 80% of the region's population; other important groups are the Chuvash, Mordvin and Tatars. The region's population fell from 3.25 million in 1991 to 3.18 million in 2008, a decline of 2.3%, substantially less than the 4% national population decline in the same period. (Rosstat 2010a)

The Samara region includes vast and fertile agricultural land, and its economic and social history of the 19th and early 20th centuries is intimately tied to grain production and the commercialization of grain employing Volga river transport. (Figes 1989; Gerschenkron 1970) The Volga barge pullers *(Burlaki)* of Ilya Repin's famous painting were painted from life along the Volga near Samara. Rail lines constructed in the 1880s reinforced the trading links of the middle Volga cities of Samara and Saratov to central Russia, the Urals, Siberia and the Caucasus. Volga shipping and crucial rail infrastructure were part of reason Togliatti (then called Stavropol on the Volga) was the site chosen by Khrushchev in 1966 for the AvtoVaz car manufacturing joint venture with Fiat (and of course for renaming the town in honor of the Italian Communist party leader). The ruins of Stavropol on the Volga lie submerged under a vast reservoir created by a major Soviet-era hydroelectric project.

Much of the population has come to the region from elsewhere, beginning with the relocation of defense-related industries in aviation in WWII and continuing with the foundation and growth of AvtoVaz. (McFaul and Petrov 1997) Because Samara grew up as a trading center for agricultural commodities, in the early 1900s it was sometimes called the Russian Chicago. Governor Konstantin Titov revived the comparison of Samara to Chicago in his quest to attract foreign investment and advertise the region's economic dynamism. (Orttung 2000) In the same vein, the troubled automotive capital, Togliatti, could be called the Russian Detroit.

Because of its defense-related industry, Kuibyshev was a closed city from 1935 to 1991. The city of Togliatti, for its part, epitomizes the pervasive Russian phenomenon of the *monogorod,* a city built in the Soviet period around a single industrial plant, with extensive social infrastructure for its huge workforce. The Samara region is one of several Russian regions where regional administrations' main preoccupation has been coordination with a single 'structurally crucial' enterprise. (Mau and Stupin 1997) The social and political implications of the restructuring of AvtoVaz have been central to the region's politics since 1991. Even in its much-reduced state, AvtoVaz represented in 2007 nearly 40% of the region's industrial output and a large share of the region's tax revenue. (Lapina and Chirikova 2002; Russia: All Regions Trade and Investment Guide – Samara 2008)[2] Dozens if not hundreds of other enterprises were related to AvtoVaz, making its survival crucial to the region's economic and social stability.

Appointed in 1991 and elected in competitive races in 1996 and 2000, Governor Konstantin Titov left office in 2007 as one of the leading survivors of the Yeltsin period and a figure of national stature, closely identified with market economic reforms, including small business development. Titov was perforce engaged in open politics and the balancing of interests, in part because the municipalities of Samara and Togliatti were, for most of Titov's time as governor, led by elected mayors asserting their own jurisdictional prerogatives.

Titov's successor, Vladimir Artyakov, appointed by Putin in August 2007, was board chairman and later CEO of AvtoVaz from 2005 to 2007, having served as deputy director of one of AvtoVaz's principal shareholders, the state-owned conglomerate Rossoboroneksport from 2000–2006. Rossoboronoeksport has since been expanded and renamed Rosstekhnologii and, as implied by the name change, has moved beyond its leading role in the defense sector to acquire industrial enterprises not specifically related to defense or armaments. The director of Rosstekhnologii, Sergey Chemezov, is said to have strongly backed the appointment of Artyakov as governor. (Nikolaeva 2009) The other two principal shareholders of AvtoVaz are Renault-Nissan and the Russian investment bank Troika Dialog. In the crisis of 2009, the federal government provided substantial emergency financing to AvtoVaz. Renault-Nissan increased its 25% share in AvtoVaz to 50% plus one share by the end of 2012.[3]

Modernization and defense conversion in the region's 'incumbent' defense related manufacturing enterprises was a leading theme of Titov's early years as governor. The best known of these companies, AviaKor, which produces Tupelev aircraft had 15,000 employees in the mid-1990s. (McFaul and Petrov 1997)

The Samara region has substantial oil and gas reserves, refineries and associated industries. A key stronghold of Russia's once preeminent private oil giant Yukos, the region has become an important base for the principal beneficiary of Yukos's liquidation, state-owned Rosneft. Metallurgy, chemicals/fertilizer, machine building and confectionary are the region's other leading industrial sectors. (Russia: All Regions Trade and Investment Guide – Samara 2008) Samara's integration into the large company networks of the broader national economy has been considerable from the early 1990s onward.[4] In no sense was the Samara region an enclave or fiefdom for regional business interests protected by the governor and his administration. This is in part because Togliatti and AvtoVaz inherited national significance from the Soviet period, as did the defense and aviation enterprises of Samara.

The Samara region has been called the 'birthplace of the oligarchs.' The first substantial business venture of the late arch-oligarch Boris Berezovsky was Logovaz, an AvtoVaz car dealer, along with a chimerical scheme to produce the AVVA, a small economy model that would, Berezovsky claimed, turn AvtoVaz around. Berezovsky, who had an advanced degree in mathematics, came to Togliatti in the late 1980s to help then-AvtoVaz director Vladimir Kadannikov write his doctoral dissertation. (Freeland 2000) Kadannikov was appointed deputy prime minister in 1996 and returned to the region to lead AvtoVaz in its joint venture with General Motors, retiring in 2005.

By the mid-1990s, the production and sales activities of AvtoVaz were allegedly linked to a whole 'nest' of criminal groups. (McFaul and Petrov 1997) As was the case for many Soviet industrial assets remaining in state hands, private intermediaries appropriated the enterprise's income stream while the enterprise itself sank deeper into debt. By 2002, law enforcement in the region had managed to wrest away from Togliatti-based criminal groups the control they had gained over sales from AvtoVaz. (Lapina and Chirikova 2002)

Companies of national stature dominate the business landscape in the Samara region. In 2009, the regional edition of the business magazine *Delovoy Kvartal* asked prominent local experts to name the region's most influential businessmen. The seven chosen were, in rank order: Vladimir Avetisyan, from the electrical power sector and a close associate of Anatoly Chubais; Sergey Chemezov of

Rosstekhnologii; Yuriy Kachmazov, whose business is linked to AvtoVaz; Sergey Bogdanchikov, then president of Rosneft; Oleg Dyachenko, president of a Samara-based bank; Leonid Mikhelson, CEO of natural gas producer Novatek; and Igor Komarov, AvtoVaz president. Of the seven men making the list, only three had business activities principally or exclusively in the Samara region: Avetisyan, Kachmazov and Dyachenko. (Dyachenko was also deputy speaker of the regional legislature.) Chemezov and Bogdanchikov headed national state-owned companies with large investments in the Samara region, and Komarov was appointed AvtoVaz director from the senior ranks of Rosstekhnologii headed by Chemezov. Leonid Mikhelson headed a nationally significant private natural gas company with significant business in the Samara region. Chemezov in particular epitomizes that part of the national business elite that rose up in the Putin era, in that he heads a state-owned company and has close career associations with the defense and intelligence establishment.

The presence of these large Moscow-based companies and their significance in the regional economy means that regional politics in Samara have been integrated to an unusual degree with national politics even in the years when many regions in Russia functioned as economic enclaves and political fiefdoms. Apart from the surviving enterprises in the defense and aviation sector whose restructuring and modernization is incomplete, and the still unfinished story of AvtoVaz itself, the Samara region's incumbent enterprises have been absorbed into profitable large companies of national scale, whether private or state owned.

The Samara oblast is also one of Russia's most successful at generating new small companies. The extensive development of local financial institutions and the penetration by national and international banks has presumably been of importance in SME development. The micro-lender FINCA, originally supported by USAID, has used the Samara region as its base for expansion in other regions of Russia. The EBRD-supported small business lender KMB, acquired by the Italian commercial bank Intesa in 2010, has also long been active in the region.[5] According to FINCA's market survey of Samara-Togliatti in 2011, there are 105 credit institutions ranging from non-bank micro-lenders FINCA and SIGAL up to Citibank, Raffeisen and national majors Sberbank, VTB and Alfabank. (FINCA 2010, 2011)

Impulse: the democratic breakthrough and its institutionalization

We have seen that the extent of the democratization in the period 1991–2001 was crucial to the scope of development of small firms over the period 2000–2008. The Samara region shows both a fairly decisive break in 1991 and a tendency to be 'polycentric' over much of the ensuing period. (Lapina and Chirikova 2002) Twice-elected and once-appointed Governor Konstantin Titov and his administration represented only one of several centers of political authority and economic power in the region. Extensive elite interviews conducted by Lapina and Chirikova in Samara and Togliatti in 2000–2001 pointed in particular to the existence of a complex partnership between business and political leaders. After the crisis of 1998, they reported, regional business interests had moved away from *ad hoc* and improvised lobbying to demand instead the application of legal guarantees while attempting to bring their own business into compliance with tax and other laws. (Lapina and Chirikova 2002)[6]

The collapse of the putsch in August 1991 upset the prevailing order in regional power structures, making or breaking the fortunes of contenders for political leadership. The extent of local mobilization and organization of democratic movements, proto-parties and independent news media influenced Yeltsin's choice in appointments of regional leadership. (Fish 1995; McFaul 2001; McFaul and Petrov 1997) Konstantin Titov had been elected in partially competitive elections to the city legislature *(gorsovet)* in 1990 and was elected chairman from among the membership. From this position, he publicly supported Yeltsin against the 1991 coup plotters, becoming as a result one of Yeltsin's first new appointees to head a regional administration. Titov was an avowed supporter of Yeltsin's intended course of democratic and market reforms.

Born in Moscow in 1944, and raised in Stavropol on the Volga, Titov studied at the Kuibyshev Aviation Institute (later the Samara Aerospace University) and worked as an engineer in that industry. He became active in Komsomol and was engaged in the scholarly and practical aspects of economic reforms in the perestroika period including having a hand in drafting of the landmark 1988 Law on Cooperatives. (Central Electoral Commission Russian Federation 2001; Samara Regional Government 2005)[7]

Yeltsin's appointment of Titov frustrated the ambitions of Viktor Tarkhov, then the chairman of the oblast executive governing committee *(obispolkom)*, suspected (his supporters say unfairly) of supporting the 1991 putsch. (McFaul and Petrov 1997) The continuing intra-elite political contestation in the Samara region is, in part, due to the rallying of some factions of the region's democrats to the leadership of Tarkhov from this early phase. With a long background in the oil and gas sector, Tarkhov, born in Kuibyshev in 1948, belongs to the camp of post-Soviet Russian political leadership drawn directly from the ranks of company directors. Beginning in 1992, Tarkhov returned to the oil industry as refinery director, and from 1994 was a vice president of Yukos. (McFaul and Petrov 1997)[8]

The pro-putsch regional CPSU first secretary, Valentin Romanov, was to be Titov's principal opponent in the election of 1996, paralleling the national recovery of fortunes by the CPRF and Zyuganov's potent challenge to Yeltsin. Titov's comfortable victory in that race showed the region's electorate was more disposed to support of democracy and economic reform than was then the case in Russia as a whole. Titov was a member of the pro-Yeltsin, pro-reform Democratic Choice of Russia (DVR) in the early 1990s, and from 1994 served as national deputy chairman of the centrist 'party of power,' Our Home Is Russia (*Nash Dom Rossiya,* or NDR). Having served as chairman of the budget and tax committee in the Federation Council, he nevertheless declined an appointment as deputy prime minister in the wake of his impressive showing against Romanov. (McFaul and Petrov 1997)

In February 1999, in preparation for the state duma elections of that year, Titov formed an electoral bloc of 14 governors who, while shunning Moscow mayor Luzhkov's initiative to draw governors into his Fatherland party, nevertheless sought to assert, from what Titov called a 'right of center' position, the rights and prerogatives of regional authorities relative to the center and calling for greater devolution or genuine federalism. Among those joining Titov's bloc, called the Voice of Russia, were Perm governor Igumnov and Rostov governor Chub. Receiving financial backing from Yukos's Khodorkovsky and aluminum magnate Oleg Deripaska, the 'Voice' bloc joined an electoral alliance with the liberal pro-business party Union of Right Forces (SPS). (Orttung 2000)

Titov chose to run for president against Yeltsin's anointed successor Vladimir Putin in 2000, having been a vocal critic of Putin's conduct of the second war in Chechnya. (Orttung 2000) Titov came third with 20% of the vote in the oblast, but received only 1.5% nationally, checking definitively Titov's national political ambitions. In a controversial maneuver, Titov resigned his office in order to run for a new term as governor in a snap election in July 2000. Titov's principal opponent, Viktor Tarkhov, then a prominent member of the regional legislature, came in a distant second. According to Lapina and Chirikova, Yukos backed Titov's re-election, and Titov appointed a Yukos executive to serve as deputy governor after his re-election. (Lapina and Chirikova 2002)

Titov may have called the snap election in 2000 in part because he feared that Putin would engineer his removal by canceling governors' elections. (Konitzer 2005; Lapina and Chirikova 2002) The defeated Tarkhov unsuccessfully challenged the election result in court on grounds that holding the snap election gave unlimited rein to the governor's incumbent advantages including the liberal use of 'administrative resources.' (Konitzer 2005) Neither Titov nor Tarkhov (nor for that matter, the other three candidates in the 2000 gubernatorial election) was formally associated with a party. Tarkhov's affiliation was given as the president of the autonomous non-commercial manufacturers' "Association of Agricultural and Industrial Enterprises of the Volga Region." (Central Electoral Commission Russian Federation 2001)

Konstantin Titov's disappointing performance in the 2000 presidential election weakened his authority relative to other regional contenders for power.[9] His diminished standing provoked more contention among political clans represented in regional and municipal legislatures, often with backing from business interests. Despite his avowed 'right of center' orientation in economic matters, Titov nevertheless affiliated briefly with Gorbachev's Social Democratic Party, disappointed at the failure of the pro-business liberal party SPS to endorse his presidential run in 2000. (Golosov 2004) After a period of gradual reconciliation, Putin extended Titov's term as governor in 2005 (Petrov 2006).

The Transparency International survey in 2002 of perceived and actual 'everyday' and business-related corruption in forty regions of Russia found the Samara region not particularly plagued by petty bureaucratic corruption but performing much more poorly on business-related corruption. (Transparency International and INDEM Foundation 2002) Titov's critics alleged he favored business activities by his wife and his son, a prominent banker.[10] Samara mayor Georgiy Limans-kiy's media assets were seen as inconsistent with his role as mayor of Samara, and the influence of Yukos and AvtoVaz in political life was pervasive. Nevertheless, the region's business climate was counted among Russia's best, bringing tangible results in attracting foreign investment by international companies ranging from Nestlé and Pepsi-Cola, to General Motors and Alcoa.[11]

The appointment of Vladimir Artyakov to replace Titov in 2007 reflected two important national trends: the recentralization of Moscow's power over regional administrations and the elevation of the paradigm of governor as 'manager' rather than politician. Artyakov projected the image a seasoned and effective manager, but he showed little aptitude for political leadership in the sense of understanding and reconciling the interests of socially engaged citizens and stakeholders in regional or municipal elected office. Although no doubt a share of Titov's credibility derived from his ability to be heard in Moscow, especially in defense of AvtoVaz, Artyakov's authority among regional elites seemed to derive directly from his close association with the presidential administration under Putin, and above all from his ability to leverage substantial new investment in industrial modernization and revival through his professional links to the state conglomerate Rosstekhnologii.

In the October 1993 crisis that pitted Yeltsin against the Congress of People's Deputies, the majority of the Samara regional legislature, also held over from the last semi-free elections of late perestroika, sided with the Moscow deputies. Titov dissolved the regional legislature and the first fully competitive legislative elections were held in 1993. An electoral coalition called *Ob'edininie Podderzhki Reform* (OPR) was formed to mobilize the region's democrats under Titov's leadership. Among its leaders was Oleg Sysuev, a factory director also in banks and other interests. (McFaul and Petrov 1997).

Sysuev was elected mayor of Samara in 1994 and re-elected in 1996. He left office to accept an appointment as deputy prime minister for social affairs and minister of labor in Chernomyrdin's cabinet in 1997, triggering a special mayoral election in Samara. The victor was Georgiy Limanskiy, director of the regional telecommunications company *Svyazinform,* deputy speaker of the municipal duma and a supporter of Aleksandr Lebed. (McFaul and Petrov 1997) Limanskiy's 'populist' policies tended to worsen the business climate in the city of Samara, home to more than half of the oblast's small businesses, which together accounted for 18% of the city's employment. (Lapina and Chirkivova 2002) From his position as mayor, Limanskiy challenged Titov's policy direction from the left. Limanskiy in turn met opposition from business lobbies in the regional duma led by Tarkhov, elected to the legislature in 2001. (Golosov 2004)

Tarkhov kept up a steady barrage of criticism of Limanskiy, and the battle took the form of public *kompromat* (leaked press reports alleging corruption). Tarkhov based his successful electoral challenge to Limanskiy on these allegations of corruption against Limanskiy, the candidate of United Russia. Tarkhov won the mayoral election of 2006 under the banner of the Party of Life, later merged into the Just Russia (SR) party. Electoral setbacks such as this one for United Russia by this time were quite rare.

Tarkhov's was an exceptional case of an elected mayor who did not switch over to United Russia and nevertheless stayed in office. His tenure as mayor was an irritant to United Russia's regional party organization. Some local observers claim, for example that the regional administration withheld or delayed budgetary transfers to the city to undermine Tarkhov's standing. Tarkhov's last two years as mayor saw him constantly under investigation for alleged mismanagement of city finances. (Gutorova 2010)

Tarkhov's quixotic fight to win re-election in 2010 under the banner of Just Russia met determined opposition from United Russia. The process of candidate selection by United Russia was opened to the party's general membership (of several thousand Samara residents) in a primary contested by two main candidates, Duma speaker and political veteran Viktor Sasonov and the much younger former Samara deputy mayor and regional environment minister Dmitry Azarov.

Lapina and Chirikova (2002) found Togliatti to be the clear leader of the two cities in terms of average living standards and the extent and quality of social services provided by the administration. Several interviewees for the present study contended that Togliatti had withstood the acute economic crisis of the 1990s better than Samara. Today, the most casual visitor is immediately struck by how much shabbier and more depressed Togliatti appears by contrast to Samara.

The city of Togliatti has been more than usually plagued by organized crime and unsolved murders of both politicians and journalists, and scandal-ridden local politics. Much of this is likely traceable to the rich takings available from the long-running problems of AvtoVaz. (McFaul and Petrov 1997) In 2002, two editors in chief of the independent newspaper *Tol'yatinskoe Obozrenie (Togliatti Observer)* were murdered. The murders, never solved, are widely believed to have been related to the paper's investigations of corruption including by the city administration. (Trifonov 2002) The first of the men killed, Valeriy Ivanov, aged 32, was also a member of the municipal duma.

Although his alleged financial dealings made him a target of the investigations of the *Togliatti Observer,* Togliatti's mayor, Sergey Zhilkin, first elected at the age of 34 in 1994 and re-elected in 1996, was an advocate of democratization and economic reform who cooperated closely with western technical assistance programs such as EU-TACIS and the U.S. Peace Corps while in office.[12] After leaving office in 2000, Zhilkin studied public administration in the United Kingdom, was elected president of the Rotary Club of Togliatti and became the rector of Togliatti State University. Zhilkin's successor Nikolai Utkin, elected in 2000, was forced to resign in 2007 on being charged with corruption and was imprisoned.[13] Utkin's supporters believed that his arrest and removal were due to his attempts to remain politically independent relative to powerful business influences.[14]

By comparison to Samara's municipal legislature, Togliatti's city duma exercised more genuine oversight over budgetary and policy matters, pointing to even greater dispersion of political power there than in Samara. (Lapina and Chirikova 2002) Mayor Anatoliy Pushkov was elected in 2008 to succeed Utkin. He was the candidate of United Russia and a former AvtoVaz executive. Press accounts indicate that the city duma and public challenges of Pushkov's performance were common.[15]

Comparative overview of small business development

The Samara region is one of only eight regions where the numbers of small companies increased every year through the second half of the 1990s. (GosKomStat *Regiony Rossii* 2001) In 1995, the region had 17,400 small companies and by 2000, they numbered 27,600, although the total number of such companies across Russia rose only insignificantly over the same five years.[16] The other regions where the number of small companies rose each year over this period were the cities of Moscow and St. Petersburg and the Moscow, Kaliningrad, Nizhniy Novgorod, Chelyabinsk and Novosibirsk regions. All except the city of Moscow and the Moscow region are also among the strongest performers on the regional democracy index.[17]

Table 4.1 shows the numbers of incorporated small companies in the Samara oblast per 1,000 of the labor force in selected years with the average (mean) of this statistic for all regions of Russia.

These figures show clearly the comparatively strong performance of the Samara region relative to the average across all Russia's regions from 1995 onward and suggest a decree of sustained legal, political and economic reforms that generated persistent business confidence. The figures for the city of Samara itself show a 30% increase in the numbers of small businesses from 2000 to 2006, and in 2007, the city had more than 17,000 small companies, or 58% of the regional total, as well as 19,000 individual entrepreneurs. Incorporated small companies employed 27% of the city's workforce. Taking into account individual entrepreneurs and their employees brought this proportion to almost 40% of the workforce. (Samara City Administration 2007) A catalog of small businesses distributed at the launch of the city's small business incubator in 2010 includes profiles of about 450 companies, organized by sector. (Samara City Administration 2009)

According to the director of the city's small business development programs, Larissa Ermolenko, the Samara regional administration has had an SME development program run by a department within the administration since 1993. Ermolenko and OPORA Samara co-president Vladimir Tikhonov attribute the expansion in numbers of small companies throughout the 1990s in part to the

Table 4.1 Samara Small Firms Concentration

Number of Incorporated Small Companies per 1,000 of Labor Force						
Years/Region	*1995*	*2000*	*2002*	*2004*	*2006*	*2008*
Samara region	11.19	16.19	18.13	20.43	17.05	21.99
Average	11.64	9.48	9.32	11.05	10.76	14.91

Source: Goskomstat 2001, Rosstat *Regiony Rossii* 2002, 2008, 2010

sharp contraction in the region's defense industry, which they said drove highly qualified and talented people into small businesses, at first mainly as traders. They also emphasized the role played by AvtoVaz, which over the years has turned increasingly to small companies for inputs and services. Ermolenko said there were in 2010 more than 300 small companies whose 'customer' was AvtoVaz.[18] The experience of the Samara region illustrates well the social significance of SME development in generating employment in conditions of dramatic economic dislocation.

The small business of the Samara region is, as elsewhere in Russia, dominated by services including retail and wholesale trade, construction, property sales and leasing, and transportation/communications. In 2008, these four sectors accounted respectively for 41%, 12%, 20% and 6% of small businesses, with another 10% in manufacturing and processing. This distribution tracks very closely with the distribution of small businesses by sector nationally in 2008. (Rosstat 2009) Data on medium-sized companies (under the formal definition established by the 2007 SME support law) were collected for the first time in 2008, when the Samara region had 311 such companies out of a total of 14,170 in Russia. (Rosstat 2009)

Because the Samara region was a leader in adoption of economic reforms, it attracted substantial early interest from aid donors interested in promoting financial sector development and nourishing the incipient small business community through microcredit and small business finance. One of the leaders in this field is the U.S.-based non-profit microcredit agency FINCA, which adopted Samara as the center of its operations in Russia. FINCA's director American Timothy Tarrant, based in Samara, related how FINCA was the leading provider of very small loans to individual entrepreneurs and small companies in the region, was also active in Tomsk and Kazan and was expanding into Rostov and Krasnodar regions.[19] FINCA estimated the population of eligible small entrepreneurs in the Samara region in 2010 to be about 120,000, mainly working in 45 large bazaars. (FINCA 2011) Although FINCA was fairly secure in its niche as a non-bank provider of small loans (ranging up to about $20,000), competition among lenders to small business clients was intensifying.

Business associations and small business advocacy – bonding and bridging 'civic-ness'

The study of the Samara region's business associations follows the rationale and analytical approach laid out in Chapter 3. The evidence used to develop the study is personal interviews, observation of public events involving business association leaders, review and analysis of associations' documentation and websites, media reports and project documents from the CIPE small business advocacy program in which all the associations in the study participated. The key analytical questions related to associations concern their 'internal' or bonding functions and their 'external' or bridging functions. Because business associations' effectiveness is inextricably tied up with the degree of receptiveness or openness by governmental officials to policy recommendations and redress of grievances, the regional and municipal small business development programs and the various channels and structures for consultation with business associations are also discussed. The three leading associations that represent small entrepreneurs in the Samara region are the OPORA affiliate, the Chamber of Commerce of Togliatti and the Chamber of Commerce of the Samara Region.

OPORA Samara region

Having headed a regional association of manufacturing and agricultural enterprises, Viktor Tarkhov, unsuccessful challenger to Konstantin Titov in the 2000 gubernatorial election, was elected to the regional duma in 2001. He became the head of the regional chapter of OPORA when it was formed in 2002. Tarkhov remained the titular head of OPORA's regional chapter after he was elected mayor of Samara in 2006. From around 2005 onward, Viktor Tarkhov's principal business interest has been in the manufacture of small civil aircraft.[20]

Vladimir Tikhonov, who had been executive director of OPORA Samara from its foundation and a close associate of Tarkhov, became co-president and in effect the head of the regional chapter when Tarkhov became mayor. Tarkhov appointed another leading figure in the regional OPORA chapter, Larissa Ermolenko, to head Samara's municipal small business development programs. Tikhonov and Ermolenko worked together very closely, on behalf, respectively, of OPORA Samara and the Samara city administration.

As we have seen, the city of Samara is home to the solid majority of the oblast's small businesses. Having the serving mayor of a major city as the head of an OPORA regional affiliate was not typical, but was welcomed by the national leadership of OPORA.[21] Tarkhov's leadership of OPORA in Samara exposed the organization to tensions with the regional administration especially as his campaign against United Russia's preferred candidate for mayor intensified in mid-2010, culminating in Tarkhov's defeat in October.[22] Despite the barely concealed political tensions between the city and regional administration, the reputation of OPORA nationally and its leadership by Tikhonov made it a respected partner of the regional administration on issues related to small business. Still, Tarkhov's leadership of OPORA's regional organization is likely to have limited the appeal of the association to entrepreneurs outside of the city of Samara and to have made OPORA more relevant in a municipal than in a regional context. Because OPORA's regional affiliates are financed exclusively by members' dues, any factor that inhibits membership must on balance tend to reduce the effectiveness of the association.

Tarkhov's leadership of OPORA as mayor suggests that he considered small business to be important in the context of the city's economic development, as indeed it is by measures of company tax revenue and employment. Based on the comparison of municipal small business development programs in this study (programs of Rostov, Perm and Smolensk) the Samara municipal program is exemplary, in terms of its display of initiative and public visibility.[23]

Vladimir Tikhonov, a sociology professor and enthusiast of small business development, devoted considerable energy to his role of co-president of OPORA.[24] His cellphone never ceased to ring with requests and questions related to OPORA business, and his schedule was packed with meetings of the many established consultative bodies where OPORA represents small business concerns. Tikhonov said the regional OPORA affiliate has about 80 members.[25] The organization, he said, responded regularly to requests for help and advice from nonmembers, and advocated for the interests of all small companies. Tikhonov's remarks and work program suggested he understood OPORA's priorities to be the persuit of legal and regulatory reforms, transparency and effective governance. OPORA's Samara organization served as coordinator of the CIPE small business advocacy program for the region, with both Tikhonov and Ermolenko as important and active participants.[26]

The website of OPORA Samara does not give any information about the internal structure of the organization, such as a governing board or the existence of committees among the membership. The only documents are on the work of the regional association related to public meetings where Tikhonov has spoken on behalf of the organization.[27] Under the Tarkhov-Tikhonov tandem, OPORA's considerable influence in Samara seems mainly to have been as a provider of expertise and policy input, including by ensuring that the national organization's expertise and research were taken into account in policy formulation in Samara and the region. The organization's principal sources of influence appeared to be the link to the resources of city administration and the link to the considerable lobbying power of OPORA at the federal level.

At a meeting at the business incubator on June 2, 2010, Tikhonov and Ermolenko both expressed optimism about developments at the federal level in Russia, advocated by OPORA, to support and encourage small business. The main accomplishment was the passage of the 2007 law on SME promotion under which the federal Ministry of Economic Development (MED) co-finances small business development programs with regional administrations. They praised the commitment and talent of the Ministry's program director Andrey Sharov, as a key partner for OPORA. They also welcomed the new push by MED and OPORA to foster technology-based start-ups.

Tikhonov said that OPORA's national president Sergey Borisov solicited input from OPORA Samara in formulating OPORA's reactions to various drafts of federal laws affected small business. They also cited the laws of 2008 limiting the scope of inspections and the removing of MVD (police) from any role in business inspections as having been accomplishments of OPORA's lobbying efforts.

Tikhonov serves as a very effective and energetic advocate for small business, but the regional OPORA affiliate seems nevertheless to be under-developed organizationally in terms of membership engagement, especially outside of Samara itself. On balance, OPORA's regional chapter seems to have sacrificed building of a broad-based organization to exploit instead the avenues of influence opened by Tarkhov's position as mayor, including in the shaping of the city's SME development efforts.

Togliatti chamber of commerce and industry

The Togliatti Chamber, set up in 1994 immediately on passage of the national legislation setting out the role and structure of Chambers of Commerce, was one of the first municipal Chambers. By 2010, there were 220 municipally based Chambers, usually in cities other than regional capitals.[28] The Togliatti Chamber has approximately 700 members. Most are incorporated companies, but some individual entrepreneurs are also members.

Chamber President Vladimir Zhukov headed Togliatti's municipal administration beginning in 1991 and was closely involved in organizing the city's first mayoral elections.[29] He is the former head of the regional Yabloko party and was in 2010 serving a second term in Togliatti city duma, one of six members of the so-called Decembrist faction.[30] Zhukov started, and later sold, a company producing construction materials. He has served on the national presidium of the TPPRF. A photo prominently displayed in the office shows Zhukov and Mayor Pushkov receiving TPPRF President Primakov at the Togliatti Chamber's offices.

In an interview with the author in 2010, Zhukov recalled how he and longtime friend and colleague Aleksandr Rybakov, head of the TPPRF department for relations with regional and local Chamber affiliates, were part of a group that travelled to the United States in the early 1990s, where, among other encounters with American groups and individuals, they were introduced to the Rotary Club in Maryland.[31] On his return home, Zhukov started an association in Togliatti called the American House. It was on the basis of this association that the Togliatti Chamber was founded.

The roots of the Togliatti Chamber in voluntary civic engagement may explain why the full list of the Chamber's members has long been available on its website.[32] Other civil society organizations engaged in charitable, environmental and other fields are comparatively dense and active in Togliatti, perhaps, as Zhukov and then-Vice-President Vitaly Matveev suggested, because of the retreat of AvtoVaz from its formerly overwhelming role in providing social programs and employment. Matveev said that much of Togliatti's population came from other parts of the Soviet Union in AvtoVaz's heyday. This mixing of strangers supported, he thought, the development of formal associations as opposed to traditional networks.

AvtoVaz is a member of the Togliatti Chamber, but no longer is the clear leader it once was of the business community in the civic sphere. According to the Chamber, around 34,000 employees still lived in AvtoVaz housing and enjoyed at least some company-provided social services as of late 2010, but this was a sharp decline from the 115,000 people AvtoVaz once employed. Zhukov confirmed that about 300 SMEs are suppliers to AvtoVaz and many are Togliatti Chamber members. Togliatti's AvtoVaz suppliers have formed a 'cluster' to generate efficiencies, share expertise and hasten the adoption of newer technologies. In helping member companies find markets outside the region or abroad, the Chamber also tries to promote their adoption of more advanced technologies.

The Togliatti Chamber advocates for its members principally vis-à-vis the mayor and municipal duma. Zhukov and Matveev suggested that, by contrast to

Chambers open to companies from an entire oblast, municipal Chambers enjoy a greater measure of independence from regional administrations. The Chambers at a municipal level were, they believed, more evenly matched with, and therefore more influential upon the decisions of, their governmental counterpart – the city administration – than regional Chambers typically are with respect to regional administrations.

Zhukov and Matveev pointed to the fact that the Togliatti Chamber and other civic groups had worked with the administration on a city development plan in 2010. This initiative had come from the city duma, the Chamber and other civic organizations. The city's leadership has been, according to the Chamber, interested in small business development, not, as is sometimes the case among officials, primarily as a source of tax revenue, but rather as a means of diversifying and reviving Togliatti's economy. The Chamber was a principal partner in these efforts. Zhukov argued that further reforms to revenue sharing between municipalities and regions would help to encourage small business further.[33] On the May 25 Entrepreneurs Day observance in 2010, the Togliatti Chamber organized a conference to review the work of the city's small business development program of 2010–2015 entitled "Society-Business-Government" and invited commentary on its online forum. (Chamber of Commerce and Industry City of Togliatti 2010)

Zhukov said that, despite the passage of the 2007 federal law on SME support and other signs of progress, conditions for entrepreneurship and small business in Russia were still very difficult. Those small businesses that had prospered had typically done so in spite of bureaucratic obstacles, not because of any official support or encouragement. Successful small entrepreneurs were, he said, Darwinian survivors. He argued that the resolution of fundamental problems, such as regulatory and tax burdens and abuses such as '*reyderstvo,*' should be the priority tasks of small business development.

Following on the approaches originated by INDEM under the CIPE program, the Togliatti Chamber provides input to draft legislation at the municipal level with a view to reducing the scope for the corruption allowed by unchecked or arbitrary enforcement or oversight. The Chamber found this approach helpful to its members, including in consultations with the local prosecutor's office.

Chamber of commerce and industry of the Samara region

The Chamber of Commerce of the Samara region traces its origins to the enactment by the Provisional Government in early October of 1917 of the statute "On Chambers of Commerce and Industry" based on legislation first proposed in 1910. The 1917 statute allowed for formation of Chambers with elected leadership in Russian provinces. Several prominent deputies of the Constituent Assembly, freely elected and forcefully dissolved after its opening session by the Bolsheviks, founded in Samara on June 8, 1918, a government claiming to rule all of Russia on behalf of the Constituent Assembly, provisional upon the full restoration of the elected parliament.

The regional Chamber in Samara was established in 1918 when the Samara region and much of the middle Volga was governed by this anti-Bolshevik authority, called the *Komuch* (*komitet chelenov uchreditelnogo sobraniya* – Committee of Members of the Constitutional Assembly). The founding membership of regional entrepreneurs had as one of its aims the collection of resources for support of the armed forces of the *Komuch*. The first elected president was Konstantin Neklyutin, just 31 years old in 1918 and a leader in the Samara business community.[34] This brief idyll of months when the Samara regional Chamber's 'ancestor' existed is highlighted on the Chamber's website. This antecedent Chamber was dissolved with the imposition of Soviet power in the region late in 1918.

The revival of the Chamber in the Samara region began with efforts at reforming and restructuring the Soviet Chamber of Commerce and Industry (TPP-USSR) beginning in 1988. The Samara Chamber's immediate antecedent was a new affiliate of the TPP-USSR for the middle Volga established in 1990. Rather than arising as many other Chambers did from the initiative of local private businesses when these became common by around 1992, the Samara Chamber emerged from an expansion and reform of the role and functions of the Soviet Chamber.

As governor, Konstantin Titov encouraged and fostered the growth of the regional chamber, and in 1998 the Chamber emerged in its current form as the Chamber of Commerce and Industry for the Samara Region with the election of its first president, Boris Vasil'evich Ardalin, owner of a construction company and also founding president of the Samara Rotary Club.[35] Chamber President Valery Petrovich Fomichev was elected to succeed Ardalin in 2005, with the support of Governor Titov, having served in the regional administration. Ardalin served as transport minister under Titov in his last two years in the governor's office and then resigned.

The 19-member board of the Samara regional Chamber is chaired by Fomichev and has 5 other members, including Matveev, president of the Togliatti Chamber and two other members who head sector-specific business associations. Both 'incumbent' and 'new' sectors of business are represented, and among the board members is the regional representative of Alcoa.[36] There are three branches under the direct leadership of the Samara Chamber: Syzran, Zhigulevsk and Chapaevsk.

Seven committees of the Samara Chamber are devoted to appraisal (of real property and equipment), expertise and analysis, youth entrepreneurship, construction, tourism and communal services sectors, budget and audit. An eighth committee set up 2010 provides legal support and advice to entrepreneurs and invites participation by non-member entrepreneurs and business associations. Svetlana Spicenok, as director for development of entrepreneurship at the Chamber, is closely involved with this committee's work.[37] The Samara regional Chamber's website began in 2011 to feature a list of the roughly 220 member companies organized by sector.[38]

In an interview with the author in 2010, Fomichev said he saw the Chamber's effectiveness for business mainly in the advocacy on behalf of all member companies in a given sector.[39] He expressed doubts about the usefulness of policy advocacy on behalf of small business as a whole. Small business owners did not tend to see the benefit of joining the regional chamber, because they tended not to be well informed about the laws and norms of business practice that the Chamber sees itself as protecting.

The Samara Chamber is an instrument, Fomichev said, of 'informed and professional' representation of the interests of members. The many regular structured consultations between government agencies and organized business were very important, and the regional Chamber played a leading role in all of them. He said that the Chamber had no reason to interact with the Samara municipal administration; its representations on behalf of business were exclusively vis-à-vis the governor and regional administration.

Other associations representing the business community

Table 4.2 gives the names of the associations that took part in the Samara regional coalition of business associations formed under the CIPE-USAID small business advocacy project in 2003.

This list of organizations points to considerable institutional diversity and involvement of a wide range of locally organized small associations of entrepreneurs in Samara, Togliatti and several smaller cities. OPORA Samara – under the leadership of Tikhonov and Ermolenko – was chosen by coalition member

Table 4.2 Coalition Member Organizations

OPORA Rossii - Samara chapter
Chamber of Commerce and Industry of the Samara Region
Chamber of Commerce and Industry – City of Togliatti
Non-commercial credit fund "Kredo"
Non-commercial Partnership of artisans and craftsmen
"Sredevolskaya Assotsiatsiya Masterov"
Regional social movement "Razvitie Predprinimatel'stva"
Non-commercial partnership "Samara Union of Scrap-Metal Markets"
Consumer Union of Mutual Financial Support "Lyubimyy Gorod" Togliatti
Non-commercial fund "'Stavropol' Biznes"
Consumer Union of Mutual Financial Support "KS-Samara"
Non-commercial organization "Liga Dela" Kinel'-Cherkasskiy Rayon, Samara Oblast
Fund for Small Entrepreneurship "Progress" city of Otradnyy
Council of Entrepreneurs, city of Chapaevska
Center of Small Business Development, Sergievskiy Rayon, Samara Oblast
Association of Business Cooperation "Sozidanie" Togliatti
Agency of Support for Small and Medium Business – Samara Region
Social organization for support of entrepreneurship "Initiativa" Samara city
Non-commercial organization "Samara Oblast Business Incubator"
Non-commercial social organization for consumer protection "Traditsiya"

Source: Center for International Private Enterprise (CIPE)

organizations to coordinate the coalition's work and its interactions with CIPE.[40] The coalition attracted associations from among consumer protection groups and credit unions, and only two of the groups on the list are governmental or quasi-governmental: the Agency for Support of Small and Medium Enterprise and the Samara regional business incubator. Based on interviews in the region, it seems that several of the voluntary associations which took part in the coalition were no longer active in 2010, reflecting the attrition that is common among civil society associations in Russia.

The Samara regional branch of the national organization for medium-sized enterprises, Delovaya Rossiya, is headed by prominent businessman Gennady Kiryashin, CEO of the regionally based cellphone company Smarts and former president of the Samara Rotary Club.[41] Labor unions representing employees in small business are also part of the network of associations involved in encouraging SME development. Aleksandr Afanasenko, president of the small business council of the regional union federation, and Iranda Gusakova, president of the regional union of workers in trade and entrepreneurship 'Torgovoe Edinstvo,' took part in the opening of the Samara city business incubator in October 2010. Under new features of the labor code, employees in small business and OPORA are included in some aspects of the tripartite bargaining that has heretofore concerned only RSPP representing the country's largest employers.

Business associations' dialogue with regional and city administrations – contributions to the openness of policy formulation

Business agenda

The first product of the coalition of business associations advocating for small business in the Samara oblast was a policy declaration, the Regional Business Agenda, setting out the principal problems faced by small business and obstacles to the expansion in the contribution of small business to the regional economy and employment. (Samara Regional Business Association Coalition 2004) The Samara coalition's 'Agenda' was formulated based on results of a survey of small business people (including incorporated companies and individual entrepreneurs) in the region.

The program calls for the regional administration to lift administrative barriers, simplify laws and regulations, make credit more accessible, reduce the tax burden, curb anti-competitive abuses by some market actors and help open up opportunities for small companies to compete as suppliers for large industrial concerns. As we will see in the next section, some of these purposes are adopted in the Samara regional administration's programs of small business promotion. The associations' agenda also sets aims for the business community itself, including attracting broad participation from entrepreneurs' associations in shaping regional policies, developing more complete and current information on laws and regulations as well as market opportunities for small business, and developing training and other initiatives to raise the management and other professional capacities of entrepreneurs and potential entrepreneurs.

In a second phase of the CIPE project, the same regional coalition of business associations drafted and publicized their anti-corruption program. (Samara Regional Business Association Coalition 2004) This part of the Samara regional coalition's work was supported by policy input from the INDEM foundation, including through various studies on the scope of corruption and through training sessions on how entrepreneurs should deal with bribe-seeking officials.[42] OPORA conducted its national monitoring study on small business and corruption and produced a set of recommendations based in part on insights from the work of the coalitions in the CIPE project. (OPORA 2008) OPORA Vice President Dina Krylova, a recognized expert on the problem of corruption as it affects small business, partnered with INDEM in training sessions of regional business association coalitions devoted to anti-corruption efforts.[43]

A major part of the remedy for pervasive corruption identified in the Samara coalition's anti-corruption program is the role of the media, and of business associations and other civic organizations, in publicizing instances of corruption. The program envisages use of all available consultative avenues to raise the issue with regional and local executives and legislatures. It also points to the utility of expert analysis by legal experts from business associations to remove 'corruption engendering' formulations from draft legislation affecting business *('korruptsia-gennost')*. This is a central recommendation devised by INDEM as a means of bringing greater oversight from the business community over the performance of regional and local officials.

The Samara coalition's anti-corruption program adopted the specific goal of reducing corruption in the region's construction sector.[44] In adopting this purpose, the business associations argued that their objectives were aligned with the broader social concern about the short supply and high cost of housing in the region. The program suggests that corruption in the sector is in part due to contradictions between federal and regional laws applied to project approvals, gaps exploited by corrupt officials.

Regional administration's small business development efforts

The Samara Regional Administration's program for "Development of small and medium enterprise in the Samara Region" for 2009–2010 was adopted under the provisions of the 2007 federal law on SME support. (Samara Regional Administration 2009b)[45] The 2007 federal law's provisions allow regional SME promotion programs to be partly funded by the federal Ministry of Economic Development. The Ministry decides on the extent of its support for any given program on the basis of the quality and design of the programs.

The Samara region's program covering two years was funded with 195.42 million rubles, of which 72.6 million came from the federal budget. The program funded credit subsidies and other measures to ease small business financing as well as the creation of four business incubators aimed at supporting new companies, especially in technical and engineering fields and in agricultural processing.

Small business promotion efforts in the Samara region are the responsibility of the Regional Ministry of Economic Development, Investment and Trade headed by Minister Gabibulla Khasayev. Khasayev was a deputy governor under Titov's administration and has been closely associated with market-oriented economic reforms in the Samara region. (McFaul and Petrov 1997) Ministry department head Yevgeny Borisov has direct responsibility for the small business development program and for the region's policy toward small business development in general.

Minister Khasayev and department head Borisov participated in a national conference on SMEs organized in Moscow on May 25–26, 2010 by TPPRF and OPORA.[46] Borisov spoke at a first-day panel on institutional supports for small business development, which compared the experiences of several Russian regions and foreign countries' approaches to small business promotion. Participants were entrepreneurs, financiers and business association leaders. Laying out the Samara regional administration's small business development program, Borisov urged entrepreneurs themselves to participate more actively in giving input to policies to support small business development.

Borisov belongs to the generation of Russian entrepreneurs that came of age in the cooperatives movement. OPORA's Vladimir Tikhonov joined an improvised meeting with the author in Borisov's ministry office in 2010, and the two evidently worked together frequently and on a collegial footing.[47] Borisov alluded jovially to his business experience in the late 1980s, importing consumer goods into the Samara region, initially from East Germany and later from reunified Germany. He said it had been a no-holds-barred struggle *('boi bez pravil')* for the first entrepreneurs.

The Samara region, he said, had started early and produced more than its share of small businesses, but it was now clear that developing small business required institutional and infrastructural support from the federal and regional levels. Without an active policy of support, the scope of Russian small business would not expand decisively beyond the few sectors where it had established itself – wholesale and retail trade and consumer services. Encouraging outsourcing and industrial 'clustering' was one promising avenue to generate new areas of small business activity.[48] Another was to address the inadequacies of leasing finance for equipping new companies. Yet another avenue being pursued in the region was to ensure transparent and competitive access for SMEs to government procurement contracts at the regional and municipal level to SMEs. Finally, small business could play a much bigger role in contracting to provide 'communal services' such as water supply, heat, refuse collection and other services to apartment dwellers. The spinning-off of these services to private providers at affordable costs to consumers has been a major issue on the structural economic reform agenda in Russia since the early 2000s.

Borisov explained that the oblast's small business development program aimed to link the science and technology research of local universities into potential commercialization by entrepreneurs. Of some two hundred new ventures using advanced technology across Russia, 20 were based in the Samara region. He acknowledged the risk, however, that active state support for new small businesses could make firms dependent on soft conditions and unable to become fully competitive.

Borisov said the regional administration also promotes contacts for the region's SMEs with potential partners in other countries, including through including small business in trade delegations organized within Russia and abroad. For example the region's small business people participated in the regional administration's regular meetings with Turkish business delegations.

Borisov cited OPORA Rossii and its Samara regional organization as a key source of ideas for federal and regional policies. Other entrepreneurs' associations in the region were, he said, more local in focus, and tended to interact principally with their municipal administrations, where most of their concerns could be addressed. A regional association of SMEs in innovative (advanced technology based) sectors had recently been formed. The established sector-specific associations also remained important partners for the regional administration. OPORA, he said, helps to synthesize the views of all entrepreneurs into a coherent set of proposals. The regional Chamber was, he concluded, no longer the only business community interlocutor for the regional administration.

Samara city small business development program

The city of Samara's SME development program for 2008–2010 was approved by the city duma on September 27, 2007, with quarterly progress reviews assigned to the municipal duma's economics committee. (Samara City Administration 2007)[49] The head of the city's department for Industrial Policy, Entrepreneurship and Communications, Larissa Ermolenko, was responsible for implementing the program, which was funded at 149 million rubles.[50]

The program's main aims were to improve and simplify the legal-normative framework for small business, develop supportive institutions, provide training and information, support access to credit (by guaranteeing collateral) and develop access to foreign markets and attract foreign investors.[51] The regional Chamber of Commerce based in Samara, OPORA and other (unspecified) business associations are cited as partners in carrying out program objectives. A principal stated aim of the program was the establishment of a business incubator in Samara, funded by the city's revenues. This seems to be exceptional, as business incubators are generally projects of regional administrations.

The city's business incubator opened on June 2, 2010 with public information sessions.[52] Located in an extensively remodeled former school building, the incubator has several company office suites and large conference rooms. The competition for business start-ups to be sited at the incubator had just opened. The incubator carries on an active program of forums and information sessions disseminated via e-mails to interested people in the community and beyond. The incubator has launched a busy series of training and information sessions open to all local entrepreneurs. It functions in effect as an institution for exchange and coordination between entrepreneurs and the city administration. Vladimir Tikhonov and OPORA were closely involved in the launch of the incubator as well.

Channels and structures for small business associations' advocacy

Business associations in the Samara region are involved in advisory or consultative bodies vis-à-vis the governor and regional legislature, as well as with mayors and municipal legislatures, on the theme of improving the climate for small business development. There are also regular opportunities for policy discussions with the militia, prosecutors' offices and the regional representation of the Federal Anti-Monopoly Service.[53] Municipal engagement with small business in Samara is centered on the business incubator and its information and training programs, while in Togliatti the Chamber and business community are involved in promoting economic development in a general sense (as evidenced by their work on a long-term city renewal plan in 2010) and philanthropic initiatives with other civil society actors, as in *Fond Togliatti* (discussed later in this chapter).

Oleg Borisov, who served three terms in the Samara city duma and chaired the economic committee there, is chairman of the regional legislature's committee on industry and entrepreneurship. From this position, he has frequent contacts with OPORA and other business associations. On a regular basis, the regional administration is called upon to report to this committee on progress in the implementation of its program of SME development. Representatives of business associations are invited to speak at these hearings and offer policy suggestions.[54]

Tikhonov of OPORA, Fomichev of the Samara regional Chamber, representatives of the Russian Employers' Union (affiliate of the national RSPP), and two women entrepreneurs representing Samara-based entrepreneurs associations spoke at one such legislative hearing on October 13, 2009, chaired by Speaker Viktor Sasonov. The regional administration distributed to participants in the hearing a summary report of funds spent against program goals under the regional program to date. (Samara Regional Administration, 2009a)

Yevgeny Borisov presented a detailed program update on micro-credit and property lease/sale developments, the work of regional business incubators (one in Togliatti for technology-based companies and a newly established one for agro-businesses) and the launch of a consulting service for entrepreneurs funded by the administration. He discussed several new measures introduced to deal with the effects of the economic downturn on small business. Key specific problems as he saw it were the credit crunch, the affordability of gas and electricity tariffs and the devolution of some regulatory responsibilities to the newly formed self-regulating organization of construction companies. He acknowledged the chronic problem of changes in the tax regime and inspections by tax and other authorities.

Borisov pointed to the availability of subsidies for the long-term lease of premises and to regulations protecting tenant enterprises from dramatic changes in lease terms. The region was promoting credit access through its guarantee fund for micro-credit loans and was moving into funding micro-credit directly. The administration supported credit evaluation by lenders and partially guaranteed borrowers' collateral. New grants were available for entrepreneurs from among the unemployed or new college graduates. The competition for these had attracted more than 500 applications.

The presentations by business association leaders acknowledged the sincere efforts of the regional program but reported ongoing problems facing small business, especially in view of the sharp economic slowdown in 2009. Speaking for OPORA, Tikhonov emphasized the high tax burden and excessive inspections. Regulations and approvals needed to be further simplified, and punitive fines for infractions were too high. He said that new market supporting infrastructure was needed to develop the potential for small companies in agricultural processing companies in the region. Speaking also for small businesses in Samara, Nadezhda Suleimanova of the association *Vzaimodeystvie* criticized the city administration's performance on dealing with the leasing or purchasing of buildings and land, complained about utility tariffs and credit access. She suggested a special outreach to support women entrepreneurs.[55] Elena Solomko, leader of another small business group, cited many of the same concerns.

Speaking at the same session, the leader of the regional Union of Employers (RSPP) said the regional administration should sponsor the creation of technoparks to support clusters in various industrial sectors. He suggested that the opportunities for large firms to sponsor and develop smaller ones had not been fully exploited and submitted detailed proposal in writing. Samara Chamber president Valery Fomichev told the committee that the Chamber would submit two proposals for adapting legislation affecting small business.

Entrepreneurs in regional and municipal political office – contributions to the dispersion of regional and local political authority

As we have seen, regional politics in Samara have accommodated a degree of competition between governor and his administration, mayors of Samara and Togliatti and regional and municipal legislatures. In this section, we look at the role played by entrepreneurs or former entrepreneurs in the regional legislature.

As is well known, political parties have generally failed to take firm hold in structuring political competition in Russia's regions. (Golosov 2004; Hale 2006) However, parties have been more influential in regional legislative elections than in gubernatorial, mayoral or municipal legislative elections. Nevertheless, Konstantin Titov invested considerable effort in building a programmatically reformist party in the Samara region in his early years in office. To contest legislative elections in late 1993, Titov supported the formation of a regional proto-party, the *"Ob'edinenie Podderzhki Reform"* (Union of Support for Reform). (Golosov 2004) A leading OPR member was Oleg Sysuev, elected mayor of Samara in 1994. Reformists fared much better in Samara's regional legislative election of 1993 than in the national legislative elections held simultaneously.[56] The OPR was transformed into the regional chapter of Russia's Democratic Choice (DVR) headed by Oleg Borisov and RUFIL' Ibragimov in late 1994. (McFaul and Petrov 1997)

Biographies of all members of the regional legislature elected in 2007, along with their party affiliations and committee assignments are available on the legislature's website.[57] Half of the 50 deputies were elected by party lists, and the other half in single mandate races. The party list voting reflects a fair degree of dispersion of party support in the region, at least by comparison with the picture in Russia as a whole. Of the 25 seats apportioned from the party lists, United Russia had 11, CPRF 5, Just Russia 4, LDPR 3, and SPS and Greens 1 each. United Russia nevertheless had a commanding majority in the body by virtue of the affiliation of members elected from single mandate races.

The biographies of eight members clearly identify them as having founded or headed a business. Nine others are senior managers of privatized or state-owned industrial enterprises.[58] Of the entrepreneur-deputies elected from party lists, two were from United Russia, two were from Just Russia (SR) and one (Rufil' Ibragimov) was elected from the Union of Right Forces (SPS) as head of that party's list. From the single mandate deputies with entrepreneurial backgrounds, two joined the United Russia faction and the other, a female environmental activist, gave no party affiliation. Two of those entrepreneurs in the Just Russia caucus noted work experience with Yukos. Two entrepreneur-members cited experience in civic associations as well. Prominent banker Oleg Sinitsyn was Samara regional Rotary Club president and a leader of the regional banking association. Another member of the United Russia caucus, Dmitry Arishhenko founded in 2006 an NGO involved in community development called 'Initiativa.'

OPORA Samara's Tikhonov mentioned that OPORA worked closely in its lobbying work with around eight deputies in the regional duma who were receptive to OPORA's concerns because of their own entrepreneurial backgrounds. The legislative committee dealing with small business issues, and with which OPORA and other business associations have structured as well as informal interactions, was chaired by Oleg Borisov. Borisov, a strong proponent of small business development, and a key partner for OPORA and other business associations, was a leader in the democratic politics of the early 1990s in the region and an early advocate of market reforms. Oleg Borisov, now in his early 50s, joined the United Russia faction in the legislature.[59]

Rufil' Ibragimov, the sole deputy elected from the SPS party list, is an entrepreneur who emerged from the cooperatives movement and a member of the committee chaired by Borisov that dealt with small business issues. With Borisov, Ibragimov headed the region's branch of the liberal party DVR. (McFaul and Petrov 1997) Ibragimov's official biography shows that he was the regional party leader for Russia's Democratic Choice from 1993–2001, head of SPS in the oblast and headed SPS's successor party *Pravoe Delo.* The continued participation in regional politics of Borisov and Ibragimov, both central figures in the region's democratic politics of the early 1990s as well as being entrepreneurs, undoubtedly reinforced the favorable environment for entrepreneurship in the region.

Business, society and the press in the Samara region

The business community in Togliatti has an unusually strong participation in civic and social activism. Many of the Chamber's members are also active members of the Chamber-affiliated Mercury Club of Togliatti, which supports civic and charitable work as well as serving as an informal network for discussion and exchange of views about local developments.[60] The Togliatti Chamber's public events, such as the conference "society-business-government" held on the May 26 National Entrepreneurs' Day holiday in 2010, generate considerable interest and public discussion.[61] The Chamber's president sits on the board of the charitable foundation *Fond Togliatti.* This non-profit institution supports community revival in Togliatti by mobilizing charitable giving from corporate sources and awarding grants to local organizations on a competitive basis.[62] *Fond Togliatti* cooperates with the British Charities Aid Foundation and has also received funding from the Ford Foundation.

Rotary Club chapters in both Samara and Togliatti are engaged in civic and charitable activities.[63] Both clubs show all members with photos and professional affiliations at their websites. The Togliatti club has 47 members and the Samara club has 18. These Rotary Clubs count as members some of the most prominent owners of 'new' businesses in each city: companies in retail, services, finance and, in Samara's case, the leading regional cellphone company. The membership also encompasses journalists, professors, lawyers and a few local or regional officials. Women are well represented. The Togliatti club's civic work includes fundraising for a monument to the memory of the murdered mayor, Sergey Zhilkin, who was president of the Rotary club in 2006–2007 and rector of the university.

The regional press

A comprehensive list of periodicals published in Samara region lists 103 titles.[64] Twenty-five newspapers cover political, economic and social news in the region, of which 14 are published in Samara, 6 in Togliatti and 5 in other cities of the region. Of the newspapers published in Samara, five are local editions of the national newspapers, *Kommersant, Vedomosti, Moskovskiy Komsomolets, Komsomol'skaya Pravda* and *Argumenty i Fakty.* Two independent newspapers are the weeklies *Samarskoe Obozrenie* and *Togliattinskoe Obozrenie,* also appearing in online editions.[65] There are a number of online-only publications, including independent regional and national political and economic reporting.[66]

There are seven publications produced in Samara for a business readership and two in Togliatti. One of the seven is a regional edition of *Ekspert,* a leading national business magazine. Articles in these publications typically address problems facing business as well as opportunities, interview or profile noteworthy entrepreneurs, report on and analyze business and investment developments. These publications play a significant role in shaping the self-awareness of entrepreneurs and managers. *Delovoy Kvartal,* which has editions covering Samara and Perm among other regions, covers regional politics from a business perspective.

The relationship of the press to small business is most obvious for those publications (20 in Samara and 4 in Togliatti) consisting exclusively of classified advertisements. Another seven in Samara and one in Togliatti advertise houses and apartments for sale or rent, as well as remodeling or home repair services. Rounding out the categories of publication are those devoted to entertainment, lifestyle, fashion, family matters and culture and the arts. There are 16 such publications in Samara and 3 in Togliatti.

Civic memory: entrepreneurs and the 'usable' past – ideational antecedent conditions

From the beginnings of Russian settlement in the 16th century, the Volga region was a "frontier." Figes provides a vivid description of the human crosscurrents of the region in the 18th century, emphasizing its remoteness from imperial rule and its restiveness:

> During the eighteenth century the European settlement of the Volga region was increased by the establishment of the German colonies; by the imposition of serfdom in the north-western areas; and by the arrival of Russian and Ukrainian runaway serfs, debtors, political fugitives, Old Believers, and escaped convicts, seeking refuge in the remote areas by the Volga River, bordering the 'kingdom of the nomads'. The presence of these people, the volatility of the Cossacks, the grievances of the non-European population against the Russian rule, the newness of serfdom, and the consequent weakness of the state in the Volga region all helped to turn it into a bastion of banditry, libertarianism and anti-centralism.
>
> (Figes 1989:23)

The rich grain-producing land of the Samara *gubernia* (region) made it a leader in embracing commercial farming for export via the Volga river port at and near the city. Gerschenkron (1970) emphasizes the socio-economic and political consequences of the schismatic Old Believers in the Volga region and in Moscow in the first phase of Russian capitalist development in the middle of the 19th century. Their fortunes were based on the milling and transport of grain to the markets of central Russia and St. Petersburg. There were 203 merchants of the first and second guilds in Samara and about 3,000 in the gubernia by the end of the 19th century. (Samartseva 1994)

The Samara *gubernia* was the source of 14% of Russia's grain exports at the turn of the 20th century. (Samartseva 1994) The introduction of modern farming methods can in part be traced to the settlement of Germans in the Volga region beginning in the reign of Catherine the Great. Lankina (2010) uses historical data to explain divergences in regional democracy in contemporary Russia by reference to the extent of German settlement, which she claims have been associated with greater availability of primary education and literacy. The whole lower and middle Volga region was a beneficiary of this trend. The census of 1897 showed that 8.1% of the population of the Samara gubernia was German, 68.9% Russian, 8.7% Mordvinian, 6% Tatar, 2.1% Bashkir, 3.3% Chuvash and 0.06% Jewish. (Figes 1989)[67]

Land in private peasant ownership more than doubled to approximately 800,000 hectares from 1877 to 1905 and increased by a further 250,000 in the years 1905–1914. (Figes 1989)[68] The Samara gubernia far outstripped the other three Volga gubernii on this measure. Nevertheless, much of the Volga peasantry remained highly radicalized by the suppression of peasant uprisings in 1905–1907.

A vivid illustration of the presence of the past in contemporary elite awareness in Samara is the deputies' anteroom of the *Gubernaya Duma* (regional legislature). Occupying a remodeled historic building, formerly a college, the Duma displays an exhibition first mounted in 2006 as part of a national commemoration of the centenary of Russian parliamentarism, featuring portraits and brief biographies of members of the region's legislative assemblies beginning with the *zemstva,* and proceeding through the four pre-revolutionary state dumas, the Soviet-era legislatures and the four regional legislatures elected since 1994. The portraits show the merchant-industrialists, landowners and lawyers of the region's pre-revolutionary politics.

During 1918, Samara became the base for what Figes calls the "Ghost of the Constituent Assembly," which had been freely elected in 1917. The Samara region was a stronghold of the agrarian based Socialist Revolutionary SR, several of whose leaders came from the Volga region. In the Samara region, the SR party had won the elections to the Assembly overwhelmingly (Figes 1989) As touched upon in our discussion of the antecedents of the Samara Chamber of Commerce, some deputies elected to the short-lived Constituent Assembly took refuge in Samara and, in June 1918, formed a government claiming to rule all of Russia on behalf of the elected Constituent Assembly. They were defended by about 40,000 anti-Bolshevik Czech and Slovak troops. The authority formed was called the Committee of Members of the Constituent Assembly, the *Komuch.*

Viktor Mikhailovich Chernov, a native of the Samara region, was elected chairman of the Constituent Assembly at its first and only session on January 5–6, 1918. Having fled to Samara, he became the head of the *Komuch* and was proclaimed the 'leader of democracy' by his supporters. Figes notes that "it was hoped he would become the figurehead of a national crusade." (Figes 1996:578) The authority of the *Komuch* spread in June–August of 1918 to the Simbirsk, Kazan, Ufa and Saratov regions. Thousands of so-called former people, especially right SR members, flocked to Samara. By the end of its four-month reign, 100 members of the dissolved Constituent Assembly had come to Samara to join the *Komuch.* (Figes 1996)

The *Komuch* authorities' rule represented a program of moderation and compromise in impossible conditions. Much of the region's peasantry withheld their support, suspicious of any accommodation with former landowners. Urban factory workers were already squarely in the Bolshevik camp. (Figes 1989; Suny 2011) In municipal duma elections across the Samara region in August–September 1918, the SR party maintained its dominance while the liberal-conservative parties performed fairly well in larger cities. (Figes 1989)

The Red victory in the civil war was in part decided by the failure of the *Komuch* to consolidate its rule and defend its territory and allow the white armies of Denikin in the South and Kolchak in Siberia to join up and control the strategic agricultural potential and transportation networks of the Volga. (Figes 1989) "The survival of the Samara government, and arguably the whole anti-Bolshevik movement, depended on the union of the anti-Bolshevik forces on the Southern and Eastern Fronts." The Red triumph and the White loss was, as Figes concludes, "a damned close-run thing." (Figes 1989:182)

Chernov and the right SRs ended their uneasy alliance with the White forces with the November 1918 coup installing Kolchak as ostensible leader of Russia. Thus ended definitively what Suny calls "the moderate, 'democratic' phase' of the civil war," a phase in which the Samara region had played a principal role. (Suny 2011:92)

During the period of *Komuch* rule, Viktor Chernov lived in a suite at the gracious National Hotel in the main avenue of Samara's historical center. The hotel was built in 1910 by one of Samara's leading merchants, Vasiliy Mikhailovich Suroshnikov, who, like many of Samara's early merchant-industrialists, made his fortune in bread production and trade. He was elected to the regional duma and headed the Samara regional chapter of the Red Cross.

Having failed to roll back the Kolchak coup, Viktor Chernov and many other right SRs carried on their political work from exile in Prague and later in France. Chernov moved on to New York, where he died in 1952. Having spent decades as the Intourist Tsentralnaya, the historic National Hotel has been freshened up by its private owners and welcomes budget conscious tourists, business travelers and the odd American academic researcher.

The region and the model – conclusions

The Samara region closely approximates the paradigmatic case shown as Figure 3.1. The democratic 'impulse' engendered a strong 'reply' in the form of private entrepreneurship in the region. The decisive break from Soviet-style governance represented by governor Konstantin Titov's assumption of regional leadership was reinforced and institutionalized in repeated genuinely contested elections, including those of the first mayors of Samara and Togliatti, with relatively clear programmatic choices available to voters. The Samara region saw the rise of a cadre of reformist elites, among them entrepreneurs, some of whom remained in prominent positions nearly two decades later.

The 'feedback' effect running from entrepreneurs to regional democratization is, as we have seen, likely to operate principally on four aspects of democratization: openness or transparency in the exercise of power, the independence and diversity of media, the range and activism of civil society organizations and the dispersion of political authority. These together can be considered a single factor, *civic-ness*. Business associations representing entrepreneurs function both to create a group identity among entrepreneurs and to express their interests in public relative to municipal and regional governments. They therefore are part of the contribution of small business owners to civil society activism. Through their lobbying activities, they also make a contribution to openness in policy deliberations at the regional and municipal level.

The role of municipal administrations in larger cities relative to small business lobbying is a crucial component of the feedback arrow in the Samara regional case. In Samara *de facto* and in Togliatti *de jure* the most active business associations representing the interests of small business are doing so relative to the municipal rather than the regional administration. OPORA Chairman Viktor Tarkhov was at the same time the mayor of Samara, and the Togliatti Chamber's Vladimir Zhukov a long-standing member of local duma and former head of city administration.

Business associations' work in the Samara region has been conducted in public and has generated competition among various groups for representation of entrepreneurs' interests. Business advocacy seems to have had some modest success in shaping policies at the municipal level in both Samara and Togliatti. Cooperation between the Chamber and broader social and civic activity is particularly pronounced in Togliatti.

The Samara oblast's economy is dominated by nationally prominent big companies and by substantial foreign multinational investment, but the significant inroads of 'new' business into economic life is in some ways mirrored by the entry of entrepreneurs in considerable numbers into the regional duma. This participation represents the contribution of small business owners – elected to legislative or executive office – to the dispersion of political power. Viktor Tarkhov as mayor of Samara was receptive to small business development and spearheaded with OPORA the city's small business incubator and other small business promotion programs. The role of the regional legislature in sustaining the priority of small business development is probably due at least in part to the effectiveness of associations' lobbying and policy proposals. The case of Tarkhov as business association leader and as mayor makes explicit the association between contested politics and the defense of entrepreneurs' interests.

The relative dispersion of political authority among the governor, regional legislature and the local administrations in Togliatti and Samara is reflected by an associational environment that is more plural and competitive than the norm. The defense of the prerogatives of local government and elected mayors in both Samara and Togliatti, as well as the unwillingness of Togliatti to play second fiddle to Samara, seems to create conditions where institutional channels for consultation between business and government on such questions as entrepreneurship promotion are multiple, productive and public. Meetings with and observations of the interactions among the business associations and the regional and municipal governments in the region were marked by considerable openness, informality and reciprocal confidence.

The Samara case is also paradigmatic because the antecedent social conditions and historical experience are supportive of democracy and private enterprise. The

Samara region is among the country's most urbanized, industrialized and educated. These are among the structural antecedent conditions that seem to predispose a region toward both greater and more open political contestation and larger numbers of incorporated small firms. At an ideational level, the region's 'distance' from the centralizing tradition of Russian statehood is manifest in its role in anti-Bolshevik politics in the Civil War period and in the recovered histories of Samara's merchant-industrialists.

Titov's survival in office until 2007 and Tarkhov's quixotic obstruction of regional re-centralization in Samara until 2010 are both manifestations of a degree of political pluralism in the region. Titov never locked down contestation among other centers of power and cultivated the input of business and other public groups. His failed presidential bid against Putin caused even bolder public feuding and vying among various interests, which was healthy from standpoint of participation by groups such as entrepreneurs' associations in political and civic life.

Regional legislators involved in issues related to the business climate, in particular Oleg Borisov and RUFIL' Ibragimov, have their roots in the early democratic movements of the 1990s and are certainly a part of the explanation for the fairly lively and substantive consultative channels for small business, of which the Duma hearing recounted in this chapter is an example. Yevgeny Borisov and Larissa Ermolenko, the directors of the regional and municipal small business development programs, have backgrounds in small business or business associations and are therefore open to and interested in taking input from business associations and entrepreneurs. The importance of the region to early capitalist development in the pre-revolutionary period and its centrality to Russia's last democratic experiment in 1918 are present in the awareness of many entrepreneurs as well as business, academic and governing elites. In Togliatti, business lobbying on behalf of small business is tightly linked to civic and charitable work through the Fond Togliatti, Rotary and Mercury Club.

Notes

1 The Samara region is also the most urbanized of the four cases in this study, with the Perm Region *(Kray)* in second place at 75% in 2009.

2 Lapina and Chirikova reported that the share of regional budget revenue from AvtoVaz in 2002 was 55%, the same figure cited in personal interviews in 2009 with several sources in Samara and Togliatti.

3 "Renault and Nissan in Parts Tie-Up with AvtoVaz" *Financial Times,* July 20, 2011. Renault itself, nationalized after WWII, was long the French 'national champion' and dominated its home market. This is likely the role sought by the Russian state shareholder, Rosstechnologii, for a revamped, modernized and profitable AvtoVaz. A cooperative arrangement between General Motors and AvtoVaz was not successful.

4 This point is emphasized in the opening remarks of then Deputy Governor Gabibulla Khasayev to a 2005 regional development conference in Samara. (Grigor'ev 2005)

5 Italian BancaIntesa was among the earliest foreign banks in the Russian market and in 2006 acquired a large stake in KMB (Kredit Malogo Biznesa), launched by the EBRD in 1993 and acquired KMB fully in 2010. In 2010 Intesa's Russian subsidiary was the sixth largest financier to SMEs in Russia.

6 Frye (2002) concluded, on the basis of entrepreneurs' surveys in eight regions, that a model of 'exchange' (as opposed to either state capture or business capture) character-ized the relations between companies and regional administrations. Evidence for a sub-stantial shift toward rules-based lobbying by companies is also presented in Yakovlev (2006).

7 http://www.adm.samara.ru/en/gubernator/1511/?printable=1. Accessed November 10, 2009.

8 Tarkhov biography at Samara Business Consulting website http://smbc.ru/samara/peoples/tarhov_viktor_aleksandrovich/. Accessed September 1, 2011.

9 Personal interviews, Alla Chirikova, May 22, 2010 and Alexey Titkov, May 20, 2010, Moscow.

10 Aleksey Titov's interests in banking in the region are said still to be considerable. http://63.ru/rich/57.html. Accessed September 12, 2011.

11 A list of American Chamber of Commerce in Russia members based in the Samara region in 2010 gives 56 company names, one of the largest for any region outside Moscow.

12 http://www.chaskor.ru/p.php?id=1214. Accessed September 3, 2011. States that Zhilkin has been a 'cult figure' in Togliatti and that his death in 2008 marked a defini-tive end to the democratic hopes of the 1990s. The site also links to the national televi-sion news report (*Vesti*) of the still unsolved murder by two knife-wielding assailants.

13 http://www.kommersant.com/p796106/r_500/Togliatti_Mayor_Corruption/. Accessed August 30, 2011.

14 Comment made on Radio Svoboda by Lyudmila Kuzmin of the independent electoral observation NGO Golos. http://www.svobodanews.ru/content/transcript/2058583.html. Accessed September 3, 2011.

15 For example "Pod Merom Tol'yatti Zagorelos' Kreslo" *Kommersant* (Samara) 147:4445, August 13, 2010 reports on a petition for Pushkov's resignation.

16 GosKomStat (2001) gives the number of small companies in 1995 as 877,300 and in 2000 as 879,300. Although they are not analytically as relevant to this study as small incorporated companies (for reasons elucidated in Chapter 3), it is nevertheless important to recall that individual entrepreneurs are not included in these statistics and outnumber registered companies by around 3 to 1.

17 Over period 1995–2000, Smolensk and Perm regions saw declines in the numbers of small companies and Rostov saw a rise from 21,400 in 1995 to 25,000 in 2000 (but with two years where numbers of companies fell).

18 Personal interview, Vladimir Tikhonov and Larissa Ermolenko, June 2, 2010, Samara.

19 Personal interviews and e-mail communications, Timothy Tarrant, October 13, 2009 and June 2, 2010, Samara.

20 Company website http://www.vvv-avia.ru/rus/skorost-komfort-i-bezopasnost.html. Accessed September 1, 2011.

21 Personal interview, Olga Plotnikova, Director, Regional Association Development, OPORA Rossii, June 28, 2010, Moscow. Leaders of OPORA and Chambers of Com-merce, as will become clear from the case studies, often have previously served in regional legislatures, ministries or as mayor.

22 In an informal conversation on May 20, 2011 in Washington, OPORA Vice President for International Relations, Sergey Moiseev, mentioned that OPORA's Samara regional chapter was no longer headed by Tarkhov.

23 See the discussion of Samara's small business program on below. The author receives e-mails weekly on the training and networking events of the Samara business incubator.

24 This is based on spending two working days with Tikhonov in Samara in June 2010 and several interviews in October 2009.

25 Personal interview, Vladimir Tikhonov, October 12, 2009. In case this number of mem-bers seemed small, Tikhonov hastened to add that the (prerevolutionary liberal) Kadet

party never had mass membership. As is typical across OPORA regional branch leaders, Tikhonov seemed to focus much more on effectiveness and access than on expanding membership.

26 Larissa Ermolenko's husband, Igor Ermolenko, a professor at Samara State University, is regional chairman of the Yabloko party and the author of an informative blog commenting on regional social and political issues.

27 http://www.opora.ru/regional/#view/regional/764/. Accessed September 9, 2011.

28 Extended personal interviews on June 1, 2010 with Chamber President Vladimir Zhukov (now the governing board chairman) and Vice President Vitaly Matveev (who became Chamber president in 2011).

29 The 1993 constitution sets out the broad outlines of municipal 'self-government' *(samoupravlenie)*, and this was further elaborated in a 1995 federal law (Gel'man, Ryzhenkov, Belokurova and Borisova 2008: 13–24).

30 Zhukov's biography on the Togliatti city duma website http://dumatlt.ru/deputies/dep_v/zhukov.phpof. Accessed September 2, 2011. The choice of the name 'Decembrist' by the faction signals a liberal-constitutional outlook and is another example of the self-conscious reference of today's politics to 19th-century democratic aspirations.

31 Rybakov, also interviewed for this project on October 7, 2009, has been one of the national Chamber's principal partners with the CIPE program and is the author of a book placing the TPPRF's structure and mission in the context of global approaches to organizing Chambers (Rybakov and Fedotov 2009).

32 http://www.ccitogliatti.ru/. Accessed September 11, 2011. In the course of 2011, the Samara regional Chamber began listing all members on its site as well.

33 OPORA Rossii President Sergey Borisov made the same point in his speech to the plenary session of the OPORA-TPPRF Small Business Conference in Moscow, May 26, 2010.

34 http://tppsamara.ru/about-tpp-so/history. Accessed August 9, 2011 as well as interview with staff director at the Samara Chamber Svetlana Spicenok, May 31, 2010, Samara. Spicenok mentioned with pride that the Samara chamber is the oldest in Russia. Neklyutin, heir to a prosperous family business in grain trade and bakeries, was later a minister in the Kolchak cabinet, emigrated to the United States where he had success in business in Seattle and died in 1978. http://www.hrono.ru/biograf/bio_n/neklyutin.php Accessed June 10, 2010.

35 Biographical sketch of Ardalin http://63.ru/rich/5.html. Accessed September 3, 2011.

36 http://tppsamara.ru/about-tpp-so/pravlenia. Accessed August 9, 2011.

37 http://tppsamara.ru/komitets/cpp invites participation by entrepreneurs in this committee and gives the names and affiliations of its principal members. Accessed September 1, 2011.

38 http://tppsamara.ru/reestr. Accessed September 10, 2011.

39 Personal interview, Valeriy Fomichev, President Samara Regional Chamber, May 16, 2010.

40 Personal interviews, Aleksandr Raevsky, CIPE Moscow office director and CIPE project documents.

41 http://www.deloros.ru/main.php?mid=157 and http://www.rotarysamara.ru/. Accessed September 15, 2011.

42 A practical guide is the brochure produced by Chamber of Commerce and Industry, Novorossisk Region (2006) "U Vas Proverka?" (Are You Being Inspected?)

43 Personal interview, OPORA Rossii Vice President Dina Krylova, September 23, 2009, Moscow.

44 The World Bank Group's annual "Doing Business" studies have identified construction permitting and licensing as well as urban land tenure as one of the most burdensome issues affecting the conduct of business in Russia.

45 Program text at the regional Ministry of Economic Development, Investment and Trade (MEDIT) site http://www.economy.samregion.ru/programm/obl_p/pro_2009/. Accessed September 20, 2011.

46 Attended by the author.

47 Personal interview, Yevgeny Borisov, June 2, 2010, Samara.

48 Minister Khasayev's speech at the plenary session of the Chamber-OPORA small business conference in Moscow on May 26, 2010 stressed the oblast's interest in 'clustering,' which OPORA's Tikhonov noted that OPORA Rossii had embraced at the organization's 2006 meeting in Irkutsk.

49 Program documents available at http://city.samara.ru/administration/program/1151. Accessed August 10, 2011.

50 Ermolenko continued to serve as department head under Tarkhov's successor as mayor Dmitry Azarov.

51 Small business is an important source of tax revenue for the city. According to the program document, most of the small companies in the city of Samara pay the ENVD tax *(edinnyi nalog na vmenennyi dokhod)*, 90% of which goes to the city's budget.

52 Attended by the author. Around 40–50 people were seated in the meeting room to hear Ermolenko's introductory presentation.

53 Interview, Vladimir Tikhonov, June 2, 2010. These structures are fairly standard across all four cases in this study. They differ mainly in associations' assessments of the sincerity and commitment of the government agencies involved. The Samara region's principal distinction is in the sincere engagement of municipal administrations in both Samara and Togliatti as well as in the openness and substance of legislative review at the regional level of small business development programs.

54 Attended by the author as a guest of OPORA Samara.

55 Suleimanova was a member of the oblast's *Obshchestvennaya Palata* (Social Chamber) from 2008–2011.

56 See Table 3.1 on page 54.

57 http://samgd.ru/deputies_c/. Accessed August 21, 2011. This is the fourth *gubernskaya duma*; its predecessors having served in 1994–1996, 1997–2000 and 2001–2006. The membership of all four bodies is available on the site.

58 Nine other deputies are senior managers of privatized or state-owned industrial enterprises.

59 A series of reports on "Samara's 100 richest" gives Borisov's principal interests initially in retail and later in commercial real estate and most recently in finance. This report also states that he was detained for two years during which a criminal case against him was investigated and dropped. http://63.ru/rich/11.html. Accessed September 12, 2011.

60 http://ccitogliatti.ru/. Accessed September 20, 2011.

61 One of the Chamber's networking events has been an annual chartered cruise on the Volga. A pastiche of Repin's painting (Burlaki), with the faces of those taking part in one of the cruises replacing those of the original barge-pullers, hangs in Zhukov's office.

62 Fond Togliatti website http://www.fondtol.org/. Accessed September 20, 2011. When the author arrived to interview Chamber President Zhukov and Vice President Matveev, Zhukov was wrapping up a meeting with Fond Togliatti officials and a Swiss children's charity. Zhukov's place on the foundations' board has now been assumed by Matveev as Chamber president.

63 http://www.rotarytlt.ru/index.html and http://www.rotarysamara.ru/. Accessed September 2, 2011.

64 http://www.media-atlas.ru/regionmedia/Regional. Accessed July 25, 2011.

65 http://www.63media.ru/ and http://www.tltoboz.ru/. Accessed August 1, 2011

66 http://www.politsamara.ru/.

67 American descendants of Volga Germans are among the professors of agricultural sciences from the University of South Dakota working with counterparts at Samara State University on reviving and developing the region's agriculture.
68 Converted from the Russian measure *desiatina,* equal to 1.09 hectares.

References

Central Electoral Commission Russian Federation. (2001) *Vybory v Organy Gosurdanst-vennoy Vlasti Sub'yektov Rossiyskoy Federatsii 1997–2000.* Moscow.

Chamber of Commerce and Industry City of Togliatti. (2010) *Gorodskaya Conferentsia "Obshchestvo-Biznis-Vlast'"* http://www.ccitogliatti.ru/news/theme/day?n3603. Accessed June 15, 2010.

Chamber of Commerce and Industry, Novorossisk region. (2006) *U Vas Proverka: Shkola Vyzhivanniya Predprinimatelya.* Novorossisk, Russian Federation.

Figes, Orlando. (1989) *Peasant Russia, Civil War: The Volga Countryside in Revolution (1917–1921).* Oxford, UK: Clarendon Press.

Figes, Orlando. (1996) *A People's Tragedy: The Russian Revolution 1891–1924.* New York: Penguin Books.

FINCA. (2010) *Russian Client Slides.* Samara, Russia.

FINCA. (2011) *Market Review Samara 2011.* Samara, Russia.

Fish, M. Steven. (1995) *Democracy from Scratch: Opposition and Regime in the New Russian Revolution.* Princeton, NJ: Princeton University Press.

Freeland, Chrystia. (2000) *Sale of the Century: Russia's Wild Ride from Communism to Capitalism.* New York, NY: Crown Business.

Frye, Timothy. (2002) Capture or Exchange? Business Lobbying in Russia. *Europe-Asia Studies* 54 (7):1017–1036.

Gel'man, Vladimir, Sergey Ryzhenkov, Elena Belokurova and Nadezhda Borisova. (2008) *Reforma Mestnoy Vlasti v Gorodakh Rossii, 1991–2006.* St. Petersburg, Russia: European University in St. Petersburg.

Gerschenkron, Alexander. (1970) *Europe in the Russian Mirror: Four Lectures in Economic History.* Cambridge, UK: Cambridge University Press.

Golosov, Grigoriy. (2004) *Political Parties in the Regions of Russia: Democracy Unclaimed.* Boulder, CO: Lynne Rienner.

Goskomstat Rossii. (2001) *Regions of Russia (Regiony Rossii).* Moscow: State Committee of the Russian Federation for Statistics.

Grigor'ev, Leonid. (ed.) (2005) *Aspekty Regional'nogo Razvitiya: Vzglad Iz Samarskoi Oblasti – Regiona-Lidera.* Moscow, Russia: Moskovskiy Obshchestvennyi Nauchnyi Fond.

Gutorova, Mariya. (2010, October 11) "Resurs na Rasput'e" *Kommersant Vlast* 40 (894).

Hale, Henry E. (2006) *Why Not Parties in Russia? Democracy, Federalism and the State.* Cambridge, UK and New York: Cambridge University Press.

Independent Institute for Social Policy (IISP). (2008) *Regional "Portrait" – Samara Oblast* http://atlas.socpol.ru/portraits/samar.shtml. Accessed October 25, 2009.

Konitzer, Andrew. (2005) *Voting for Russia's Governors: Regional Elections and Accountability Under Yeltsin and Putin.* Washington, DC and Baltimore, MD: Woodrow Wilson Center Press and Johns Hopkins University Press.

Lankina, Tomila. (2010) *Historical Influences on Regional Democracy Variations in Russia: The Forgotten Legacies of Western Engagement.* Paper presented at American Political Science Association Annual Meeting, Washington, DC.

Lapina, Natalia and Alla Chirikova. (2002) *Regiony-Lidery: Ekonomika i Politicheskaya Dinamika*. Moscow: Institute of Sociology, Russian Academy of Sciences (IS-RAN).

Mau, Vladimir and Vadim Stupin. (1997) The Political Economy of Russian Regionalism. *Communist Economies and Economic Transformation* 9 (1):5–25.

McFaul, Michael. (2001) *Russia's Unfinished Revolution: Political Change from Gorbachev to Putin*. Ithaca, NY: Cornell University Press.

McFaul, Michael and Nikolai Petrov. (eds.) (1997) *Politicheskiy Almanakh Rossii: Sotsialno-Politicheskie Portrety Regionov*. Moscow: Carnegie Moscow Center.

Nikolaeva, Lyudmila. (2009, September 29) Oborona Vladimira Artyakova. *Delovoy Kvartal* 10–14. Samara.

OPORA Rossii. (2008) *Razvitie Malogo i Srednogo Predprinimatel'stva v Regionakh Rossii "Index OPORY"*. Moscow.

Orttung, Robert W. (ed.) (2000) *The Republics and Regions of the Russian Federation: A Guide to Politics, Policies and Leaders*. Armonk, NY and London, UK: M.E. Sharpe.

Petrov, Nikolai. (2006) Naznacheniya gubernatorov: itogi pervogo goda. *Carnegie Moscow Center Briefing* 8 (3).

Petrov, Nikolai and Alexei Titkov. (2006) *Demokratichnost' Rossiskikh Regionov*. http://atlas.socpol.ru/indexes/index_democr.shtml. Accessed Novermber 10, 2010.

Petrov, Nikolai and Alexei Titkov. (2013) *Reyting Demokratichnosti Regionov Moskovskogo Tsenta Karnegi: 10 Let v Stroyu*. Moscow: Carnegie Moscow Center. http://carnegie.ru/publications/?fa=55853. Accessed December 1, 2014.

Rosstat (Federal'naya Sluzhba Gosudarstvennoy Statistiki). (2002, 2008, 2010a) *Regiony Rossii: Sotsial'no-Ekonomicheskie Pokazateli*.

Rosstat (Federal'naya Sluzhba Gosudarstvennoy Statistiki). (2009) *Maloe i Srednee Predprimatel'stvo v Rossii*.

Rosstat (Federal'naya Sluzhba Gosudarstvennoy Statistiki). (2010b) *Goroda Rossii*.

Russia: All Regions Trade and Investment Guide. (2008) Samara Region. London, UK: CTEC and Effective Technology Ltd.

Rybakov, A.M., and V.I. Fedotov. (2009) *Vovlechenie v Chlenstvo*. Moscow: National Endowment for Democracy and CIPE.

Samara City Administration. (2007) *Tselevaya Programma Podderzhki i Razvitiya Malogo i Srednego Predprinimatel'stva Gorodskogo Okruga Samara na 2008–2012 Gody*. Samara.

Samara City Administration. (2009) *Katalog Predpriyatiy Malogo i Srednogo Biznesa Gorodskogo Okruga Samara*. Samara: Samara Business Incubator.

Samara Regional Administration. (2009a) *Realizatsiya Meropriyatiy oblastnoy Tselevoy programmy "Razvitie Malogo i Srednogo Predprinimatel'stva v Samarskoy Oblasti" na 2009–2010 na 2009 godu": Discussion paper for October regional parliamentary committee hearing.*

Samara Regional Administration and Ministry of Economic Development Investment and Trade. (2009b) *Regional Program for "Development of Small and Medium Enterprises in the Samara Region" 2009–2010*.

Samara Regional Business Association Coalition. (2004) *Samarskaya Regional'naya Antikorruptsionnaya Programma Delovogo Soobshchestva (Samara Regional Anticorruption Program of the Business Community)*. CIPE small business advocacy project document.

Samara Regional Government (Pravitel'stvo Samarkoy Oblasti). (2005) *Konstantin Titov – Brief Biography* (in English).

Samartseva, Olga. (1994) *History of Entrepreneurship in Samara Region*, Samara State University, Samara.

Suny, Ronald Grigor. (2011) *The Soviet Experiment: Russia, the USSR, and the Successor States*. Second ed. Oxford, UK: Oxford University Press.

Transparency International and INDEM Foundation. (2002) *Corruption Perceptions Index for Russia's Regions*. Moscow, Russia.

Trifonov, Vlad. (2002, May 29) "Journalist Is Killed by His Own Subject: Why Editor of Togliatti Observer Was Killed." *Current Digest of the Russian Press* 18 (54):2–12.

Yakovlev, Andrei. (2006) *Agenty Modernizatsii*. Moscow, Russia: State University Higher School of Economics.

5 The Smolensk region

Small business and the uses of adversity

About one third of the Smolensk oblast's almost one million inhabitants live in the city of Smolensk. The city lies on the main rail link running from Warsaw through Minsk to Moscow and the main Moscow-Minsk highway. The region has several other cities of between 40,000 and 50,000 inhabitants. (Rosstat 2010b) Three of them, Vyasma, Safonovo and Yartsevo, lie on the eastward route toward Moscow. The other principal city, Roslavl, is on the route south toward Bryansk. The two largest cities after Smolensk, Vyasma and Roslavl, are referenced in historical documents of the 12th century and founded in their modern form in the 18th century. In the southern part of the oblast near Roslavl, the town of Desnogorsk founded in 1974 is home to the nuclear power station, a major industrial asset. (Chamber of Commerce and Industry Smolensk Region 2008c; Smolensk Regional Administration, Departments of Economic Development and Trade and International and Interregional Cooperation and Tourism 2009)

The oblast's population fell from 1.16 million in 1991 to 983 million in 2008, a decrease of 18%, as against the 4% decline for Russia as a whole in the same period. (Goskomstat Rossii 2001; Rosstat 2002, 2010a) Conversations about the region's challenges often dwell on the problem of population loss, especially from rural areas. The decline in the region's population reflects the attractiveness of study and work in Moscow, St. Petersburg, or abroad for the region's most talented graduates.

The Smolensk region stands out for the strong electoral performance of conservative and traditionalist politicians in the freely contested elections of the early 1990s.[1] From a political economy standpoint, it may be that the traditionalism and conservatism of the Smolensk region stems in part from the fact that the region's industry had been oriented toward consumer markets in the USSR, and, unlike the natural resource extraction and processing industries in such regions as Samara or Perm, or the large scale agriculture of regions such as Rostov, the Smolensk region's industrial enterprises could not readily be reoriented to new markets. On the other hand, voters in manufacturing centers such as Vyasma and Yartsevo were more favorable to the liberal economic reforms of the early Yeltsin years than was the city of Smolensk itself. (McFaul and Petrov 1997)

Economic geography and business history – antecedent structural conditions

The earliest written records of the city of Smolensk date from the year 863, when it was a settlement of an eastern Slavic people, the *Krivichi*. On the heights above the Dnieper River, early Smolensk was a vital link in the legendary early trading route "from the Varangians to the Greeks," or from the Baltic and Scandinavian north to the Black Sea.

The leading industrial sector in Smolensk's early 20th-century economy was textile production, much of which was based on local cultivation of flax. Famed British observer of Russia in the early 20th century, Donald Mackenzie Wallace was surprised on a visit to the region in 1903 to find how flax cultivation had spurred the adoption of advanced agricultural techniques even by smallholders. He noted the evident prosperity of much of the countryside compared with many other rural regions of Russia at the time.[2] The textile industry in the city of Yartsevo became a center of worker agitation in 1905 and again after the Tsar's abdication in 1917. (Fainsod 1958)

Hickey (1996) discusses how the liberal landowners strongly represented in the Smolensk *zemtsvo* since the 1890s held the reins of leadership in the spring of 1917 with support from various civic organizations including the merchants and the nascent industrialists' association. He argues that the liberals' notion of the common interests of citizens irrespective of social class or occupational status in a justly governed and undivided 'society' (*'obshchestvo'*) was overwhelmed by the revolutionary parties' insistence on class conflict and the redress of social injustice. Carr (1980) argues that liberalism failed in late imperial Russia because the commercial elements that underpinned it in other national contexts were never strong enough. This may apply to the city of Smolensk, where, according to a 1914 business guide there were only 30 enterprises. (Hickey 1996)

The overwhelmingly agrarian economy of the region and the dominance of nobles in the region's liberal parties may have contributed to the very weak association between capitalist development and liberal politics in the Smolensk region. (Hickey 2004) Ethnic divisions within the ranks of the commercial and industrial elite may also have played a role. Owen (1991) argues that the prominence of members of ethnic and national minorities – Jews, Germans, Poles and others – in capitalist development in the last half-century of Tsarism contributed to the political inertness and defensiveness of business elites. The Jewish share in the population of Smolensk in 1914 was between 7–10%, with the majority being industrial workers, artisans or small tradesmen. In the first decade of the 20th century, ten Jewish merchant-industrialists had been admitted to the First Guild, more than in any city outside the Pale of Settlement. (Hickey 1998)

Although the oblast's population is today overwhelmingly Russian by ethnicity, the city of Smolensk and the western districts of the oblast have been closely linked historically to neighboring Belarus.[3] The transformation of the provincial border between the oblast and Belarus into an international boundary provoked human and economic dislocations. During the first troubled decade after the Soviet Union's collapse, many Smolensk residents tended to see Belarus as better governed and managed than their own city, riven as it was by contract killings and scandals. According to many observers and analysts, the long and porous international border helped to create a special susceptibility of the region to smuggling and other criminalized business.

The failure of regional agriculture, especially flax cultivation, to recover has spurred relentless rural depopulation. Throughout the Soviet period, the eastern city of Vyasma was a center for linen textile production based on local flax. Other agricultural ventures, such dairy and meat production, have recovered more than flax cultivation and have attracted some investment. (Russia All Regions Trade and Investment Guide 2008)

The nuclear power station at Desnogorsk and associated electricity generation and distribution assets meet the region's power needs and account for about 30% of the region's industrial production. (Russia All Regions Investment Guide 2008) The power station is held by one of the power generating companies spun off in the dissolution of UES, the former national electricity monopoly. The diamond cutter and jewelry maker Kristall is the best known and most resilient of the region's large companies from the Soviet era, remaining to date fully state-owned and having well-established relations with the principal diamond mining concern Alrosa.[4] Kristall's production is almost entirely for export, and it is a leading employer in Smolensk. Soviet-era manufacturing enterprises such as Smolensk's refrigerator manufacturer and the automotive ZIL assembly plant at Roslavl have had some success in restructuring, but are well below the employment and production levels of their Soviet heyday.

As there was little heavy industry in the Smolensk region, there was also little in the way of defense-related industry, by comparison at least with such regions as Samara, Perm and Rostov. Nevertheless, on a human and social level, the dissolution of the Soviet military left a deep trace on the Smolensk region. Smolensk residents interviewed for this project observed that, although the region was never settled by large numbers of workers from elsewhere in USSR, service in the Soviet military did bring some outsiders to Smolensk in the post-war years. Among the small businesspeople interviewed by the author, previous military service, or family relations to service members, was common.

Smolensk's institutions of higher learning were a major source of local pride in the Soviet period, and their recovery is very important to the talent base upon which entrepreneurial activity is built. The city's medical and dental schools are still a particular source of regional pride but are strapped for resources. A vivid illustration is the case of a physician and former medical school professor, who now finds a comparatively comfortable income running a small fee-paying clinic in the city's bustling central market.[5] The salaries of doctors, teachers and professors employed by the state have notoriously failed to keep pace with pay for comparable work in the private sector. In the face of these developments, Smolensk's locally trained dentists have embraced private provision of care, opening a profusion of busy private clinics.

The economic recovery in Russia from 1999 to 2008 gathered pace in Smolensk region in its final years. The numbers of incorporated small companies relative to the workforce increased sharply from 2006 to 2008.[6]

For Smolensk, the French saying could be turned on its head: "Plus ça reste la meme chose, plus ça change." The public square called in Tsarist times Bazarnaya Ploshchad (Market Square), still bears its Soviet name Kolkhoznaya (collective farm) square. According to a grisly photograph at the WWII museum lodged in the city's Kremlin walls, resistance suspects were hanged on this square under the occupation. Nearby, the crowded and cheerfully chaotic market, focus for local individual entrepreneurs, sells affordable agricultural produce, household goods and clothing. The city's newer retail stores and supermarkets attract the comparatively well heeled, while the market serves bargain shoppers. Kolkhoznaya Ploshchad was the site chosen for McDonald's first restaurant in Smolensk.

Impulse: the democratic breakthrough and its institutionalization

Lallemand (1999) found many in the Smolensk region deeply ambivalent to the democratic and market reforms of late perestroika and the early Yeltsin years.[7] The fact that Smolensk region elected unrepentant supporter of the 1991 putsch Anatoly Lukyanov to the state duma elections three times is a particularly vivid illustration of the thoroughgoing rejection of the course set by Yeltsin by much of the region's electorate. One source of the prestige of Sergey Antufyev, appointed governor of the Smolensk region in 2007, might be that he had decisively defeated Lukyanov's bid for re-election in 2004.[8] The Smolensk region thus shed its long-standing role as "buckle of the red belt."

Late perestroika had seen, however, the emergence of a tentative democratic movement and of several avowedly pro-reform political leaders. Electoral results from across Russia in the 1990s typically show democratic forces at their strongest in regional capitals and weaker in the rural hinterlands. The city of Smolensk is distinctive in that its voters in the 1990s were not markedly more pro-reform than the rest of the region. (McFaul and Petrov 1997) Within the Smolensk region, the electorate has tended to be 'redder' as one proceeds westward, with the regions bordering Belarus returning the highest share of votes for the CPRF. The eastern part of the region, which borders on the Moscow oblast and includes the city of Vyasma, gave greater support for pro-reform parties.

Following Schumpeter, some democratic theorists consider the holding of contested elections where the outcome is unknown in advance the *sine qua non* of democracy. (Schumpeter 1942) As it happens, the Smolensk region measures up fairly well against this narrow definition of democracy. Since 1991, the region has had five governors: Valeriy Fateev, Anatoliy Glushenkov, Aleksandr Prokhorov, Viktor Maslov and Sergey Antufyev. Glushenkov, Prokhorov and Maslov defeated incumbents in tightly contested races and won by weak pluralities. Fateev was appointed by Yeltsin and Antufyev by Putin.

Pyle (2009) employs a regional democratic index, the Democratic Audit of Russia, designed by Public Expertise Institute, INDEM and the Merkatur Analytical Center, rating regions on the competiveness of elections held regionally and locally from 1995 to 2005. On this scale, the Smolensk region is the second best performer in Russia.[9] The Petrov regional democracy index, as we have seen, weighs a range of factors including the quality of elections, and considers the Smolensk region to be a lackluster performer, with no clear trajectory of improvement or decline from the 1990s through 2008. The Petrov ratings reflect the endemic problems of governance that have plagued the Smolensk region, including indecisive and weak administration, corruption and lawlessness. (Petrov and Titkov 2006, 2013)

Political challenges to the ruling CPSU began with the spring 1989 elections to Congress of People's Deputies. The Smolensk Popular Front was formed from the democratic platform within the CPSU and the newly formed Democratic Party of Russia in the region in September 1989. However, neither at this point nor later was the dominance of the conservative flank of the CPSU seriously undercut by these developments. (McFaul and Petrov 1997)

The senior ranks of the CPSU leadership in the Smolensk region included no obvious Yeltsin allies after the failed putsch of August 1991. Following some weeks of consultations among the Smolensk region's fledging pro-reform circles, Yeltsin appointed Valeriy Fateev to head the regional administration. Born near Gorky (Nizhniy Novgorod) and a graduate of the physics department at Gorky University, Fateev had also earned a doctorate in economics and served as director in small factories. In February 1990, Fateev, as factory manager, led a protest by the Vyasma factory's workers of the policies of the national and regional leadership. He resigned from the CPSU in early 1991 and led a strike of the Vyasma factory over the regional administration's appropriation of enterprise revenues. This brought him regional celebrity, and the factory collective, the region's fledging democratic parties, Democratic Russia, the Popular Front and the Democratic Party of Russia petitioned Yeltsin to appoint him governor.[10] (McFaul and Petrov 1997)

Fateev's performance as governor – including a push to privatize enterprises quickly – won high marks from the economic reform team then headed by acting prime minister Yegor Gaidar, but implacable hostility from much of the region's still entrenched political elite. Fateev's confrontations with the regional legislature created such a deadlock that the federal authorities acquiesced in the Smolensk legislature's call for elections to the governor's post. Ironically, then, the Smolensk region, a stronghold of the more conservative factions of the CPSU and opposition to Gorbachev's perestroika reforms, was among the first of Russia's regions to hold gubernatorial elections.

Going into these elections in early 1993, Fateev enjoyed full support of the federal center, the region's democrats, and the so-called administrative resources of the governor's office. Nevertheless, he lost the election to Anatoliy Glushenkov, then director of the Smolensk refrigerator manufacturing enterprise, one of the region's most prominent employers. The region's beleaguered democrats decried Glushenkov's victory as the return of the 'underground' oblast committee of the CPSU. Glushenkov did have the endorsement of the regional CPRF (in the second-round contest with Fateev) but represented much the same social and economic forces that were to be united under the centrist NDR. Glushenkov's defeat of Fateev, then, was not a traditionalist revanche but rather a parallel development to the move in Moscow from the radical reformist Gaidar to the centrist Viktor Chernomyrdin. (McFaul and Petrov 1997; Orttung 2000)

In the aftermath of the showdown in October 1993 between Yeltsin and the Congress of People's Deputies, the Smolensk region's democrats had another shot at the governor's post. Predictably, the Smolensk regional duma had publicly sided with the anti-Yeltsin forces in the standoff with the Congress of People's Deputies, and new elections for the governor's post were set for December 1993. Fateev, having become federal deputy minister of economy, returned to Smolensk to oppose Glushenkov, and again was defeated. In both of these electoral contests of 1993, Glushenkov won a far-from-crushing plurality, and Fateev won about one third of the vote. In December 1993, Glushenkov received 39.3% and Fateev 33.8%. (McFaul and Petrov 1997) The one third of the electorate supporting Fateev in the two elections of 1993 was to be the high-water mark for the region's democratic movement. In both elections, there were five candidates.

The pro-Fateev opposition remained influential during Glushenkov's term as governor. Important figures included deputy mayor of Smolensk and former Yeltsin representative to the region Aleksandr Manoim, the founding editor of the leading independent newspaper *Smolenskie Novosti*, S. V. Novikov, then also a member of the regional legislature, and the general director of the television company "Smolensk" V. Meshcheryakov. Entrepreneur Leonid Prokopovich succeeded Fateev as head of region's branch of the pro-reform Russia's Democratic Choice (DVR) party. (McFaul and Petrov 1997)[11]

The democrats of the early to mid 1990s left little lasting trace on the region's politics by the late 2000s. The weak plurality won by Glushenkov in 1993 and his failure to win re-election in 1998 point to the failure as well of moderately conservative or centrist forces to build any stable political organization with effective leadership, at least until the founding of United Russia.

Glushenkov was to lose his bid for re-election in April–May 1998 to Aleksandr Prokhorov, then the 45 year-old mayor of Smolensk. If Fateev represented the (weak) Yeltsin reformers of 1991–1992 and Glushenkov the centrist Chernomyrdin current of NDR, Prokhorov, although not formally a member of CPRF, enjoyed that party's support. (Lallemand 1999)[12] The most prominent backer of Prokhorov's challenge to Glushenkov was the diamond cutter and jewelry maker Kristall, whose director, Aleksandr Shkadov, member of the regional legislature and financier of charitable causes and sports teams, was second in power and prominence only to governor Glushenkov.

The assassination of Shkadov in August 1998, at the height of his notoriety and influence, is still unsolved, and, judging by conversations in Smolensk, has contributed to a persistent sense of insecurity. The fact that this murder and others like it remained unsolved may help to explain why Viktor Maslov, head of the regional branch of the Federal Security Service (FSB), was able to defeat Prokhorov for re-election in 2002. Maslov's electoral appeal had a great deal to do with his perceived ability to restore order and curb crime and corruption. Maslov defeated Prokhorov with 41% of the vote to Prokhorov's 34.3%.[13] Putin extended Maslov's term in office by 16 months in 2005. (Petrov 2006) Maslov was eased out in 2007 with Putin's appointment of Antufyev.

Although Antufyev was not elected to the post of governor, he had served as a deputy mayor of Smolensk and had been elected to the regional duma, becoming chairman in 1994.[14] Antufyev's time in office allowed the Smolensk regional administration to achieve some level of continuity and by most accounts improved the delivery of services, financial management and other aspects of governance. The appointment of Antufyev as governor also ushered in a period of more predictable and less turbulent administration, which may have generated greater business confidence, even if problems of state capacity and corruption remained acute.

The pattern, familiar in many Russian regions, of tension between governor and mayor of the regional capital has been present in Smolensk regional politics. High municipal office in Smolensk was a springboard to the governor's post for Prokhorov and was the first step in Antufyev's political career. For much of the time since 1991, the mayor of Smolensk was elected from among the elected members of the city legislature rather than directly. This was the case for Prokhorov, who nevertheless was able to mount a successful electoral challenge to Glushenkov in 1998. Prokhorov was charged with misuse of public funds in 2004, and in 2009 he came second in the mayoral election in Smolensk.

Direct popular election of the mayor of Smolensk in 2009 brought a young, previously little-known entrepreneur Eduard Kachanovskiy to the office. Kachanovskiy ran under the United Russia banner, but without having been endorsed by the party's local organization. His brief period in office ended with his arrest on charges of corruption in 2010 and the return to a system under which the mayor would be elected from among the city legislature's members. In elections held in March 2010 for city duma, eight of the 25 deputies elected ran as United Russia members and another 16 declared themselves United Russia 'supporters.' The sole member elected with a party affiliation other than United Russia was from Just Russia.[15]

Comparative overview of small business development

Several industrial concerns of the Soviet era are very prominent within the regional business community. The Smolensk region has been relatively untouched by entrepreneurs of the 'oligarch' type so influential elsewhere, most likely because of the relative insignificance of natural resource extraction or metallurgy to the region's economy. For better or worse, succession to directorships seems mainly to have been by orderly handover, rather than by insurgent style privatization.

Many of the region's leading companies, even if privatized, bear Soviet-sounding names such as RossSelKhozBank, Smolensk Shoe Factory or Road Construction Machinery Factory named after Kalinin. Prominent business people heading *de novo* or substantially restructured companies in sectors such as retail, light manufacturing, agro-processing or finance are present in the region as well.[16]

Although the leadership of big business in the region has a strong 'retro' flavor, numbers of small companies relative to the labor force increased sharply, beginning in 2004.

Table 5.1 Small Firms Concentration

Incorporated Small Companies per 1,000 Economically Active Population						
Year	*1995*	*2000*	*2002*	*2004*	*2006*	*2008*
Smolensk region	7.17	4.56	4.65	5.64	6.99	11.37
Average (all regions)	11.64	9.48	9.32	11.05	10.76	14.91

Source: Rosstat *Regiony Rossii*, various years

As of January 2010, the Smolensk regional administration reported that there were 37,327 small businesses, of which 10,769 were incorporated small companies and 26,558 were individual entrepreneurs.[17] Employment in small and medium-sized enterprises, – without counting microenterprises (those with ten or fewer employees) – was 58,781 in 2009, or 23% of the workforce. The turnover of these companies rose by one third in 2009 compared with 2008, showing that such companies weathered the economic contraction of 2009 surprisingly well. Tax revenue from all small business (incorporated companies and individual entrepreneurs) to the regional budget was 1.75 billion rubles in 2009. (See also Chamber of Commerce and Industry Smolensk Region 2008d, 2010b.)

Data concerning medium-sized companies as defined by the 2007 federal law on SME support were reported by Rosstat for the first time for the year 2008. (Rosstat 2009) In 2008, the Smolensk region had 128 medium-sized companies, of 14,170 such companies across the whole of Russia. The Smolensk region was relatively rich in medium-sized enterprises relative to the size of its population and economy, and its incorporated small firms were more disposed than the national averages to be in manufacturing relative to trade and consumer services sectors. 13% of the Smolensk region's small businesses and 43% of its medium businesses were in manufacturing, as opposed to 10% and 24% respectively for Russia as a whole in 2008. Smolensk's small businesses in trade and services had about a 20% share as compared with more than 40% nationally.

Among those entrepreneurs interviewed for this study were two whose experiences typified adaptation to the sweeping changes of the 1990s and business conditions that remain very difficult. A primary school teacher in her mid-40s on the train journey from Moscow to Smolensk in October 2009 recounted how she and her unemployed husband bought and sold goods through much of the 1990s to supplement her meager salary, living in one room with their infant daughter. She remembered being mortified when pupils saw her after school hours selling produce from a kiosk. She and her now-married daughter have launched a new business making and selling herbal soaps.

A particularly vivid story is that of Sergey and his wife, who have a men's shoe shop in the Smolensk market, just across from another shoe shop run by their son and his wife.[18] Both shops are in a newly constructed commercial building housing about a dozen small shops like theirs. A group of merchants had jointly financed the building's construction, and they own it in common on land leased from the city. Sergey joked that if the city raised the lease charges, they would have to pick up the building and carry it away.

A deeply devout Orthodox Christian, Sergey served in the Soviet military from 1973 based near Smolensk. He recalled that Dmitry Likhachev had written about how, within one century, it had been Russians' fate to attempt to rebuild on the ruins, first of capitalism and then of socialism.

In early 1994, Sergey and his son, then age 14, took a bus to Poland, spent all the money they had scraped together to buy exactly 11 pairs of shoes in the wholesale market, brought them back to Smolensk and sold them. With the proceeds, they began shuttling back and forth to Poland to buy shoes, cigarettes and food items to sell. Over the next three years, they travelled to Poland and back 57 times. Most of the shuttle traders of those days were women, he recalled that, loaded down with goods, and bearing the heavy burden of supporting their families. Men among the shuttle traders of those days were few, he said, clicking his finger on his throat to say that many men instead fell into heavy drinking.

Sergey and his son still travel regularly by bus to a Moscow wholesale market to stock their shoe shops. Sellers extend credit on these purchases with confidence, because he and his son have carefully established their reliability. Sergey insists that honesty and knowing one's customers is the only sure road to success. His son had taken to business well, allowing Sergey and his wife to have worry-free time away. The younger couple has two other shops within the market as well.

Business associations and small business advocacy – bonding and bridging 'civic-ness'

Applying the analytical framework laid out in Chapter 3, the following discussion probes the 'internal' and 'external' dimensions of business associations' activities, as well as the associational landscape.

Chamber of commerce and industry of the Smolensk region

The Smolensk regional Chamber, created in 1993, gives the following succinct mission statement:

> The Chamber is a non-commercial, non-state organization, the founding goals of which are advancing the socio-economic development of Smolensk oblast, the forming of a modern industrial infrastructure, the creation of favorable conditions for entrepreneurial activity, the scientific-technical and economic links between the entrepreneurs of Smolensk and its region with those of other

Russian regions and foreign countries and also the representation of and protection of the legal interests of the Chamber's members to state structures.[19]

Membership in the Smolensk Chamber stands at just under 300, having approximately doubled since 2003.[20] The large majority of members of the Smolensk Chamber – 80% according to Chamber President Vladimir Arkhipenkov – are small and medium-sized companies. (Matveev 2009) The Smolensk Chamber was formed in 1993 on the basis of an already-existing local entrepreneurs' association. A review of numerous Chamber documents and published materials reveals that its most frequently stated goal is support of entrepreneurship.[21]

The Chamber's founding president was Oleg Vladimirovich Lukevich, whose business was in wholesale trade. Lukevich was charged and convicted of an offense related to the conduct of his business in 2006 and forced to resign from the Chamber presidency. Arkhipenkov, who had served as Lukevich's deputy, became president of the Chamber on Lukevich's resignation. Vladimir Pinyugin, Chamber vice president, is a retired military officer who served in Smolensk but comes from the far eastern Chitinskaya province. In a neat illustration of the salience in Smolensk's popular consciousness of military valor and determination, a published profile of Chamber President Arkhipenkov and Vice President Pinyugin claims the two draw inspiration from the dictum of legendary Tsarist general Suvorov: "Forward is my favorite direction." (Chamber of Commerce and Industry, Smolensk Region 2008g)

The Smolensk Chamber has a very full agenda of roundtables, public events and seminars. Where many regional Chambers organize their consultations with regional authorities through sector-based committees representing well-established industrial concerns, the Smolensk Chamber emphasizes improving the business climate in general, especially as it affects smaller companies. The large share of membership by small companies and also some individual entrepreneurs is an indication of an encompassing and open approach to representing business. An important secondary focus of Chamber activities seems to be the encouragement of higher standards of business ethics and active attempts to increase membership. Arkhipenkov is also active in an informal club uniting directors of Smolensk's larger companies.

The Smolensk region was brought into the CIPE small business advocacy program in 2005 and, as had been done in the other participating regions, a coalition of business associations was formed to agree on common objectives. In Smolensk, leadership of the coalition remains very much a part of the Chamber's *modus operandi*. The Smolensk Chamber's website, redesigned in 2010, includes links to the list of associations in the coalition and to the text of the business community's anti-corruption program.[22]

The Smolensk Chamber participates actively along with several others in the anti-corruption programming sponsored by CIPE. This approach devised by INDEM emphasizes the development of legal drafting expertise by business associations' leadership. The Chamber held a conference on how business can contribute to reducing corruption in June 2010, based in large part on the approaches recommended by INDEM. The background for this conference was a 2010 survey of lawyers in the Smolensk region funded by CIPE. A principal finding of this survey was that the inadequate legal preparation of regional and municipal administrations was the most significant obstacle to resolving issues on behalf of business clients. (Chamber of Commerce and Industry, Smolensk Region 2010a)

The 12-member governing board of the Smolensk Chamber elected in March 2010 has strong representation by small business.[23] Only one member of the board – director of the automotive parts manufacturer ZIL – is drawn from one of the Soviet-era enterprises that still dominate the landscape of larger companies in the region. Other members include the Mikhail Bagrov of the security company Mangust, Yuriy Malik of the baked goods company Elizabeta and Aleksandr Kochergin, director of the national park Smolenskoe Poozer'e (Smolensk Lakelands), which aims to build up eco-tourism in the region. Deputy Governor Aleksandr Dolgov is also a board member.

The Chamber's departments carry out the core services that all Chambers provide for both members and non-members. These include providing quality certifications, appraisals of land and other assets, provision of certificates of origin and other documentation required by exporters, voluntary dispute arbitration, mounting trade shows and missions within Russia and abroad, and making available to members a directory of reliable partners to assist in finding suppliers, customers and potential investors. The Chamber received in 2009 the full accreditation of the national Chamber (TPPRF) for the quality and professionalism of the provision of these services. Chamber president Arkhipenkov serves on the TPPRF governing board, whose members are selected from among the ranks of regional or municipal chambers' leadership.

The Smolensk Chamber organizes frequent training sessions and seminars to build the capacity and skills of entrepreneurs and has begun over the last three years to provide free legal advice to businesspeople, including non-members. It produced with the Regional Administration in 2008 a handbook laying out the steps in such issues as company registration, licensing requirements and lease or purchase of buildings and land. (Smolensk Regional Administration, Department of Economic Development and Trade, and Smolensk Region Chamber of Commerce and Industry 2008a)

One major theme of the Smolensk Chamber's international trade and investment development work is deepening business links with Belarus, through exhibitions and trade missions and cooperation with the Belarus Chamber of Commerce. The Chamber's interventions are explicitly related to the national political aim of greater integration of Belarus and Russia. (Chamber of Commerce and Industry, Smolensk Region 2010e) Another initiative by the Smolensk Chamber is to involve Chambers from cities along the Dnieper in both Belarus and Ukraine (including Kiev) in joint efforts to promote greater trade and business links. Seven Ukrainian Chambers of Commerce (including the Kiev Chamber) and three from Belarus joined Smolensk in this initiative.[24]

The Smolensk Chamber's connectedness and relevance to the small business community was illustrated at an improvised discussion meeting arranged by Chamber Vice President Pinyugin on October 28, 2009, including several entrepreneurs and OPORA Smolensk head Moskovtseva. A local grocery store owner, formerly a high school teacher, recounted having disputed an unjustified tax assessment in court and having prevailed. He had formed an association of about 20 local grocers facing some of the same issues and had sought advice from the Smolensk Chamber. He said he and other entrepreneurs wanted also to be able to meet the competition from larger supermarkets more effectively. Another participant, young lawyer Ilya Matveev, represented a new association of retailers in a Smolensk suburb, formed to pool members' access to legal services. (This association joined the Smolensk Chamber during the author's second visit in June 2010.) Also participating in the discussion was Chamber member Mikhail Bagrov, founder of the security firm Mangust.

At a ceremony attended by the author on June 24, 2010, ten new members joined the Chamber, including three individual entrepreneurs (two women and a young man), lawyer and business association leader Ilya Matveev, as well as the regional representative of the Moscow-based major cellphone company MTS. The reception, hosted by the Chamber after the ceremony, included newly inducted members, board members Malik, Bagrov and Kochergin and the regional minister of economy.[25]

The idea of rebirth is manifest in the choice of the phoenix as emblem for the Chamber's logo and publications. The Smolensk Chamber's publications make frequent references to trade as central to Smolensk's ancient foundation.[26] The Chamber attempts to 'nudge' the region's contemporary business culture toward adopting 'civilized' business conduct by reference to the pre-revolutionary past. As a follow-up to a roundtable in early 2009 around the theme "Problems in the Adoption of Corporate and Social Responsibility by Smolensk Business," the Chamber delved further into the role played by Russia's early merchant-industrialists, arguing these figures' high ethical standards in the conduct of business, and their devotion to country and charitable causes, were both admirable and part of their business success.[27] This is part of a pattern of recuperation or rehabilitation, observed in all four of the case study regions in this project, of the reputations of the merchant industrialists of early 20th century.

Drawing upon the experience of the guilds of late Tsarist Russia, the article suggests that the universal adoption of business ethics will foster a transformation in the behavior of state authorities and promote stronger economic growth. The ethical code proposed is based on the principle that an effective state is required for the successful conduct of business. Profits earned in violation of law, by recourse to violence or threats of violence or by a no-holds-barred approach to competitors are, the article argues, destructive of the business climate and inhibit the emergence of a business community able to demand better laws and fairer dealings from government authorities.

The Chamber has focused particular effort on making public through its own publications and the media, the full scope of its work. The publications are a quarterly magazine *Vedomosti Smolenskoy Palaty* and a monthly newspaper *Predprinimatel'*. Cooperation with the academic community is also a significant part of the Smolensk Chamber's work. The Smolensk Humanitarian University, established in 1992, the region's leading private university and a Smolensk Chamber member, carried out entrepreneurs' opinion surveys in 2007 and 2008, for the Chamber funded by the regional administration, that helped to shape the Chamber's programs as they relate to corruption and other issues, as well as the regional and municipal administrations' small business promotion efforts.[28] (Chamber of Commerce and Industry Smolensk Region 2008b)

The Smolensk Chamber works in close cooperation with the regional and municipal administration and is a source of expertise and advice for these. By becoming engaged in the CIPE regional business associations project, already well established in several more economically advanced regions of Russia by 2005, the Smolensk Chamber seems to have been able to anticipate and prepare the ground for the effects in Smolensk of the new wave of interest from Moscow in SME development following the adoption of the 2007 federal law on support for small and medium businesses. The watershed for the Smolensk regional authorities in embracing the cause of SME development seems to have been the visit to the region by then-President Medvedev in July 2008 and his speech in the city of Gagarin on the imperative of supporting small business development.[29]

OPORA Smolensk region

Elena Moskovtseva, an attorney whose clients are principally small business owners, has headed OPORA Smolensk since 2008.[30] OPORA Smolensk's office is co-located with Moskovtseva's law practice. Moskovtseva assumed the association's leadership from her friend Yelena Nikolaevna Slobodskova, who founded OPORA Smolensk with five members in 2005. Slobodskova, a pioneer of Smolensk's small business community, owned a popular restaurant. Optimistic that the passage of the federal SME support law of 2007 would bring new energy to the Smolensk regional administration's small business development efforts, Slobodskova joined the regional administration as director of the administration's first small business development program in 2008.

Membership in the regional branch of OPORA has held steady for some time at about forty members, the majority of them women from Smolensk and regional cities of Gagarin, Vyasma and Yartsevo. About half are in retail or wholesale trade, and the second largest group is in light manufacturing (such as clothing or food products). The members are mainly incorporated companies (rather than individual entrepreneurs) and tend to be on the larger end of the spectrum of small companies. Moskovtseva said that the association's membership is a collegial network, exchanging frequent e-mails as well as meeting formally as needed. The author met Moskovsteva and one of her leading members, Lyudmila Pushkareva, owner of garment manufacturer Lakos, at the TPPRF-OPORA entrepreneurs' conference in Moscow May 25–26, 2010.

Moskovtseva participates on behalf of OPORA in the various consultative bodies set up by governmental bodies to hear the views of business and provides input to legislation and programs.[31] She said OPORA Smolensk had pressed for simplifications in tax administration and fewer punitive fines.

Moskovtseva said that many small businesspeople doubt the usefulness of formal associations such as OPORA or the Chamber. OPORA's members in the Smolensk nevertheless valued their link to an association that enjoys a respectful hearing of its views at the federal level. President Medvedev and the federal Ministry of Economic Development under Minister Elvira Nabuillina were, she believed, sincerely committed to SME development, and receptive to engagement with OPORA.

A preoccupation of many small companies, both members of OPORA and others, was, Moskovtseva said, the implementation of the 2008 federal law that allows firms leasing premises from municipalities to be able to purchase those premises, including buildings and land.[32] (Russian Federation 2008) Many entrepreneurs occupy municipally owned land or buildings without a formal lease, and so must in the first instance petition the city to receive a lease and begin paying rent before moving to complete a purchase.

Other business associations

The list of associations in the coalition formed under CIPE's small business advocacy program as of 2007 is shown in Table 5.2:

Table 5.2 Association Members of Small Business Coalition – Smolensk Region

Smolensk Regional Chamber of Commerce and Industry
Non-commercial fund for the development of civil society "Patronat"
Smolensk regional union of employers "Nauchno-promyshlennyi Soyuz"
Smolensk regional fund for support of small business
Non-commercial partnership "Soyuz Predprinimateley" city of Gagarin
Smolensk fund for social support of military servicemen, family members and employees "Paritet"
El'inskaya Guild of Conscientious Enterprises
Fund for support and development of small business, city of Vyasma
Non-commercial partnership "Soyuz Predprinimateley" city of Desnogorsk
Non-commercial partnership "Soyuz Predprinimateley" city of Roslavl
Non-commercial partnership "Soyuz Predprinimateley" city of Safonov
Non-commercial partnership "Smolensk Business Club"
Association of Advertising Agencies.
Association of Road Transportation Enterprises "Smolavtotransport"
Non-commercial partnership "Smoloblturist"
Association of Small Farmers "Sodeystvie" of the Smolensk region
Non-commercial partnership "Vyazemskiy Soyuz Promyshlennikov i Predprinimateley" (city of Vyasma)
Association of Private Dentists

Source: CIPE Moscow office. 2007.

Although OPORA Smolensk is not formally a member of the coalition, there is still a fair degree of collaboration between the Smolensk Chamber, the formal members of the coalition and OPORA locally. Interviews with the Chamber and with OPORA suggest slightly different outlooks and approaches between the two, which may explain why OPORA Smolensk did not join the coalition. By contrast to the Chamber, OPORA's local organization has a much lower public profile, and it concentrates its efforts mainly on tackling specific problems – usually of a legal nature – faced by member entrepreneurs.

The participation in the coalition by small self-organized entrepreneurs' groups in the region's smaller cities such as Vyasma, Roslavl, Safonovo, El'nin, Gagarin and Desnogorsk is a mark of inclusiveness. The coalition includes the RSPP affiliate in for the Smolensk region, the Scientific-Industrial Union *(Naucho-Promyshlenniy Soyuz),* which represents the interests of the larger industrial employers. The Smolensk Business Club is an informal grouping of heads of senior business leaders in which Chamber President Arkhipenkov is active. This club is perhaps the best approximation in Smolensk of what the Rotary Club is in larger Russian cities such as Rostov, Samara, Togliatti or Perm. The association of dentists in private practice and sector-based groups in agro-processing, tourism, trucking and advertising are all locally organized and reflect some of the areas of relative success for private entrepreneurs in the region. In several interviews, Chamber Vice President Pinyugin emphasized the frequent contacts of the Chamber with coalition member associations. The Smolensk branch of Delovaya Rossiya is headed by Yuriy Vekshin, director of the vodka-producing company Bakhus.[33]

Business associations' dialogue with regional and municipal administrations – contributions to the openness of policy formulation

Business agenda

The organizing theme of the policy program run by the Smolensk Chamber on behalf of the coalition of business associations is anti-corruption, formulated into a detailed program in 2008.[34] The anti-corruption program was formulated in part on findings of a survey, funded by the regional administration and conducted by Smolensk Humanitarian University, of 1,500 local small business owners in September– November 2007. A survey of 3,000 small business owners followed in 2008. (Chamber of Commerce and Industry, Smolensk Region 2009a; Smolensk Regional Administration, Department of Economic Development and Trade, and Smolensk Region Chamber of Commerce and Industry 2008b)[35] In both surveys, substantial numbers of respondents cited corruption of state and municipal officials, the exploitation of special, unfair advantages by competing businesses, and criminal rackets, including some involving law enforcement officials, as obstacles to business. A list of the major forms of corruption cited by respondents to the 2007 survey is reported in the anti-corruption program's text and includes extortion, bribe-taking, abuse of legal authority, conflicts of interest and official favoritism or nepotism.

The list of problems which the business community program identifies are deficiencies in the regulations affecting business, lack of information on the part of businesses caused in part by lack of transparency on the part of government, excessive bureaucratic procedures or administrative barriers to the conduct of business, abuse by authorities empowered to inspect businesses' operations, and competition from businesses closely associated with government 'organs'. (Smolensk Regional Coalition of Business Associations, and Smolensk Region Chamber of Commerce and Industry 2008)

Recommendations of the business community with respect to these problems are laid out in the program and include winning acceptance from government to allow legal experts from business to comment upon legal drafts and review existing legislation and regulations to eliminate provisions that open opportunities for arbitrary or unchecked discretion. The program notes that this implies as well the training of greater numbers of experts in the legal profession prepared to provide such expertise. The coalition calls for regular surveys of entrepreneurs to contribute to the administration's awareness of the problems faced by business. The administration, for its part, should make information about laws and regulations more readily available, including through passage of a regional law on the right to information, and development of its own publicly declared enforcement measures against official corruption. New rules should ensure, for example that tenders for municipal or regional contracts are open to all potential bidders, including through official websites. The business community commits to using its own publications and the local media to raise awareness of the problem of corruption and encourage the public and business to become less tolerant toward it. For example the business association coalition will sponsor an annual competition entitled 'Business Beyond Corruption' to recognize the best reports by the press of the problem of corruption as it affects regional businesses.

The business community in its program undertakes to offer concrete suggestions for streamlining and simplifying regulatory procedures to minimize opportunities for corruption. They propose to include business and government agencies in a discussion on the design and implementation of anti-corruption programs through organizing public roundtables and conferences devoted to this theme. They also call for formation of standing consultative bodies between the regional and local governments and business to design and to monitor such programs, including through provision of information about specific cases of official conflicts of interest. (Chamber of Commerce and Industry Smolensk Region 2008f, 2009c, 2009d, 2009e, 2010d)

The anti-corruption program of the Smolensk coalition, although independently elaborated using local information, bears the hallmarks of the approach developed by CIPE and implemented with expert input and training by INDEM. (See also OPORA 2008.) The adoption of this program in 2008 was followed by a series of roundtables and other events open to business and usually attended by senior regional or municipal officials, or both.

A conference in July 2010, supported by CIPE, to review progress on anti-corruption efforts came at the initiative of the Smolensk Chamber. Anti-corruption is a prominent theme in the Chamber's publications and speeches, whereas the regional and city administrations' publications and public statements tend to address the problem only obliquely, by reference to necessary improvements in laws and regulations, lowering administrative barriers and protecting the rights of business owners in the conduct of inspections by government agencies.

In the second monitoring study conducted in 2008, a sample of 3,000 businesses, of which two thirds were individual entrepreneurs, showed 29% believed the problems of small business in the region were typically managed through illegal payments and special protection for favored players. The poll indicated that 10–20% of business income has to be paid in bribes to officials. Most respondents said they themselves solve any problems they confront either alone or with help from better connected business contacts. The role of business associations in such cases is considered important by only 124 respondents, although another 315 respondents would turn to consultants or attorneys. This result is perhaps not surprising, because two-thirds of the 3,000 respondents in the survey are individual entrepreneurs, who, as we have seen, are considerably less inclined than owners of incorporated firms to join business associations. (Chamber of Commerce and Industry, Smolensk Region 2009a)

Smolensk regional small business development program

By comparison with the priority given to small business development efforts since the early to mid 1990s in regions such as Samara, Rostov and Perm, the Smolensk regional administration's interest in these issues is weak, and the availability of program information on its website quite limited. The urging of the Smolensk Chamber, the growing contribution of small and medium companies to regional economic activity and employment and the federal imprimatur brought to small business promotion by the 2007 law on SME support together produced some actions by the Smolensk administration to create better conditions for entrepreneurship. (Smolensk Regional Administration 2009a, Smolensk Regional Fund for Support of Entrepreneurship 2009)

A key event spurring an escalation of interest in SME development on the part of the Smolensk regional administration was President Dmitry Medvedev's speech in Gagarin and televised conversation with Governor Antufyev on small business development in July 2008. The passage of the SME law in 2007, and the fact that it offers federal funding support for regional programs of SME development, may help explain be the rapid growth in numbers of incorporated small companies in the late 2000s.

The regional administration's first SME support program covered the period 2007–2009 and was succeeded by the program covering the years 2009–2012. (Chamber of Commerce and Industry, Smolensk Region 2010c) According to the director of the Regional Administration's department of economics and trade, in 2009 the program disbursed 99 million rubles from the regional budget and 95 million transferred from the federal Ministry of Economy. (Smolensk Regional Administration Department of Economic Development and Trade 2009b)

According to a brochure published by the Regional Administration in 2009, the total funding for the program over the four years 2009–2012 was to be 1.2 billion rubles from the regional budget, supplemented by 233 million from the federal budget. The program was to have disbursed 611 million in 2009 from the regional budget. (Smolensk Regional Administration 2010)[36]

The regional administration's program for small business development funds subsidies to new businesses and development of micro-finance institutions, establishes a guarantee fund to provide collateral and thereby ease access by qualifying businesses to bank loans, and provides interest rate subsidies for small business borrowers who otherwise qualify for bank credit. A specialized financial agency established by the regional administration, The Smolensk Regional Fund for the Support of Entrepreneurship implements the small business finance and advisory aspects of the regional administration's program.[37] In addition, the Smolensk regional administration holds an annual forum, which attracted 600 participants in 2009, focused on the role of small business to the region's economy. The regional administration supported roundtables organized by the Chamber publicizing the availability of support for entrepreneurs from the program and other issues affecting small business. The regional and municipal websites posted full information on how to apply for these programs as well as a new link to tenders for regional and city contracts. A 2010 survey of entrepreneurs and attorneys was designed to test the impact of the region's efforts as seen by their intended beneficiaries. (Chamber of Commerce and Industry, Smolensk Region 2010a) This survey, as mentioned earlier, found that inadequate professional preparation on the part of regional and municipal personnel implementing the SME development programs and otherwise interacting with business owners was the most serious impediment to the effectiveness of programs to encourage small business.

The region's program to advance SME development emphasizes support for generating new small companies through subsidies and credit guarantees. Although this is welcome, the monitoring of the concerns of small business carried out by the Chamber on behalf of the regional administration shows that the availability of financing is not the most pressing problem cited by respondents. It is important to remember that a large share of the respondents are individual entrepreneurs whose appetite for formal financing is small and whose needs would be best met by the expansion of micro-finance. The 2010 survey and anecdotal evidence suggest that many small businesspeople are unaware of the existence of the subsidy programs, despite the efforts of the regional administration, helped by the Chamber, to publicize them.

The regional small business development program adopts both the approach of encouraging the role of small business in sub-contracting work for larger companies and the improvement of access by small companies to bidding on competitive open tenders for projects (e.g. road construction, transport services) of the regional budget. Both of these concerns have been urged at a national level as a means of promoting faster development of small business.

In all, the Smolensk region seems to be a case where initiatives and proposals from the organized business community, in particular the Chamber, have been influential. As we have seen earlier, the business coalition proposed and pushed the adoption of several key pieces of legislation related to business conditions and was closely involved in their drafting including in employing best practices to eliminate provisions seen as opening opportunities for corruption. Two examples are the regional law 'On Development of Small and Medium Entrepreneurship in the Smolensk Region' adopted November 26, 2008 and a law passed on April 30, 2009 resolving an issue raised by small businesses on the applicability of the simplified tax system to certain kinds of income. (Smolensk Regional Duma 2008, 2009)

The regional program began in 2010 to incorporate more ambitious initiatives in line with the priority given at the federal level to building supportive institutional infrastructure to generate new start-ups in manufacturing and especially in technologically advanced activities. This new programmatic emphasis will absorb greater resources from the budget and includes promoting industrial clustering and building business incubators. In this vein, the regional government funded a training center in the city of Yartsevo in cooperation with the Smolensk Institute for Business and Entrepreneurship aimed at developing skilled employees for businesses.[38] (Smolensk Regional Administration, Department of Economic Development and Trade 2009b)

Smolensk municipal small business development programs

The regional administration provides funding to municipalities to support the conduct of their own small business development programs. In the city of Smolensk, there have been two such programs, the first for 2007–2009 and the second for 2010–2012. The city government's Department for the Consumer Market and Development of Entrepreneurship is responsible for program implementation. The city of Smolensk is home to 70% of the oblast's small businesses – including incorporated firms and individual entrepreneurs. In 2008, small business provided more than half of all retail trade and 70% of restaurant turnover, 40% of employment and a rising share of tax revenues. (Smolensk City Administration, Department for the Consumer Market and Development of Entrepreneurship 2008b)[39]

A report on progress in implementing the city's program throughout 2008 puts the growth in tax revenues from small business at the very top of the report's findings. (Smolensk City Administration 2009) According to this report, in 2008, taxes from small business provided 14% of the city's revenues. The city administration has authority to resolve the problem that many small businesses consider the most acute: the conditions for lease or purchase of land and buildings. As discussed earlier, this process has been unusually prolonged, forcing entrepreneurs to spend large sums on legal costs.

The program of the Smolensk municipality emphasizes improving the availability of information for entrepreneurs. (Smolensk City Administration Department for the Consumer Market and Entrepreneurship Development, 2008a, 2008c, 2009a, 2009b) This focus corresponds well to the priorities set by the small business respondents in the monitoring studies run by the Chamber in 2007 and 2008. Beginning in 2008, the city has organized a large annual conference 'Small and Medium Business of the City of Smolensk.' Speakers' remarks are published and distributed. In addition, the conference has in each year distributed a handbook *(spravochnik)* in which the full texts of federal, regional and municipal legislation and regulations affecting business and entrepreneurship are published as well as contact information for various government agencies, banks and business associations.[40]

An exemplary contribution to public information by the municipal program is a glossy catalog of the city's small businesses published in 2008 featuring profiles of around 200 small businesses, of which most are incorporated companies, but many are individual entrepreneurs. The catalog lists firms in manufacturing in the first section, showing the priority that policy attaches to encouraging the emergence of more small businesses outside of retail and wholesale trade where they continue to be concentrated. (Smolensk City Administration 2008)

The city program's activities emphasize such issues as workforce training as it affects small business. The difficulty in finding qualified and reliable employees was cited as very serious by more respondents than any other problem including corruption in the 2008 entrepreneurs monitoring study. The declared purposes of the city's small business development program in 2007–2009 were improving the laws and regulations affecting business, development of credit availability including a subsidy program, support for new companies in 'innovative' (technology- or ideas-based) fields, adapting educational programs to the training of entrepreneurs and the labor force, development of the infrastructure of small business support, support for improving the public image of entrepreneurs, the staging of exhibitions with small business participation, continued monitoring of the opinions of entrepreneurs through surveys and subsidizing entrepreneurial projects by youth and the unemployed.

The same purposes with slight modifications are carried over in the 2010–2012 program. (Smolensk City Administration, Department for the Consumer Market and Development of Entrepreneurship 2010) Both programs were funded at about 15 million rubles annually. (Smolensk City Administration 2006, 2009)

Style, channels and institutional forms of business – state coordination

Deputy Governor of Smolensk Region Dolgov sits on the board of the Smolensk Chamber and the director of the regional administration's department of economic development and trade spends a lot of time at the Chamber's offices. Chamber Vice President Pinyugin easily arranges meetings with working-level regional and municipal officials engaged in small business development. The Chamber seems to be recognized as a source of expertise among these officials and among many business people.

Roundtables and conferences on themes of business relations with government organized by the Chamber, jointly with the regional or city administrations, provide very frequent opportunities for business people including non-members of associations to interact with policymakers, get updated information and express concerns. The engagement of the associations' legal experts in proposing and vetting legislation is a productive, if less inclusive, form of interaction intermediated by the Chamber. Business associations also are active in the councils on entrepreneurship vis-à-vis the governor and the mayor of Smolensk.

An agreement between the Chamber and the regional administration, signed by Governor Antufyev and Chamber President Arkhipenkov, lists a series of events and interactions that will take place in a one-year planning horizon. These include joint work on a draft law on public information availability (an aim of the business coalition's anti-corruption program) and the establishment of advisory councils of business association leaders to the heads of municipalities throughout the Smolensk region.

In general, the evidence suggests that the Chamber and business association coalition has been an initiator of activities and generator of ideas in small business development and anti-corruption efforts. However, much of this work awaited the passage of the 2007 law on SME promotion and the appointment of Antufyev as governor. Clearly, the receptiveness of the regional administration and the national priority given to SME development has been important.

Entrepreneurs in regional and municipal politics and administrations – contributions to the dispersion of regional and local political authority

As we saw in the Samara case study, turnover or renewal of the ranks of political elites through entry by entrepreneurs heading restructured privatized companies or *de novo* firms has enhanced the political weight of regional and municipal legislatures and checked executive power. New entrants to political office from *de novo* business supported and enhanced the comparatively dispersed or 'polycentric' pattern of regional political power in the Samara region.

The Smolensk region's first governor, Valeriy Fateev, himself a reform-oriented company director, pursued privatization actively, against strong opposition from the bulk of the region's industrial managers. Fateev's successor as DVR party head in 1994 was entrepreneur Leonid Prokopovich. Prokopovich's company, Sitall, a glass manufacturer located near Roslavl with 600 employees, is one of the exceptional cases of successful privatization and restructuring of a larger industrial concern in the Smolensk region. The European Bank for Reconstruction and Development took a 30% equity share in 1996 and the French company St. Gobain a 10% interest in 2004.[41] Prokopovich is a rare holdover in the region's political life from the small circle of democratic activists of the early 1990s. He is serving his second term as a member of the regional duma, elected a second time in 2007 from his Roslavl district, is affiliated with United Russia and serves on the economic development committee. He served in the Roslavl municipal legislature from 1996–2002.

The regional duma elected in 2007 (the 4th since 1991) has 48 members, half elected from districts on a majoritarian basis and half by proportional representation from party lists. Of the single-mandate members, all but two – one from Just Russia and one from the CPRF – belong to United Russia. United Russia has 15 of 24 of the seats elected by party lists, the CPRF has 5, and Zhirinovsky's LDPR has 4. A breakdown of their occupational or professional backgrounds is shown in Table 5.3:

Table 5.3 Occupations of Regional Legislators

Occupation	Single Mandate	Party List
Industrial directors	7	3
Entrepreneurs	3	3
Doctors, teachers	5	3
Professional politicians	6	12
Other	3	3
Total	24	24

Source: http://www.smoloblduma.ru/. Accessed June 15, 2011.

The regional duma's website lists with committee affiliations the members from the three previous dumas, but not their party affiliation. The share of entrepreneurs in the membership of the earlier dumas seems to have been somewhat greater, reflecting the overall sense in Smolensk in the last two regional duma elections of a 'restoration' of the region's traditional leadership. The unseating of the previously dominant CPRF by United Russia in the ranks of the duma has in some cases been accomplished by defections from the CPRF to United Russia. On the other hand, some political figures from the democratic camp of the early 1990s have also rallied to United Russia.

The age distribution of the regional duma membership is shown in Table 5.4:

Table 5.4 Smolensk Regional Legislature: Age Distribution of Members

Birth Decade	Single Mandate Members	Party List Members
1940s	8	5
1950s	9	11
1960s	4	3
1970s	2	2
1980s	0	3

Source: http://www.smoloblduma.ru./ Accessed June 15, 2011. One single mandate seat is vacant because of a resignation.

The heavy representation of people age 60 and over is telling in several ways. The single mandate races return a large share of members who have long careers in their fields and high local standing. United Russia has been able to incorporate almost all of these into its ranks. In the party list races, United Russia has evidently made an effort to offer places to younger people, but these younger deputies seem, based on their occupational profiles, to be United Russia activists rather than entrepreneurs, managers or professionals. In fact, the preponderance of party list members having no professional or occupational role other than duma membership is likely a marker of a widening gap between professional-ized administration and society at large. In particular, the very limited participa-tion of entrepreneurs in elected political office provides a tangible correlate for the widely expressed lack of confidence by business people in the institutions of local governance in terms of either their capacity for or interest in effecting real improvements in the business climate.

The popular election of Smolensk's mayor in 2009 produced a surprise victory for Eduard Kachanovskiy, who ran as a member of United Russia, but was not the party's chosen candidate. The mayor's term was cut short by his arrest in February 2010 on charges related to the awarding of a commercial lease on attractive terms of a city-owned apartment, allegedly on the basis of having received a bribe.[42] This event had been preceded by earlier controversies including Kachanovskiy's alleged failure to cease operating his business when he became mayor.

After a brief few days of protests by small numbers of supporters, it became evident that most Smolensk residents were untroubled by the imprisoned mayor's plight. The author's conversations in Smolensk in June 2010 found interlocutors generally convinced that, at a minimum, Kachanovskiy violated the rule that pre-vented him from continuing to run his own business while in office. With a voter turnout of only around 20% and Kachanovskiy's winning plurality so small, he must have seemed to many, and perhaps to himself, the accidental victor.

Whatever the facts of Kachanovskiy's guilt or innocence, the reaction to his arrest provides yet another indication of a corrosive lack of mutual regard between elected officials and the broader society. The institution of an elected mayor for Smolensk had not been well established to begin with, and has been replaced with a chief executive elected from among the members of the elected municipal duma.

Business, society and the press in the Smolensk region

Identical surveys investigating popularly held values in eight Russian regions under the overall direction of Russian Academy of Sciences Sociology Institute's Nikolai Lapin and L.A. Belyaeva included both the Smolensk and Perm regions and provide insights into the 'civic cultures' of each region. (Vinokurov and Blagovestova 2009) The researchers asked respondents in each region to define their own personal attach-ment to a given value (such as freedom, family or tradition) by reference to a 5-point scale, where a score of 5 would mean that value was cherished above all else. The regions where the survey was carried out were Smolenskaya, Kurskaya, Vologods-kaya, Karelia, Ul'yanovskaya, Chuvashkaya, Permskiy kray and Tyumenskaya.

The editors of the collection of regional sociocultural portraits, Lapin and Bely-aeva, devised a scheme for interpreting these results, categorizing the proposed values as modern, universal or traditional. According to this scheme, the results showed that the Smolensk region was the most 'traditional' of those surveyed.[43] Table 5.5 shows that Russia taken as a whole is quite 'traditional,' but that the Smolensk region is markedly more so. The Russian terms that the respondents were given are shown for reference in parentheses.

These findings comport with impressionistic evidence of the generalized traditionalism in Smolensk and are consistent with the electoral history of the

Table 5.5 Intensity of Adherence to Selected Values – Smolensk and Russia Compared

Russia	Smolensk Region
family (семья) 4.69	family 4.72
order (порядок) 4.69	order 4.60
sociability (общительность) 4.51	sociability 4.52
life (жизнь) 4.37	well-being 4.28
tradition (традиция) 4.34	tradition 4.18
freedom (свобода) 4.25	freedom 4.17
independence (независимость) 4.14	independence 4.15
work (работа) 4.08	work 4.04
initiative (инициативность) 4.0	human life 3.97
self-sacrifice (жертвенность) 3.99	integrity 3.92
well-being (благополучие) 3.68	initiative 3.74
integrity (нравственность) 3.66	self-sacrifice 3.64
strong will (своевольность) 2.24	authoritativeness 2.53
authoritativeness (властность) 2.06	strong will 2.06

Source: Lapin and Belyaeva 2009

late perestroika and early years of the Yeltsin presidency. Adopting the contrast drawn in the international comparative values surveys of Inglehart and Welzel (2005) between 'survival' and 'self-realization' values, clearly, survival values are more dominant among Smolensk respondents than among Russians generally. This is evident for example in the greater weight given in Smolensk to 'well-being' and the lesser weight given to 'initiative' or 'freedom.' A striking difference, too, is the lesser weight given in Smolensk to the value of 'life,' which means the preservation of the life (of others) and is given the greatest weight of all values by respondents in the most 'modern' of Russian regions, Karelia, Tyumen and Perm.

A crucial role in social and charitable work in the Smolensk region is played by the extremely vigorous revival of the Orthodox Church. The national significance of the Orthodox Church in the region was enhanced by the election of Metropolitan Kyrill of Smolensk to become Patriarch, succeeding Alexey in 2011. Among its other forms of social engagement, the diocese '*eparkhia*' of Smolensk and Vyasma has had a role in sponsoring the idea of the social usefulness of private entrepreneurship, for example in the production by the Church's own television studio – *Telestudia Svyatoy Merkuriy* – of an informative 2009 broadcast on small business development, covering President Medvedev's 2008 visit and speech on SME development and profiling several Smolensk small manufacturing enterprises.[44] (Artemenko 2009)

A second pillar of the traditional order related to the social engagement of business people in Smolensk region is the military, or, more precisely, the veterans of military service, who are perceived as having borne an unduly heavy burden of hardship in the aftermath of the collapse of the Soviet Union. 'Paritet,' a charitable fund devoted to social support for veterans and their families, is one of the members of the coalition of business associations whose programs and objectives were outlined earlier. Several small business people in Smolensk have either served or have family members who have served in the military, who reportedly focus their personal charitable activity toward military pensioners and their surviving spouses.

The noteworthy exception to the usually discreet and individualized form of charitable engagement practiced by entrepreneurs in the region is the work for the Smolensk Chamber on behalf of the region's orphanages. Beginning in the 1990s the Smolensk region saw a great number of foreign adoptions from its orphanages. By the late 2000s these had reportedly declined, leaving a greater role for private charity from local donors including from business.

The Smolensk region has, relative to its population, a large volume of newspapers and magazines.[45] Eight general newspapers are published in Smolensk and three others in other cities in the region. Three of the eight in Smolensk are regional editions of the popular national papers, *Argumenty i Fakty, Moskovkiy Komsomlets* and *Komsomolskaya Pravda*. These three papers report news in a somewhat irreverent and entertaining style and attract a mass readership in Russia as a whole. Among local publications, *Smolenskie Novosti* launched in 1990 gives priority to seriousness, objectivity and independence. There are 26 magazines published locally on life-style (home décor, family, fashion, health) and five free newspapers with large print runs devoted exclusively to small business and individual advertisers. Only two publications are addressed to entrepreneurs and managers as such. One of them, *Portfel'*, has a youthful chat-space on the social network site livejournal and is led by a recent graduate of the Smolensk Humanitarian University. The underdevelopment of the business press in the region is presumably part of the reason why the Smolensk Chamber publishes its own newspaper and magazine.

Civic memory: entrepreneurs and the 'usable' past – ideational antecedent conditions

The Smolensk region's fate is to lie on the route of invaders, and it has styled itself the gateway to, or shield of, Moscow. In the city stand memorials to the role Smolensk played in the war of 1812 when, after a bloody and inconclusive battle, it was overrun by Napoleon's advancing forces. Intensely loyal to the Russian Empire, the region was to prove one of the most stubbornly loyal to preserving the Soviet Union.

In the living memory of some of its residents, the city fell to Nazi invaders in 1941 after bitter fighting. After nearly two years of cruel occupation, Smolensk was almost completely devastated on being retaken. The city only recovered its pre-war population levels in the mid-1960s. The survivors of the war seem to have returned to rebuild in Smolensk, with a relatively small role being played by newcomers from other parts of Russia. (McFaul and Petrov 1997) The post-war restoration of the historic center and especially of the Kremlin walls reinforces the status of the city as one of the 'hero-cities' of the USSR. Identical monuments to each of these cities stand along Smolensk's Kremlin wall, near the WWII museum.

Liberal-constitutional politics of the final decades of imperial rule period attracted some support from the business community in the Smolensk region, but the region's politics were, by virtue perhaps of the still predominantly agrarian base of the region's economy of the time, dominated by ethnically Russian noble landowners or professionals of noble origin. (Hickey 1996) A plaque placed in 2003 near the entrance of the graceful historic Glinka concert hall on Smolensk's central square honors Nikolai Alekseevich Khomyakov, a prominent leader of the moderate-liberal Octobrist party, native of the Smolensk region, leader of the regional nobles' assembly (which met in what is today the Conservatory), director of the Russian Red Cross and chairman of the 3rd duma.[46] A supporter of the White forces in the Civil War, Khomyakov emigrated and died in Dubrovnik in 1925. The placement of the plaque in his honor is an indication of a reassessment in post-Soviet Smolensk of the significance and value for current generations of the constitutional and parliamentary experiment of the early 20th century.

The civic landscape of Smolensk, unlike that of Perm, Samara or Rostov, does not give pride of place to early merchant-industrialists of the late 19th and early 20th centuries. The sole partial exception to this is the museum housing the art collection and the nearby country estate of Maria Tenisheva, patron of the arts and wife of a Bryansk textile factory owner. In the early 20th century, Tenisheva set up a school for peasant children and a workshop for traditional artisans, now a museum.

The region and the model – conclusions

The modified scheme shown in Figure 5.1 attempts to capture the principal ways in which the Smolensk case differs from the paradigmatic case:

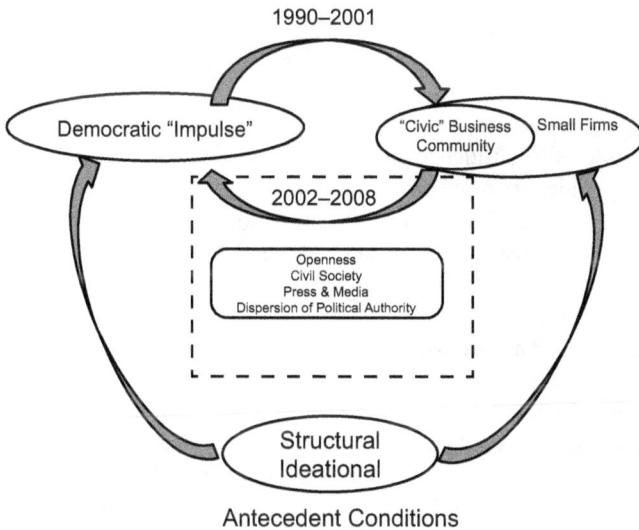

Figure 5.1 The Elaborated Model: Smolensk Case

In general terms, the Smolensk case conforms to the balanced picture of the paradigm, but most of the posited relationships are weak. The tenure of the pro-Yeltsin reformist governor Valeriy Fateev was brief, and the small cadre of reformist political leadership in Smolensk confronted entrenched traditionalist opponents, mainly in the well-organized and popular CPRF.[47] The tentative political opening and economic reforms of Fateev's tenure, pursued to some degree by his successor, Anatoliy Glushenkov, were followed by thoroughgoing 'restoration' from the mid-1990s, accompanied by deepening social malaise and nostalgia on the part of many for the Soviet Union.

The 'feedback' from entrepreneurs to democratization in the Smolensk case is, however, stronger that what would be anticipated. The Smolensk Chamber has worked with small self-organized entrepreneurs' associations in its public advocacy for improved governance. The civic engagement of organized business community reinforced what would otherwise be a weaker outcome on the variables of civil society, openness of the conduct of government, and diversity/independence of the press. The Chamber is in one sense an implementer of the regional and city small business promotion efforts, but at the same time has generated program substance and initiatives, in particular through its relations with Smolensk Humanitarian University, the roots of which lie in the initial, albeit weak, democratic experiment of the early 1990s.

The fact that most of the region's 'incumbent' businesses inherited from the Soviet period were unable to execute a rapid and successful reorientation to profitable activities in new markets (because they were based on manufacturing for the domestic Soviet and Eastern bloc markets) has left scope for small businesses to carry more weight in the business community than they otherwise could have. This is a 'structural' advantage that has tended to enhance the influence of the Smolensk Chamber relative to the regional and municipal administration.

The model as applied to Smolensk falls somewhat short because it does not take into account the diffusion effects from outside the region influencing both the administration and the business community. While Rostov, Perm and Samara are all large enough to be considered economic centers in their own right, disposing of considerable self-confidence and tax resources, the Smolensk region's development and policies are more susceptible to direction from Moscow, as well as to diffusion of precedents from other Russian regions. The activism of the business community in Smolensk region has been affected decisively by its adoption of the experiences and models for business advocacy from other regions, specifically under the CIPE program.

The Smolensk Chamber was able to build on the experiences of Chambers such as Perm, where social attitudes were more open toward business and where the economic reforms of the 1990s and the political opening had been greater. As the regression line in Chapter 3 (Figure 3.3, p. 69) shows, the Smolensk region had, in the middle of the 2000s, relatively few small firms per the workforce and relatively weak performance on the democratic index. The vigorous development of small firms since 2006 shows the effects of dissemination of new social norms through the process of national integration promoted by associations such as TPPRF and OPORA and the development of entrepreneurs' associations' influence, including through the CIPE sponsored coalition.

The Smolensk regional administration, for its part, signaled a new awareness of and interest in the development of small business beginning in 2006 and decisively so after the adoption of the 2007 federal law on SME support and on the 2008 visit to the region by then-President Medvedev. The Smolensk city administration, because of the growing role of small businesses in employment and tax revenues, has been at least as active in small business development and promotion efforts as the regional administration. Small business weighs even heavier in employment in the region's smaller cities such as Vyasma, Safonov and Yartsevo than in Smolensk, which explains the role played by entrepreneurs from these cities in business association activity.

Only on the dimension of enhancing the dispersion of political power does the emergence of private entrepreneurship in Smolensk fail to generate any significant positive influence on the extent of regional democratization. The role of private entrepreneurs from *de novo* companies in politics or administration has been weak in the Smolensk region, and the extent of pessimism and cynicism of businesspeople about the political class mirrors that of much of the public. Small business development and the emergence of entrepreneurs as an organized interest group has had to proceed against strong cultural headwinds in the region, as borne out in the comparative study of regional political cultures. (Vinokurov and Blagovestova 2009)

The rich and fascinating history of the Smolensk region is neither particularly supportive of democratization nor of private entrepreneurship, because it is dominated by the intense awareness of sacrifice in national struggle and with a culturally distinctive rootedness in pre-modern Russian traditions. The unique historical role of Smolensk as 'shield' and its identification with the traditions of military valor as well as its pining for the former intimacy with Belarus color the entire region's traditionalism.

Of the Smolensk region's impressive pantheon of cultural heroes – Glinka, Tvardovsky, Tukhachevsky, Khomyakov, Przevalskiy to name a few – only one, Maria Tenisheva, is related (by her marriage) to the merchant-industrialist elite of the late 19th and early 20th centuries. This marks a clear contrast with the celebrated merchant-industrialist legacy that is part of the civic landscape in Perm, Rostov and Samara. The 'reimagining' of the immediate pre-revolutionary decades to reinforce the identity of today's entrepreneurs is less advanced in Smolensk than in the three other cases in this study.

Notes

1 See the comparative elections results Table 3.1 for case study regions, Chapter 3, p. 54.
2 Fainsod (1958:21) quotes Wallace's observations.
3 McFaul and Petrov (1997) put the share of ethnic Russians in the oblast at 94%.
4 Company information at http://www.kristallsmolensk.ru/about/. Accessed August 15, 2011.
5 Personal interview, June 24, 2010.

6 See Figure 3.6, p. 74.

7 Lallemand (1999) compares the regional politics of the Smolensk region with that of its neighbor the Bryansk region also in the so-called 'redbelt.'

8 Savenok, Svetlana. January 7, 2004. "Era of the 'Perennial Communist' Is Over" *Current Digest of the Post-Soviet Press.* 49 55:2–3. The foregoing discussion of the region's politics and governance is drawn from the cited sources and also synthesizes the views of interviewees in the region in 2009 and 2010.

9 Pyle (2009) shows the ratings on the Democracy Audit scale for all Russian regions.

10 A brief biography of Fateev is at http://www.biografija.ru/show_bio.aspx?id=127810. Several Smolensk interviewees mentioned he had until recently been teaching economics at Smolensk Humanitarian University.

11 Meshcheryakov's biographical sketch indicates he still heads 'Smolensk' television and Novikov is still editor in chief of *Smolenskie Novosti.* http://pusk.by/bbe/82144/ and http://www.smol-news.ru/. Accessed August 20, 2011. Aleksandr Manoim died in 2004. Biography at http://arhivatvt.smolensk.ru/aat/a68/manoim.htm.

12 Because Fateev, Glushenkov and Prokhorov all had been members of the CPSU, Lallemand joins Olga Kryshtanovskaya and others in considering them all to have been part of the survival of an undifferentiated 'nomenklatura' class into the elite ruling circles of Russia.

13 Stroganov, Yuriy. June 19, 2002. "FSB Men Are Crowding Out Communists" *Current Digest of the Post-Soviet Press.* 54 21:10.

14 http://admin-smolensk.ru/. Accessed August 8, 2011.

15 Interview June 21, 2010, Alexey Nikolaevich Seriy, Executive Director, United Russia, Smolensk chapter.

16 Chamber of Commerce and Industry Smolensk Region. (2009f) Calendar 'Vlast' i Biznes Smolenskaya Oblast' produced with the Regional Administration, notes the birthdays of noteworthy regional and local officials and businesspeople with their photos and affiliations.

17 Even given continued rapid growth in their numbers from 2008, the figure of 10,769 given by the regional administration seems high relative to the official Rosstat number of just under 6,000 in 2008.

18 Interview June 24, 2010, Smolensk market.

19 http://smolenskcci.ru/about-us. Accessed September 1, 2011.

20 Chamber of Commerce and Industry Smolensk Region. (2008e) *Small Business in the Smolensk Region,* PowerPoint presentation.

21 See, for example Chamber of Commerce and Industry Smolensk Region, 2008a "Role of Entrepreneurs' Associations."

22 http://smolenskcci.ru/2009–12–16–23–01–25. Accessed September 5, 2011.

23 A link to the list of board members is at http://smolenskcci.ru/about-us. Accessed September 5, 2011.

24 http://smolenskcci.ru/ has a link to this grouping of associations. Accessed September 5, 2011.

25 Malik's company Elizabeta (producer of Scandinavian style crispbread crackers) was one of the winners of the national Mercury prize in 2009, sponsored by the TPPRF, honoring outstanding small companies.

26 Chamber of Commerce and Industry, Smolensk Region 2009b "New Possibilities" is one example.

27 "Printsipy Vedeniya Del v Rossii" (Principles of the Conduct of Business in Russia) *Vedomosti Smolenskoy Torgovo-Promyshlennoy Palaty,* issue 31, September 2009. (Chamber of Commerce and Industry, Smolensk Region 2009g)

28 Smolensk Humanitarian University http://www.shu.ru/?nii. Accessed August 10, 2011 and interview October 28, 2009 with Aleksandr Katrovskiy, professor and director of Smolensk Humanitarian University Institute of Regional Studies.

29 Medvedev speech http://www.kremlin.ru/news/990. Accessed September 5, 2011.
30 Personal interviews, OPORA Smolensk President October 2009 and June 2010. Also based on a personal interview with Olga Plotnikova, OPORA Rossii director for relations with regional OPORA chapters on June 28, 2010, Moscow.
31 She had, for example been asked to comment on a draft paper from the regional administration on enhancing competition.
32 http://www.gov.ru/main/page4.html. Accessed August 15, 2011.
33 http://www.deloros.ru. Accessed June 4, 2011.
34 Smolensk Regional Coalition of Business Associations (2008) "Anti-Corruption Program of the Business Community of the Smolensk Region" (22-page brochure). The program is also published in *Vedomosti Smolenskoy Palaty* July 2008 (15th anniversary issue) no.28, pp. 40–50.
35 These two documents, the first a brochure for public distribution and the second a text shared by the Chamber with the author report and tally the results of the 2007 and 2008 monitoring surveys of entrepreneurs in the Smolensk region in detail.
36 By the end of 2009 the implementation of the program had presumably lagged so that program disbursements from the regional budget in 2009 were only 99 million rubles with a similar amount from the federal budget. The economic downturn of 2009 may be a reason for this shortfall.
37 Personal interview, Vladimir Mal'tsev, Smolensk Regional Fund for the Support of Entrepreneurship, October 27, 2009.
38 Smolensk Institute of Business and Entrepreneurship rector Valeriy Grushenkov is a member of the governing board of the Smolensk Chamber.
39 Presentation by department head Cheberyak to the 1st Municipal Small Business Conference May 26–27, 2008. This was the first observance of Entrepreneurs' Day.
40 An introductory meeting at the municipal office in charge of the program on October 28, 2009 of the produced useful documentation.
41 http://www.sitallsmolensk.ru/default.phtml?name=about. Accessed June 15, 2011.
42 "Arestovan Mer Smolenska" VOAnews.com. February 27, 2010.
43 Lapin and Belyaeva (2009:671) defines as 'traditional' the values of tradition, family, self-sacrifice and strong will, as 'modern' the values of life, freedom, independence and initiative, and as 'all-human' the values of order, well-being, work, sociability, integrity and authoritativeness.
44 Conversations with small businesspeople and several of the association leaders across the region found many of them to be strongly committed to the Orthodox faith, whether more so than the region's general population is not clear.
45 http://www.media-atlas.ru/regionmedia/. Accessed June 20, 2011. The Rosstat data on numbers of newspapers printed by year also suggest that the Smolensk region has more than its share of locally produced publications.
46 Profile at http://news.yandex.ru/people/khomyakov_nikolaj_2.html.
47 This is evident from the election results Table 3.1 in Chapter 3.

References

Artemenko, Viktor Ivanovich. (2009) *Malyi Biznes Smolenshiny (Small Business of the Smolensk Region)*. Smolensk: Telestudia "Svatoy Merkurii" Compact Disc: television documentary profiling regional small businesses.
Carr, F. H. (1980) *From Napoleon to Stalin and Other Essays*. New York: St. Martin's Press.
Chamber of Commerce and Industry, Smolensk Region. (2008a) *Role of Entrepreneurs Associations and Social Organizations in Resolving Questions about the Support of Small and Medium Enterprises in the Smolensk Region*. Smolensk.

Chamber of Commerce and Industry, Smolensk Region. (2008b) Ob Itogakh Regional'nogo Issledovaniya Sub'ektov predprinimatel'skoy Deyatel'nosti. *Predprinimatel' Smolenitsiny.*

Chamber of Commerce and Industry, Smolensk Region. (2008c) *Brief Basic Information on the Smolensk Region.* Smolensk.

Chamber of Commerce and Industry, Smolensk Region. (2008d) *Small Business of the Smolensk Oblast' in the Language of Figures.* Smolensk.

Chamber of Commerce and Industry, Smolensk Region. (2008e) *Small Business in the Smolensk Region* (PowerPoint presentation). Smolensk.

Chamber of Commerce and Industry, Smolensk Region. (2008f) *Resolutsiya "kruglogo stola" – "Aktualnye Voprosy bezopasnosti predprinimatel'skoy deyatel'nosti i protivodeystviya korruptsii".* Smolensk.

Chamber of Commerce and Industry, Smolensk Region. (2008g) Nota Bene: Smolensk Chamber of Commerce and Industry – 15 Years Together with the Region's Businesses. *Vedomosti Smolenskoy Torgovo-Promyshlennoy Palati*, July, 17–22.

Chamber of Commerce and Industry, Smolensk Region. (2009a) *Results of the Survey of Regional Entrepreneurs.* Smolensk.

Chamber of Commerce and Industry, Smolensk Region. (2009b) *Novye vozmozhnosti dlya vashego biznesa.* Smolensk.

Chamber of Commerce and Industry, Smolensk Region. (2009c) *Rol' Delovogo Soobshchestva v Realizatsii Anti-Korruptsionnoy Politiki v Smolenskoy Oblasti.* Smolensk.

Chamber of Commerce and Industry, Smolensk Region. (2009d) *Informatsiya ob Uchastii Predprinimatel'skogo Soobshchestva Smolenskoy Oblasti v Profilaktike Pravonarushenii.* Smolensk.

Chamber of Commerce and Industry, Smolensk Region. (2009e) *Biznes i Vlast': Problemy i Perspektivy.* Smolensk.

Chamber of Commerce and Industry, Smolensk Region. (2009f) *"Vlast' Biznes" Calendar.* Smolensk.

Chamber of Commerce and Industry, Smolensk Region. (2009g) Printsipy Vedeniya Del v Rossii. *Vedomosti Smolenskoy Torgovo-Promyshlennoy Palati,* September, 8–9.

Chamber of Commerce and Industry, Smolensk Region. (2010a) *Analytical Report of the Results of the Survey on the Effectiveness of State and Municipal Services to Entrepreneurs in the Smolensk Oblast.* Smolensk.

Chamber of Commerce and Industry, Smolensk Region. (2010b) *Small and Medium Business in Smolensk Region in Figures: Third Quarter 2009.* Smolensk.

Chamber of Commerce and Industry, Smolensk Region. (2010c) *Maliy i Sredniy Biznes Smolenskoy Oblasti v Tsifrakh i Faktakh.* Smolensk.

Chamber of Commerce and Industry, Smolensk Region. (2010d) *Conference Program "Vzaimodeystvie organov gosudarstvennoy vlasti Smolesnkoy oblasti s institutami grazhdanskogo obshchestva po formirovaniyu sredi grazhdan neterplimogo othoshenniya k korruptsii".* Smolensk.

Chamber of Commerce and Industry, Smolensk Region. (2010e) *Otchet o rabote Smolenskoy Torgovo-promyshlennaya Palaty v 2009 godu.* Smolensk.

Fainsod, Merle. (1958) *Smolensk Under Soviet Rule.* Boston: Unwin Hyman.

Goskomstat Rossii. (2001) *Regions of Russia (Regiony Rossii).* Moscow: State Committee of the Russian Federation for Statistics.

Hickey, Michael C. (1996) Discourses of Public Identity and Liberalism in the February Revolution: Smolensk, Spring 1917. *Russian Review* 55 (4):615–637.

Hickey, Michael C. (1998) Revolution on the Jewish Street: Smolensk 1917. *Journal of Social History* 31 (4):823–850.

Hickey, Michael C. (2004) The Rise and Fall of Smolensk's Moderate Socialists: The Politics of Class and the Rhetoric of Crisis in 1917. In Wade, R.A. (ed.) *Revolutionary Russia: New Approaches*. Wade. New York and London: Routledge.

Inglehart, Ronald and Christian Welzel. (2005) *Modernization, Cultural Change and Democracy: The Human Development Sequence*. Cambridge, UK: Cambridge University Press.

Lallemand, Jean-Charles. (1999) Politics for the Few: Elites in Bryansk and Smolensk. *Post-Soviet Affairs* 15 (4):312–335.

Lapin,N.I. and L.A. Belyaeva. (eds.) (2009) *Regiony v Rossii: Sotsiokulturnye Portrety Regionov v Obshcherossiskoy Kontekste*. Moscow: Institute of Sociology, Russian Academy of Sciences (IS-RAN).

Matveev, Sergey. (2009, October 23) "Vlast' Podderzhit Biznes" Interview with Chamber President Vladimimir Arkhipenko. *Smolenskaya Nedelya* 2.

McFaul, Michael and Nikolai Petrov. (eds.) (1997) *Politicheskiy Almanakh Rossii: Sotsialno-Politicheskie Portrety Regionov*. Moscow: Carnegie Moscow Center.

OPORA Rossii. (2008) *Maliy Biznes i Korruptsionnye Otnosheniya: Perspktivy Preodoleniya Korruptsii: Otchet po Resultatam Issledovaniya*. Moscow.

Orttung, Robert W. (ed.) (2000) *The Republics and Regions of the Russian Federation: A Guide to Politics, Policies and Leaders*. Edited by E.W. Institute. Armonk, NY and London, UK: M.E. Sharpe.

Owen, Thomas C. (1991) Impediments to Bourgeois Consciousness in Russia, 1880–1905: The Estate Structure, Ethnic Diversity and Regionalism. In Clowes, E.W., Kassow, S.D. and West J.L. (eds.) *Between Tsar and People*.

Petrov, Nikolai. (2006) Naznacheniya gubernatorov: itogi pervogo goda. *Carnegie Moscow Center Briefing* 8 (3).

Petrov, Nikolai and Alexei Titkov. (2006) *Demokratichnost' Rossiskikh Regionov.* http://atlas.socpol.ru/indexes/index_democr.shtml. Accessed Novermber 10, 2010.

Petrov, Nikolai and Alexei Titkov. (2013) *Reyting Demokratichnosti Regionov Moskovskogo Tsenta Karnegi: 10 Let v Stroyu*. Moscow: Carnegie Moscow Center. http://carnegie.ru/publications/?fa=55853. Accessed December 1, 2014.

Pyle, William. (2009) Organized Business, Political Competition, and Property Rights: Evidence from the Russian Federation. *Journal of Law, Economics, and Organization* 27 (1):2–31.

Rosstat (Federal'naya Sluzhba Gosudarstvennoy Statistiki). (2002, 2008, 2010a) *Regiony Rossii: Sotsial'no-Ekonomicheskie Pokazateli*.

Rosstat (Federal'naya Sluzhba Gosudarstvennoy Statistiki). (2009) *Maloe i Srednee Predprimatel'stvo v Rossii*.

Rosstat (Federal'naya Sluzhba Gosudarstvennoy Statistiki). (2010b) *Goroda Rossii. Osnovnye Sotsial'no-Ekonomicheskie Pokazateli Gorodov*.

Russia All Regions Trade and Investment Guide. (2008) *Smolensk Region*. London, UK: CTEC and Effective Technology Marketing, Ltd.

Russian Federation. (2008) Federal Law 159-ф3 *Ob Osobennostakh Otchuzhdeniya Nedvizhmogo Imushchestva, Hakhodyagosya v Gosudarstvennoy Sobstvennosti Sub'ektov Rossiiskoy Federatsii ili v munitsipal'noy sobstvennosti i arenduemogo sub'ektami malogo i srednogo predprinimatel'stva*. Moscow: Federal Assembly of the Russian Federation. http://www.gov.ru/main/page4.html. Accessed June 20, 2010.

Schumpeter, Joseph. (1942) *Capitalism, Socialism and Democracy*. New York: Harper.

Smolensk City Administration. (2006) *Programma "Poderzhka i Razvitiye malogo predprinimatel'stva v gorode Smolenske na 2007–2009 god) No. 430*. Smolensk, Russia: Smolensk City legislature (Gorodskoy Sovet).

Smolensk City Administration. (2008) *Malye predpriyatiya goroda Smolenska – katalog.* Smolensk.

Smolensk City Administration. (2009) *Otchet o Vypolnenii Programmy "Razvitie i Poderzhka malogo i srednogo predprinimatel'stva v gorode Smolenske na 2007–2009 gody" za 2008 god.* Smolensk.

Smolensk City Administration, Department for the Consumer Market and Development of Entrepreneurship. (2008a) Spravochnik Predprinimatelya Goroda Smolenska In *First City Conference "Small and Medium Business in the City of Smolensk"*. Smolensk.

Smolensk City Administration, Department for the Consumer Market and Development of Entrepreneurship. (2008b) *Materialy 1-y gorodskoy konferentsii Maliy i Sredniy Biznes goroda Smolenska.* Smolensk.

Smolensk City Administration, Department for the Consumer Market and Development of Entrepreneurship. (2008c) Katalog Innovatsionnykh Proyektov. In *First City Conference on Small and Medium Business in the City of Smolensk*. Smolensk.

Smolensk City Administration, Department for the Consumer Market and Development of Entrepreneurship. (2008d) *Pamyatka Nachinayushchemu Predprinimatelyu*. Smolensk.

Smolensk City Administration, Department for the Consumer Market and Development of Entrepreneurship. (2009a) Spravochnik Predprinimatelya Goroda Smolenska In *Second City Conference "Small and Medium Business in the City of Smolensk"*. Smolensk.

Smolensk City Administration, Department for the Consumer Market and Development of Entrepreneurship. (2009b) *Materialy 2-oy gorodskoy konferentsii Maliy i Sredniy Biznes goroda Smolenska.* Smolensk.

Smolensk City Administration, Department for the Consumer Market and Development of Entrepreneurship, and Smolensk Region Chamber of Commerce and Industry. (2009c) *Vystavka-Prezentatsiya "Predprinimatel'stvo goroda Smolenska"*. Smolensk.

Smolensk City Administration, Department for the Consumer Market and Development of Entrepreneurship. (2010) Entrepreneur's Handbook for the City of Smolensk. In *Third City Conference "Small and Medium Business in the City of Smolensk"*. Smolensk.

Smolensk Regional Administration. (2010) *Itogi i Perspektivy Razvitiya sub'ektov malogo i srednogo predprinimatel'stva v Smolesnkoy Oblasti v 2009–2010*. Smolensk.

Smolensk Regional Administration, Department of Economic Development and Trade. (2009a) *Development of Small and Medium Entrepreneurship in Smolensk Oblast*. Smolensk.

Smolensk Regional Administration, Department of Economic Development and Trade. (2009b) *Oblastnaya Programma "Razvitie konkurentsii v Smolenskoy oblasti na 2010–2012*. Smolensk.

Smolensk Regional Administration, Department of Economic Development and Trade, and Smolensk Region Chamber of Commerce and Industry. (2008a) *Spravochnik Predprinimatelya (Entrepreneur's Handbook): Current Aspects of the Process of Organizing a Small Business*. Smolensk.

Smolensk Regional Administration Department of Economic Development and Trade, and Smolensk Region Chamber of Commerce and Industry. (2008b) *Itogi provedeniya Monitoringa Deyatel'nosti Sub'ektov Malogo i srednogo preprinimatel'stva na territorii smolenskogo oblasti*. Smolensk.

Smolensk Regional Administration Departments of Economic Development and Trade and International and Interregional Cooperation and Tourism. (2009) *Karta Gostya: Biznes i Istoriya Smolenskoy oblasti.* Smolensk.

Smolensk Regional Coalition of Business Associations, and Smolensk Region Chamber of Commerce and Industry. (2008) *Antikorruptsionnaya Programma Delovogo Soobshchestva – Vy Mozhete Ostanovit' Korruptsiyu.* Smolensk.

Smolensk Regional Duma. (2008) *Law 153-з "O razvitii malogo i srednogo predprinimatel'stva v Smolenskoy oblasti".* Smolensk.

Smolensk Regional Duma. (2009) *Regional Law no. 32-з "O nalogovykh stavkakh dlya nalogoplatel'shchikov, primenyayushchikh uproshchennuyu sistemu nalogooblozheniya, v sluchae esli ob'ektom nalogooblozheniya yavlayutsya dokhody ymen'shennye na velichinu raskhodov".* Smolensk.

Smolensk Regional Fund for Support of Entrepreneurship. (2009) *Vmeste k Uspekhu: Nasha Podderzhka – Reshenie Vashykh Problem!*

Vinokurov, A. I. and T. E. Blagovestova. (2009) Smolenskaya Oblast'. In Lapin, N. I. and Belyaeva, L. A. (eds.) *Regiony v Rossii: Sociokulturnye Portrety Regionov v Obshcherossisskom Kontekste.* Moscow Akademia.

6   The Rostov region

Limits of patrimonial exchange

The Rostov region is home to more than 4 million people and is one of the leading agricultural regions of Russia, encompassing 160,600 sq km. The city of Rostov, with a population just over one million, lies near the mouth of the Don River as it opens onto the Azov Sea, leading onward to the Black Sea. By virtue of its history and commercial importance, Rostov is the acknowledged 'capital of the Russian south.' The city owes its early economic development to agricultural commodity processing, trading and finance, on the basis of its role as a commercial port. In this it is analogous to Samara, but whereas 19th century Samara was instrumental in the development of internal Russian economic integration – among the other Volga cities and with Moscow – Rostov seems always to have been facing outward, toward trade with the Caucasus and the Black Sea basin, especially Turkey. (IISP 2006)

The region's main export markets are Turkey, Ukraine, Kazakhstan, Venezuela, Egypt, Italy, Greece, India, Bangladesh, Georgia, Azerbaijan, Israel, Germany and Spain. (Russia All Regions Trade and Investment Guide Rostov, 2008) Rostov is the southward rail and road 'Gateway to the Caucasus.'

The oblast's population has been stable, in contrast to the declines that are the norm elsewhere in Russia. In 2008, the population stood at 4.3 million, compared with 4.25 million in 1991. In 1998 about one third of the oblast's population came from outside the region, and one fifth of those born in the Rostov region lived elsewhere in Russia or abroad. (McFaul and Petrov 1997)

Although per capita incomes in the Rostov region remain below the national median, the oblast's economic growth from 1999 to 2008 made it one of 24 'catch up' regions in a study of the dynamics of regional growth in Russia. (World Bank 2009)[1] The gross regional product of the Rostov oblast more than doubled from 1996 to 2006, compared with a 67% increase for Russia as a whole. (World Bank 2009)

The Rostov case is a puzzle from the standpoint of our model, because large numbers of small companies relative to the workforce arose with only a brief and equivocal democratic opening in the early 1990s. The solution seems to lie in the 'patrimonial' character of business-government relations in Rostov, a pattern not uncommon in Russia. The patrimonialism of the Rostov region under the leadership of long-serving governor Vladimir Chub supported the entrepreneurialism that underpinned the region's strong performance in per capita income growth and attendant poverty reduction.

Economic geography and business history – antecedent structural conditions

The city was founded in 1749 around a fortress overlooking the Don. In the 19th and early 20th centuries, Rostov vied with Odessa as a center of Tsarist Russia's southern trade. The restored central commercial district of Rostov is a monument to its pre-revolutionary economic dynamism. From the center of the city, the streets slope steeply downward through unrestored historical neighborhoods to the re-developed boardwalk along the Don.

The Rostov region was a forward redoubt of the Russian empire, intensely loyal and traditionalist in outlook, but its economic orientation and location made it somewhat detached from Moscow. The Rostov's region's most well-known cultural distinction is, however, not the merchants of Rostov and Taganrog, but the Don Cossacks, whose unofficial capital is Novocherkassk. The Cossacks, ethnic Russians with a distinct culture, represent at most 15% of the region's population. In Tsarist times, the territory of today's Rostov oblast was the 'Don Cossack Armed Forces region,' with its capital at Novocherkassk. In the Civil War of 1918–1922, the Don Cossack ataman Kaledin and the Don Cossacks were among the most effective fighters in support of the White cause, but also those most committed to a full restoration of the traditional *ancien regime*. (Suny 2011)[2] A stronghold of the White forces in the Civil War, the Rostov region also is well represented in Russia's overseas diaspora.

Ethnic diversity underpins the outward orientation of the city of Rostov. Armenian settlers in the time of Catherine the Great founded the town of Nakhchivan, directly adjacent to Rostov along the Don, and it became a bustling port in its own right. The streets of this district are lined with gracious 19th-century mansions, now in some cases restored. Nakhchivan and Rostov were fused together as both grew, so that Nakhchivan became a neighborhood of Rostov. With exquisite irony, the Soviets renamed this quintessentially bourgeois district *Proletarskaya* and it still bears that name.

Other major cities of the oblast are commercial port and industrial center Taganrog and the industrial and mining centers Shakhtiy and Novocherkassk. Nearby Taganrog is sleepier but similar to Rostov in its generally commercial and outward-looking orientation. Taganrog lost to Rostov in the race to be the most important port on the Azov, but 'won' the title of most European of the region's cities by virtue of being the birthplace of Chekhov. (McFaul and Petrov 1997)

Along its western border, the oblast shares with Ukraine the coal-rich Donbass district. The Rostov region, along with the neighboring Krasnodar and Stavropol regions, has benefited from federal policies favoring social and economic development to dampen contagion from the volatile north Caucasus. In this vein, Rostov has become the base of the Southern State University, a consolidation of several regional universities aimed at creating a regional center of higher learning with national prestige.

The Rostov oblast inherited from the Soviet period a very substantial number of nationally significant 'incumbent' industrial enterprises, including combine harvester manufacturer Rosselmash, power generation equipment maker Energomash-Atommash, the electric locomotives plant at Novocherkassk, the automotive (formerly agricultural vehicles) plant at Taganrog and others. These enterprises traversed a period of deep crisis in the 1990s and survived in varying states of soundness, in some cases absorbed or partnered with larger Russian firms or having attracted foreign strategic investors.

For example, the French manufacturer Alstom holds a 25% stake in the locomotive factory in Novocherkassk, the remainder of which was acquired by the Moscow-based ZAO TransmashHolding, whose principal is Iskander Makhmudov. (Chamber of Commerce and Industry, Rostov Region 2009a)[3] This locomotive plant was the site in 1962 of the forceful suppression of a strike, a tragedy 'erased' from official media until perestroika but remembered acutely in the region. (Baron 2001)

The agricultural machinery manufacturer, Rosselmash, had repeated brushes with bankruptcy and absorbed both federal and regional financing in the 1990s, but still faces major challenges. The Hyundai investment in the production of cars at a re-tooled agricultural machinery plant – the Tagaz project – is widely reported to be in serious trouble, suffering a heavy blow in the economic downturn of 2009. Alcoa has a joint venture in metallurgical enterprise Belaya Kalitva. (Russia: All Regions Trade and Investment Guide, Rostov Region 2008)

The region's next most important industry is agro-processing, including vegetable oil production, flour mills, dairy and meat operations. This sector seems to have weathered the crisis of the 1990s with greater success than heavy industry, benefitting, as did all industries in the consumer sector, from the ruble depreciation following 1998. Agriculture accounts for 12% of the region's economy and 84.5% of the region's territory. The region ranks second in Russia for grain production and produces a quarter of the Russian crop of sunflowers for oil production. Commercial scale livestock and poultry production has shown impressive development in the region. (Russia: All Regions Trade and Investment Guide, Rostov Region 2008)

The Rostov region, and southern Russia as a whole, has fared well in SME development since the early 1990s, drawing, according to many observers, on long-standing cultural dispositions and economic geography. In the Rostov region, small firms are active in agro-processing, as well as in trade, construction and transport. The Rostov region has one *de novo* large enterprise, casual clothing manufacturer and retailer Gloria Jeans. This enterprise, founded and led by Rostov native Vladimir Melnikov, traces its origins to a Rostov cooperative that traded in imported jeans, and has expanded across Russia. In press interviews, the colorful Melnikov breezily acknowledges having served two brief prison sentences in Soviet times for 'black market' activity. (Filatova 2007)

The World Bank (2009) praises the Rostov region's strong growth performance but mentions the reliance of many of the larger enterprises in the region on close cooperation with and various forms of support from the regional administration. The model of growth in the Rostov region from 1999 to 2008 was, according to the World Bank's analysis, built to a large extent on the recovery of the internal, regional market rather than on full integration with, and exposure to competition from, extra-regional or international competition.

Impulse: the democratic interlude and the Chub 'restoration'

In the competitive federal and regional elections of the 1990s, the Russian south was an area of relative strength for the Communist party and for the nationalist LDPR. The conformity in general terms of the Rostov region with this observation is evident from the electoral results shown in Chapter 3 (see Table 3.1). Voters in the Rostov oblast showed, however, a somewhat greater disposition toward reformist parties in national elections in the 1990s than did neighboring regions of the Russian south, such as the Krasnodar or Stavropol regions. In the city of Rostov, the Yabloko party, founded on the basis of an entrepreneurs' and a student association in 1995, had one of its stronger organizations, reflected in Duma election results through 1999 and in Yavlinsky's presidential support in 2000. (McFaul and Petrov 1997)

Vladimir Chub, the Rostov oblast's governor from 1991 to 2010, was born in 1948 in the Belarusian SSR but claims Don Cossack ancestry. He started his career in the 'Krasniy Flot' shipping enterprise in Rostov in 1971 and rose in CPSU ranks in Rostov's Proletarskaya district, becoming a member of both city and regional legislatures by 1985. He was elected chairman of the city legislature in 1990. Chub's political base was the city of Rostov and the Proletarskaya district, where merchant traditions are strongest in the Rostov region, which might account in part for his relative reformist and pro-democratic stance in the early 1990s, at least against the background of a quite conservative CPSU senior regional leadership.[4]

The crisis of August 1991 and its aftermath produced a shake-up of ruling elites in the Rostov region. In an emergency session of the legislature, Chub embraced the view of the region's 'democrats' and declared the putsch unconstitutional, recognizing only the authority of the Russian president. In return for this show of support, Yeltsin appointed Chub to the post of governor. Yeltsin appointed Chub after consultations with leaders of the democratic movement in Rostov, which was divided over whether the seasoned 'apparatchik' Chub, having resigned from the CPSU in August 1991, was the right choice to lead the region. (McFaul and Petrov 1997) After the failed coup, senior regional CPSU officeholders resigned or were dismissed and the party dissolved.

The political memoir of former Rostov mayor Yuriy Pogrebshikov (2007) contains a vivid account of how the previously closely guarded Central Committee headquarters, a handsome historic building in the heart of Rostov, was left suddenly empty and undefended after the failed putsch and the outlawing of the CPSU.[5] According to Pogrebshikov, governor Chub's administration decided not to reoccupy the building, concerned that doing so could be seen as a *de facto* restoration of the CPSU authority associated with that building. After the events of August 1991, Pogrebshikov writes, the former party headquarters building was

> practically devastated and occupied by different organizations, including Cossack groups, which had no legal right to this unique building. In addition, as a consequence of these groups' occupation, there reigned disorder and bad management (*beskhozyaystvennost'*). Everything that could be stolen had been.

> (Pogrebshikov 2007:254)

As mayor, Pogrebshikov moved the city administration into this building, where it remains.

Chub stood down challenges from more reformist or liberal contenders for power in the first half of the 1990s. Yeltsin's appointed regional representative, radical democrat Vladimir Zubkov, resigned in 1994. The other important alternative political figure was Rostov mayor Pogrebshikov, appointed by Yeltsin on the recommendation of the Rostov members of DemRossiya in 1991. Pogrebshikov had been an enterprise director and was a "tough technocrat not inclined to compromise and with ambitious plans for the reorganization of the city's life." (McFaul and Petrov 1997:798) Pogrebshikov clashed with Chub and resigned in 1994. In his memoir, Pogrebshikov expresses particular disappointment that the Rostov entrepreneurs, who had benefited from the city administration's aggressive privatization program, did not leap to his defense when it became clear that the regional administration was moving to curb his authority.

On his resignation, Pogrebshikov became head of the newly formed 'Don Association of Privatized and Private Enterprises.' He remains a member of the business group 'Club 2015' even though he now lives in the United States. He served on the governing board of the Chamber of Commerce of the Rostov region until 2008.

Mikhail Chernishev, head of the regional administration of the Proletarskaya district, succeeded Pogrebshikov as Rostov mayor. A long-time close associate of Governor Chub, Chernishev brought the city under full subordination to the regional administration.

In the crisis of October 1993, the Rostov regional legislature sided with the Moscow parliamentarians in their standoff with Yeltsin. Chub dissolved this legislature having once more astutely stayed loyal to Yeltsin. The region's first freely elected regional legislature was elected in March of 1994. In this 'founding' democratic election in the region, deputies were elected on a majoritarian basis, and with any reference to party affiliation on the ballot expressly forbidden. An average of five candidates ran for each of the 45 seats. Almost half of the 45 deputies elected were regional or municipal officials, and another third were industrial plant directors. (McFaul and Petrov 1997) With the governor's support, this assembly extended its initial two-year term until 1998.

Chub decisively defeated his main opponent, CPRF candidate Leonid Ivanchenko, in 1996 elections, decried by the CPRF as having been falsified in favor of the incumbent. The official tally gave Ivanchenko 32% of the vote, and, although a State Duma investigation did not support the Communists' allegations of fraud, there can be little doubt that Moscow's backing, local patronage and media bias played heavily in Chub's favor. In November 1997 and January 1998, the regional CPRF initiated a referendum to call for Chub's impeachment. (Orttung 2000)

Chub became a leading figure in the pro-Yeltsin party NDR and served in the Federation Council from 1996 to 2001. By the time Chub ran for re-election in 2001, he had fully consolidated authority around himself, and he won 78% of the vote. President Putin appointed him to a third five-year term in 2005.

Chub seems to have been a guarantor for the region's big industrial firms, getting support from the federal budget and also warding off potential competitors while welcoming foreign strategic investors. The Rostov regional administration under Chub's leadership embraced small business development early and steadily, as a means of employment generation and poverty alleviation. He became a member of United Russia's senior governing council in 2003.

The replacement of Chub by Medvedev appointee Vasiliy Golubev in May 2010 suggested potential erosion in the insulated and protected status of the region's business elite. Although born in the Rostov oblast, Golubev had been a deputy governor in the Moscow region. His appointment confirmed the trend toward integration of the region's economy, with attendant new competitive pressures to be felt locally.

The genuine prospect of a communist *revanche* up to and through first gubernatorial election in 1996 seems to have generated tactical support for Yeltsin appointee Governor Vladimir Chub from the region's numerically weak democratic forces. Elections held for the legislature in 1994, where parties were expressly banned, frustrated democratic progress, and, by the time the second legislative elections were held in 1998, Chub had restored to the region's politics an unchallenged, if comparatively enlightened, monocentrism. Incrementally, over his nearly two decades as governor, he consolidated power and neutralized potentially competing sources of political authority, such as the legislature or the Rostov mayor's office. In interviews with regional officials in 1999, Chirikova and Lapina were told that a 'monocentric' governing structure with a strong dose of authoritarianism was "optimal and corresponded to the traditions of the regions of the Russian south where, already in Soviet times, a strict subordination to regional authority was in place that was not softened by the [subsequent] period of market reforms." (Lapina and Chirikova 2002:117) This was in distinct contrast to the 'polycentrism' the same authors found in the Samara region.

Comparative overview of small business development

Strong traditions of entrepreneurship in the Rostov oblast are frequently cited as the source of the dynamic development of small business in the region after 1991. This tradition survived in informal and semi-legal forms through the Soviet period, to re-emerge beginning in the late 1980s. (World Bank 2009) The region's entrepreneurs, several interviewees for this book claimed, had a commercially oriented, 'Southern Russian' mentality and long-established, trustful and resilient personal networks. Lending credence to the notion of a distinctive southern Russian business culture is the fact that Rostov's southern neighbor, the Krasnodar region, has exceeded even the Rostov region with respect to the prevalence of small firms.

Table 6.1 shows the number of incorporated small firms per 1,000 of the labor force compared with the average (mean) for all regions in the same year. (Rosstat 2002, 2004, 2008, 2010a)

These data show that the Rostov oblast has generally outperformed the national averages. However, apart from the years 2004 and 2006, the region does not exceed the national average by very much. In particular, it is interesting to observe that the Rostov region did not experience the big increase in small company registrations between 2006 and 2008 that brought the national average up to near parity with the Rostov figure. These data do not by themselves justify the region's reputation for unusually strong entrepreneurialism.

Stronger evidence for the claim that the region is culturally supportive of entrepreneurship comes rather from the numbers of unincorporated individual entrepreneurs relative to the workforce. Table 6.2 shows that the Rostov region exceeded the national median and national mean on this measure by a very wide margin in 2008.

These data show that the Rostov figure for individual entrepreneurs relative to the workforce went from being close to the average for Russia as a whole in 2004 to being in the 94th percentile in 2008. The fact that, under strong encouragement from the federal authorities since 2007, the numbers of new small companies did not grow by much, while the numbers of individual entrepreneurs rose steeply, is

Table 6.1 Rostov Region: Incorporated Small Firms per 1,000 Persons in Labor Force

	1995	*2000*	*2002*	*2004*	*2006*	*2008*
Rostov oblast	11.24	11.79	11.99	13.57	14.73	15.04
All-region average	11.64	9.48	9.32	11.05	10.76	14.91

Source: Goskomstat Rossii 2001; Rosstat *Regiony Rossii* 2006, 2010

Table 6.2 Independent Entrepreneurs: Rostov Region 2004 and 2008

	2004	*2008*
Independent entrepreneurs for 1,000 workforce	39	51
Rostov region national percentile ranking	59th	94th
Median (national)	37	36
Mean (national)	37	37

Source: Russian SME Resource Center 2004, 2006, Rosstat 2009a

an indication of inadequacies in the institutionalization of formal rules related to the conduct of business.

The status of individual entrepreneur serves many important economic functions in employment and poverty reduction, and a strong role for individual entrepreneurs is in no sense to be deplored. However, it seems fair to say that individual entrepreneur status in Russia has been closely associated with a transitional period during which entrepreneurship and markets were relatively novel. Among our four case regions, their numbers relative to the workforce in 2008 as compared to 2004 fell in Samara and Smolensk and held steady in Perm. Only in Rostov did they rise substantially. In addition to pointing to inadequacies of the business climate, the rise of individual entrepreneurs relative to the Rostov region's workforce may be related to the considerable inflow into the region of people fleeing the instability of the North Caucasus. It is reportedly common for such newcomers to work as market traders. The prevalence of independent entrepreneurs relative to incorporated firms may also support the widely held view that the region has a large and unmeasured informal sector that relies for resolution of its problems on informal, *ad hoc* recourse to personal networks rather than on formal institutions applying generalized rules.

As shown in Chapter 3 (Table 3.9), the Rostov region had 450 medium-sized enterprises in 2008, a larger number of such companies than in the Perm or Samara regions. This outcome is consistent with the generalized picture of a regional administration favorably disposed to the emergence of indigenous new companies, because by law a medium-sized company may have no more than a 25% shareholding by any large company 'parent.'

In 2007, the World Bank sponsored a survey of 535 firm owners or managers in the Rostov region, with 70% of the firms having fewer than 50 employees. (World Bank 2009) The survey revealed that small business respondents generally considered the business climate to be better than large companies did. Neither group, however, saw substantial improvement in the business climate in the period 2005–2006. The areas of greatest perceived deterioration were, in order of seriousness: breach of contract, unfair competition, organized crime, street crime/theft/disorder and corruption. Improvements were recognized in availability of credit, cost of credit and telecommunications services. The researchers noted that, "Some of the areas of greatest perceived deterioration correspond to variables related to market institutions of law and order." (World Bank 2009:35–36)

In their assessment of the regional business climate, both big and small companies in the World Bank survey pointed to the relative stability of the 'rules of the game' for business in the region. The close relations between big companies and the regional administration, according to the authors, may have limited the size of outside investment into the region. The fact that representatives of bigger companies in the Rostov region judged the business climate more harshly than did small firm owners could be in part due to the anticipated greater penetration by, and competition from, firms from outside the region, as national economic integration proceeds. The fact also that all firms rated the business climate in Rostov better than in other neighboring regions while giving low marks on most of the specific areas of state performance (e.g. corruption, courts, land tenure) may also suggest that business conditions depend on *ad hoc* bargaining rather than formal rules. (OPORA 2008b)

The World Bank and International Finance Corporation *Doing Business* reports compare the ease or difficulty of procedures such as registering a company, obtaining construction permits, registering property or exporting/importing goods by firms in capital cities (or main business cities) of World Bank member countries. (World Bank and International Finance Corporation 2009, 2010) In 2010, this report for the first time included nine Russian cities besides Moscow: St. Petersburg, Kazan, Rostov, Perm, Voronezh, Irkutsk, Tomsk, Tver and Petrozavodsk.[6] The results show that business conditions vary considerably across Russia. The city of Rostov ranked first among the ten Russian cities studied in ease of registering a new company and had the shortest average time and the fewest procedures to permit construction of a warehouse. Rostov was in second place in ease of procedures and costs of exporting or importing but was in last place on documenting the transfer (sale) of property. To the uninitiated, it must come as a surprise that Moscow, Russia's undisputed business capital (and the subject of all the forgoing *Doing Business* surveys), was 10th, 8th, 7th and 10th on the same measures.

Rostov economist Sergey Shneider questioned owners of micro, small and medium firms on business conditions in the Rostov and neighboring regions in a survey sponsored by the Rostov Regional Chamber of Commerce and Industry. (Shneider 2008)[7] The 509 respondents from the Rostov region included 431 from the region's cities and 78 from its rural districts. The respondents also included 318 from the Krasnodar, Volgograd, Stavropol and Astrakhan regions and 85 from the North Caucasus republics. Nearly two thirds of those surveyed were microenterprise owners, about one quarter represented small companies (i.e. with 11–100 employees), and 11% headed medium-sized companies. The respondents were presented with a list of factors that they could identify as serious obstacles to the conduct of business. The factors that were cited most frequently are shown in Table 6.3 below, along with the percentage of respondents who cited each factor:

Table 6.3 Survey of Rostov and 'Southern' Entrepreneurs: Main Obstacles to Business

High levels of corruption in government 'organs' and regulatory bodies	50%
Presence of real and hard to overcome administrative barriers	36%
High level of administrative protection of favored enterprises	36%
Access to long-term credit on attractive terms	31%
Absence of transparent access to state procurement opportunities	28%
SME access closed to some sectors closed (industry, communal services, public transportation)	18%

Source: Shneider 2008. The survey results are reported for all respondents, including those from elsewhere in the Southern Federal District. Rostov respondents represented about 55% of those surveyed.

The respondents were asked to define the factors of competitiveness in the current business climate and those that they anticipated would be influential when Russia joined the WTO. The factors that were considered important to competitiveness in the current business conditions were good relations with governmental authorities *(vlast')*, access to state contracts, the presence of highly placed patrons *(pokroviteley)* and access to state subsidies. The respondents saw these factors fading to insignificance after accession to the WTO, with other factors growing dramatically in importance: the application of modern technology, high labor productivity, improved management, and probity *(chistota)* and transparency in the conduct of business.[8]

The evidence from these three studies suggests that the Rostov region's rapid growth has drawn on a store of entrepreneurial talent and culturally favorable conditions, as well as on a pro-business and stable administration whose authority is unchallenged by contenders such as mayors or legislators. The pro-business stance is manifest in the relatively lighter regulatory procedures highlighted in the *Doing Business* ranking of the city of Rostov. However, the World Bank (2009) and Shneider (2008) surveys of entrepreneurs' attitudes and outlooks suggest that the institutions applying formal, public and impartial protections to all firms are weak. Moreover, the favorable business climate may have been based to some degree on inhibiting competition from outside the region.

Business associations and small business – bonding and bridging 'civic-ness'

The following discussion assesses the performance of business associations with respect to 'internal' issues such as leadership, initiative, expertness and leadership, and 'external' issues of interest representation vis-à-vis state institutions and visibility to the broader public. The associational landscape is assessed as well as the role of institutions serving as functional substitutes for business associations.

Chamber of commerce and industry of the Rostov oblast

The Chamber of Commerce and Industry of the Rostov Oblast (Rostov Regional Chamber) was formed in 1994, based on a local business organization set up in 1992 by three local businessmen. One of the three original founders of the regional Chamber, Andrey Skorik, is also a founding and continuing member of the Rostov OPORA association and of the Rotary Club.[9] Skorik resigned from the Chamber after its first few years to become the regional director of the U.S. based and USAID-supported Center for Citizen Initiatives (CCI) program promoting entrepreneurship. Skorik said that, in this initial period, the Chamber was not energetically expanding its membership or engaging in public advocacy on behalf of small companies.

The national Chamber leadership considers the contemporary Rostov Chamber, led since 2001 by president Nikolay Prisyazhnyuk, to be one of its most effective affiliates.[10] Completing technical studies in Novocherkassk, Prisyazhnyuk worked as an engineer and manager of a food-producing enterprise and then as head of the local food products trading board. He was elected mayor of Novo-cherkassk and served in this position from 1999 to 2001, when he was elected Chamber president. Prisyazhnyuk has also served on the governing board of the national Chamber (TPPRF). The Rostov Chamber employs a professional staff of about 20 people.

Economist Sergey Shneider was a deputy to Prisyazhnyuk in the city admin-istration of Novocherkassk and remains a close friend and colleague. In an inter-view with the author on June 9, 2010, Shneider said that, as mayor, Prisyazhnyuk had strongly pushed for small business development and produced good results.[11] Schneider said the Rostov Chamber was strongly committed to improving condi-tions for small business. Nevertheless, conditions for small business remained very tough.

According to its annual report for 2009, the Rostov Chamber considers among its main accomplishments the expansion of Chamber membership, expanding demand for and provision of services, the shaping of federal and regional leg-islation as well as building its downtown headquarters, managing finances and providing training for employees. (Chamber of Commerce and Industry, Rostov Region 2009a) The Chamber publicizes its meetings and publications on its web-site, from which membership applications may be downloaded.[12]

In 2009, the Rostov Chamber's membership stood at 493, of which 24 are business associations, 24 are official agencies, 388 are incorporated compa-nies, 35 are individual entrepreneurs and 8 are 'other.' [13] This membership tally incorporates the membership of the functionally independent Chambers based in other regional cities: Taganrog, Novocherkassk, Shakhtiy, and Kaminsk-Shakhtinsky. The business association members of the Rostov Chamber include the local affiliate of RSPP representing big business as well as industrial branch associations that lobby both through the Chamber and independently for poli-cies affecting their sectors. (Chamber of Commerce and Industry Rostov Region 2009c, 2009d)

This structure of membership of the Rostov Regional Chamber reflects the significance of big established industrial and agricultural concerns in the region relative to small companies even though, as we have seen, small com-pany development in the region is also fairly vigorous. The fact that the Cham-ber has attracted 35 individual entrepreneurs to its ranks indicates a measure of inclusiveness.

The governing board *(pravlenie)* is elected by the full membership and sets policy and direction for the Chamber. The board elected in 2010 has 34 mem-bers, three of whom are women.[14] A long-serving member of the board is Vasiliy Vysokov, whose CentreInvest Bank has been the leading source of small business finance in the Rostov region since its creation in early 1990s. Sergey Shneider and OPORA regional president Yuriy Roshkovan are also board members. (Chamber of Commerce and Industry Rostov Region 2011)

By category of principal affiliation, the governing board members break down as shown in Table 6.4:

Table 6.4 Affiliations of Members of Rostov Chamber Governing Board

Leaders of the Rostov Regional Chamber or of chapters in regional cities	6
Leaders of business or professional associations	5
Entrepreneurs, managers (total) *of which*	21
'incumbent' industrial	*6*
finance, services, agro-processing	*13*
subsidiaries of national companies	*2*
Academics	2

Source: http://www.tppro.ru/about/structure/. Accessed June 24, 2011

Comparing this list with the governing board that preceded it (Chamber of Commerce and Industry, Rostov Region 2009a) shows that the 14 new members of this board are mainly entrepreneurs from the services sector, in which companies are always new and frequently small.

Members of the Rostov Chamber participate in 16 committees. Seven of these committees are defined by sector: media, agro-processing, tourism, wholesale and retail trade, transport and logistics, advertising, energy and high technology. The other nine committees deal with membership, social policy and healthcare, foreign trade and exhibitions, investment policy, natural resources and the environment, dispute arbitration, law, and small business development. OPORA regional branch president and owner of and agro-processing company OOO Rostov, Yuriy Roshkovan heads the agro-processing committee, economist Schneider the investment committee. All but two of the committees are headed by members of the governing board.[15]

Although the TPPRO website does not include a full list of members, the Chamber's annual yearbook *Biznes Dona 2009* features detailed profiles and contact information for 85 member companies from industry and agro-industry as well as construction, finance, consulting, retail and wholesale trade, education and media. There are few industrial giants among those profiled; companies in construction and design, finance, insurance, law, consulting, retail and media are heavily represented.[16]

The Rostov Chamber's services to business and much of its expert staff are managed by a principal vice president. Chamber president Prisyazhnyuk concentrates on public policy questions, as well as interactions with the committees. Vladimir Kochura heads the legal department, which directly advises the president.

In the first of several conversations with the author on October 15, 2009, Kochura said the TPPRF's high regard for the Rostov Chamber is in large part due to the range and volume of services it provides to companies. The Chamber's calendar was full of anticipated events where businesspeople would confer on issues and give policy input. The author was invited to join a full-day seminar on utility tariffs policy. The following day a session was set to air Chamber members' concerns about *reyderstvo* (illegal company takeovers).

Kochura's legal department cooperated closely with CIPE's anti-corruption programs beginning in the mid-2000s. Kochura has been accredited by the

Ministry of Justice to provide expert input on behalf of the Chamber to legal drafts at the federal and regional level aimed at reducing the scope for the corrupt exercise of discretion in the application of law. According to Kochura, the opening of the drafting process of legislation to expert input from business attorneys was in place in more than 30 regions before being adopted at the federal level in 2009. The TPPRF and OPORA had both lobbied heavily for this decision. (Rostov Regional Business Association Coalition 2007)

Kochura's department gives legal advice to Chamber members, and the *arbitrazh* (commercial) courts took input on particular cases from the Chamber.[17] Kochura said that the *arbitrazh* courts had become very professional, and that the mentality of businesspeople had also changed remarkably in recent years. The Chamber's legal department was working with a newly formed regional association of jurists. The Rostov Chamber's fee-based business dispute mediation service *(Treteyskiy Sud)* is quite active. The Chamber sponsors the training of new mediators through local universities.[18]

Although the Rostov Chamber embraces most of the region's major enterprises and an appreciable number of smaller ones, here, as elsewhere in Russia, many companies are not members. The Chamber derives most of its income not from members' dues but from the provision of fee-based services (discounted for members).

OPORA – Rostov region

The OPORA association in the Rostov region was founded in 2002 with Petr Proydakov as president, and a handful of small business activists including Andrey Skorik, then the regional director for the U.S.-based non-profit Center for Citizen Initiatives, as founding members.

Petr Proydakov, in his mid-40s, owns a flour mill near Taganrog. His flour, under the brand name Pudoff, is sold throughout Russia.[19] Proydakov said he had begun trading foodstuffs in the market and, from that experience, had developed a grocery business. By the year 2000, he began milling flour from local wheat. Proydakov made several visits to the United States in the 1990s under the CCI program and built his company based in part on examples he encountered in the United States.

Proydakov is an active member of OPORA; however, he says business associations are hard to develop because by definition businesspeople are pressed for time. Being a member of OPORA was worthwhile, because from the outset the federal authorities had indicated their willingness to listen to its members. The same respect was accorded to the TPPRF, and that was why these associations could deliver something for members.

Proydakov said many business owners doubt the effectiveness of OPORA or the Chamber. They saw these associations as implicitly 'political' and felt business should steer clear of politics. One of his acquaintances, for example, had been a vocal critic of OPORA and was now an active member. This friend is successful in business and sees OPORA membership as a step toward running for the city duma.

In 2006, Yuriy Roshkovan was elected to succeed Proydakov as president of OPORA Rostov. Roshkovan's company OOO Rostov is a grain and livestock producer in the village of Dar'evka in the Rodiono-Nesvetayskogo district. The company was formed on the basis of a cooperative founded by Roshkovan. He has invested in advanced agricultural technology and management and frequently speaks to the media about the problems of agricultural modernization in the region.[20]

Roshkovan also heads the Rostov Chamber committee on agro-processing and serves on its board. He served on the elected local legislature in his home district, until failing in his bid for re-election in 2010. Founding members Petr Proydakov and Andrey Skorik remain very active in OPORA and credit Roshkovan's leadership with having expanded membership. Some members mentioned that Roshkovan exceled in advancing OPORA's objectives through the collaborative and discreet consultative processes favored by the regional administration.

The Rostov regional OPORA chapter has roughly 100 members. As always, these are dues-paying individual business owners. Ten members head local subgroups in their cities or localities. Taganrog is the largest of these subgroups, with about ten members.[21] Roshkovan opened the spacious first floor of his home in central Rostov to serve as the offices of the OPORA chapter.

Yuriy Yevchenko, OPORA Rostov's executive director, served as international liaison for the regional administration in the very early 1990s and later as advisor to several EU-TACIS regional technical assistance programs. He was also the executive director of the business organization Club 2015 in Rostov.[22]

In an initial interview with the author on October 16, 2009, Yevchenko said OPORA's development in the region was constrained by finances, because the sole source of funding is membership dues. Persuading the regional administration that OPORA speaks for all small business depended to some extent, he thought, on expanding membership. OPORA also struggled to convince cynics who see association members as promoting only their individual careers, but at times had to discourage some potential members who actually would see membership in exactly that light.

At the same time, here, as elsewhere, OPORA tried to ensure that members represent businesses that eschew bribe paying, have no non-transparent official 'sponsorship,' pay taxes in full and apply all legal protections to their employees. New members must be recommended by two existing members in good standing. As Andrey Skorik noted, OPORA is a 'brand' that has to be preserved in order for the institution to do its work.[23] In this sense, OPORA both represents the concerns of existing small business while shaping an 'aspirational' collective identity for its potential constituency.

According to Yevchenko, OPORA has to contend with the belief among many entrepreneurs that business is only about no-holds-barred competition, rather than cooperating to improve the rules of the game for all.

Chamber of commerce and industry Taganrog area

The Taganrog Chamber, founded in 1994, occupies offices above a bank in a newly built commercial district. The president, Aleksandr Amerkhanov, was previously the director of external and international relations in the municipal administration, a member of the city legislature and is a member of the governing board of the national Chamber (TPPRF).[24] The Taganrog Chamber, somewhat analogously to the Chamber in Togliatti, finds a productive alignment of interests and priorities with the local administration. The mostly young staff members, including many women, talk eagerly about the Chamber's work.

The Taganrog Inter-regional Chamber of Commerce and Industry (Taganrog Chamber) is, like the Togliatti Chamber discussed in Chapter 4, scaled to a municipal level in a regional 'second city.' Taganrog is about an hour by commuter train from Rostov on the Azov Sea. (Chamber of Commerce and Industry Taganrog 2009) Interviewed by the author on June 10, 2010, the Chamber's business information department director, Irina Zakharchuk, explained that her department provides small business owners with legal, customs and tax expertise as well as information on the municipal micro-finance program. Zakharchuk and other staff members said that, of the approximately 70 Chamber members, around 30 are small businesses, including individual entrepreneurs. Members participate in the work of various committees, of which the most active were devoted to agriculture and innovation/higher education. A Chamber working group of lawyers from member companies provides expert input to proposed regional and municipal draft legislation. The Taganrog Chamber participates in the business cooperation aspects of the inter-governmental Black Sea Economic Commission (BSEC) and also in an International Black Sea Club involving Chambers in Ukraine, Trans-Dnistria, Abkhazia, Turkey and Romania. The Chamber runs a popular internship-training course for local university students.[25]

Club 2015

Established as a non-commercial partnership, Rostov's Club 2015 is a group of entrepreneurs and managers united by a desire to cooperate in developing high standards of management and business ethics and to contribute to regional economic development. The 28 members of the club are pictured along with brief profiles on the Club's website. They include OPORA president Roshkovan, two people who have served on the Rostov Chamber's board, and the former mayor of Rostov, Yuriy Pogrebshikov. The membership includes three women, is generally under 50 years old, and is drawn mainly from such 'new' sectors as consulting, finance, construction, trade, agro-processing, media, IT and telecommunications.[26] Club 2015 has some limited lobbying functions and holds public forums, but its principal mission seems to be business networking, mutual help and professional development of members from the standpoint of management and leadership. The Rostov's Club 2015 is a partner of Club 2015 in Moscow, which has a similarly prominent and relatively young membership.

According to Club 2015 member and executive director Yuriy Yevchenko, the Rostov Club was formed under the leadership of Vladimir Melnikov, founder-owner of Gloria Jeans. In numerous press interviews, Melnikov has advocated an open and collegial style of business leadership and management. Although interested in adopting western management innovations, he also claims to base his business ethics on his strong Orthodox faith. According to Yevchenko, Melnikov also launched the regional chapter of Delovaya Rossiya.

Rostov regional agency for entrepreneurship support (RRAPP)

This agency is not an association of members, but can be seen as having some of the functions of an association with respect to small business. Like the Chamber or OPORA, the RRAPP provides information on laws and regulations and can help 'match' potential business partners. Unlike either of these associations, the RRAPP's principal focus is entrepreneurship training and professional development. Director Natalya Krainova enjoys a reputation of very sound and qualified leadership.[27]

The RRAPP was formed in 1998 at the behest of the regional administration, but its principal achievements came after Krainova became director in 2003. (RRAPP 2009) The agency provides, under contract with the regional administration (through competitive tender in which other organizations also participate), services related to the implementation of the region's small business development programs. There are 17 employees, of whom seven are consultants to business. The number of individual consultations saw a three-fold increase from 2008 to 2009, rising to over 9,000. There is a telephone 'hotline' for those seeking help to resolve urgent business problems.[28]

According to deputy director Kovalenko, the RRAPP provides a sort of bridge to publicize and build participation among businesses in the regional administration's small business development programs. Using the funding it receives from the regional administration, the RRAPP gives advice on all aspects of launching and running a small business, holds training courses, helps firms apply for bank loans or micro-finance and recruits firms for and manages two regional business incubators. The incubators are a base for 26 new companies, mainly in manufacturing or agro-processing. The RRAPP participates in a web-based network of potential customers, suppliers and partners among EU firms accessible by the Rostov region's business community. The RRAPP is modeled on and works closely with the Russian Agency for Support of Small and Medium Entrepreneurship *(Rossiyskoe agenstvo podderzhki malogo i srednogo biznesa),* founded in 1992 and headed by Viktor Ermakov, chairman of the TPPRF small business development committee and a member of OPORA's governing board.[29]

According to deputy director Kovalenko, RRAPP has funding for some of its work from the Rostov-based CentreInvest Bank, a leading source of small business finance. Russia's largest retail bank, Sberbank has also provided support for legal support that RRAPP has provided to small businesses.

CentreInvest bank

The Rostov region is home to one of the few regional banks in Russia with a founding mission to lend to small business. Founder of the bank in 1992, board chairman Vassiliy Vysokov was and remains a university professor and was a leading designer of privatization policies in the oblast in the 1990s. He has served as a vice president of the Rostov regional Chamber and has long served on its governing board.

The European Bank for Reconstruction and Development has used CentreInvest Bank as intermediary for its small business lending programs in the region and has a minority equity stake in the bank and a seat on its board. CentreInvest has also been a partner of USAID's programs to expand small business lending. Although he is a native of Rostov, Vysokov was active in the very early phase of cooperatives development in Moscow. Because Vysokov was already a figure of national standing in 1992, the bank has a degree of institutional autonomy and independence vis-à-vis the regional administration. The initial financial backing for the bank was from outside the Rostov region and, according to some accounts, the national electrical power generation and distribution company UES played a major role.

The bank's SME lending department head, Elena Pontankova, said that the bank's loans to small businesses have consistently represented about 40% of its portfolio. Another 30% of the portfolio is in the growing area of consumer credit and mortgages. CentreInvest has branches throughout the oblast and has expanded into the Krasnodar, Stavropol and Volgograd regions. Pontankova said that CentreInvest and Sberbank together accounted for almost all of the small business lending in the Rostov region, but CentreInvest's average small business loan is smaller (2 million versus 5 million rubles).[30]

Although it is a for-profit business, CentreInvest Bank plays a key role in advocating for better business conditions for small entrepreneurship. Vysokov is active in support of small business development, including by offering the bank as platform for entrepreneurship forums and other events. He and CentreInvest are members of the regional administration's policy-shaping body, the Entrepreneurship Council. The regional administration solicits advice from CentreInvest on expanding credit availability to small business.

Other associations representing SMEs

In addition to the Chamber of Commerce and Industry and branches of OPORA outside of Rostov, many of the region's cities are home to at least one association of entrepreneurs. Sector-based associations are also numerous and seemingly well established in the region. Delovaya Rossiya is present in Rostov and headed by owner of a successful local supermarket chain. Non-commercial partnerships, structured along the same lines as the RRAPP, are found across the Rostov oblast and provide entrepreneurs with legal advice, training and consulting services, with municipal and regional funding.

Business associations' dialogue with regional administrations – contributions to the openness of policy formulation

Business agenda

The Rostov Chamber lists its four principal priorities for 2008–2010 as advocating on behalf of businesses in structured consultative coordination bodies and through legal drafting input; raising the social and civic responsibility of business; bringing business input to national projects such as healthcare, housing and education development; and developing policy input to expand the role played by small business (through lowering administrative barriers, lowering taxes and designing regional and municipal programs to support small firms.) (Chamber of Commerce and Industry, Rostov Region 2009) These objectives are broadly shared by OPORA and the other principal institutions representing or advocating on behalf of business in the Rostov region, including RRAPP and CentreInvest Bank.[31]

A typical instance of how the Rostov Chamber provides a platform for business to give input to policy is an all-day seminar held October 15, 2009 on the problem of the affordability and predictability of power and gas utility tariffs to industry. The forum brought Chamber member companies together with representatives of the Federal Anti-Monopoly Service (FAS) and regional administration as well as academic specialists on the issue of 'natural monopoly' pricing and resulted in a set of specific policy recommendations. (Chamber of Commerce and Industry, Rostov Region 2009b)[32] Several business interlocutors in Rostov praised the Federal Anti-Monopoly Service for having setup its own structured consultative process for small business. Business association leaders in all four case study regions cited the FAS as open to policy input from business and genuinely committed to generating a more competitive business environment conducive to new companies' development.

A principal example of legislation based partly on policy suggestions from the Chamber and organized business community is the regional law "on countering corruption in the Rostov region" adopted in May 2009. The regional law closely parallels the provisions of the federal law (173-f3) 'on anticorruption expertise of laws and draft laws' adopted in July 2009. (Rostov Regional Legislative Assembly 2009)[33] The Rostov regional law also calls for greater public access to information, creates a standing commission on anti-corruption involving non-governmental groups and introduces more transparent procedures for regional government procurement.

Regional administration's small business development efforts

As was mentioned earlier, Microfinance Center Director Mikhail Mamuta, SME Resource Center Director Igor Mikhalkin, and OPORA's director of regional development Olga Plotnikova all cite the Rostov regional administration's small business development programs as being among Russia's most effective and innovative. Part of the reason may be that the regional administration generated and designed its own set of approaches at its own initiative and pursued them for more than a decade before the passage of watershed 2007 law on SME promotion. The Rostov regional legislature passed a law "on support for small entrepreneurship in the Rostov region" in June of 1997.[34] This law was one of the first adopted in a period dominated by work on electoral laws, budgets and the regional 'constitution' *(ustav)*.

The region's Deputy Minister of Economy, Anna Palagina, played a key role in spearheading SME development through the principal vehicle for coordinating policy and receiving the input of organized business, the Council on Entrepreneurship of the Regional Administration, established by a declaration *(polozhenie)* of the Governor in 2002. (Rostov Regional Administration 2008) Chaired formally by a deputy governor and the minister of economy, the 27 member Council worked under the *de facto* leadership of Palagina and Rostov Chamber President Prisyazhnyuk.[35] Other members included OPORA President Roshkovan, CentreInvest President Vysokov, RRAPP Director Krainova, the regional RSPP leader, and representatives of sector-based business associations. Other members come from the regional legislature, higher education institutions and regional administration agencies. The agenda of each meeting of the council as well as the presentations by participants are posted on the regional administration's website.[36]

The regional administration's Small Business Development Program for 2009–2013 funds similar interventions and uses performance measures analogous to those in the Samara regional SME program discussed in Chapter 4.[37] (Rostov Regional Administration 2011) The regional budget funds to the program for five years are to be 1.3 billion rubles, and the federal budget's contribution would be 473 million rubles. From non-budgetary sources – commercial banks – the program expects to receive the vast majority of its funding – a total of 391 billion rubles in credit to small business over the five years of the program.

The program's main emphasis and the reason for the substantial bank funding is the perceived need to improve the availability of credit to SMEs on accessible terms. This is addressed through the creation of a guarantee fund to ease access to bank credit and expansion of micro-finance resources. Other main activities are provision of subsidies for innovative (high technology) firms, support for SME export and inter-regional trade, support for institutions (such as RRAPP) that advise and provide professional development to entrepreneurs and sponsorship of public events. The program includes an elaborate formula for assessing its impact through the rise in economic activity and therefore of tax revenues to the regional budget from the boost to SME development. Both the OPORA Regional Index of 2008 (see Table 3.5) and the World Bank and International Finance Corporation (2010) *Doing Business* comparison of the business climate in ten cities indicate that entrepreneurs consider credit access a less pressing problem in Rostov than in many other cities or regions. (OPORA 2008a)

A persistent criticism raised by businesspeople is that programs of regional support seem to focus more on fostering new businesses through subsidies and other interventions than on tackling the problems of intrusive inspections, heavy regulation and inadequacies in the judicial system. The Rostov regional program does envisage activities aimed at publicizing and addressing these problems and makes explicit the participation of business associations in this work. The activities include a continued review of legislation and regulation to reduce excessive controls or inspections and to encourage and further institutionalize the provision of input from legal experts from business to proposed and existing legislation, the development of specific policy program input to municipal governments, opening the provision of communal services to SMEs, the conduct of surveys of entrepreneurs' perceptions of the business climate and pressing municipal governments to accelerate the sale of business premises to lease-holders. This range of activities in the program addresses the kinds of issues entrepreneurs consider most pressing, based for example on the OPORA regional index survey in Rostov, the World Bank's survey reported in World Bank (2009) and the Shneider survey of entrepreneurs in Rostov and neighboring southern oblasts. One concrete achievement along these lines has been the regional administration's inclusion on its website of tender announcements for regional and municipal contracts open to small firm bidders.

The seriousness and commitment of the Rostov regional administration is clear in its early espousal of the cause of SME development and in its strong contribution to institutional innovations such as the active Entrepreneurship Council and especially the development of the training and information services of the RRAPP. The region has been especially favored also by the presence of CentreInvest Bank, a profitable enterprise with clear social and developmental aims. The leadership of this bank created vital links through the EBRD and USAID with best practices in small business lending and may have played a role in attracting Sberbank, with its much larger resources, into the field of SME finance.

It is nevertheless clear that much of the small business community remains untouched and possibly even unaware of the effects of the regional administration's efforts to improve the business climate. Some of this may be due to the relatively weak development of the regional press and media, discussed in greater detail in the following sections. The results of the survey study by Shneider (2008) discussed earlier provide an interesting insight into this issue. About one quarter of Shneider's respondents thought that the activities of the regional administration with respect to SMEs were very or somewhat helpful, more than half thought they had no effect, and about 15% found the regional administration to be a hindrance to their business. Municipal administrations rated even lower, which is likely to be related to their perceived obstruction of the process of land acquisition by businesses. Asked what they would like governments to be doing, more than half said they favored direct financing, credit guarantees, access to regional and local government procurement, legal information and training services, and 40% also cited the need for "transparent, fair rules for the conduct of business applicable to all." (Shneider 2008:25–26)

The Rostov regional administration has taken pains to hear from the business association leaders, but the interactions within the Entrepreneurship Council are not publicized enough to allow the vast numbers of businesspeople who are not in associations to learn how their interests are being pursued and become themselves more engaged in the process, and less convinced that nothing meaningful ever changes except through informal means. The principal shortcoming of the program of SME development in the Rostov region is the centralization of all activity in the regional administration, leaving limited scope for autonomous action by municipal authorities.

As has been stressed elsewhere, the most obvious and potentially productive interaction with government for many small businesses is at the municipal level. It is probably not accidental that Rostov Chamber President Prisyazhnyuk and Taganrog Chamber President Amerkhanov came from municipal administrations. In the city of Rostov itself, the municipal administration seems to be eclipsed by the regional administration with respect to shaping small business development policies.

As has been emphasized the regional administration under Governor Chub was unusually hierarchical. Several interlocutors in Moscow and in Rostov mentioned that access to regional officials in Rostov is difficult, and that officials sometimes seem cautious and unwilling to speak informally or offer personal views. A small indication of greater openness since 2010 is that the regional Ministry of Economy has begun soliciting comments and input from businesspeople on its website and also has a page urging businesspeople to take part in the policy dialogue through membership in the Chamber, OPORA or other associations. This gesture may suggest that the regional administration is trying to improve the so-called '*obratniy svyaz*' (feedback loop) from the business community.[38]

Entrepreneurs in regional political office – contributions to the dispersion of regional and local political authority

The regional legislature and elected municipal office are the obvious entry points for renewal of the political elite, where entrepreneurs are most likely to seek and win office. The first regional legislature was elected in March 1994, with an average of five candidates running for each of the 45 seats. The electoral law set up all these races as majoritarian and therefore based on local districts. Candidates could not be proposed by parties, but only by groups of voters by petition. None of the entrepreneurs or bankers who ran was elected, although nine industrial enterprise directors were. (McFaul and Petrov 1997) As was typical in first elections to regional legislatures, many of those elected in the Rostov oblast were either from regional or local administrations.

The 'closing' of the only tentatively opened path for new elites proceeded in the re-election of 21 of those sitting in the second assembly to the third and of 25 of those in the third assembly to the fourth. Five of the deputies elected in 1994 were re-elected in the subsequent elections in 1998, 2003 and 2008. The opening to competitive politics and party development that took place in the 1990s therefore has left comparatively little residual impact on the composition of the regional legislature in Rostov. The share of deputies aged 50 or over rose from one quarter in 1994 to almost two thirds in the assembly elected in 2008. The Rostov regional assembly website does not give the professional affiliations of its members but does state that 11 of the current deputies have no employment other than their duties as legislators.[39] With the introduction of proportional representation and party lists to the regional elections in 2003, the United Russia faction had overwhelming majorities – 34 of 45 in the third assembly and 45 of 50 in the fourth assembly. The only other party faction in the legislature is the CPRF.

The Rostov municipal duma gives the professional affiliations for the current members but no party affiliations. Of the 35 deputies, 22 give a professional affiliation with an incorporated company, either an OOO, OAO or ZAO. However, several of these are either large industrial concerns or incorporated public infrastructural enterprises such as the port, energy distribution or central markets. In a study of the composition of regional and municipal legislatures in the Southern Federal District in 2008, Shneider found that some directors of medium-sized companies served in legislatures because of their dependence on preferential access to public procurement contracts or other forms of support. Shneider's inference is plausible for companies in the construction and remodeling fields as well as in public transportation (e.g. bus) services. (Shneider 2009)

The professional profiles of six of the 35 deputies in the Rostov city legislature suggest that they are heads of small companies because they are involved in retail or consumer services. The committee of four members devoted to "trade, restaurants, consumer services and small entrepreneurship" includes three of these four members, the other member being the dean of the economics faculty at Rostov's Southern Federal University. These members are unlikely to be involved in direct contracting with the municipality and are more likely to be pressing for the interests of small business as a whole in better governance and rule of law. One of the other deputies from small business is on the committee dealing with municipal property, where the ongoing troubles with the divestment of buildings leased by the municipality to businesses is surely on the agenda. The presence of small business owners in the municipal duma and their absence in the regional assembly is yet another indication of the importance of local governments in affecting business conditions and in serving as entry point for new political elites.

Business, society and the press in the Rostov region

Organized or public philanthropy by individual businesspeople or by business associations in the Rostov region is fairly subdued compared with the situation in the Samara, Perm and Smolensk regions. The actual level of philanthropic activity is not necessarily lower, but such activities are not publicized as widely or made a major focus by business associations. Entrepreneurs such as Gloria Jeans founder Melnikov reportedly support the philanthropic activities of the Orthodox Church. The RSPP, whose membership includes many extra-regional (national) Russian companies, has in addition to its principal social role of promoting and sustaining employment, a certain public emphasis on social and charitable activity.

The Rostov chapter of the Rotary Club unites a fairly small number of young businesspeople and professional men and women in charitable activities. Press releases from their meetings suggest the organization is well established with an active membership. An 'initiative' group from Taganrog is also working to start a Rotary Club in that city.[40]

An area of public engagement that receives greater emphasis from the Rostov region's business community is the development of entrepreneurship among the young. The May 26 National Entrepreneurs' Day – established in 2008 on the 20th anniversary of the adoption of the Cooperatives law – was observed by a conference convened at a private business school, the Rostov International Institute of Economics and Management (Rostovskiy Mezhdunarodniy Institut Ekonomiki i Upravleniya) sponsored by the regional OPORA chapter. (Rostov International Institute of Economics and Management 2010) The institute, established in 1996, is headed by rector and founder Elina Liss.[41] Liss has worked to create business internships for the institute's students. She said that many of her students, who come from across Russia, are the children of founders of small firms.[42]

The regional press

The press and media play an important role in the formation of business identity as well as in explaining business to society and vice versa. On a strictly commercial level, advertising in the press is crucial to linking customers to business. The publications in the category 'lifestyle' in Table 6.5 include those devoted to entertainment, home decoration and remodeling, fashion, health and fitness, family life and child rearing, and automobiles. All of these are clearly related to certain aspirational forms of consumption and therefore are a sort of generic advertisement.

Nevertheless, it is striking that the critical and analytical content in the regionally produced press remains weak. The major exception is the business and economic publication *GorodN*, which carries analytical, investigative and critical content, including in its online edition. The effects of the general weakness of the regionally produced press is also mitigated by weekly Southern Russia editions of *Kommersant* and other national 'quality' papers, which have grown in importance with the economic dynamism of the region and the growth in numbers and sophistication of the business readership.

Table 6.5 gives an overview of the print media in the Rostov region by category and city of publication:

Table 6.5 Press in Rostov Oblast by Category and Place of Publication

Publication Type	National	Rostov	Other Cities
Political-social	7	4	16
Business-professional	2	10	0
Lifestyle	0	34	6
Advertising only	0	24	7

Source: http://www.media-atlas.ru/regionmedia/. Accessed June 29, 2011.

The city of Rostov is a large media market and the capital of the Russian south, which explains why seven national newspapers publish weekly regional editions with inclusion of regional and local reporting from Rostov and neighboring southern regions. The seven journals and their circulation numbers are given in Table 6.6:

Table 6.6 National Papers Published in Southern Editions in Rostov

Newspaper	Circulation
Moskovskiy Komsomlets	31,000
Argumenty i Fakty Rostov	70,000
Komsomolskaya Pravda	75,000
Trud	15,000
Vedomosti Yug (South)	2,000
Kommersant Yug (South)	7,000
Rossisskaya Gazeta	N/A

Source: http://www.media-atlas.ru/regionmedia/ accessed June 29, 2011

As is evident from the circulation figures, the first four of these newspapers are oriented toward a mass readership, while *Vedomosti, Kommersant* and *Rossisskaya Gazeta* are aimed at the business or official elite. Relative to the population of nearly four million people in the Rostov region alone, none of these papers has a large circulation, although all are also available online.

The four Rostov-based newspapers (all published weekly) are shown in Table 6.7:

Table 6.7 Newspapers: Rostov Region

Newspaper	Circulation	Date of First Publication
Vecherniy Rostov	30,000	1958
Molot	13,000	1917
Nashe Vremya	20,000	1921
Ofitsialniy Rostov	10,000	1994

Source: http://www.media-atlas.ru/regionmedia/. Accessed June 29, 2011.

Of these four, *Vecherniy Rostov* most closely approximates an independent quality newspaper, but it is stylistically very 'retro' and lacks analytical or in-depth reporting. It is particularly telling, relative to the flowering of print media in the late perestroika and early 1990s, that the only general audience newspaper still published in Rostov from that period is *Ofitsialniy Rostov*, published by the municipal administration. The online publication donnews.ru is the functional equivalent of a general interest newspaper as comprehensive as *Vecherniy Rostov* and stylistically more contemporary.

In keeping with the general picture of Rostov as a place where business is better developed than would seem commensurate with the strength of the public or civic sphere, the business press in Rostov has produced analytical journals covering politics and economics as well as business in depth and with considerable editorial independence. The four journals, also available in web editions are *GorodN, Realniy Biznes, Delovoy Kvartal* and *Rostovskiy Biznes Zhurnal.*

Civic memory: entrepreneurs and the 'usable past' – ideational antecedent conditions

The Rostov region is a patchwork of political cultures formed by the merchant cities of Rostov and Taganrog, the culturally distinct Don Cossacks around Novocherkassk, the coal-mining eastern Donbass and the vast grain-producing rural hinterland. The diagram at the beginning of the chapter depicts the strong support of antecedent conditions for entrepreneurship but at best only weak or ambivalent support from antecedent conditions for democratization.

The region's contribution to the White Cause in the Civil War of 1918–1921 distances it from the Soviet norm and underpins an alternative political culture, in some senses freedom loving, but compatible nevertheless with a political system based on protection and patronage. This was most manifest in the turbulent years of 1992–1993, when Cossack descendants seized and occupied buildings in downtown Rostov, claiming pre-revolutionary ownership.

The orientation of the littoral cities of the Rostov region toward trade on the Black Sea and beyond, the region's Western diaspora born of the Civil War emigration and the role of centuries-old Armenian and Greek settlement have supported entrepreneurial traditions. A billboard in downtown Rostov reads, "Rostovians of the world, unite!" The newest and shiniest office tower in Rostov was financed and built by Rostovians from the United States.

The relatively small natural resource endowment of the Rostov region has created scope for the formation of a business community that is diverse to both sector and company size. It has not, however, in all cases generated companies that will cope well with the advancing national and international integration of Rostov's economy, developments that will continue to expose the limitations of the traditional patrimonial style of governance.

Rostov is exceptional among major Russian cities in having preserved right at the city's heart the massive Orthodox cathedral built in 1885, topped by a huge golden cupola. Worshippers and visitors thread through the throngs of shoppers to reach the cathedral, surrounded on all sides by a vast area of market stalls covered with blue tarp and full to bursting with fresh fruit, vegetables, meat, spices in bulk, inexpensive clothing and housewares. This uncomplicated cheek-by-jowl cohabitation of Orthodoxy and entrepreneurship says a great deal about the business community at all levels in Rostov.

Like their pre-revolutionary antecedents, the organized business community in the Rostov region seems to be attempting a synthesis of Russian traditionalism with efficiency, competitiveness and technological modernization.

The region and the model – conclusions

The Rostov case diverges from the paradigmatic or ideal case in several important ways, crucial for producing an outcome where, contrary to the model's predictions, large numbers of small companies relative to the workforce emerged and persisted where there was only a brief and limited initial democratic 'impulse.'

Figure 6.1 represents the model shown in Chapter 3 (Figure 3.1) adapted to the Rostov case:

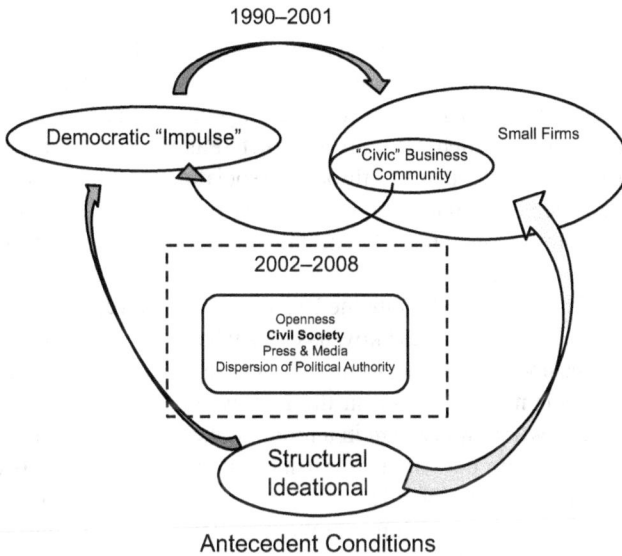

Figure 6.1 The Elaborated Model: Rostov Case

The extent of democratization depicted here is modest relative to the numbers of small firms, illustrated by having the 'democratic impulse' smaller and the arrow signifying the generation of small firms in the 1991–2001 base period thinner than in the ideal case. The small firms 'balloon' is roughly the same size, producing the 'lopsided' outcome that characterizes the Rostov case. Antecedent conditions, both structural and ideational, are depicted as supporting the emergence of small business but as having a much weaker relationship to the process of democratization. The 'civic business community,' moreover, is small relative to the number of small firms.

Business associations other than the Chamber of Commerce are not well established in the region. The regional chapter of OPORA is less influential than might be expected in a region where small business is comparatively well developed. The interactions of business associations with the administration in Rostov takes place in a framework qualitatively distinct from that anticipated by our model and founded upon support for small business not influenced by social pressures but essentially technocratic and top-down in nature.[43]

The relations of the regional administration with business associations are governed by an ethos of professionalism and expertise rather than of civic participation. The regional Chamber and OPORA are not less representative or inclusive than in the other three case studies, but the preferences of the administration and the centralizing of authority affect the nature of their 'external' (bridging) functions. The regional press is also weak in terms of the availability of critical or analytical content, failing to play an adequate role in building confidence with respect to any public engagement among the vast numbers of entrepreneurs not involved in business associations.

The structures of formal business-state coordination in the Rostov region are, to a greater degree than in the other three case study regions, orchestrated and led by the regional administration's exogenous policy agenda. Because of this, the 'feedback' arrow in our modified diagram is depicted as weak in all aspects except for the contribution civic business, through associations and otherwise, makes to broader civil society. The interactions of the civic business community with the regional administration tend to be bound into an agenda set by the preferences of the regional administration.

Lapina and Chirikova (1999) cite the Rostov region, as well as Tatarstan under Shamiev and Moscow under Luzhkov, as cases where the relations between state authority and business took the form of 'patronage' or selective sponsorship. Business-government coordination in the Rostov region operates in an 'expert' and discreet framework, rather than in a more public and therefore inclusive one. The entry of elites from new or small business into political office is also fairly weak in the region, and possibly played a minor role in the political monocentrism of the region under the stewardship of Governor Vladimir Chub, consolidated and hardened after the mid-1990s.

Notes

1 Vigorous growth in per capita money incomes can be seen in case study per capita income table in Chapter 3, Figure 3.4, p. 73. Among the regions where industrial growth and per capita income growth exceeded the national averages from a starting point in 1999 of below median per capita incomes were five other regions in the Russian south: Krasnodar, Stavropol, Kabardino-Balkaria, Adygea and Dagestan. Among the four case study regions in the present study, Samara and Perm regions saw their rate of industrial growth fall in 2004–2006 relative to 1999–2003, but their per capita GRP started and remained well above the Russian median. The Smolensk region saw industrial growth above the Russian median in 1999–2003, but below the median in 2004–2006. Per capita GDP in Smolensk was just below the median level of Russian regions in 2008. (World Bank 2009)

2 This period is of course immortalized in the classic *And Quiet Flows the Don.* According to Suny (2011) a weakness of the White cause was that the ultra-conservative counter-revolution of the Southern region, buttressed by German support, had little in common with the anti-Bolshevik forces of the Volga and Siberia, who were promoting the Constituent Assembly.

3 Makhmudov is number 11 on the *Forbes* Russia billionaires list in 2010 with an estimated net worth of $8.5 billion.

4 Chub's roots in the Proletarskaya district with its historical association with Armenia may also be part of the explanation for the sister city relationship between Rostov and Yerevan.

5 Pogrebshikov's memoir is at http://www.horse-rostov.ru/konkur/2007/all_.htm and offers a firsthand account of the momentous first years of post-Soviet Rostov, including claims for restitution of property and in some cases occupation of city buildings by Cossacks claiming descent from pre-revolutionary owners. (pp. 245–255)

6 http://subnational.doingbusiness.org. Accessed September 1, 2011.
7 Shneider has worked on the World Bank's Russian regional development programs in the region, as a professor and researcher.
8 About one quarter of respondents nevertheless favored immediate WTO accession, about one third expressed some reservations, and 37% thought the benefits of joining were doubtful.
9 Personal interview, Andrey Skorik, June 8, 2010.
10 Personal interview, Alexander Rybakov, TPPRF Vice President, Regional Development, October 7, 2009, Moscow.
11 Personal interview, Sergey Shneider, June 9, 2010.
12 http://www.tppro.ru. Accessed September 10, 2011.
13 Document shared with author October 15, 2009
14 http://www.tppro.ru/about/structure/. Accessed June 24, 2011.
15 http://www.tppro.ru/about/committees/. Accessed June 24, 2011.
16 Companies that chose to be profiled are likely to be among the more active members of the Chamber. They include 15 from industry; 12 from agro-industry; 9 from energy, transport or communications; 12 from construction or architecture; 5 from finance or insurance; 9 from law or consulting; 9 from research or education; 7 from retail or wholesale trade; 5 from media companies; and 1 each from tourism and medical services.
17 The World Bank survey found that 40% Rostov oblast business owners had been either defendants in or had initiated court cases in the last two years. This far exceeded the 27% in a similar study across the whole of Russia in 2005. (World Bank 2009)
18 A Chamber leaflet (Chamber of Commerce and Industry Rostov Region 2009e) lists the names of recently trained and accredited business dispute mediators.
19 Personal interview, Petr Prodakov, Taganrog and Rostov, June 10, 2010.
20 Interview with Yuriy Roshkovan, published in Foodnewsweek December 12, 2008 "Sel'skoe Khozyaystvo Dolzhno Stat' Biznesom" http://www.foodnewsweek.ru/staraya-versiya/tmpl2.php?PN=doct.php&dout=text&dsubj=28&dtype=4&nid=29248
21 The list of local chapters includes several rural districts, suggesting that agro-processors such as Roshkovan's company are well represented. http://www.opora.ru/regions/rostov. Accessed September 10, 2011.
22 Several personal interviews with Yuriy Yevchenko in October 2009 and June 2010.
23 Personal interview, Andrey Skorik, June 8, 2010.
24 http://tpprf.ru. Accessed September 1, 2011.
25 Personal interview, Irina Zakharchuk and Taganrog Chamber staff, June 10, 2010.
26 Members' profiles, as well as mission statement, at http://www.2015.ru/1209183. Accessed August 20, 2011.
27 This assessment was offered in personal interviews by Russia Microfinance Center Director Mikhail Mamuta May 25, 2010, and Russian SME Information Center Igor Mikhalkin October 6, 2009.
28 Personal Interview, RRAPP Deputy Director Natalya Kovalenko, October 14, 2009. RRAPP website: www.r911.ru. Accessed August 9, 2011.
29 Ermakov's professional biography at his organization's website http://www.siora.ru/about/about_ermakov.php.
30 Personal interview, Elena Pontankova, Director SME lending, CentreInvest Bank, June 7, 2010.
31 Although the Rostov Chamber actively participated in the CIPE project to develop associations' advocacy for small business, the Rostov Chamber does not seem to have adopted the approach of leading an explicit 'coalition' of associations. However, the Chamber and OPORA have good and frequent working contacts and coordinate their input to the regional Entrepreneurship Council.
32 Seminar program and text of agreed resolutions.
33 Article 9 addresses the issue of expert input from business association representatives.

34 A list of the laws passed by the regional legislature since 1994 is at http://www.zsro.ru. Accessed July 6, 2011.
35 After the new governor assumed office in mid-2010, Palagina was succeeded on the Council by a new department head.
36 http://www.donland.ru/Default.aspx?pageid=79086 gives composition and purposes of the Entrepreneurship Council. Accessed March 1, 2012.
37 http://www.donland.ru/Default.aspx?pageid=87183 is the text of the Regional SME program. Accessed March 1, 2012.
38 http://www.mbdon.ru/ accessed March 1, 2012 is the regional Ministry of Economy's updated and inviting website providing information for small business owners.
39 The legislature's website gives names of deputies in all four sessions since 1994. http://www.zsro.ru. Accessed June 26, 2011.
40 http://rotary2220.com/. Rostov Rotary website accessed June 15, 2011, interview with Andrey Skorik, Rotary member.
41 The Institute is a member of the Rostov Chamber. A company profile appears in *Bisnes Dona* 2009:132.
42 Personal interview, Elina Liss, Insitute rector, June 11, 2010.
43 Of the four regional case studies, Rostov was the one where getting access to regional officials was most difficult. Meeting with business and business-supporting organizations, by contrast, was as easy as in any of the four cases.

References

Baron, Samuel H. (2001) *Bloody Saturday in the Soviet Union: Novocherkassk 1962*. Stanford, CA: Stanford University Press.

Chamber of Commerce and Industry, Rostov Region. (2009a) *Biznes Dona*. Rostov.

Chamber of Commerce and Industry, Rostov Region. (2009b) *Effektivnaya Tsenovaya i Tarifnaya Politika kak Instrument Realizatsii dolgosrochnogo sotsial'no-ekonomicheskogo razvitiya Rossii*. Rostov.

Chamber of Commerce and Industry, Rostov Region. (2009c) *Sootnoshenie Chlenov TPP Rostovskoi oblasti po organizatsiono-pravovoi forme*. Rostov.

Chamber of Commerce and Industry, Rostov Region. (2009d) *History and Structure of the Rostov Regional Chamber, List of Members, Summary of Programs in Support of Small Business*. Rostov.

Chamber of Commerce and Industry Rostov Region. (2009e) *Biznes bez konfliktov*.

Chamber of Commerce and Industry, Rostov Region. (2011) *Struktura i Pravlenie 2010*. http://www.tppro.ru/about/structure and http://www.tppro.ru/about/committees/. Accessed August 4, 2011.

Chamber of Commerce and Industry, Taganrog. (2009) *Taganrogskaya Mezhraionnaya Torgovo-Promyshlennaya Palata: Otchet o Deyatel'nosti za 2003–2008 gody*. Taganrog, Rostov Oblast.

Filatova, Natal'ya. (2007) Kapitalist po Klichke 'Intelligent" – Profile of Vladimir Mel'nikov. *Russkiy Reporter* 54 (7):1017–1036. http://www.rusrep.ru/article/print/134156. Accessed January 15, 2010.

Goskomstat Rossii. (2001) *Regions of Russia (Regiony Rossii)*. Moscow: State Committee of the Russian Federation for Statistics.

Independent Institute for Social Policy (IISP). (2006) *Regional 'Portrait' – Rostovskaya Oblast'* http://atlas.socpol.ru/portraits/rost.shtml. Accessed May 25, 2011.

Lapina, Natalia and Alla Chirikova. (1999) *Regional Elites in the Russian Federation: Models of Behavior and Political Orientation (Regional'nye elity v RF: Modeli povedeniia politicheskie orientatsii)*. Moscow: INION RAN.

Lapina, Natalia and Alla Chirikova. (2002) *Regiony-Lidery: Ekonomika i Politicheskaya Dinamika.* Moscow: Institute of Sociology, Russian Academy of Sciences (IS-RAN).

McFaul, Michael and Nikolai Petrov. (eds.) (1997) *Politicheskiy Almanakh Rossii: Sotsialno-Politicheskie Portrety Regionov.* Moscow: Carnegie Moscow Center.

OPORA Rossii. (2008a) *Razvitie Malogo i Srednogo Predprinimatel'stva v Regionakh Rossii "Index OPORY".* Moscow.

OPORA Rossii. (2008b) *Maliy Biznes i Korruptsionnye Otnosheniya: Perspktivy Preodoleniya Korruptsii: Otchet po Resultatam Issledovaniya.* Moscow.

Orttung, Robert W. (ed.) (2000) *The Republics and Regions of the Russian Federation: A Guide to Politics, Policies and Leaders.* Armonk, NY and London, UK: M. E. Sharpe.

Pogrebshikov, Yuriy B. (2007) *I Ver', i boisya, i prosi – Political Memoir.* http://www.horse-rostov.ru/konkur/2007/all_.htm. Accessed June 30, 2011.

Rosstat (Federal'naya Sluzhba Gosudarstvennoy Statistiki). (2002, 2004, 2008, 2010a) *Regiony Rossii: Osnovnye Sotsial'no-Ekonomicheskie Pokazateli Gorodov.*

Rosstat (Federal'naya Sluzhba Gosudarstvennoy Statistiki). (2009a) *Maloe i Srednee Predprimatel'stvo v Rossii.*

Rostov International Institute of Economics and Management. (2010) *Molodozhnoe Predprinimatel'stvo – Novyy Vektor v Razvitii Rossiiskogo Biznesa.*

Rostov Regional Administration. (2008) *Polozhenie o sovete po predprinimatel'stvu pri Administratsii Rostovskoi oblasti.* Rostov.

Rostov Regional Administration. (2011) *Oblastnaya dolgosrochnaya Tselevaya programma razvitiya sub'ektov malogo i srednogo predprinimatel'stva v Rostovskoi oblasti ha 2009–2013 gody.* Ministry of Economy, Trade and Foreign Economic Relations, Rostov Oblast. http://www.donland.ru/Default.aspx?pageid=87183. Accessed March 1, 2012.

Rostov Regional Agency for Entrepreneurship Support (RRAPP; Rostovskoe Regional'noe Agentsvo Podderzhki Predprinimatel'stva). (2009) *Program brochures and policy documents of the Non-Commercial Partnership RRAPP.* Rostov.

Rostov Regional Business Association Coalition. (2007) *Regional Anti-Corruption Program.* Rostov: Chamber of Commerce and Industry Rostov Region.

Rostov Regional Legislative Assembly (Zakonodatel'noe Sobranie). (2009) Regional Law no. 213-ZS of May 12, 2009 "O protivodeystvii korruptsii v Rostovskoy oblasti".

Russia: All Regions Trade and Investment Guide. (2008) *Rostov Region.* London, UK: CTEC and Effective Technology Marketing, Ltd.

Shneider, Sergey. (2008) *Voprosy konkurentnosposobnosti malogo i srednogo biznesa Rostovkoi oblasti.* Rostov na Donu: Chamber of Commerce and Industry, Rostov Region.

Shneider, Sergey. (2009) *Otchet o monitoringe sistem gosudarstvennogo upravleniya b Iuzhnom federal'nom okruge 2008.* Rostov na Donu: Southern Federal District Resource Center – Monitoring Department.

Suny, Ronald Grigor. (2011) *The Soviet Experiment: Russia, the USSR, and the Successor States.* Second ed. Oxford, UK: Oxford University Press.

World Bank. (2009) Russian Federation Regional Development and Growth Agglomerations: The Longer Term Challenges of Economic Transition in the Russian Federation. *Country Economic Memorandum.* Washington, DC: World Bank.

World Bank and International Finance Corporation. (2009) *Doing Business in Russia 2009.* Washington, DC.

World Bank and International Finance Corporation. (2010) *Doing Business 2010: Comparing Regulation in 183 Economies: Russian Federation.* Washington, DC.

7 The Perm region

Entrepreneurship and elite transformation

With the full incorporation of the formerly semi-autonomous Komi-Permyatskiy *okrug,* what had been the Perm oblast became the Perm *kray* (territory) in 2006. In 1991, the population of the Perm region (including the Komi-Permyatskiy *okrug*) was 3.045 million, and by 2010 it had declined to 2.72 million, a change of 10.8%, exceeding substantially the roughly 4% decline for Russia as a whole over the same 17-year period. The population of the city of Perm was 986,000 in 2010, or more than one third of the population of the *kray.* The Perm region's population decline, rates of tuberculosis, alcoholism and narcotics addiction, and high reported crime rate are serious social challenges. The UNDP index of human development for Russia's regions shows the Perm region moving from 17th place in 2000 to 20th place in 2008. (Lapin and Belyaeva 2009) With a strong majority of ethnic Russians, the region is nonetheless a geographic meeting place of Finno-Ugric and Turkic populations. The *kray* borders the Udmurtskaya Republic, Tatarstan and Baskortostan.

The Komi-Permyak autonomous okrug's population numbered 136,000 in 2002, of which 59% were of the 'titular' Finno-Ugric linguistic and ethnic group. (Independent Institute for Social Policy 2008) Most of the population is either in small farms or works in the 'budgetary' sector (e.g. teachers, doctors, administration). This is among the poorest regions of Russia. Its full merger with the Perm oblast was pressed by Moscow and intended to transfer some of the fiscal burden to the Perm regional, as opposed to the national, budget.

The share of industry in the Perm region's economy is greater than that in the Russian economy as a whole. In 2005, industry's share in the regional economy was 41%, compared with 31% for Russia as a whole. (Independent Institute for Social Policy 2008) Lapin and Belyava (2009) put the share of industry in the Perm region at greater than 50% and employment in industry at 40%. Much of the region's diversified industry is oriented toward export, including oil, gas, petrochemicals, potassium fertilizer, pulp and paper. Forests cover 70% of the region's territory. (Russia All Regions Trade and Investment Guide, Perm 2008) There are no fewer than 16 industrial monocities in the Perm region.

On the measure we have called 'small firm prevalence,' the Perm region is an underachiever. The fact that industry has a larger share of employment in the Perm region than in Russia as a whole implies that the services sector is comparatively less significant here than in much of the rest of the country. Because this sector is where small companies are typically concentrated, there are fewer small businesses in the Perm region than in many regions where the disposition of the authorities to small business is worse – where 'political' constraints are much more formidable.

The Perm region has been among the best performers on the regional democracy index. (Petrov 2002; Petrov and Titkov 2006, 2013) The region is among Russia's richest as measured by per capita income, but its economic growth rate was slower in 2004–2008 than in several regions in the Southern and Central Federal Districts. (World Bank 2009)

Economic geography and business history – antecedent structural conditions

Settlement of the Perm region by ethnic Russians began in the 15th century, and the city of Perm was founded in 1780. Perm is situated on the heights above a navigable river, the Kama, important both for trade and for defense. Much of the region's vast territory is sparsely populated and covered by forests. Perm, considered the Urals' 'most European' city, is center of commercial, industrial, financial, civic and cultural life. The region's second city by population, Berezniki, lies north of Perm on the Kama as well. (Rosstat 2010b) The river joins the region to the White, Caspian, Baltic and Black Seas. The largest of tributaries of the Volga; the navigable Kama has long compensated to for the remoteness of Perm and the Urals from the heart of European Russia. According to historian Dominic Lieven,

> The river system both aided the Russian expansion and determined some of its axes. Siberia could be crossed and conquered within a few decades because its rivers allowed rapid and relatively easy movement of people and goods. The Urals could become the world's leading iron-producing region in the eighteenth century despite its remoteness because its produce could flow down the Kama to the Volga, and thence by river and canal to St. Petersburg and to European export markets.
>
> (Lieven 2000:205)

The region's indigenous Finno-Ugric people mined copper in and near today's city of Perm. According to a local historian and businessman, the cast iron roofs of the palaces of the 1900 Paris world exhibition were produced in Perm foundries.

Berezniki and the nearby city of Solikamsk are industrial centers based on extraction and processing of mineral resources. The prominent Stroganov family's fortune was built in part upon the extraction of salt from mines around Berezniki beginning in the 16th century. (Colton 2008) Soda and potash were mined beginning in the 19th and early 20th centuries from the same areas, and this industry was intensified in the 1930s with exploitation of penal labor.[1] The Perm region, long considered very remote from Moscow, was home to penal or prison colonies in Tsarist and Soviet times. (Lapin and Belyaeva 2009)

The region's leading large companies in the natural resource field are Lukoil and its refining and petrochemical affiliates, Uralkali and Sil'vinit in potassium fertilizer (these two companies merged early in 2011) and VSMPO-Avisma in titanium. (Vokhrintsev 2008) The principal export markets for the region in 2006 were China, Finland, Kazakhstan, Ukraine and Switzerland. Almost half the region's imports – mainly of capital equipment – came from EU member countries in 2006, with Germany accounting for over one quarter. (Russia All Regions Trade and Investment Guide, Perm 2008)

The city of Berezniki is dominated by a single company, Uralkali, one of the more successful regional enterprises and the source of the fortune of one of Russia's younger billionaires, Dmitry Rybolovlev, born in 1966.[2] Son of physician parents, Rybolovlev graduated from medical school in Perm. Although Rybolovlev was reportedly close to Governor Igumnov, the company maintained a low profile in Perm regional politics and played no discernable role in organized business lobbying at the regional level. According to a Perm academic expert, the company has important influence within the Berezniki municipal administration.

An interesting illustration of the significance of industry and manufacturing to the region is the annual publication *"Ekonomika Prikam'ya"* funded by the regional administration. In 2008, this publication profiled large industrial concerns across the spectrum from machine building to metallurgy to petrochemicals to fertilizer to pulp and paper. The introductory essay by the director of *Politkom,* the organization that produces this publication, claims that industry and manufacturing are the only genuine measures of development and progress. (Vokhrintsev 2008)

Impulse: the democratic breakthrough and its institutionalization

The politics of the Perm region opened wider and stayed more open than is the norm in Russia, in terms of elections, media, the quality and access to information and analysis, and public organizations' activism. According to McFaul and Petrov,

> The [Perm] oblast, considered calm and rarely showing up in the chronicles of scandal, nevertheless must be counted as among those with the most democratically structured political life due to the "mildness" (*myakost'*) of the governing authorities, the organization of the interests of managers and entrepreneurs, and the diversity and freedom of political parties' activity.
>
> (McFaul and Petrov 1997:779)

The authors note that the oblast's electoral support for 'democrats' in the early 1990s came above all from the city of Perm, and to a lesser extent from the Berezniki/Solikamsk area. (McFaul and Petrov 1997)

A leitmotif in the region's politics since the late 1980s is generational change among elites. Interviewed by the author on the first of several occasions on

October 22, 2009, leading political scientist Oleg Podvintsev opined that the Perm region's reputation as one of Russia's most democratic is based largely on the fact that elections at crucial junctures have overturned incumbents and elected challengers.

Two near contemporaries from the generation that came of age in the 1980s epitomize the newer elite of the Perm region: former governor Yuriy Trutnev, born in 1956, and prominent businessman and financier Andrey Kuzyaev, born in 1965. The regional elites of the incumbent generation created permissive conditions for their rise, and Trutnev in turn fostered the careers of promising younger leaders. A prominent example is Trutnev protégé Nikita Belykh, former national leader of the pro-business, liberal SPS party and governor of the neighboring Kirov region.

The first contested elections for the Soviet Congress of People's Deputies in 1989 unseated CPSU regional chairman Yevgeny Chernishev. (McFaul and Petrov 1997) The Perm region's deputies to the Soviet parliament of perestroika period were mainly enterprise directors and had been among the strongest in support of Gorbachev's reforms. (McFaul and Petrov 1997) The region elected two deputies in 1989 who joined the reformist inter-regional group of deputies in the Soviet legislature (Congress of People's Deputies – CPD). The region's first democratic proto-party, 'Perm City Voters' Committee,' was formed under CPD deputy Sergey Kalyagin's leadership in early 1990 to contest the regional legislative elections. These elections brought to political office for the first time future Perm mayor and regional governor Yuriy Trutnev. (Filatov 2002)

Yeltsin appointed Boris Kuznetsov to head the regional administration in 1991, in a compromise between communists and democrats. Kuznetsov, then the director of the Kama river shipping enterprise, was a "manager, little known in politics, who for almost five years in his office did not encounter any serious opposition, but did not turn into a strong personalized ruler and even lost an election to the Federation Council in 1993." (McFaul and Petrov 1997:778) Kuznetsov came in third in the 1993 elections to the Federation Council, behind two candidates from the democratic camp: Vitaly Zelenkin, head of International Fund for Cooperation in Privatization, and entrepreneur Sergey Levitan. Elected to the State Duma in 1995 from the centrist NDR party list, Kuznetsov was the only regional governor who willingly resigned from the post of governor to take his duma seat, leaving the governor's office to his chief deputy, Gennadiy Igumnov. (McFaul and Petrov 1997)

Igumnov decisively defeated his main opponent, entrepreneur and former Federation Council member Sergey Levitan, in the first popular election for governor in December 1996. The first election for the office of mayor of Perm was held along with the gubernatorial election in December 1996. Yuriy Trutnev, at that time 40 years old, won with 61.2% of the vote.

With both parents in the oil industry, Trutnev studied in the oil and gas institute.[3] In 1979, he joined Komsomol, and by 1985 had become the leader of the Komsomol committee for university youth, and soon afterwards the chair of regional CPSU administration's sports committee. Trutnev resigned these party and Komsomol positions in 1988 to found one of Perm's first cooperatives, running a chain of sports clubs and importing exercise equipment. He also organized and headed the Perm Association of Cooperatives. Trutnev's business expanded to a broader retail business called "EKS Limited," still very prominent in the region. Trutnev's itinerary was not exceptional: in the turbulent early 1990s in Perm, "Everyone traded something." (Podvintsev 2005)

Podvintsev argues that the achievement by cooperatives entrepreneurs such as Trutnev of a measure of economic autonomy allowed them to step in and fill a 'vacuum' of political leadership after the October 1993 showdown in Moscow, without themselves espousing any very clear political program, but instead basing their appeal to the electorate only on their relative youth and business success. (Podvintsev 2005) In 1994, presenting himself as a 'fighter' and a force for renewal, Trutnev had been elected to the regional and city legislatures simultaneously. He chaired the economic committee in the regional legislature.

Elected mayor of Perm in 1996, Trutnev staffed his administration with other young leaders and enjoyed strong popular support for reformist and pro-business policies. From the mayor's office he mounted a challenge to incumbent governor Igumnov in 2000. Both men broadly favored democratic and market reforms and had been fairly compatible in their respective roles. According to political scientist Petr Panov, the essence of Trutnev's challenge was youth, renewal and dynamism.[4]

Trutnev did not join any party to run for mayor or governor, but was endorsed by the liberal Yabloko party in 2000. Trutnev joined United Russia after his appointment to the post of Minister of Natural Resources in 2004.[5] As governor, Trutnev did not, as many predicted he might, roll back the authority of mayors and municipalities. A study of municipal administration in 1991–2006 concludes that the city of Perm had considerable scope for independent policy and disposition over its own tax resources independent of the regional administration. (Gel'man et al. 2008)

Trutnev defeated Igumnov, who represented the NDR party, in the 2000 gubernatorial election. The contest was decided only in the second round where Trutnev won a bare majority of 51.48%. In a conversation with the author, sociologist Alla Chirikova related that, among the elected governors she interviewed in her research on regional politics, Trutnev was one of the very few she judged to have really impressive leadership qualities, in terms of articulating and pursuing goals.[6]

Closely paralleling Trutnev's rise in the political elite was the ascent of Andrey Kuzyaev to head Lukoil's Perm affiliate, the single most prominent company in the region. Kuzyaev graduated from the economics department of Perm State University (PGU) in 1987 and went on to form and lead the Perm Commodities Exchange, which in 1993 became the Perm Financial Production Group (PFPG). This group was able to acquire through voucher privatization the enterprise Perm-Neft, which was to become the regional subsidiary of Lukoil. Kuzyaev headed Lukoil Perm from 1996 to 2003 and in 2000 was named president of Lukoil Overseas. With interests in communications and real estate as well as in the oil industry, Kuzyaev as head of PFPG had a reported net worth in of about $850 million in 2010.[7] Kuzyaev served two terms in the Perm regional legislature. He provided strong backing for Trutnev in the gubernatorial race in 2000.

After his defeat, Igumnov became a vice president of Lukoil Perm until his retirement. According to Olga Deryagina, editor in chief of the regional paper *Novyy Kompan'on,* Igumnov, eclipsed by Trutnev's rise, should be recognized for having been both effective and reformist as governor.[8] The rise of Trutnev and his embrace of the tradition of 'mildness' in power can nevertheless been seen as having opened doors for a continued renewal of elites in the Perm region, including the emergence of younger leaders across business, politics and academia.

Comparative overview of small business development

Table 7.1 shows the numbers of incorporated small companies per 1,000 of the labor force in selected years with the average (mean) of this statistic for all regions.

These data show that the Perm region has fewer than average small companies relative to the labor force, even though the region's leadership enacted liberal economic reforms and policies to promote and encourage entrepreneurship from the early 1990s onward. The fact that small firm development has been less vigorous in Perm than in other economically dynamic regions is highlighted for example in the regional administration's small business development program. (Perm Regional Legislature 2008)

There is evidence that the Perm region compares more favorably with other fairly prosperous Russian regions with respect to the numbers of larger small firms (those with more than 15 and up to 100 employees) than on numbers of microenterprises (those with fewer than 15 employees). A comparison of the regions within the Privolzhe Federal District (which includes the Samara and Perm regions) in 2009 shows that the Perm region has about the same number of small firm employees as Samara does but only about one third the number of microenterprises. (Rosstat, Perm Regional Office 2010)[9] The region also is roughly on par with the Samara region as to the number of medium-sized companies (those with 101–250 employees).[10]

Small and medium-sized firms are concentrated in the regional capital, Perm, which in 2009 accounted for 61% of the incorporated small firms in the region and nearly three quarters of the turnover. The city is home to only about one third of the 304 medium-sized companies in the region, but over 70% of the turnover of these companies. (Perm City Administration 2009)

A peculiarity of the Perm region is the continued importance of independent entrepreneurs in the small business community. The figures in Table 7.2 show

Table 7.1 Perm Region: Incorporated Small Firms per 1,000 Persons in Labor Force

	1995	*2000*	*2002*	*2004*	*2006*	*2008*
Perm region	8.95	5.74	6.38	7.96	8.41	10.23
All-regions average	11.64	9.48	9.32	11.05	10.76	14.91

Source: Goskomstat Rossii 2001, Rosstat *Regiony Rossii* 2006, 2010

Table 7.2 Independent Entrepreneurs: Perm Region 2004 and 2008

	2004	2008
Independent entrepreneurs for 1,000 workforce	41	40.7
Perm region percentile ranking	78th	75th
Median (national)	37	36
Mean (national)	37	37

Source: Russian SME Resource Center 2004, 2006, Rosstat 2009

that their numbers relative to the workforce held steady from 2004 to 2008. By comparison, independent entrepreneurs relative to the labor force fell steeply in Samara and Smolensk, while they rose in the Rostov region.

This outcome, along with the small numbers of microenterprises, suggests that many *de facto* microenterprise owners have opted in the Perm region for the status of individual entrepreneur. The fact that their numbers have held steady in the Perm region may be an indicator of limited competition in the region's retail sector. Some critics of former governor Trutnev suggest that the retail trade sector has been inhibited by favorable treatment of the retail activities of 'EKS Limited,' the company he founded. These critics also point to the absence in the Perm region of Russia's national supermarket chains.

Small companies represented 18.5% of turnover of all companies in the Perm region in 2009, but 61.2% of turnover in wholesale and retail trade and consumer services. Small firms produced 12.5% of GRP in the Perm region in 2008, compared with 15.1% in Russia as a whole. (Rosstat, Perm Regional Office 2010) According to the regional administration, in 2009, 190,000 people worked for 14,800 incorporated small businesses, and another 82,300 people were individual entrepreneurs. This means that 272,300 people – one fifth of the region's 1.4 million strong labor force – worked in small businesses. (Perm Regional Ministry for Entrepreneurship, Development and Trade 2010)

The 2008 OPORA regional comparative survey of small business owners discussed in Chapter 3 ranked 35 regions by the conditions for small business development. (OPORA 2008) The Perm region was found to be the fifth most favorable to small business development among those studied. The region was ranked eighth in terms of real property and infrastructure, sixth on human resources, 8th on administrative barriers and sixteenth of the availability of credit. As shown in the discussion in Chapter 3, the entrepreneurs of Samara, Perm and Rostov regions differed in revealing ways on the weight of political versus economic challenges they identified.

The single most distinctive outcome for Perm is the role entrepreneurs cite for the demands of regulatory bodies. The interpretation of this impediment may vary from one regional setting to another, because, on the one hand, it could be that the demands of regulators are legitimate in the interests of public safety or consumer protection, or, on the other hand, it could be that they are burdensome and a means of extracting resources either legally as fines or illegally as bribes.

The question put to respondents in the OPORA 2008 survey leaves open both possible interpretations.

The World Bank and International Finance Corporations's *Doing Business* report (2010) supports the evidence from the OPORA survey with respect to the regulatory environment for business in the city of Perm. As discussed in the Rostov case study, this study compared ten Russian cities, including Moscow and St. Petersburg, in terms of the cost and duration of legal and regulatory procedures related to starting a business, dealing with construction permits, registering property, and trading across borders.

The study found the city of Perm is the most costly and time-consuming of the cities studied for establishing a business. Perm was in fourth place for the costs and duration of getting construction permits, in third place for ease of transferring property, and in eighth place for the cost and time involved in importing or exporting. The overall outcome supports the idea that regulations on the conduct of business are heavy relative to the national norm in the city of Perm, and by inference in the Perm region. This may help to explain why incorporated micro-enterprises are relatively few and individual entrepreneurs relatively numerous, as shown earlier.

The comparison of Rostov and Perm in the OPORA and *Doing Business* studies shows that administrative barriers and corruption are not always reliably or predictably related, even if the existence of complex and lengthy formal procedures creates conducive conditions for the arbitrary exercise of power. Rostov performs well on the ease of doing business, and its entrepreneurs do not complain about regulatory requirements. Nevertheless, they cite corruption as a problem more often than do the survey respondents in cities with higher formal administrative barriers. It seems that Perm's entrepreneurs face more complex regulations than in Rostov, but do not tend to associate these rules with egregious abuse of power or monopolization by a favored few. Table 7.3 compares Rostov and Perm with each other by their rank among the ten cities covered by *Doing Business* 2010. The rankings of Moscow and St. Petersburg are shown for comparison.

It is possible that the regulatory burden in Perm is at least partly symptomatic of the attempt of the authorities to be responsive to the broader public (beyond the business community) or even to organized civic groups advocating for environmental or consumer safety concerns. This issue became even more acute after a

Table 7.3 World Bank 2009 Rankings of 10 Russian Cities by Ease of Doing Business

City/Rank	Starting Business	Construction Permits	Transferring Property	Trading Across Borders
Perm	10th	3rd	3rd	8th
Rostov	1st	1st	10th	2nd
St. Petersburg	9th	8th	6th	1st
Moscow	8th	10th	7th	10th

Source: World Bank and International Finance Corporation Russian subnational *Doing Business* 2010.

fire in a popular Perm nightclub, *Khromaya Loshad'* (Lame Horse) killed 150 on December 5, 2009. The owners of the nightclub, near the regional administration building, were found to have egregiously violated fire safety standards. The incident dominated national and regional headlines for weeks.

Business associations and small business advocacy – bonding and bridging 'civic-ness'

The discussion of business associations in the Perm region is structured as in the preceding three case studies. As in those cases, we assess the performance of business associations with respect to leadership and structure, 'internal' (bonding) issues such as representativeness, usefulness and inclusiveness and 'external' (bridging) issues of interest representation vis-à-vis state institutions and visibility to the broader public. The associational landscape is assessed, as well as the role of institutions serving as functional substitutes for business associations.

Chamber of commerce and industry of the Perm region

The Perm Regional Chamber of Commerce and Industry was organized at a conference in 1991 of 60 members of the *Uralskiy Torgovo-promyshlennaya Palata,* a branch of the Soviet Chamber of Commerce and Industry. Because the Perm region was home to major exporting enterprises, it was one of the exceptional regions where the Soviet Chamber had a regional affiliate.

With an initial membership dominated by engineering firms, the Chamber focused much of its early work on defense conversion and the adoption of modernized technologies by the region's industrial enterprises, including through attracting foreign investment. (Chamber of Commerce and Industry, Perm Region 2011b) The Chamber has continued its steady emphasis on trying to use the region's strong tradition of engineering and technical education to generate local technological innovations and on the importance of intellectual property protections. The Chamber's membership grew from 60 in 1991 to 490 in 2010. Over this period, the preponderance of technical and engineering enterprises within the Chamber was diminished as smaller companies joined. By 2010, 65% of the Chamber's member companies were either incorporated small firms or individual entrepreneurs.[11] The Chamber has affiliates in several other regional cities.

In an interview with the author on October 19, 2009, the Chamber's founding President Viktor Zamaraev and board chairman Pavel Kudryavtsev discussed the Chamber's role and goals. They said widespread asset stripping had laid waste to many otherwise viable industrial enterprises during the voucher privatizations of the early 1990s. The defense and machine-building base had been spared, because the voucher privatization program did not cover them. One of the Chamber's core priorities had been to help generate new manufacturing firms to apply new technology and ideas, building on the region's industrial tradition and human capital base.

The election of Marat Bimatov, born in 1971, to succeed Zamaraev as Perm Chamber president and governing board chairman in early 2011 marked both a generational change and the continued shift of the center of gravity of the Chamber's membership and representations on behalf of business toward newer and smaller firms in the services sector, with a somewhat diminished focus on the interests of the engineering firms in its initial constituency. Founder of an advertising company, Bimatov headed the regional affiliate of Delovaya Rossiya and was the regional minister of economy and entrepreneurship, a post from which he was one of the region's leading advocates of small business promotion. This smooth generational succession again typifies the pattern of elite transformation in Perm as a whole. Viktor Zamaraev remains the Chamber's honorary president.

The regional Chamber's governing board elected in early 2011 has 25 members. Table 7.4 organizes the members into four categories and gives their organizational affiliation:

Table 7.4 Perm Chamber Governing Board by Organizational Affiliation

Category	Number of Board Members
Chamber president and officers	2
Large industrial companies	6
Small or 'new' business	14
Academics, NGOs	4

Source: www.permtpp.ru/about_chamber/board/. Accessed July 8, 2011.

The 'incumbent' industrial enterprises have significant representation on this board as they did on the previous one. (Chamber of Commerce and Industry, Perm Region 2011a) Prominent businessman Aleksey Andreyev, the president of the regional employers' organization *Sotrudnichestvo,* was reelected to the Chamber's board. Of the other five representatives of industrial enterprises on the board, three are from engineering firms, and the other two from the oil and gas sector (Lukoil and Gazprom's regional affiliate). Among the 'new' sector companies represented on the board are two large companies in telecommunications and banking. The remaining 12 represent smaller new businesses in advertising, retail, finance and insurance, construction (residential and commercial), consumer goods production and media. Also included is the director of the agency for entrepreneurship development, which implements the regional administration's small business credit programs. Two newer and smaller companies are closely associated with the engineering and oil refining industries. Two women are on the board: the director of motor-oil producer (*Kamski Zavod Masel*) and the director of the *Mayskiy Zhuk* (Maybeetle) advertising group. One board member, Aleksandr Gimervert, director of an engineering firm, is a municipal legislator in Perm and another, Sergey Klimov, CEO of the city's exhibition center, serves in the regional legislature. The generally younger membership of the board under Bimatov's leadership represents the partial incorporation of many leaders of companies that belong to Delovaya Rossiya.

The theme of representing small business and promoting entrepreneurship through the Perm Chamber was embraced with the founding of the committee on small business development in 2000. In that year, the Chamber held its first roundtables and seminars devoted to the problems of small business. In 2003, under the program organized by CIPE, the Chamber became the coordinator of the "Coalition of Business Associations for the Protection of Interests of Entrepreneurs of Perm Oblast."

In the first of several interviews with the author on October 20, 2009, the Chamber's External Relations Director Pavel Zaitsev said that contacts among the associations in the coalition helps the Chamber to identify new issues and problems being encountered by small business. In turn, he said, the Chamber gives coalition organizations greater lobbying leverage by lending its weight to their concerns.

The list of associations in the coalition at its founding in 2003 follows in Table 7.5:

Table 7.5 Coalition Member Organizations 2003 – Perm Region

Perm Association for Support of Individual Entrepreneurs
Non-commercial Organization "Fund for Support of Small Entrepreneurs" Nytvenskiy rayon
Perm Association "Society for Development of Entrepreneurial Initiatives"
Municipal Fund for Support of Small Business, city of Krasnokamsk
Perm Regional branch of Russian Union of Workers in Medium and Small Business
Perm Regional Association Business Club "Edinenie"
Dobryanskaya Association for Support of Small Business "Partner"
Perm Regional Chamber of Commerce and Industry
Non-commercial Partnership "Perm Guild of Conscientious Enterprises"
Non-commercial Partnership "Union of Conscientious Ferry Operators Prikam'e"
Association for Small Business Development, city of Berezniki

As coalition coordinator, the Perm Chamber formalized the coalition's work within a standing small business committee. As of late 2010, the composition of the small business committee of the Perm Chamber was as shown in Table 7.6:

Table 7.6 Small Business Committee Members and Affiliations

Baranov, Aleksey Ivanovich*	Chairman of Committee, Individual Entrepreneur
Mironova, Elena Aleksandrovna	Vice President of Perm Chamber
Galitsky, Denis Grigor'evich	Leader of "Society for Development of Entrepreneurial Initiatives"
Gusev, Valeriy Vasil'evich*	General Director OOO "Khemi" President, Guild of Conscientious Enterprises

(*Continued*)

Table 7.6 (Continued)

Dobrolyubov, Igor Konstantinovich*	Managing Director, Perm regional affiliate of OAO "TD" Lukoil
Zaitsev, Pavel Vladimirovich	Director, External Relations, Perm Chamber
Churakova, Irina Aleksandrovna	Director, OAO Perm Center for Entrepreneurship Development
Okunev, Konstantin Nikolaevich	Member, Perm regional legislature
Orlova, Elena Yaroslavovna	President, Perm regional affiliate of Russian Union of Employees of Medium and Small Business
Popov, Aleksey Mikhailovich*	Director of Krasnokamsk Municipal Fund for Support of Small Business Director, TD "Lider"
Slobodskiy, Roman Efimovich*	Director OOO "Basma-N"
Fridman, Yevgeny Mikhailovich	Head, Perm regional OPORA
Sasonov, Dmitry Valer'evich	Deputy Minister, Trade and Entrepreneurship
Khusid, Andrey Gennad'evich	Executive Director, Perm regional affiliate of Delovaya Rossiya

* Also members of the Chamber's governing board of 2010.

Source: Chamber of Commerce and Industry Perm Region (2010b)

The breadth of this committee's membership reflects the institutionalization of a 'coalition' approach to small business advocacy. The participation of Lukoil at a senior level illustrates the civic corporate policies of Lukoil alluded to by many analysts. (Peregudov 2005) Another member of the committee, Konstantin Okunev, was a member of the "*Solidarnost*" faction in the regional legislature, in opposition to Governor Chirkunov and United Russia. Okunev owns a supermarket chain in direct competition with the Sem'ya supermarkets, part of the EKS group of former governors Trutnev and Chirkunov. Another critic of the region's political leadership on the committee is Denis Galitsky, an outspoken and prominent social activist in support of entrepreneurship as well as other issues in urban development in Perm. The objectives, leadership, activities and effectiveness of those business organizations represented on the committee are discussed in detail in the following sections.

As stressed throughout these case studies, participation by individual entrepreneurs in business associations is fairly weak. It is noteworthy therefore that the chairmanship of this committee is held by individual entrepreneur Valeriy Baranov, also a member until 2011 of the Chamber's governing board. In an interview with the author, Baranov explained that he deals in tableware and dishes, the former made in Russia, and the latter imported. He had drawn on the Chamber's services as he sought to expand his supplier network into China. His customer base has expanded beyond the Perm region and employs substantial numbers. Nevertheless, like many other individual entrepreneurs, he has not sought to incorporate his business. Baranov praised the receptiveness of the regional administration to the concerns of small business as expressed through the Chamber's small business committee.[12]

Chamber Vice President Elena Mironova's work has been focused on representing small business since the formation of the coalition in 2003. In an interview with the author, she discussed having launched in 2010 a club of women company directors *(Klub Zhenshin Rukovoditeley)* from among Chamber members. At its founding, this group had 31 members, almost half of whom were from companies in such new sectors as construction, real estate development, finance, insurance, tourism, consulting and retail. Five are from companies either in or building upon the mainstream industrial sectors of natural resource processing or manufacturing. The remaining eight members represent associations such as the Chamber itself (Mironova and one colleague), the Kungur entrepreneurs association, the regional women's council, educational institutions and the Governor's staff. (Chamber of Commerce and Industry, Perm region 2010a)[13]

Sotrudinichestvo

Sotrudinichestvo is the Perm region's employers' union, founded under the provisions of the federal law of 2002 "on employers' associations." (Perm Regional Association of Employers 2006) The purpose given in the law for the formation of employers' unions is to participate in 'social partnership,' which means negotiations with labor unions around wages and conditions of work. Sotrudnichestvo was registered in its current form in 2004, on the basis of its antecedent organization with the same name, set up as a non-commercial partnership in 1996, at the initiative of the directors of enterprises in the defense sector.[14] Although Sotrudnichestvo is the regional affiliate of RSPP, because of its 'indigenous' founding by regional actors, the organization has built its own well-recognized 'brand' and is the most influential and best-known business association in the region.

Peregudov (2005) reports on extensive interviews with members and leaders of Sotrudnichestvo related to the question of interest representation by big business in Russia's regions. He concluded that this organization brought "a substantial contribution to the development of the partnership between the regional business and regional government and with civil society." (Peregudov 2005:19)

In an interview with the author, Sotrudinichestvo Vice President Igor Savrasov explained that, in addition to periodic sector-based contract negotiations with labor unions, the organization has active committees on safety, education, research and development and the implementation of newly adopted legislation. He said Sotrudnichestvo does not advocate for or defend the interests of individual member companies but takes positions on broad issues of policy affecting all members or those in a particular sector. Issues such as curbing corruption were not as prominent in the concerns of Sotrudnichestvo as among the smaller companies in the Chamber or in OPORA.[15]

The president of Sotrudnichestvo is Aleksey Andreyev, perhaps the best known representative and advocate for the interests of the engineering firms in the region. As noted earlier, he also serves on the board of the Perm Chamber. Born in 1947, Andreyev trained as an engineer and studied economics in the 1980s.[16] The enterprise Andreyev heads, OAO 'PNPPK,' designs and manufactures precision instruments, including navigation instruments for aviation and shipping. The enterprise was founded in 1956 and seems to have been restructured as an OAO by direct acquisition by its management.[17] Andreyev was elected to the regional legislature for two terms beginning in 1997 and has served on the Social Chamber *(Obshchestvennaya Palata)* for the Perm region. According to scholars Oleg Podvintsev and Irina Semenenko, Sotrudnichestvo has financed social and educational programs in close coordination with the regional administration.[18]

The 60-member presidium of Sotrudinichestvo is dominated by the heads of large industrial firms in either engineering or natural resource extraction or processing. There are several instances of interpenetration between the Perm Chamber and Sotrudnichestvo. Two vice presidents of Sotrudnichestvo and one member of presidium have served or are serving on the Chamber's board. Chamber founding president Viktor Zamaraev and former board chairman Pavel Kudryavtsev are also listed as members of the presidium, as is the president of another business association, the Perm Guild of Conscientious *(dobrosovestnikh)* Enterprises.[19]

In principle, any company or organization that is a substantial employer can join Sotrunichestvo.[20] The member companies and organizations include 22 in machine building or metals fabrication; 5 in metallurgy; 15 in chemicals, petrochemicals and natural gas; 6 in electrical power generation and transmission; 7 in construction and manufacture of construction materials; 2 in wood and paper; 14 in banking and insurance; 7 in project design; 12 educational institutions (mainly with a technical or engineering focus); 4 companies in information technology; 4 in media or advertising; 7 in medicine or pharmaceuticals and 11 in trade and consumer services. From this list it will be evident that Sotrudinechestvo's ranks have not been penetrated to a great degree by companies the 'new' (services) sectors.

In 2000, Sotrudnichestvo and the Chamber jointly launched of a specialized institute to train managers and technical leadership for companies, the Institute for Raising Qualifications (Institut Povysheniya Kvalifikatsii) RMTsPK.[21] A public-private partnership with the regional administration, the institute has continued sponsorship by the Chamber and Sotrudnichestvo, as well as support from Andreyev's company. The institute's director serves on the Sotrudnichestvo presidium and on the Chamber's board. Peregudov (2005) interprets the creation of this institute as forming a politically significant links between the region's responsible business community and the talented and ambitious younger generation entering senior ranks of companies. (Peregudov 2005)

Delovaya Rossiya of the Perm region

As we have seen in Chapter 3, Delovaya Rossiya was formed to represent businesses in the 'new' sectors of the economy – services, finance, mobile telecommunications and light manufacturing – focused on the domestic market. Its members are individuals, not companies, and its objectives are the most openly 'political' of any of the business associations, in that its explicit agenda is to promote diversification away from resource extraction. This political agenda is reinforced by the fact that Delovaya Rossiya's founding national president, Boris Titov, was one of three senior leaders in the now-defunct pro-business liberal political party Pravoe Delo. Delovaya Rossiya has regional chapters in Samara and Rostov regions, where its leadership is locally very prominent. In neither of the other two cases, however, does the local chapter approach the level of visibility and activism of Delovaya Rossiya in the Perm region

Delovaya Rossiya's Perm chapter was launched and headed by Marat Bimatov, who continued as president after he became regional Minister of Trade and Entrepreneurship. The chapter's executive director is Andrey Khusid, who, in his mid-20s, has a public relations agency "Projector."[22]

In the first of several interviews with the author on October 20, 2009, Khusid and several other young members of Delovaya Rossiya said membership opened the possibility of participating in changing policies affecting business. These new members were drawn into Delovaya Rossiya under the wing of Marat Bimatov.[23] One focus for the new members led by Khusid was to generate new businesses from among the graduates of Perm's universities and institutes with an emphasis on innovative technologies. In June 2010, Delovaya Rossiya was among the sponsors along with Microsoft of a business plan workshop to critique young entrepreneurs' ideas for web-based startups. Andrey Khusid chaired the presentations at this event attended by about 50–60 young people, backed by the Moscow-based company StartupPoint.[24]

Delovaya Rossiya and the regional Ministry of Trade and Entrepreneurship were among the sponsors of an exhibition devoted to innovation and youth entrepreneurship, the 'Permskiy Molodozhniy Innovatsionniy Konvent' on October 23, 2009. A roundtable discussion at this event, took up the question of the value of associations representing and advocating for entrepreneurs. One speaker argued that formal business associations were not as important in practical terms as the informal business community, of which, he said, everyone at the table was a member. Several participants mentioned that entrepreneurs are not well regarded by the public, and that associations could help change this. Marat Bimatov suggested that business associations' role had been pre-empted by the relatively pro-business political leadership of the Perm region. It might be the case, he thought, that small businesspeople were content and had little reason to mobilize around a small business association.[25]

OPORA – Perm region

The history of OPORA in the Perm region follows the pattern of generational succession and elite promotion we have discerned elsewhere. An OPORA chapter was established in Perm in 2002, but by late in the decade, it had dissolved in all but name as its original leaders moved on. Reportedly, several of the local OPORA's original leaders are members of the regional legislature. The long lapse in activity by OPORA, the leading association advocating for small business, is nevertheless surprising given the general strength of civil society organizations in the region.

In 2009, young entrepreneur Yevgeny Fridman initiated the effort to revive and reconstitute OPORA in the Perm region.[26] A medical school graduate, Fridman owns a fleet of vehicles equipped as ambulances, serving municipalities by contract. He also publishes the regional edition of the national newspaper *Kommersant.*

After some discussion, Fridman won endorsement from OPORA's national leadership, and he moved fairly swiftly to rebuild the membership base.[27] Having formally launched the chapter in early 2010, the membership stood at 100 in July. According to Fridman, one could easily enroll 1,000 members, but OPORA's reputation demanded that only dynamic, active and reputable businesspeople become members. In 2011, Fridman publicized the work of OPORA Perm and pursued the expansion of the chapter through frequent Facebook posts and through the association's website.[28] Member entrepreneurs form committees in OPORA Perm on construction, restaurants, outsourcing and information technology.

Fridman said that the regions small business had been hard hit by the 2008–2009 financial crisis. In his view, OPORA's role was to let entrepreneurs know about the programs and support available from the regional administration. OPORA-Perm participates, according to Fridman, in various advisory councils to municipal, regional and federal agencies.

Fridman said OPORA members valued in particular the ability to interact with federal agencies, leveraging OPORA's standing as a national organization. He cited the Federal Anti-Monopoly Service as a key partner. The regional administration and the legislature's anti-corruption committee were also important channels for OPORA's policy input. Fridman praised the regional administration for its accessibility, due, he believed, to the pro-business outlook of Governor Chirkunov and many of his close associates. OPORA was able to have frequent informal exchanges with senior leaders in the administration. Fridman sought a role for OPORA in shaping programs to foster technical innovation, following a precedent set in the Irkutsk region.

OPORA Perm publicly supported the elimination of direct elections for the office of Perm mayor, a move that ensured the incumbent mayor's extension of his tenure. Fridman defended this position by arguing that direct elections are subject to 'black PR' and fraud. Under a system where the mayor would be elected from among the elected members of the local legislature, Fridman argued, a majority of legislators could remove an ineffective mayor at any time. Fridman further argued that management skills were more important in political office than ideology, and that elections do not reliably select the most effective managers.

Guild of conscientious enterprises

The Perm Guild of Conscientious *(dobrosovestnykh)* Enterprises aims to project a public commitment to high quality and safety standards to consumers. The 42 company members of the Guild are all producers of consumer goods (such as meat or poultry processing) or providers of consumer services, including pharmacies, construction or insurance companies. The 10th anniversary publication in 2006 gives full company profiles and histories of member companies. (Perm Guild of Conscientious Enterprises 2006) At the founding in 1996, there were six members. The Guild's president since 2006 has been Valeriy Vasil'evich Gusev, general director of the "KhEMI" (paint producing) holding. Gusev is a member of the Perm Chamber's governing board and the presidium of Sotrudnichestvo.[29]

Executive Director Valeriy Gulayev said the name "Guild" had been chosen with self-conscious reference to the merchant and industrialist guilds of the Tsarist period. The Guild had been created on the passage of the first federal law on consumer protection in 1994. The organization had adopted the motto of the First Guild of the Tsarist period "Honor is Higher than Profit" *(Chest' prevyshe pribyli)*. They distribute to visitors a collection of reproductions of period photos of the leading First Guild merchants of Perm.

According to Gulyaev, regional consumers' faith in locally produced food and other consumer products collapsed in the early and mid 1990's. The founding of the Guild was seen as a means of restoring the market position of local companies relative to imports. Governor Igumnov had been a strong supporter of these aims, because he was concerned about employment and also about improving the quality of affordable local foodstuffs to lower income consumers in the region.

In retirement, Igumnov remains on the Guild's board of directors. The Guild also received strong support from regional Vice Premier Elena Gelazova, a former business associate of Governor Chirkunov and the predecessor to Marat Bimatov as regional Trade and Entrepreneurship Minister. (Perm Guild of Conscientious Enterprises 2010)

Kungur entrepreneurs' association

The city of Kungur, an hour and half's drive from Perm and with a population of 67,000, is home to the Kungur Association of Entrepreneurs. The association, headed by Galina Teklyuk, has 42 members, including both incorporated firms and individual entrepreneurs. Teklyuk is also a member of the Perm Chamber and businesswomen's club. She owns and runs a travel agency in Kungur, which, in addition to organizing national and international travel for Kungur clients, is working to generate interest from Russian and international travelers in visiting Kungur, on the Trans-Siberian rail route. Teklyuk's travel agency, *"Kungur i Mir"* employs a youthful staff of six people on the third floor of a newly built building, shared with a beauty salon and a children's clothing store.

Association leader and entrepreneur Teklyuk explained that the majority of her association's members are in wholesale or retail trade, but some are in construction or light industry. The association's offices are co-located with those of the city administration's small business support program, which administers a fund to support new companies as well as a business incubator. Kungur has no heavy industry, leaving the small business community as a major source of the local economy and employment. The city's public relations brochures highlight the role of the small business association and point out that the revival of small business is the restoration of the city's merchant tradition.[30]

The city flourished in the 19th century when local merchants imported tea and sold Russian manufactured goods in an overland trading route through Kungur with Asia. A museum in the city commemorates the lives and work of these merchants, displaying period clothing, documents and artifacts from the merchants' households. According to Teklyuk, Kungur's first elected mayor, Makhmudov, had raised the monument to Kungur's most prominent merchant Aleksey Semonivich Gubkin in the city's square adjacent to the museum. A Kungur historian's 2008 biography of Gubkin is entitled "*Kungurskiy Rotshild.*" (Mushkalov 2008)[31]

Teklyuk said the main obstacle to small business development is the unavailability of credit on reasonable terms. Most successful small businesses in Kungur had found ways to self-finance, which meant that they usually remained small. Teklyuk illustrated the difficult conditions for entrepreneurs by citing the case of the owner of Kungur meat processing, a member of the Perm Guild. He had invested in modernized equipment for the Soviet-era factory and vastly improved the quality of his products, popular throughout the region. He had successfully contested an adverse tax ruling in court, but his plans for expansion had been delayed as he fended off a renewed inquiry by tax inspectors.

Union of employees in small and medium business

The Perm regional affiliate of the national labor union for workers in medium and small businesses *(Rossiiskaya Profsoyuz Rabotnikov Srednego i Malogo Biznesa)* is headed by Elena Orlova and has been an active participant in the coalition led by the Perm Chamber on behalf of small business. Orlova is a veteran of the earliest phase of the cooperatives movement in Perm and a strong advocate for better conditions for small business and the expansion of the share of such business in employment. According to Orlova, of the 30,000 or so people employed in small business in the region, 7,000 (from 110 different companies) are represented in the Union. Orlova sees the Union as a defender of small businesses in a general sense, because the growth of the sector means more secure employment, better pay and more new jobs. Her association with the Perm Chamber has, she said, helped her to solve problems for companies whose employees belong to the Union.[32]

Orlova explained that the Union chapter in Perm had been established in 1989 at the same time as the founding national conference. The organization was originally called the Union of Employees in Cooperatives, since this was the only form that legal small business took at the time. The national union has chapters in 44 Russian regions.

According to Orlova's account, Yuriy Trutnev was one of those who pushed for setting up a union for cooperative employees, through his leadership of the cooperative association in Perm and its participation in the founding of a national cooperatives association in the late 1980s.

Business associations' dialogue with regional and city administrations – contributions to the openness of policy formulation

Business agenda

In 2008, the Perm regional coalition of business associations produced and disseminated its 'Anti-Corruption Regional Business Agenda.' (Perm Regional Coalition of Business Associations 2008) A distinctive element of the Perm program (as compared with those adopted in Samara or Smolensk for example) is the strong emphasis on shaping public opinion: in particular addressing the public perception that business itself bears most of the responsibility for corruption. The program addresses itself also to shaping the business community's own attitudes, so that paying bribes will not be considered routine.

While recognizing that the problem of corruption in the Perm region is not as acute as in many other parts of Russia, the program points to official sponsorship of favored enterprises as widespread, especially on the part of municipal governments. Another major problem cited is 'corruption barriers in land and real estate transactions,' an issue typically under the control of municipalities. The program recognizes the criminal liability of both bribe payers and bribe exacters, but places its emphasis on prevention rather than on punitive law enforcement. The program alleges that laws and regulations are deliberately drafted to create opportunities for the corrupt exercise of discretion. The remedy proposed for this is for business associations' legal experts to review proposed and existing legislation.

The coalition of business associations claims to have played a role in the regional legislature's passage of the regional law 'on countering corruption in the Perm region' in 2007. (Center for International Private Enterprise 2008) Like the business program, the law emphasizes curbing corruption through changing public and official attitudes. It enacts the provision, proposed by business associations, allowing legal experts from business and other citizens' associations to advise on legal drafts. The law emphasizes the need to consult with and accept the view of civic associations and establishes permanent 'organs' in the executive and legislature to pursue anti-corruption objectives, conduct monitoring and receive the input of civic associations committed to reducing corruption. This regional legislation is not able directly to affect the many challenges for small business lying in the jurisdiction of municipalities, however.

The principal consultative structures for small business in the Perm region are the governor's council *(kraevoy sovet po razvitiyu predprimatel'stva pri gubernatore),* a body formed by the Federal Anti-Monopoly Service *(obshchestvenno-konsultativniy sovet pri Permskoy FAC Rossii)* and, in the city of Perm itself, the mayor's council *(gorodskoy sovet po razvitiyu predprimatel'stva pri glave goroda).* (Perm Regional Ministry of Entrepreneurship, Development and Trade 2010)

The Regional administration's program for development of small and medium entrepreneurship for 2008–2011 called for total expenditure of approximately

1.5 billion rubles spread over the four years, with about 473 million from the region's budget, 840 million from the federal budget, 63 million from municipal budgets and 139 million from non-budgetary sources (from regional and municipal financial agencies such as the *Permskiy Tsentr Razvitiya Predprinimatel'stva* (PTsRP).[33] (Perm Regional Legislature 2008) The very substantial contribution to the Perm program from the federal budget is decided by the Ministry of Economic development on the basis of the quality of the program in terms of its design and the measureable objectives set out for it.

The declared objectives of this program are to increase the numbers, turnover and share of overall employment of small firms. The Perm program states as a principal goal the involvement of the business community in formulating small business development policy. The authors acknowledge that the Perm region lags behind other comparably prosperous Russian regions in terms of numbers of small firms, but claims substantial growth in numbers of firms, turnover and employment since 2006. Fostering small business will, according to the program, create greater economic competition and regional budget income, ensuring "the formation of the middle class – the main guarantor of social and political stability of society." (Perm Regional Legislature 2008)

The program document cites the inadequacies of the legal environment and weak protections for the rights of entrepreneurs and notes the need to tackle administrative barriers constraining the growth of entrepreneurship. The major part of the resources in the program are devoted to easing collateral requirements and repayment periods for small business loans, as well as expanding access to legal and other advisory services. Other measures in the same spirit are direct subsidies to business creation by students, the unemployed and veterans, in addition to projects in innovative technologies and the creation of a network of municipal business incubators. Regional administration funding for municipal governments' programs in small business support are to be funded by a competition *(konkurs)* based on evaluation of program features and design.

A 2010 presentation by Minister of Entrepreneurship and Trade Bimatov emphasizes creating equal conditions for all entrepreneurs, development of competition instead of applying protectionist measures and the opening of new niches for small business. (Perm Regional Ministry of Entrepreneurship, Development and Trade 2010) In a 2008 interview published in a regional business magazine, Bimatov's predecessor, Elena Gilyazova, discussed the input of business associations in the design of this program. She said 13 working groups, including entrepreneurs from various sectors, had been involved. (Yutov 2008) Gilyazova emphasized the need to ensure that the region's programs assist only those enterprises strong enough to prosper in competitive conditions.

The principal innovation in the Perm regional program beginning in 2008 was the establishment of the small business web information portal.[34] This site links to the texts of federal and Perm regional legislation affecting small business in addition to the text of the regional program, contact numbers for the ministry, a hotline for legal consultations *(skoroy pomoshch')* especially as related to inspections by tax and other oversight agencies. This latter service dispatches a small ambulance-style van to business premises.

The program of entrepreneurship support of the city of Perm for 2009–2011 is distinctly more oriented toward 'industrial policy' than the regional program. (Perm City Administration 2009) The funding for the program is 2.8 million rubles for the three-year period. The main activities funded are training and advisory services for entrepreneurs and periodic survey research on the numbers, profitability and sectoral trends in the city's small business. The mayor's council on SME development, where business associations are represented, is designated to assess the program's success.[35]

The department in the city administration responsible for the program is the Department of Industrial Policy, Investment and Entrepreneurship, under which one of three sections deals with small business development. A statement of goals of the department in a public presentation in 2007 gave the top billing to the strengthening and development of the scientific-technical, productive and intellectual potential of the city of Perm, followed by making industrial production more competitive, enhancing investment in promising sectors, deepening 'social partnership' and, in last place, the goal of developing entrepreneurial initiatives (with no mention of removing impediments or administrative barriers). (Perm City Administration Department of Industrial Policy Investment and Entrepreneurship 2007)

The Perm city small business development program makes no mention of reducing administrative limitations on business and does not address the issue of facilitating land and building purchases by enterprises holding leases on city property, a critical priority of small business. According to several Perm Chamber sources, the main interaction of the Chamber with the Perm city administration is precisely with respect to this question.

In an interview with the author on June 18, 2010, Deputy Minister of Entrepreneurship and Trade Dmitry Sasonov, about 30 years old, said he had entered the ministry at Bimatov's invitation, having already started two companies – one in tourism and the other in information technology. Sasonov said that the regional small business program identified the most committed and energetic people in municipalities and fostered their interactions with the Ministry. He said the regional program had not worked very much with the city of Perm itself, because small business was most advanced there.[36]

Entrepreneurs in regional political office – contributions to the dispersion of regional and local political authority

The Perm region has seen the promotion of larger numbers of new elites into political life from business, including 'new' business, than any of the three other case study regions, including its close peer on many measures, the Samara oblast. The following discussion covers the role of 'crossovers' from business to politics, including Trutnev's successor Governor Oleg Chirkunov, and deputies elected to the regional and Perm city legislatures from business backgrounds.

Governor of the Perm region from 2004 to 2011, Oleg Chirkunov was a partner with Yuriy Trutnev in the founding of the trading cooperative EKS Limited, later to become the EKS group of companies and today known as EKS management company. The activities of this company include commercial real estate development and the Sem'ya supermarket chain that is the market leader in the Perm region.[37]

Chirkunov, two years younger than Trutnev, shares with him a background in Komsomol ranks in Perm. Unlike Trutnev, Chirkunov has never run for office. When EKS was founded, Chirkunov was serving as a Soviet trade attaché in Switzerland. This position is widely understood, but never directly acknowledged in official biographies of Chirkunov, to indicate his having been an intelligence officer. (Latukhina 2007)

Chirkunov became acting governor in March 2004 on Trutnev's resignation and was appointed by Putin to a five-year term in 2005. According to elite interviews conducted in 2004 by Chirikova, Chirkunov's authority relied at the outset on Trutnev's, and his ascent to the governor's office was seen as a continuation of the "Trutnev project." (Chirikova 2005) Describing his relations with the regional business community as central to his anticipated success as governor, Chirkunov said that he approached the dialogue with business as a manager *(upravlenets)*. Having managed a corporation before, Chirkunov said he viewed his role as managing another "corporation" called the Perm region, the "owners" of which are the region's people. (Chirikova 2005:43–44)

Regional admirers and detractors of Chirkunov interviewed for this book in 2009 and 2010 insisted that his approach to governing is directly transferred from his business experience. Apparently bored by hierarchy and bureaucratic processes, Chirkunov launched more initiatives than could be realized. On the other hand, he had genuine enthusiasm for entrepreneurship and small business development, and brought new people, some of them from a business background, into the regional ministries.

Chirkunov fostered an open and informal network, which his supporters called the new management model *(novaya model' upravleniya)* within the administration, bypassing hierarchy through instant messaging and e-mails within the administration and with legislative committees and non-governmental actors, such as business associations. According to some, this produced confusion and bureaucratic resistance. Chirkunov's blog was one of the first by a regional governor and was reportedly drafted firsthand.[38]

One leading scholar suggests that Chrikunov behaved in office more like an industrialist-philanthropist than a public administrator. This was most manifest in Chirkunov's adoption of the goal of making Perm a capital of culture and the arts and his embrace of the project of Marat Gel'man, a Moscow gallery owner, to open the Museum of Contemporary Art in Perm.[39] Chirkunov's embrace of this cultural agenda became one of his two major political vulnerabilities. The other was the accusation that his business interests in Perm (the Sem'ya supermarkets above all) enjoyed an anti-competitive advantage.

Chirkunov declined to join United Russia and had tense relations with some of the regional leadership of United Russia. (Novikov 2009) This tension led to doubts among many that Chirkunov would be reappointed to a new term as governor in December 2010. Although he was reappointed, speculation continued to mount that Chirkunov would be removed, because he was unlikely to bring in a strong electoral result for United Russia in the state duma elections of December 2011. He faced an ominous attack on national television news program *Vesti* in fall of 2011 for alleged conflicts of interest, tolerance of corruption and neglect of social welfare. He resigned in April 2012.

Election to the Perm regional legislature has been an important point of crossover for new business elites into politics. Entrepreneurs were among the deputies elected to the regional legislature in 1994, 1997, 2001 and 2005. As noted earlier, Yuriy Trutnev began his political career as chairman of the economic committee of the regional legislature elected in 1994, and Andrey Kuzyaev served in the legislatures elected in 1997 and 2001.

In the 2005 elections, fought under a mixed-party list and single-mandate system, the ranks of United Russia had incorporated many entrepreneurs who had previously been unaffiliated or had belonged to SPS. The regional chapter of SPS also won election in the party list contest in 2005, turning in one their best performances in Russia.

The deputies elected in 1994's 'founding election' to the regional legislature were enterprise managers, entrepreneurs and representatives of local administrations. The deputies organized themselves into three principal blocs: the pro-reform Russia's Choice, the Regions bloc headed by Sergey Levitan, and the 'Patriots of Russia' incorporating the CPRF and its allies. Only 11 of the 40 deputies, all elected in single-mandate contests, were affiliated as candidates with any of the three blocs: seven from Russia's Choice, and two each from the other two blocs. Nine of those elected were entrepreneurs. (McFaul and Petrov 1997) As was typical of initial regional legislative elections elsewhere, there was substantial representation in the Perm regional legislature by municipal administrators and enterprise managers.

The elections of 1997 saw the growth in representation in the legislature by the two principal categories of big business in the region. Defense-related machine building was represented by Gennady Kuzmitskiy, then president of Sotrudnichestvo and the regional chapter of the centrist NDR. Entrepreneurs remained well represented. (McFaul and Petrov 1997)

The legislature elected in 2001, still elected by single mandates only, represented nevertheless some greater prominence of explicit political party affiliation and certainly a fuller emergence of programmatic alternatives among candidates. (Panov 2006) The organization of political competition in Perm by explicit party affiliation was, according to a survey of regional elections of the 'third cycle' (i.e. 2001) election in Perm, only 5–20%. (Panov 2006)[40] Blurring party affiliation boundaries, where these existed, deputies formed groups with clear programmatic priorities within the legislature.[41] The largest of these factions, with 18 members was "Promyshlenniki Prkam'e" (Industrialists). A five-member group 'Svobodnaya Rossiya" (Free Russia) significantly overlapped with the SPS party faction and included four members with small or new business backgrounds.[42] Two other entrepreneurs were in the group *"Budeshee Prikam'e"* (Perm Region's Future): Konstantin Okunev and cinema owner Aleksandr Fleginskiy, both vocal critics of the regional administration.

The legislature elected in 2005 was one half from party lists and one half from single mandate. The membership expanded from 40 to 60 members.[43] The United Russia faction (those elected from lists and in single-mandate races) numbered 35. The SPS, LDPR, SR factions had five members each, the CPRF had three, and two deputies were unaffiliated.[44] By comparison with its predecessors, this body had fewer senior managers from large industrial concerns, but much of the membership in the United Russia faction has some association with this part of the economy. Entrepreneurs were represented in the United Russia ranks and among the five members elected from SPS.

The most vocal opposition to Governor Chirkunov in this legislature came from the self-organized nine-member faction '*Solidarnost*,' led by entrepreneur Konstantin Okunev. Okunev owns a chain of regional supermarkets called Dobrynina and complained of unfair competition from Sem'ya, the chain owned by the EKS group. Okunov and three other *Solidarnost'* group members had no party affiliation, two were from CPRF, two from SPS and one was from Just Russia. The group also included several other business figures: Andrey Agishev, formerly of SPS and now one of the regional leaders of United Russia; Vladimir Grebenyuk, an entrepreneur who migrated from SPS to the CPRF; SPS deputy Vladimir Mal'tsev and Pavel Makarov, a CPRF deputy and owner of a construction company.

Within the legislature elected in 2005 was formed the Anti-Corruption Commission *(Komisiya po voprosam protivodeystviya korruptsii v Permskom Krae)*, with ten members drawn from all parties represented in the legislature. The Commission was mandated to review legislation from the jurisdictions of legislative committees and to offer drafting changes to reduce the potential for corrupt exercise of administrative authority. Members were drawn from the leadership of other relevant committees within the legislature. Two of the Commission's members, affiliated with United Russia, were entrepreneurs: Viktor Plyusnin and Yuriy Elokhov. This committee was a principal interlocutor for the anti-corruption work of business associations.[45]

When Trutnev became governor in 2000, Arkadiy Kamenev was elected Perm mayor in 2000. Kamenev faced criminal investigation for his handling of the sale of city property and resigned in 2005 leaving his deputy Igor' Shubin as acting mayor.[46] A former deputy governor to Igumnov and a member of the 'Industrialists' faction in the regional legislature elected in 2001, Shubin worked in the provision of gas for heating and power generation and served in the regional legislature elected in 1997 as a deputy governor to Igumnov and with the regional Gazprom affiliate after Trutnev became governor. To circumscribe the scope of Shubin's authority as mayor, Chirkunov created the post of city manager in Perm and sponsored the appointment to this post of Arkadiy Katz, a member of the city duma with a background in banking and public finance.

The city duma elected March 2011 had 36 members, all elected from single-mandate constituencies. This was the fifth Perm city duma, its predecessors having been elected in 1994, 1996, 2000 and 2006. The deputies elected Igor Sapko to serve as mayor.[47] A 1993 graduate of PGU in history, Sapko was first elected to the city duma in 1996. He is not formally affiliated with any party. Yuriy Utkin and Arkadiy Katz were elected to serve as deputy mayors. Both Utkin and Katz list themselves as 'supporters' of United Russia. (Perm Regional Legislature 2008) A physician with long involvement in health policy reform, Utkin, as deputy prime minister 2007–2009, was a leading advocate for entrepreneurship development and was well regarded by the Perm Chamber's small business committee.

The city duma's website shows 6 members and 2 'supporters' of United Russia, 21 members with no party affiliation, and 1 from the CPRF. The sole CPRF member is an individual entrepreneur born in 1991 who lists on his biographical profile that he joined the CPRF "on his own personal conviction" in 2009. Their professional affiliations as given on their official biographies are shown in Table 7.7:

Table 7.7 Perm City Duma Members by Professional Background

Principal Occupational Background	Number of Members
Entrepreneurs	8
Economists, Banking, Economic Policy	4
Senior Manager or Director, Industry	10
Professional Politician or Administrator	4
Medicine, Education, Sports	4
No Information	6

Source: http://duma.perm.ru/. Accessed July 15, 2011.

Business, society and the press in the Perm region

The Perm region was among those whose populations were surveyed in a comparative values research project. (Lapin and Belyaeva 2009) As discussed in the case study of Smolensk (Table 5.5), respondents were asked to 'rate' on a 5-point scale the importance they attach to 14 different 'values'.[48] Table 7.8 compares the results in Perm with those in Russia as a whole and to the Smolensk region.

The prominence given by respondents Perm region to values that are either universal (human life and selflessness) or related to self-realization (freedom, independence and initiative) marks a strong contrast with responses in Russia as a whole and in the Smolensk region. Attitudes in Perm may give some insight into the foundations for the Perm region's distinctive levels of public engagement, dispersion of political power and steady promotion of new elites on the basis of talent and individual achievement.

A key institutional strength that has supported the emergence of a younger generation of business and government elites in the Perm region is the quality of the Perm region's institutions of higher education. The academic preparation of

Table 7.8 Intensity of Adherence to Selected Values – Smolensk and Perm Compared

Russia	Smolensk Region	Perm Region
family 4.69	family 4.72	human life 4.64
order 4.69	order 4.60	self-sacrifice 4.58
sociability 4.51	sociability 4.52	family 4.53
human life 4.37	material well-being 4.28	order 4.50
tradition 4.34	tradition 4.18	freedom 4.35
freedom 4.25	freedom 4.17	independence 4.32
independence 4.14	independence 4.15	material well-being 4.21
work 4.08	work 4.04	work 4.15
initiative 4.0	human life 3.97	initiative 3.99
self-sacrifice 3.99	morality 3.92	tradition 3.90
material well-being 3.68	initiative 3.74	sociability 3.79
morality 3.66	self-sacrifice 3.64	morality 3.57
power, influence 2.24	power, influence 2.53	self-will 2.51
self-will 2.06	self-will 2.06	power, influence 2.47

Source: Lapin and Belaeva 2009

political leaders and business leaders from the 'incumbent' industrial enterprises is almost always in engineering and technology. By contrast, the economics, and to a lesser extent law, departments of Perm State University feature prominently on the resumes of elites born from 1965 onward. Trutnev's case was a transitional one, because his initial academic work followed in the footsteps of his parents who worked in the oil industry. Kuzyaev is a graduate of the economics department at PGU. The cases of Nikita Belykh (whose mother taught at PGU), Arkadiy Katz and many others could be cited.[49] The receptivity of scholars and officials of the Perm region to public intellectual exchange is manifest in various political and economic forums, the leading one of which is the nationally well-known annual Perm Economic Forum held each spring, featuring both Russian and foreign experts on the various panels.

As discussed earlier, the employers' union *Sotrudnichestvo,* although clearly the direct heir of the Soviet era directors' lobby, has adopted wide-ranging activities aimed at addressing social problems, such as housing and healthcare. Peregudov (2005) counts this association as one of the more sincere and effective efforts at constructing an enlightened and socially responsible role from big corporations in Russia.

Lukoil in its various local subsidiaries is by far the most visible socially and influential politically of all the large companies in Perm. According to Peregudov (2005), Lukoil has been a leader in Perm in corporate social responsibility, including through holding competitions for NGOs to design and manage community development and philanthropic activities in the region. Lukoil's advertising features prominently on the website of Perm's Eko-Permii (Echo of Perm) radio station, which, like its Moscow 'parent,' provides lively political interviews, phone-ins, blogs and debates. Lukoil is also one of the leading corporate sponsors for Perm's justly famous ballet and opera companies.

The regional press

The number of publications produced for the readership of the Perm region is not particularly large relative to the population. The regional media atlas lists 49 titles, not counting 3 that have ceased publication. Their breakdown by category is shown in Table 7.9:

Table 7.9 Regional Press by Category – Perm Region

Type of Publication	Number of Titles
Political and economic newspaper/magazines	16
Lifestyle (fashion, entertainment, family)	21
Business	4

Source: http://www.media-atlas.ru/regionmedia/. Accessed June 30, 2011.

Within the newspaper or news magazine category, there are three national papers published in special editions for the Perm region: *Kommersant, Argumenty i Fakty* and *Komsomolskaya Pravda*. In the city of Perm, there are eight newspapers or news journals. The most influential among business, academic and political elites are the weekly *Novyy Kompan'on* and *NK Magazine* (monthly), financed by Lukoil. The online-only newspaper *Permskiy Obozrevatel'* is particularly outspoken and oppositional relative to the regional political establishment.[50] The newspaper *Zvedza* has the largest circulation of any 'quality' publication (45,000). It has considerable editorial independence and analytical quality and a well-designed website. Publications on business, economics and management such as *Delovoye Prikam'e* (circulation 22,000) and *Business Class* (circulation 3,000) round out the 'quality' press aimed at established and emergent regional elites.

Civic memory: entrepreneurs and the 'usable' past – ideational antecedent conditions

The Perm region in Tsarist and in Soviet times seems to have benefited by being remote but not marginal, a center of industry based on natural resource wealth, ingenuity and culture. Chirkunov's attempt at a synthesis of art and enterprise follows in the tradition of one of Perm's towering cultural figures, ballet impresario Serge Diaghilev, son of a prominent merchant family.

The history of early industrialization and the role played by Perm's industrialist-philanthropists is prominent in the city's landscape. A 'green line' along several city thoroughfares leads to historic landmarks from this era. In its anniversary portfolio in 2006, the Perm Guild of Conscientious Enterprises celebrates the philanthropist businessmen of the late 19th and early 20th centuries. Tellingly, the Guild's publications call the contemporary regional business and commercial community "the second convening *(sozyv).*" Kungur, an old city marginalized by Soviet-era industrialization, has emerged as a sort of Russian Ark of the region's merchant-industrialist heritage. The New York–based Stroganoff Foundation is an instance of international civic partnership, related to the revival of the region's pre-revolutionary history. The city of Perm is a sister city with Louisville, Kentucky in addition to both Oxford, England and Duisberg, Germany. Like the Rostov and Samara regions, the Perm region was a base for anti-Bolshevik forces in the Civil War.

The Perm region was a place of exile and imprisonment during the Tsarist and Soviet periods, and of evacuation during WWII. The experience of welcoming exiles and free thinkers such as Aleksandr Herzen may have contributed to the openness of the political culture exposed in Perm after 1991.

The really striking thing about Perm is how young many of the people in responsible positions are. This is an indication of the intake of new elites on the basis of merit and building on the higher education assets of Perm. The analytical 'eye' turned on the region itself by its scholars, journalists and activists, and the preference of business and political elites for public forums and policy innovations, nourish a civic 'medium' within which business and entrepreneurship, past and present, make a vital contribution.

The discussion and analysis of the activities of business associations in the Perm region reveals a denser, more inclusive and more active associational framework than in the other three case study regions, and one that is exceptional in drawing large and small companies into close coordination.

The region and the model – conclusions

The Perm region presents a puzzle for the model because small firm prevalence is smaller than might be expected given the decisiveness of the region's democratic impulse. Moreover, 'endogenous' democratization in the region over the two decades since 1991 has occurred without the concentrations of small firms that our model suggests are supportive of that outcome. The version of the model shown as Figure 7.1 depicts the specificity of the Perm case in the interactions of the key variables and explains how the case might be reconciled within the terms of the model.

Comparing this diagram with the paradigmatic case in Chapter 3 (Figure 3.1) we can see that the 'impulse' is comparable, but the small firm 'reply' is weak. The case study suggests that this deficiency is compensated by the extent of the 'civic' business community. Unusually, this community in the Perm case is drawn not only from among small company owners, but from the broader business community as well.

Alla Chirikova (2007) discerns in the Perm region a distinctive pattern of business-government relations as regards social and civic initiatives, which she terms 'public liberalism.' Public liberalism defines the attitudes and roles of some of the

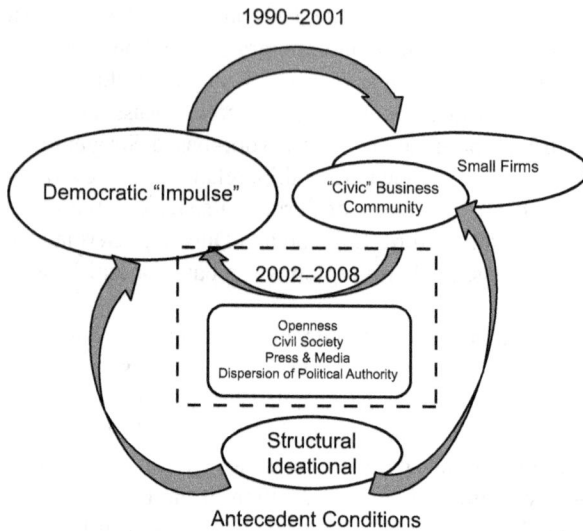

Figure 7.1 The Elaborated Model: Perm Case

region's principal large firms within the public sphere. This civic-ness is manifest in the visibility and diversity of business associations in the region, their frequent use of public forums and regional news media to articulate their proposals, an unusual degree of social legitimacy for entrepreneurs and business and the considerable intake of entrepreneurial elites into regional political office. As in the paradigmatic case, all four of these hypothesized avenues (denoted as 'openness,' 'civil society,' 'press and media' and 'dispersion of political authority') for the influence of the organized business community upon regional democratization are active in Perm. All four are highlighted in the central 'box' of the model, as in the paradigmatic case.

The business association environment in Perm is varied and, insofar as small business advocacy is concerned, characterized by the adoption by associations of a networked approach of frequent and informal consultations among interested groups, including from broader civil society. Business associations are embedded in a broader civil society and civic engagement framework, reflected also in a diffusion of political authority among institutions such as the regional administration and governor, regional legislature, municipal administration and city legislatures. The diffusion of power, availability of critical and independent media and the extent of public civic activism even on the part of big incumbent industrial concerns have worked in parallel with the associations advocating for and organizing participation by entrepreneurs.

The two arrows depicting support from antecedent conditions for democratization and for entrepreneurship are asymmetrical in the Perm case, marking another distinction from the paradigmatic case. Here, the antecedent conditions more strongly support democratization than entrepreneurship. This is because the region's rich natural resource endowment engendered the formation of large-scale industrial and engineering firms during the pre-revolutionary industrialization rather than, as in Samara or Moscow, a business elite whose wealth derived principally from commerce.[51] The level of urbanization in the Perm region stood at 74.6% in 2008, down slightly from where it stood in 1990 (77.2%), but near the national average of 73.1% in 2008 and, on this indicator, second only to Samara among our four case study regions.[52]

The solution to the Perm puzzle for our model is that the civic business community is larger than might be expected when small firms relative to the workforce are less numerous than in comparator regions such as Samara. This exceptional situation, remarked upon by scholars such as Peregudov, Chirikova and Semenenko, has to do with what we have called civic memory. This chapter has attempted to explain how a region deeply entrenched as an industrial and defense asset during the Soviet period is one of Russia's least 'Soviet' in terms of politics, economics and popularly held values. This is due to not only the new elites epitomized by Trutnev and Kuzyaev, but also the character of the 'incumbent' elite, which was much milder and more yielding than might have been expected.

The contribution of new business owners to the dispersion of political authority is greater in the Perm context than in the three others, compensating for the weaker numbers of small firms relative to the labor force and reinforcing the role played by business associations and by the quality of the regional press. Not only was Trutnev an entrepreneur, but he was also a pioneer of business associations in Perm as head of the local chapter of the Cooperatives Association. The multiplicity, visibility and inclusiveness of business associations in Perm magnify the influence of the small business community relative to its size.

Notes

1 Colton (2008:11–31) recounts Boris Yeltsin's family antecedents and early life in Berezniki.
2 *Forbes* May 2010 list of Russia's 100 Richest puts Rybolovlev's net worth at $8.6 billion.
3 Trutnev's biography is traced in Podvintsev (2005).
4 Personal interview, Petr Panov, Perm State University, June 15, 2010.
5 Trutnev is a member of UR's governing board, which includes other former or sitting governors.
6 Personal interview, Alla Chirikova, May 22, 2010.
7 *Forbes* May 2010 List of Russia's Richest Businessmen places Kuzyaev in 82nd place.
8 Personal interview, Olga Deryagina, Editor, *Novyy Kompan'on*. June 18, 2010.
9 The figures given are 5,000 and 4,400 'larger' small firms in Samara and Perm regions respectively in 2009, with the totals for small and micro firms in Samara at 46,420 and in Perm 18,174.
10 The comparison of the four case study regions as to numbers of micro-, small- and medium-sized enterprises in 2008 is in Table 3.9.
11 Personal interview, Elena Mironova, Chamber Vice President, June 16, 2010.
12 Personal interview, Valery Baranov, individual entrepreneur and Chamber member, October 21, 2009.
13 Personal interview, Elena Mironova, Chamber Vice President, June 16, 2010.
14 http://www.sotrudn.ur/ruk.htm accessed July 13, 2011 gives the names and affiliations of the leadership and governing board.

15 Personal interview, Igor Savrasov, Sotrudinichestvo Vice President, June 16, 2010.

16 http://lobbying.ru/persons.php?id=1744 accessed July 20, 2011 is a biographical sketch of Andreyev.

17 The company's website is http://www.ppk.perm.ru. Accessed June 4, 2011.

18 Personal interview, Oleg Podvintsev, June 14, 2010, Personal interview, Irina Semenenko, May 21, 2010.

19 This association, representing smaller companies in the consumer goods and services sector, is discussed below.

20 Members' list at http://www.sotrudn.ru/chl.htm accessed July 1, 2011. Sotrudnichestvo lists all its members on its website, something the Perm Chamber does not do.

21 http://rmc.edu.ru/. Accessed July 15, 2011.

22 http://vprojectore.ru/. Accessed June 10, 2011.

23 Personal interview, Andrey Khusid and three other young entrepreneur-members of Delovaya Rossiya, October 21, 2009.

24 http://startuppoint.ru. Accessed July 3, 2011.

25 Personal interview, Marat Bimatov, Minister of Trade and Entrepreneurship, Perm Kray, October 23, 2009.

26 Personal interview, Yevgeny Fridman, OPORA President, July 16, 2010.

27 The OPORA 'ustav' (by-laws) sets out the procedures for creating a local affiliate. The national organization reviews and approves the initiators' plan and goals. This process was confirmed for the Perm case in a personal interview with Olga Plotnikova, OPORA director for regional development, May 27, 2010, Moscow.

28 http://perm.opora.ru/organization/opora/council/#active_item=9820 accessed November 10, 2011 shows capsule biographies and photos of Fridman and other principal members.

29 This section draws on a personal interview at the Guild's offices with Executive Director Valeriy Gulyaev, June 16, 2010.

30 Personal interview, Galina Teklyuk, June 17, 2010 in Kungur.

31 Kungur's main tourist attraction, the remarkable Ice Cave, is also in its way a monument to the city's merchant past. The champion of opening the cave to visitors was the explorer son of a prominent local merchant, Aleksander Timofeeovich Khlebnikov, who lived for several years in Kentucky, where he got the idea about making a cave into a tourist attraction.

32 Personal interview, Elena Orlova, October 22, 2009 and June 18, 2010.

33 This program's funding is comparable to the analogous program in Samara oblast, which, like Perm, is a net contributor to the federal budget with similar GRP. The program's authors and initiators are the Ministry of Entrepreneurship and Trade, and the program's funding adopted and approved by the regional legislature on the governor's recommendation.

34 http://g2b.perm.ru/. Accessed December 1, 2011. http://g2b.perm.ru/article/show/7630 gives the text of the Regional SME program. At the site, another page http://g2b.perm. ru/section/show/6443#352 links to the texts of all federal and regional laws and decrees related to protections and support for SMEs.

35 Several interlocutors in Perm mentioned that this council has been convened very infrequently.

36 Personal interview, Dmitry Sasonov, June 18,2010. Sasonov was about to leave the ministry to write a doctoral dissertation comparing international policy models of small business and entrepreneurship promotion.

37 http://www.eks-development.ru/main/ and http://www.semya.perm.ru/. Accessed July 10, 2011. Neither website mentions the role of Trutnev or Chirkunov as past or present owners, but the EKS site gives a historical sketch of the company reaching back to 1990.

38 http://chirkunov.livejournal.com/. Accessed July 7, 2011. In October 2011, Chirkunov shifted most of his web commentary to Facebook and Twitter.

39 http://travel.nytimes.com/2011/07/24/travel/perm-russias-emerging-cultural-hotspot. html?pagewanted=all is a recent account of this cultural program, also covered frequently and critically in the Perm regional media.

40 Panov's study of the role of parties in organizing political competition in regional legislative elections in the 'third cycle' puts Perm, along with Samara, Smolensk and Rostov regions among the 37 regions where party affiliated deputies represented 5–20% of those elected. (Panov 2006:14)

41 http://old.parlament.perm.ru/deputats/. Accessed July 3, 2011.

42 They were D. Skrivanov, Viktor Plyusnin, Aleksey Chernov (founded of an investment company and close associate of Nikita Belykh) and Yuriy Elokhov, a MGIMO graduate in international business.

43 The full results can be downloaded at the Perm regional link of the Central Electoral Commission website cikrf.ru.

44 http://www.parliament.perm.ru. Accessed June 15, 2011. This website and that of the parliament elected in 2001 were not accessible after the new elections of December 2011.

45 http://www.parliament.perm.ru/meeting/?ID=149&ID2=151 gives the committee's composition.

46 Capsule biographies and links to press articles on the careers of Kamenev and Shubin at http://www.alpha.perm.ru/inform/peoples/kamenev.shtml and http://www.alpha. perm.ru/inform/peoples/shubin.shtml. Accessed June 10, 2011.

47 http://duma.perm.ru/struct/heads/2/ accessed December 1, 2011 is Sapko's curriculum vitae.

48 The six regions other than Smolensk and Perm where the survey was conducted are Kurskaya, Vologodskaya, Karelia, Ul'yanovskaya, Chuvashkaya and Tyumenskaya.

49 Many Moscow-based scholars told me that Perm was not only intrinsically interesting, but also was rewarding to study because the PGU and other academic analytical work on the region was of such a high quality.

50 http://www.permoboz.ru/ and http://www.nk.perm.ru/ are these two publications' websites.

51 The 'tilt' or asymmetry in the antecedent conditions' influence in Perm is the opposite of the case of Rostov, where a trading past, persistent even in shadowy form throughout the Soviet period, favors the resumption of entrepreneurship, but where patterns of social traditionalism do not provide any strong support to democratization.

52 As was shown in Chapter 2, the variable 'urbanization' is highly correlated with both the regional democracy scores and small firm prevalence.

References

Center for International Private Enterprise (CIPE). (2003–2009) *Semi-Annual Reports on Russian SME Advocacy Program,* USAID Moscow.

Chamber of Commerce and Industry, Perm Region. (2010a) *List of Members "Women-Executives" Club of the Perm Chamber of Commerce.* Perm.

Chamber of Commerce and Industry, Perm Region. (2010b) *List of Members of the Committee of the Perm Chamber for Development of Entrepreneurship and Work with Small and Medium Firms.* Perm.

Chamber of Commerce and Industry, Perm Region. (2011a) *Members of the Governing Board and Their Affiliations.* http://www.permtpp.ru/about_chamber/board/. Accessed October 10, 2010.

Chamber of Commerce and Industry, Perm Region. (2011b) *History of the Perm Chamber.* http://www.permtpp.ru/about_chamber/history/. Accessed June 7, 2011.

Chirikova, Alla E. (2005) Putinskie reformy i ikh posledstviya dlya regional'noi vlasti v Rossii. *Panorama Issledonvanii politiki Prikam'ya* (3):22–65.

Chirikova, Alla E. (2007) *Vzaimodeystvie vlasti i biznesa v realizatsii sotsialnoy politki: regional'naya proektsia.* Moscow: Independent Institute of Social Policy.

Colton, Timothy. (2008) *Yeltsin: A Life.* New York: Basic Books.

Filatov, Nikolay M. (2002) Fenomen gruppy "Grazhdanskoe Deystvie" na vyborakh 1990 goda kak primer praktichestkoi politiki. *Panorama* (1):42–47.

Gel'man, Vladimir, Sergey Ryzhenkov, Elena, Belokurova and Nadezhda Borisova. (2008) *Reforma Mestnoy Vlasti v Gorodakh Rossii, 1991–2006.* St. Petersburg, Russia: European University in St. Petersburg.

Goskomstat Rossii. (2001) *Regiony Rossii.* Moscow: State Committee of the Russian Federation for Statistics.

Independent Institute for Social Policy (IISP). (2008) *Regional "Portrait" – Perm Oblast and Komi-Permyatskii avtonomnyi okrug* http://atlas.socpol.ru/portraits/perm.shtml. Accessed April 13, 2011.

Lapin, Nikolay and L.A. Belyaeva. (eds.) (2009) *Regiony v Rossii: Sotsiokulturnye Portrety Regionov v Obshcherossiskoy Kontekste.* Moscow: Institute of Sociology, Russian Academy of Sciences (IS-RAN).

Latukhina, Kira. (2007) "Ya v bisnese k proverkam privyk", interview with Perm governor Oleg Chirkunov. *Vedomosti,* September 12, 2007. Perm.

Lieven, Dominic. (2000) *Empire: The Russian Empire and Its Rivals.* New Haven, CT and London: Yale Nota Bene.

McFaul, Michael and Nikolai Petrov (eds.) (1997) *Politicheskiy Almanakh Rossii: Sotsialno-Politicheskie Portrety Regionov.* Moscow: Carnegie Moscow Center.

Mushkalov, Sergey. (2008) *Kungurskii Rotshil'd: Materialy k biografii A.S. Gubkina 1816–1883.* Perm: published in 200 copies for local educational institutions.

Novikov, Evgenii. (2009) Partiinyi bilet *Kompan'on Magazine,* October. Perm.

OPORA Rossii. (2008) *Razvitie Malogo i Srednogo Predprinimatel'stva v Regionakh Rossii "Index OPORY".* Moscow.

Panov, Petr V. (2006) Rossiiskie politicheskie partii i regional'nye protsessy: problema effektivnogo predstavitel'stva. *Panorama Issledonvanii politiki Prikam'ya* 5:4–41.

Peregudov, Sergey P. (2005) Korporativny biznes Permii kak sotsial'nyi i politicheskii aktor (na primere dochernikh predpriyatii kompanii "Lukoil"). *Panorama Issledonvanii politiki Prikam'ya* (3):6–21.

Perm City Administration. (2009) Vedomstvennaya tselevaya programma "Razvitie malogo i srednogo predprinimatel'stva v gorode Permi na 2009–2011 gody. *Pravovye Akty No. 63.* Perm.

Perm City Administration Department of Industrial Policy Investment and Entrepreneurship. (2007) *O vzaimodeistvii administratsii goroda Permi s promyshlennym sektorom.* Perm.

Perm Guild of Conscientious Enterprises. (2006) *Chest' Prevyshe Pribili.* Perm: Mamontov Publishing House.

Perm Guild of Conscientious Enterprises. (2010) Zhivaya Istoriya: Interview with former governor Gennady Igumnov. *Znak Doveriya (journal of the Perm Guild),* 2.

Perm Regional Association of Employers "Sotrudnichestvo". (2006) *Normativnye dokumenty regional'nogo ob'edineniya rabotodatelei Permskoi oblasti "Sotrudnichestvo".* Perm.

Perm Regional Coalition of Business Associations. (2008) *Anti-Corruption Regional Business Agenda.* Perm: Chamber of Commerce and Industry, Perm Region.

Perm Regional Legislature. (2008) *Kraevaya tselevaya programma "Razvitie malogo i srednogo predprinimatel'stva v Permskoi krae na 2008–2011 gody."* Regional law N 352-PK 2008 Perm.

Perm Regional Legislature. (2011a) *Legislative Committees Statement of Jurisdiction and Membership* http://www.parliament.perm.ru/meeting/?ID=149&ID2=408. Accessed February 10, 2012.

Perm Regional Legislature. (2011b) *Party Factions Principles and Membership (Fraktsii)* http://www.parliament.perm.ru/meeting/?ID. Accessed June 25, 2011.

Perm Regional Ministry for Entrepreneurship, Development and Trade. (2010) *Razvitie malogo biznesa v permskom krae*. Perm Regional Administration: Perm.

Petrov, Nikolai. (2002) Permskaya Oblast' okazalas' demokratichnee Moskvy i Sankt-Peterburga. *Panorama Issledonvanii politiki Prikam'ya* (1):108–125.

Petrov, Nikolai and Alexei Titkov. (2006) *Demokratichnost' Rossiskikh Regionov*. http://atlas.socpol.ru/indexes/index_democr.shtml. Accessed Novermber 10, 2010.

Petrov, Nikolai and Alexei Titkov. (2013) *Reyting Demokratichnosti Regionov Moskovskogo Tsenta Karnegi: 10 Let v Stroyu*. Moscow: Carnegie Moscow Center. http://carnegie.ru/publications/?fa=55853. Accessed December 1, 2014.

Podvintsev, Oleg P. (2005) Yurii Petrovich Trutnev: shtrikhi k politicheskomu portretu. *Panorama Issledonvanii politiki Prikam'ya* (3):66–82.

Rosstat (Federal'naya Sluzhba Gosudarstvennoy Statistiki). (2002, 2004, 2008, 2010a). *Regiony Rossii: Osnovnye Sotsial'no-Ekonomicheskie Pokazateli Gorodov*.

Rosstat (Federal'naya Sluzhba Gosudarstvennoy Statistiki). (2009) *Maloe i Srednee Predprimatel'stvo v Rossii*.

Rosstat (Federal'naya Sluzhba Gosudarstvennoy Statistiki). (2010) *Goroda Rossii.*

Rosstat, Perm Regional Office (Territorial'nyi Organ federal'noi sluzhby gosudarstvennoi statistiki po permskomu krayu). (2010) *Deyatel'nost' malykh predpriyatii (vklyuchaya mikropredpriyatiya) Permskogo kraya v 2009 g.* Perm.

Russia: All Regions Trade and Investment Guide. (2008) Perm Region (Kray). London, UK: CTEC Publishing and Effective Technology Marketing.

Vokhrintsev, Dmitrii. (ed) (2008) *Ekonomika Prikam'ya*. Perm: Fond Korporativnykh Teknologii "Politkom" http://www.vsmpo.ru/. Accessed December 12, 2011.

World Bank. (2009) Russian Federation Regional Development and Growth Agglomerations: The Longer Term Challenges of Economic Transition in the Russian Federation. *Country Economic Memorandum*. Washington, DC: World Bank.

World Bank and International Finance Corporation. (2010). *Doing Business 2010: Comparing Regulation in 183 Economies: Russian Federation*. Washington, DC.

Yutov, Georgii. (2008) Pomogat' Sil'nym (interview with Elena Gilyazova) *Permskii Bisnes-Zhurnal*, March 4.

8   Concluding arguments

Trade is the natural enemy of all violent passions. Trade loves moderation, delights in compromise and is most careful to avoid anger. . .Trade makes men independent of one another and gives them a high idea of their personal importance; it leads them to want to manage their own affairs and teaches them to succeed therein. Hence, it makes them inclined to liberty but disinclined to revolution.

Alexis de Tocqueville
Democracy in America[1]

Processes linking small firm prevalence and democratization

The four case studies strongly suggest that the extent of the *civic business community,* within which incorporated small firms typically make a disproportionate contribution, is the means through which 'small firm prevalence' positively influenced democratization in some Russian regions by the mid-2000s. Variations in small firm prevalence serve as a quantitative 'marker' that tends *in most cases* to approximate the extent of the emergence of entrepreneurs as actors in the public or civic sphere. From the evidence of the quantitative analysis and case studies of this project, a set of processes and mechanisms can be inferred linking small firm prevalence to democratization, subject to a number of conditions and through the intermediation of the civic business community.

The first pertinent question that can now be answered is "What explains the variation across regions of the extent of the civic business community?" The first part of the explanation is variation in small firm prevalence. A second contribution to variation in the civic business community comes from differences in ideational antecedent conditions, a variable we have called '*civic memory.*'

A second question answered by our analysis is "What explains the variation across Russia's regions in small firm prevalence?" The regression evidence strongly supports the conclusion that small firm prevalence by region is largely a consequence of the extent of democratization by region in the founding decade of the Russian Federation: 1991–2001. The regressions also reveal that the structural variable, urbanization, is significant in explaining differing outcomes in small firm prevalence. The case study evidence also points to the role of antecedent structural conditions – such as economic geography, natural resource endowments, urbanization, industrialization – on the extent of small business development.

The two findings can be summarized as follows:

Claim 1

Variation in *civic business community* depends on:

Small firm prevalence (quantitative variable)

AND

Ideational antecedent conditions – '*civic memory*' (qualitative 'shading' variable)

Claim 2

Variation in *small firm prevalence* depends on

Democratic 'Impulse' (composite 'base' democracy score 1991–2000)

AND

Antecedent structural conditions

These two arguments together form a causal chain that explains how small firm prevalence and democratization are related. It is important to realize that the process begins with democratization as an exogenous 'shock' and ends in the 'endogenizing' of democratization in an ongoing process. It is also critical to understand that this model analyzes only one of many processes affecting the course of democratization; the causal claim being advanced here holds only on a *ceteris paribus* basis.

The causal chain produced can be schematized as follows:

Democratic 'Impulse'
and ⇒ Small Firm Prevalence
Antecedent Structural
          and ⇒   Civic Business ⇒ Democratization
          Civic Memory

The final link in this chain, that linking civic business to democratization, was found in Chapter 2 to relate small firm prevalence with four dimensions of democratization derived from the regional democracy index.[2] Guided by the regression findings, the four case studies traced the role of small business owners in affecting civil society development, openness to citizen participation in policy deliberations, media diversity, and independence and the dispersion of political authority among governors, mayors, and regional and municipal legislatures.

The case studies take business associations as an institutional manifestation of the civic business community. Such associations are principal actors through which small firm prevalence affects the civil society and openness/participation outcomes. Through their public information efforts and sponsorship of public forums and debates, business associations also contribute to the diversity of press and media reporting regionally.

The influence of small and new business owners upon the extent of media independence and diversity works principally, however, through the effects of a competitive business milieu on newspaper and magazine ownership and advertising revenue. In addition to owning and advertising in publications, small and new firm owners, and business in general, are prominent consumers of publications aimed at a business readership nationally and locally. The content of such publications contributes, as do business associations, to the shaping of a distinctive attitudinal and normative identity for entrepreneurs as a group, an identity claiming attributes such as initiative, creativity, determination, self-reliance and honesty with regard to employees, customers, partners and creditors. It can be said that there exists a synergy between the share of small and new firms in the business community and the diversity, breadth and financial health of the regional press.

The process through which small firm prevalence affects the dispersion of political authority in the regions works through the uptake of new elites – especially in regional and municipal legislative office – from among the ranks of entrepreneurs. In some cases, business association leadership was a stepping-stone in the political career of regional elites. Examples from the four case studies include Viktor Tarkhov in Samara and Yuriy Trutnev and Marat Bimatov in Perm. Also, not uncommonly, former office holders at the regional or municipal level lead business associations, as in the case of Rostov Chamber President Nikolay Prizyazhnyuk, Rostov OPORA leader Yuriy Roshkovan and Togliatti Chamber President Vladimir Zhukov.

Business associations as civic actors

The case study evidence shows that a principal means of civic engagement by business is business associations. Business associations are an important, if imperfect, institutional embodiment of the civic business community, which we have argued is the central mediating variable between small firm prevalence and democratization.

The interviews with business association leaders and members in the four case study regions suggest that business associations – *open to and representing small firm owners and individual entrepreneurs* – play a role in building a cohesive community of trust among members, which helps to engender a sense of shared identity for entrepreneurs both inside and outside of the associations' membership. The practice within associations of formulating policy, articulating and defending goals in negotiations with regional and city authorities, giving input to the drafting of legislation and the public advocacy of business through the media are all powerful contributors to the 'civic' outcome embodied in the civil society, openness/participation, media independence/diversity and political power dispersion sub-indicators in the regional democracy index.

Business associations are the institutional form in which business enters as a collectivity into the civic sphere. Business associations are the most direct and obvious way that small firm owners as a group would positively contribute to civil society development. However, this relationship is also likely to work through many other indirect channels. The case studies show that civic organizations involved in community development and charities attract business people as members. The spread of Rotary Clubs in many Russian provincial cities has been discussed in the case studies. The Mercury Club active in Togliatti, affiliated with the Russian Chamber, is a similar organization with a similar program. Charitable foundations based on corporate contributions and with prominent business figures on governing boards are noteworthy in Perm (Stroganoff Foundation) and in Togliatti (Fond Togliatti). Both foundations are modeled upon, and have substantial contacts with, analogous institutions in Europe or the United States.

Although tracing the penetration of small firm owners in civil society groups other than business associations is beyond the scope of this book, it seems likely that greater small firm prevalence would on balance create better conditions for the financing of broader civil society organizations, even though contributions and support for such organizations come from across all aspects of society.

Business associations individually and as part of a landscape of overlapping business associations with similar goals and constituencies institutionalize the civic business community, but they do so with varying degrees of success. Their success in embodying the civic business community depends upon their performance in the 'internal' (identity shaping, normative cohesion) and 'external' (interest representing, rule demanding) functions.

The factor analysis in Chapter 3 suggested that differences among regions in small firm prevalence (and by implication the civic business community and business associations) have a greater impact on the reinforcement of 'civic-ness' at a societal level than upon the quality of governance. Because, as we have seen, the work of business associations tends to focus on reducing corruption and improving governance, this outcome was somewhat surprising and counterintuitive. Perhaps the circle can be squared by suggesting that, in coalescing behind the identification of, and advocacy for, policy changes affecting the conduct of business, some business associations are at the same time building a normative identity for members and potential members that contributes to 'civic-ness.'

Table 8.1 is an attempt to summarize the effectiveness of the business associations encountered in the case studies. The scale adopted evaluates the associations across two sets of indicators belonging to the 'internal' and the 'external' dimensions of the functions of associations. The associations are evaluated on a scale from 1–3 on each characteristic, with 1 denoting weakness, 2 an intermediate outcome, and 3 a strong outcome. The evaluations are derived from the interviews and documents related to each association and are intended as a summary representation of the findings reported in the discussion of each association in the case studies. The assessment is shown in Table 8.1.

Table 8.1 Assessments of Business Associations

Region/Association	Internal Dimension					External Dimension		
	Representative-ness/ Inclusiveness	"Initiative-ness"	Leadership/ Governance	"Expertness"	Autonomy/ Independence	Effective Lobbying	Public Lobbying	Information Dissemination
Samara Region								
Regional Chamber	2	1	2	3	1	2	2	1
Togliatti Chamber	3	3	3	3	3	3	3	3
OPORA	2	3	1	2	2	2	3	2
Averages	2.3	2.3	2	2.67	1.67	2.3	2.67	3
Smolensk Region								
Regional Chamber	3	3	3	3	2	2	3	3
OPORA	2	2	2	2	3	1	2	3
Averages	2.5	2.5	2.5	2.5	2.5	1.5	2.5	3
Rostov Region								
Regional Chamber	3	3	3	3	2	2	1	2
OPORA	2	3	3	2	3	3	1	3
Taganrog Chamber	3	2	3	3	3	2	N/A	3
Club 2015	3	3	3	3	3	3	N/A	3
Averages	2.75	2.75	3	2.75	2.75	2.5	1	2.75
Perm Region								
Regional Chamber	3	3	3	3	3	3	3	3
Delovaya Rossiya	3	3	3	3	3	2	3	3
"Guild"	3	3	3	3	3	2	3	3
OPORA	2	3	2	2	3	2	3	3
Averages	2.75	3	2.75	2.75	3	2.25	3	3

The indices in this evaluative framework can be defined as follows. *Representativeness/Inclusiveness* means the extent to which the association represents small firm owners and 'new' business generally. *"Initiative-ness"* denotes the extent of association activity generated by its own initiative. *Leadership* denotes the skill of the association's leadership in achieving a recognized public profile, and *governance* denotes both internal organizational structures such as active thematic committees of members and the process of leadership selection. *"Expertness"* denotes the degree of special qualification (e.g. legal) expertise available in the association. *Autonomy/Independence* denotes the degree of independence from the governing regional or municipal administration. The three 'external' indices in the framework are the *effective lobbying,* which means what tangible achievements in legislation or programs the association has produced, *public lobbying,* which denotes the extent to which lobbying – whether successful or not – takes place in an open and inclusive setting. Finally, *information dissemination* denotes the availability to the public of information related to the association's purposes and functions.

The picture that emerges is of the relative importance of 'internal' (identity or group cohesion) functions in Smolensk and Rostov and a relatively greater emphasis on external functions in Perm and Samara. The weakness in the external functions in Smolensk and Rostov has two different explanations. In Smolensk, the regional administration has had weak leadership and an acute shortage of qualified staff, making it not very effective in support for small business. By contrast, in the Rostov oblast, an energetic small business development policy, adopted on the regional administration's own initiative by the mid-1990s, has tended to circumscribe the role of open and public advocacy on behalf of small firms.

The emergence of a cadre of effective and active regional and municipal Chambers in the case studies we explored seems to owe much to the national Chamber leadership of Yevgeny Primakov. For a time, he was able to find an exquisite balance between being seen as loyal by the federal political leadership and fostering genuine if incremental development of more secure property rights and legal protections by business through all sorts of instruments from public advocacy to strong contributions to the drafting of legislation affecting the conditions for entrepreneurs. Under Primakov's leadership, the TPPRF brought leaders from the Chambers of Togliatti, Smolensk, Rostov, Taganrog and Perm into the governing presidium from whence they could shape the further development of the national Chamber.

Structured case comparison

This book has argued that the civic business community has contributed to reinforcing democratization, or, at a minimum, to inhibiting its deterioration in conditions where de-democratization processes and interactions were also underway. This argument builds on the regression evidence in Chapter 2 and is traced in the case studies. The structural comparison of the case study regions found in Table 8.2 attempts a decomposition of the concept of *civic business community*

218   *Conclusion*

Table 8.2 Summary Case Comparison

Summary Case Comparison				
	Samara	*Smolensk*	*Rostov*	*Perm*
Association internal	2.1	2.5	2.8	2.85
Association external	2.7	2.3	2.1	2.75
Multiplicity/diversity associations	3	2	1	3
Elite uptake from new business	3	1	2	3
Media/new firm synergy	3	2	1	3
Small/new firms share in business community	2	3	2	1
Entrepreneurs' civic and philanthropic activism	2*	2	3	3
Entrepreneurship antecedent structural	3	1	2	2
Entrepreneurship ideational antecedent	3	2	3	3
SUM (of 27 possible)	23.8	17.8	18.9	23.6

*More developed in Togliatti than in Samara

across various dimensions and evaluates each region with respect to each component. The scale, as in the evaluation of business associations denotes a strong outcome as 3, a moderate outcome as 2 and a weak outcome as 1. The first two lines of the following table incorporate the average scores for all associations in a given region on the 'internal' and 'external' indices in Table 8.1.

The elements in this framework are related to the four sub-indicators of the regional democracy index we found to be influenced by small firm prevalence. Together they are the composite form of the underlying variable civic business community intermediating between 'small firm prevalence' and democratization. The links with the sub-indicators are shown in Table 8.3:

Let us now discuss the four regional cases by reference to the differences illustrated in Table 8.3 and to the causal chain developed in the first section of this chapter.

Table 8.3 Correspondence of the Processes Shaping the Civic Business Community with Index Sub-indicators

Correspondence of the Processes Shaping the Civic Business Community with Index Sub-indicators	
Civil society development	Association internal Multiplicity/diversity associations Entrepreneurs civic and philanthropic activism Entrepreneurship – ideational antecedent
Openness/transparency of rule making	Association external Small/new firms share in business community Entrepreneurship – Antecedent structural
Dispersion of political authority	Elite uptake from new business
Diversity, independence of media	Media/new firm synergy

In the **Samara region**, the democratic 'impulse' engendered a strong 'reply' in the form of private entrepreneurship. Small and new business, although well established relative to the workforce, is nevertheless not as large a share of the business community as a whole as, for example, in the case of Smolensk. This is because of the success of nationally prominent large private companies in the region and is due in large part to its natural resource base.

The Samara region saw the rise of a cadre of reformist elites, among them entrepreneurs, some of whom remained in prominent positions nearly two decades later. The pre-eminent role of the two cities of Samara and Togliatti in terms of their population relative to that of the region and their disproportionate share of the region's economic activity seem to have enhanced the role played by business associations, the strongest of which – OPORA of Samara and the Chamber of Togliatti – are engaged at least as actively with municipal administrations as with the regional government. The relative dispersion of political authority in the region has created opportunities for business lobbying and for elite promotion. The Samara region also compares well with the other three cases across the variables of press independence and diversity. Structural conditions such as urbanization and educational levels supported the emergence of small companies.

Ideational antecedent conditions supported the civic-ness of the business community in the Samara region. The conscious evocation of the parliamentary and constitutional experience of 1905–1917 and the explicit historical claim of the Samara Chamber to represent a revival of the Chamber founded in during the *Komuch* interlude of 1918 are examples of the relevance of an ideational or normative precedent accessible to contemporary business leaders. There is evidence that the policy recommendations of business associations have shaped the policies aimed at supporting and developing entrepreneurship at the regional level and in the municipalities of Samara and Togliatti. The interactions among the business associations and the regional and municipal governments in the region are marked by considerable openness, informality and reciprocal confidence.

Applying the two principal claims in the causal chain in the first section of this chapter to the Samara case, we can see that the civic business community was supported by greater than average 'small firm prevalence' and by favorable ideational antecedent conditions. Moreover, small firm prevalence in the Samara region emerged through the strength of the democratic impulse *and* from supportive structural conditions.

In the **Smolensk case**, the democratic impulse was weak and fleeting. Freely contested gubernatorial elections in 1993, 1998 and 2002 brought a gradual restoration of an entrenched conservative *ancien regime*. With few exceptions, new business people have not penetrated regional and municipal political elite ranks.

As we have seen, by 2008 the Smolensk region had roughly the same small firm prevalence as the Perm region, although its scores on the democracy index are more comparable to those of Rostov. The interaction of the organized business community with the regional and municipal administrations in Smolensk proved to be greater than might be anticipated, however. As the leading public advocate of improved business conditions for small companies, the Smolensk Chamber embraces an approach that engages small self-organized associations, emphasizes public advocacy for improved governance, and is welcoming to potential members. The Chamber projects a civic normative identity for entrepreneurs through the regional press, its own publications and in interaction with educational institutions.

In an unexpected sense, contemporary structural conditions for small business development in Smolensk are supportive, because the region's larger enterprises and much of its agriculture have not fared well in the competitive conditions of the post-Soviet period. This has helped to make entrepreneurs *malgré soi* out of former soldiers and primary school teachers. The growing significance of small firms in employment in the region has enhanced the opportunities for associations such as the Chamber and OPORA to offer policy input to improve business conditions.

By reference to the two principal claims in the beginning of this chapter we can see that the civic business community in Smolensk has been constrained by relatively weak small firm prevalence and by the comparatively weak support from ideational antecedent conditions. Small firm prevalence itself was weak through much of the period under study because of the weak initial democratic impulse and because the region's antecedent structural conditions were not particularly supportive of small firm development.

The vigorous development of small business in Smolensk from 2006 is a response by regional leaders to the renewed focus on regional SME development from Moscow culminating in the 2007 SME promotion law. Antufyev's tenure as governor produced a measure of predictability and continuity and the conviction that small business development could help to stem out-migration from the region and engender economic recovery.

Large numbers of small companies relative to the workforce in the **Rostov region** were generated and persisted in the absence of a decisive or durable democratic impulse. Business associations in the region function better in the internal dimension than in the external one. The association landscape is not as diverse as might be expected in an economically dynamic region, and an ethos of expertise and professionalism, rather than one of civic participation, seems to dominate the exchange between business and government. The weak effect of the emergent business community on endogenous democratization is related to the character of business-state coordination defined by the regional authorities as discreet and circumscribed in scope.

The Rostov case was a puzzle for the model because small firm prevalence did not have a significant effect on democratization. The evidence suggests that the civic business community is small relative to the business community as a whole. Nevertheless, the civic business community contributes in the Rostov case as in the others to endogenous democratization through the internal functions of business associations, drawing on strong ideational antecedents nourishing entrepreneurship. The civic business community has only very limited ability to affect openness, because the authorities have limited receptiveness to public participation. It has also failed to support the dispersion of political authority, because of the deliberate centralizing of power under long-serving Governor Vladimir Chub.

The shortcomings in the region's media environment with respect to independence and to diversity are surprising, given the strength in numbers and economic contribution of small and new business. One possible explanation is the pervasive recourse by business people at all levels to informal, improvised and discreet clientelistic networks rather than to a rules-based, open or 'categorical' resolution accessible to companies collectively.

The city of Rostov weighs less heavily in the economy and culture of its region than do the cities of Perm and Samara/Togliatti with respect to theirs. This is manifest in the lower level of urbanization of the Rostov oblast relative to the three other comparator regions. In structural terms, geography, education and ethnic diversity (the Greek and Armenian influences) pull the population centers of Rostov and Taganrog toward an outward-looking, commercial ethos. (Russia's most European writer, Chekhov, is, after all, the son of a Taganrog grocer.) Rostov and Taganrog do not, however, by themselves define the region's ideational antecedents; a significant countercurrent is agrarian, traditional and patriarchal. Strong entrepreneurial traditions in a conservative and patriarchal cultural setting are fertile ground for the persistence of patronage and clientelism as the principal mode of coordination for the region's large companies and circumscribe the influence of the region's civic business community, constituted mainly of new and small firms.

By reference to the two principal claims and causal chain in the first section of this chapter, we see that the civic business community is supported in the Rostov case by substantial 'small firm prevalence,' but diminished by ideational antecedent conditions favoring informality, discretion and personal networks to categorical, inclusive and publicly visible approaches to business-government coordination. Small firm prevalence in Rostov did not benefit from a strong initial democratic impulse, but this was compensated by relatively strong structural conditions for small business, at least insofar as the cities of Rostov and Taganrog are concerned.

The **Perm case** shows early receptivity and openness of the regional and municipal governments to public participation and the most thoroughgoing penetration of new elites from among entrepreneurs in any of the four cases. Intraelite competition, nourished by a sophisticated regional media environment, has been greater and has survived longer in electoral contests in the Perm region. The participation of the young in political, associational, business and scholarly circles in the Perm region marked a significant contrast with the other three cases in this study.

Table 8.2 shows clearly that the two regions which had high democracy index scores – Samara and Perm – are similar across most dimensions the case studies examined, and their composite score on this framework is very similar, just as their scores on the regional democracy index are. Nevertheless, the Perm region was a deviant case from the standpoint of our model in exactly the obverse sense that Rostov region was. Where in Rostov small firms were more prevalent than the model would predict in view of the brief initial democratic impulse, in Perm the case was reversed: a decisive and durable democratization process through the

1990s did not engender the reply in numbers relative to the workforce of small firms that might be anticipated.

The case study of Perm suggests that the smaller incidence of small firms in the Perm region is mainly an artifact of the structural character of the economy. The region's resource-based and engineering industries were more adaptable to the transition to market conditions than was the norm for Russia. Those entrepreneurs that did emerge found access into the transformed political elite and into the leadership of some large industrial concerns as well. The role played by associations in Perm representing small business is substantial and perhaps even more public than in Samara, but it is also strongly supported by the representation of the interests of small business in senior elected and appointed office. Examples of this are Trutnev, Chirkunov and Belykh. Moreover, the civic-ness of business in Perm extends to the leadership of large companies to an unusual degree. The civic business community therefore is out of proportion to the numbers of small firms in the region. The comparative strength in Perm of industry over commerce was balanced by a more open and pluralistic political order than the Russian norm and a distinct and measurable set of popularly held values supportive of modernization.

By reference to the causal chain in the first section of this chapter, we find that the civic business community in the Perm region was supported by favorable ideational antecedent conditions, compensating for the somewhat weak numbers of small firms relative to the workforce. Small firm prevalence in turn was encouraged by a strong and persistent democratic impulse but inhibited by structural antecedent conditions, above all the strong and diverse natural resource base and the viability of many of the incumbent industrial and engineering enterprises.

In general, the Samara and Smolensk cases were marked by structural and ideational antecedents that pulled in the same direction, and the deviant cases, Perm and Rostov, by structural and ideational cross-currents. The case studies found evidence that the accessibility and the nature of ideational antecedent conditions – civic memory – color the interaction of small firm prevalence and democratization. As we have seen, the Don, Volga and Urals regions share an association with anti-Bolshevik forces in the 1918–1921 civil war. These three regions' 'distance' in ideational terms from both Tsarist and Soviet centralizing ideals of statehood helps explain their distinctive paths since 1991. In contrast to all of these, the powerful civic myth of Smolensk is of heroic sacrifice in defense of the core national and centralizing ideal of the Tsarist and Soviet state. Smolensk's impressive pantheon of national figures bind it manifestly to the center, rather than the periphery in Russian national mythology.

The civic identity of the entrepreneurs at the center of this study has been shaped in the case study regions by specific and self-conscious evocations of the role of merchant-industrialists in the half-century before 1917. As we have seen, Chambers of Commerce and some other business associations in all four regions appealed to these traditions explicitly.[3] The city of Perm has gone farthest of the four major capitals in raising public awareness of the region's merchant-industrialists, including through the revival of the tradition of sponsorship of arts and culture by major companies.

Climbing the conceptual ladder

Let us now turn to what the regional data analysis and case studies have shown about the relevance of modernization, civic culture and comparative historical approaches to the problem as introduced in Chapter 1. The causal chain presented at the beginning of this chapter represents a specific synthesis of modernization, civic culture and comparative historical approaches to a partial explanation of democratization.

The first link in our causal chain features antecedent structural conditions as contributing to the outcome. The principal such variable whose influence has been borne out is urbanization. The evidence from Russia's regions comports with modernization theory in the influence that the extent of urbanization exerts on endogenous democratization and in the explanatory power of another structural variable related to education – the incidence of personal computers by household.

In a broader sense, however, the evidence suggests that modernization thesis holds only through the intermediation of social differentiation and attitudinal change.[4] We found that strictly economic variables such as differential rates of growth or levels of per capita income had no independent effect on democratization. The independent significance of small firm prevalence, even when controlling for modernization variables such as urbanization, students per capita and income per capita, points to the relevance of civic culture and social differentiation in democratization.

As we have seen, the regional capitals have between one quarter and one third of the inhabitants of the four regions in our case studies, and this is typical of the Russian Federation. The importance of urbanization as an explanatory factor in democratization recalls the etymology of the word 'bourgeoisie' – burghers or townspeople. The case study evidence in this project strongly suggests that the locus for the civic business community instrumental to democratization is regional capitals and principal cities. Municipal administrations and legislatures were a crucial entry point for political elites drawn from among the ranks of entrepreneurs in the Perm and Samara regions. Yuriy Trutnev is a rare example of a mayor who became governor and then a federal minister, having emerged from the cooperatives movement of the late 1980s. Samara mayor Viktor Tarkhov was a stubborn check on the executive power of Governors Titov and Artyakov.

The effectiveness of autonomous Chambers of Commerce structured at a municipal level in Togliatti and in Taganrog provides additional support for the claim that cities are especially suited to the development and expansion of the 'citizen-agent' networks which in Tilly's vision embody democratization. Democratization, Tilly writes, "consists of a set of changes in citizen-agent relations: broadening them, equalizing them, protecting them, and subjecting them to binding consultation." (Tilly, 2004:15) Business associations where successful have broadened participation in consultations with 'agents' of regional and municipal authority and helped to build a binding character for understandings through formalized agreements and legislative acts. Not incidentally, one of OPORA's long-standing proposals is for the reinforcement of the financial autonomy and independent policy authority of municipal administrations.[5]

The more typical structuring of Chambers of Commerce at the oblast level is most effective when the regional leadership itself is very pro-business, as in Perm and Rostov. In general, however, placing all the critical policy questions for small business into the regional administration reduces their relative importance, because in that context they must contend with a host of other issues and priorities for the regional administration. Small business weighs much more heavily in the employment and tax revenue of cities and towns than it does for regions as a whole, which makes some municipal officials, even with meager funding, more devoted SME enthusiasts than some regional ones. This is the case for the cities of Kungur, Togliatti, Samara and Smolensk.

While providing partial confirmation to modernization theory, the cases in our study support the claim that **civic culture** is a principal explanation for variations in (endogenous) democratization. The core variable in the causal chain introduced at the beginning of this chapter is the civic business community and the case studies focused on business associations as a major institutional locus of this community. The case studies suggest that varying prevalence of small firms is a manifestation of varying degrees of social adaptiveness and optimism. 'Small firm prevalence' tends to reinforce and support regional democratization by placing demands on the state in public, and within a framework of enlightened interest advocacy having a civic character. The case studies suggest that small firm owners tend to engender a climate of social equality and reciprocity among themselves that shapes their civic identity.

Where small firms are comparatively prevalent relative to the workforce and within the broader business community, this engenders greater rule seeking and rule-shaping efforts from business. This relates to the influence of 'small firm prevalence' upon the sub-indicator *openness,* because rules having general application tend to be developed through public or open processes. As we have seen, the demands of business on the legal system and its grievances regarding official corruption are a large part of the public debate in Russian regions.

Drawing on the insights of North, the prevalence of small firms relative to the workforce and to the business community as a whole can be understood as producing pressure for greater openness in the formulation and enforcement of rules, because informal rules based on networks of personal acquaintance are somewhat resistant to adaptation and raise 'transaction costs.' This is the essence of Auzan's remark that business associations developed when entrepreneurs expected to remain in business five years hence. Because they are new, numerous and individually small, small firm owners can, under the right conditions, produce demand for a categorical and formal, as opposed to an improvised and firm-specific, mode of business-government coordination.

The sheer numbers of companies, then, have consequences for the character of business-government coordination. New companies are less likely to have a well-established network of personal understandings with state agencies, which can substitute for institutionalized and formal rules. Moreover, as regional barriers to trade and investment have broken down with the growing integration of the national market, cozy understandings at a regional level are likely to be less durable than before. This was especially evident in the case of Rostov.

The extensive survey evidence reported in Maleva et al. (2004) offers insights into the role of small business owners and their employees in the middle class. This study found that Russians tended to self-identify as middle class by reference to several criteria: educational level, earnings, professional status, sense of adaptation to the new economic system/rules, accumulated savings, the high value given to children's educational success and social ambition. Self-declared entrepreneurs had the highest self-estimate of all participants in the study with respect to their living standard, professionalism, adaptation to new economic rules and the importance of individual effort. (Maleva et al. 2004) The study found, moreover, that 43% of those employed in small businesses with up to 100 employees belonged to the middle class as defined by the aforementioned characteristics. Moreover, a greater share of employees in private firms of any size, as opposed to state companies, satisfied all the parameters of middle class membership. (Maleva et al. 2004) However, Maleva found that two thirds of the middle class was employed by the state, including the so-called *budget-niki* (teachers, professors, doctors) as well as federal and regional officials. Maleva's survey found that in the year 2000, entrepreneurs represented 8.6% of the middle class as defined by all the aforementioned parameters. (Maleva et al. 2004)

Comparing the case of contemporary Russia to the historical precedents in 18th century England and the United States, France and Germany in the 19th centuries, Gill concludes that the putative transformational role of the commercial bourgeoisie was, in the consolidated Western democracies, quite narrow in scope:

> The bourgeoisie were not much concerned to try to bring about change in the political system. There is no evidence that either collectively or individually in large numbers they pushed in a systematic fashion for democratic reform, although many did come to support liberal causes.
>
> (Gill 2008:320)

Gill draws the familiar distinction here between liberalism (the defense of individual rights, including property rights) and democratic reform, meaning the extension of voting rights to the whole adult population. Tocqueville argued that the extension of property rights to much of the population underpinned democracy in the United States:

> Why is it that in America, the land par excellence of democracy, no one makes that outcry against property in general that often echoes through Europe? Is there any need to explain? It is because there are no proletarians in America.

Everyone, having some possession to defend, recognizes the right to property in principle.

(Tocqueville 1969/1840:238)

Having established that, in England, France, Germany and the United States, the commercial bourgeoisie's role in democratic movements was secondary and at best cautious, Gill characterizes the interactions of the bourgeoisie with state authority in this concluding passage:

It is important to recognize that the bourgeoisie did not metaphorically storm the existing political institutions, take them over, and transform them in their own image. Rather, the bourgeoisie sought to adapt itself to the existing political structures, to creep into the niches that were available to it, and to work within the structures and processes that were current; their place and role were structured by the institutional arrangements, both formal and social, with which they were confronted. Involvement in the legislature and executive, in mainstream political parties, in interest groups and business associations, and in local government were the formal vehicles for this. . . . If the class was a revolutionary force, that revolution was carried out by stealth, from within the institutions, rather than from outside by direct assault.

(Gill 2008:320)

Gill's description fits well with what we have observed in the behavior of business associations in the case studies. It is also very close to the role of changes in citizen-agent relations that Tilly posits as a mechanism of democratization.

Comparative historical analysis also enters our causal chain through the influence of *civic memory,* ideational antecedent conditions. This perspective entered our analysis through the posited implications of ideational antecedent conditions to influencing the emergence of the civic business community and therefore contributing to variations in the democratization outcome. The case studies also showed the importance of the 'usable past' in the example set by industrialists and merchants of the late Tsarist period to the emergence of the civic business community in the two case study regions where it is strongest: Samara and Perm.

Carr argues, quoting Trotsky, that Russian liberalism typified by the Kadet party could not strike social roots in Russia, and that is why it failed in the parliamentary interlude of 1905–1917. According to Carr, liberalism had been successful in Britain and the United States at a time when it was the leading and most dynamic proponent of social reform, sponsored by the unchallenged rise of the entrepreneurial class. By contrast, in late Tsarist Russia, liberalism was squeezed between the revolutionary ideology on behalf of the peasantry and workers, and the stubborn and reactionary stance of the Tsar, the Church and much of the bureaucracy. Liberalism, Carr argues, was irrelevant to the fate of an overwhelmingly agrarian country. (Carr 1989)

Hosking (1973) shows that the merchants and industrialists of Russia's cities were, insofar as they took a role in politics, aligned with the moderate liberal Octobrists, and after 1912 with the Progressists, rather than the radical liberal

Kadets. Among the Third duma members elected from the Octobrist party, according to Hosking, 15% were industrialists or merchants, a larger share than in any other party faction. (Hosking 1973) Only with the founding of the Progressist party in 1912 and in the active support by prominent businessmen for the Red Cross effort in the first years of WWI, did the organized business community enter the civic sphere decisively. These years also saw the rise of organized business lobbying and the precursor organization of the Russian Chamber of Commerce.

The evidence of the late 19th and early 20th centuries in Russia suggests that the gestation of a social basis for liberalism among commercial elites was very gradual. Only on the threshold of WWI did the commercial bourgeoisie begin to coalesce as a civic and political actor, having played a significant economic role for several decades.

Contemporary Russian entrepreneurialism emerged in the legal sphere in 1988, with the passage of the cooperatives law, together with the first flowering of self-organized groups and proto-political parties. The comparative analysis of this book gives grounds for cautious hope that the incremental development of a social basis for liberalism among the cohort of owners of new and small firms may ultimately contribute, with other social actors, to a democratic future for Russia.

Notes

1 Tocqueville (1969/1840) p. 637.
2 See regression results and discussion on regression model 4, Chapter 2.
3 This was the focus of "The Region and the Model – Conclusions" section in each of the case studies.
4 As noted in Chapter 1, Lipset drew the same conclusion. (Diamond 1992)
5 OPORA President Sergey Borisov made this point in his speech to the May 2010 TPPRF-OPORA entrepreneurs' conference.

References

Carr, E. H. (1989) "Liberalism in Alien Soil" In *From Napoleon to Stalin and Other Essays* (pp. 60–67). New York: St. Martin's Press.
Diamond, Larry. (1992) Economic Development and Democracy Reconsidered. *American Behavioral Scientist* 15:450–499.
Gill, Graeme. (2008) *Bourgeoisie, State and Democracy: Russia, Britain, France, Germany and the USA*. Oxford, UK, New York: Oxford University Press.
Hosking, Geoffrey. (1973) *The Russian Constitutional Experiment*. Cambridge, UK: Cambridge University Press.
Maleva, Tatiana, E. Avraamova, M. Mikhailiuk, L. Nivorozhkina, A. Ovsiannikov, L. Ovcharova, . . . N. Firsova. (2004) *Srednie Klassy v Rossii: Ekonomicheskie i Sotsial'nie Strategii*. Moscow: Moscow Carnegie Center.
Tilly, Charles. (2004) *Contention and Democracy in Europe, 1650–2000*. New York: Cambridge University Press.
Tocqueville, Alexis de. (1969/1840). *Democracy in America*. London: Fontana Press.

Index

For Product Safety Concerns and Information please contact our EU
representative GPSR@taylorandfrancis.com
Taylor & Francis Verlag GmbH, Kaufingerstraße 24, 80331 München, Germany

www.ingramcontent.com/pod-product-compliance
Lightning Source LLC
Chambersburg PA
CBHW071416290326
41932CB00046B/1894